S0-DJP-258

A READER FOR COLLEGE WRITERS

A READER
FOR
COLLEGE WRITERS

models
methods
mirrors

RALPH E. LOEWE

PRENTICE-HALL, INC.
Englewood Cliffs, New Jersey 07632

Library of Congress Cataloging in Publication Data
Main entry under title:
A Reader for college writers.
    Includes index.
    1. English language—Rhetoric.   2. College
readers.   I. Loewe, Ralph E.

PE1417.R35   808'.0427   79-22751
ISBN 0-13-753582-1

© 1980 by Prentice-Hall, Inc., Englewood Cliffs, N.J. 07632
All rights reserved. No part of this book
may be reproduced in any form or
by any means without permission in writing
from the publisher.
Printed in the United States of America

10   9   8   7   6   5   4   3   2   1

Editorial and production supervision: *Hilda Tauber*
Cover and text design: *Suzanne Behnke*
Manufacturing buyer: *Harry P. Baisley*

PRENTICE-HALL INTERNATIONAL, INC., *London*
PRENTICE-HALL OF AUSTRALIA PTY. LIMITED, *Sydney*
PRENTICE-HALL OF CANADA, LTD., *Toronto*
PRENTICE-HALL OF INDIA PRIVATE LIMITED, *New Delhi*
PRENTICE-HALL OF JAPAN, INC., *Tokyo*
PRENTICE-HALL OF SOUTHEAST ASIA PTE. LTD., *Singapore*
WHITEHALL BOOKS LIMITED, *Wellington, New Zealand*

Contents

3 Description 44

6 Comparison/Contrast 143

❖❖❖

7 Process Analysis 178

❖❖❖

8 Definition   *213*

❖❖

9 Cause/Effect   *245*

❖❖

Preface

To the Student

Language is a much more powerful instrument than most people realize. Today, world-wide, mastery of the written language is a major factor in upward social and economic mobility. In India riots occurred when an attempt was made to impose one national language on a country where many languages and dialects are spoken. People fear that those who already know the language well will have a distinct advantage in the job market. In Quebec the French Canadians ousted the English Canadians from power and insisted that the French language have primacy. In countries like India, China, and the U.S.S.R. English is important as a second language because it is the language of international business and finance as well as the language of advanced industrialization and science. In the U.S.A. few can succeed in the business and industrial world without mastery of English.

The purpose of this book is to help you improve your skills in reading and writing the kinds of materials required of you in the college and business worlds. Hopefully, you will also have some mind-expanding experiences and some pleasure as you read, discuss, and write about the various selections.

Reading and writing well are skills that take patience and practice—and the critical evaluation of your instructor. Reading provides the materials to write about; it broadens your vocabulary and gives you a feeling for the rhythms of your language and the many forms in which ideas can be expressed. Reading sharpens your critical faculties, makes you aware of counterfeit thinkers, and introduces you to men and women with wit, humor, and insight. Not many people become professional writers, but the writing skills you learn in this course will help you express your ideas more effectively—a quality that will contribute to both your professional and social life.

To the Teacher

A READER FOR COLLEGE WRITERS is designed to entice the student who is disinclined to read and write, and to challenge the avid reader and potential writer.

Each chapter sets objectives for both reading and writing. Each starts with easy material and builds to more difficult and provocative selections. This allows instructors to tailor their courses to the needs of individual students and to adapt the material to various kinds of classes.

Most of the many and varied questions in the text are designed to encourage students to think inductively. Some require students to write their own thesis statements, topic sentences, outlines, or summaries, because these kinds of assignments provide excellent tests of their understanding of structure as well as meaning. (To aid busy instructors, sample summaries and outlines are provided in the teacher's manual; answers to short-answer tests are also included.)

Vocabulary words to be defined are provided throughout the text to spur students to seek definitions. But a better vocabulary-building technique might be to ask students to make their own lists and to avoid using the dictionary until they have tried to define the words in context.

Not being a rhetoric, A READER FOR COLLEGE WRITERS provides lean rather than extended instruction, but the organization of the text, the many examples, and the carefully planned questions help the student become aware of the importance of structure, development, clarity, unity, and coherence.

Some college readers separate narration, description, exposition, and argumentation into four distinct groups. This text attempts to integrate them. Narration includes many expository techniques and expository writing often includes narration. Almost all rhetorical forms have elements of persuasion or argumentation in them. Since many selections can be classified as persuasion or argumentation in addition to their other classifications, no special argumentation/persuasion chapter is included. Instead, there is a brief discussion of persuasive techniques and of logical fallacies in Chapter 1, and they are discussed throughout the text in relation to appropriate selections.

This reader starts with narration for two reasons: (1) Narration plays an important part in many types of writing. (2) It is probably the easiest starting point for the reluctant writer because he or she can deal with familiar subject matter by calling on personal experience and need not provide sources. Description comes next, not because it is easy but because it is used so widely. It also helps the student focus early on the importance of detail, something that many college students tend to overlook. Example is third because it is probably the most widely used expository method.

The next chapters deal with classification, comparison/contrast, cause/effect, process analysis, and definition. They are not handled as separate entities but as parts of the whole text, each referring back to and building on the others. Finally, there is the Idea Bank. Although the entire text is an "idea bank," Chapter 10 provides material that may well stimulate students not interested in the usual run of articles. It has poems, pictures, proverbs, quotations, charts, even lists from *The Book of Lists*. The Idea Bank can be used first, last, or intermittently. It can serve as an introduction to research techniques.

Should a reader be rhetorically oriented or thematically oriented? The answer, of course, is *both*. This book makes every attempt to stimulate ideas while simultaneously emphasizing the importance of organization and development. The wide variety of subjects found in the rhetorically classified chapters and augmented by the materials in the Idea Bank are listed for convenient use in the Thematic Table of Contents. Hopefully, the combination provides the best of both worlds.

Thematic Table of Contents

Adult Challenges

Business and Work

Childhood Memories

Crime and Punishment

Death

Education and Raising Children

History

Humor

Language

Loneliness, Regimentation, Fear

Love, Marriage, Sexism

Personalities

Politics and Society

Psychology

Sports

Science

A READER FOR COLLEGE WRITERS

Evaluation Guidelines

CHAPTER 1

As you work with this book, you will be asked to evaluate what you read even as your writing is evaluated by your instructor. But aren't all of the selections well written? Besides, how do you, a student, measure the work of a professional writer?

The material in this book has been selected for many reasons: to interest a highly diverse audience, to teach various writing techniques, to challenge your imagination and spur you to write, and to provide you with ideas to write about. Not all of the selections are written with equal skill, and even highly skillful writing is open to criticism.

As a mature student you have had experiences and gained knowledge which gives you both the right and the obligation to question the ideas of others, but in order to criticize well, you must know what to look for, what factors are usually considered in the evaluative process. This chapter briefly describes the qualities found in good writing and defines many of the terms used to analyze it.

NARRATION

Narration usually relates events in chronological order. The writer may vary this order, however, to achieve a given effect. The writer may also summarize events, add commentary, and otherwise manipulate the account to make a point, to create suspense, or to entertain.

EXPOSITION

Expository writing sets forth or explains ideas as clearly as possible. Most of the writing in this text is expository.

EXPOSITORY THEME. An expository theme is a group of paragraphs unified by a single idea. It usually has three distinct parts: the introduction, the body, and the conclusion. The **introduction** tells the reader what the theme is about. It usually states the thesis (main idea). The **body** supports the thesis announced by the introduction. The **conclusion** summarizes, dramatizes, or in some manner heightens the thesis to help unify the theme. Professional writers do not always follow this exact pattern but vary it to suit their purpose. It is, however, usually wise for novices to stick to the pattern.

EXPOSITORY PARAGRAPH. An individual expository paragraph (not in the context of a theme) is like a miniature theme. It consists of a group of sentences unified around a single idea. It also usually has a definite introduction, body, and conclusion. In the context of a theme, however, a paragraph may begin and/or end with a transitional sentence linking it with the preceding or following paragraphs.

THESIS (also called the main idea, central idea, or controlling idea). The thesis is the idea around which a theme is developed. Most good writing focuses on a single point and develops it fully. A writer often tests his thesis by stating it in a single sentence (thesis statement) to be sure that it is clear and well focused. The statement may or may not be included in the theme. An unclear thesis leads to disjointed, rambling writing.

TOPIC SENTENCE. The topic sentence is to the paragraph what the thesis statement is to the theme. It states the main idea.

ORGANIZATION. Good writing is carefully organized. It is structured to support the thesis as effectively as possible. Outlining your major and minor points before you write is an invaluable aid in presenting your ideas in an organized manner. Structure is important in writing because it provides a pattern which helps the writer say what he intends and helps the reader receive the message clearly.

DEVELOPMENT. To merely state that bald people are smarter than hairy people or that nuclear power plants should be banned is not enough. Your opponent can just as flatly counter that hairy people are smarter, and nuclear plants are vitally necessary. To make your assertions believable you must support them as fully as possible. Some of the methods used to support a thesis are examples, classification, comparison/contrast, definition, cause/effect, process, description, and narration. Although more than one method of development is usually used in most kinds of writing, we examine them separately in this text to help you become more proficient at using each type.

COHERENCE. The "glue" that holds sentences, paragraphs, and themes together is called coherence. Pronouns must agree with their antecedents, and pronoun reference must be clear. Transitions should enable the reader to be aware of changes in time, place, speaker, and in ideas.

What is evident to you will not be evident to your reader unless your thoughts are placed on paper. The development of your ideas must be readily discernible in each sentence, between sentences, and from paragraph to paragraph.

UNITY. A composition has unity when the writer achieves a successful marriage of form and content. Disunity comes from such defects as an unclear thesis, failure to support a thesis effectively, incoherence, wandering from the subject, wordiness or poor word choice, and tone that doesn't fit the situation.

PERSUASION

All of your writing, whether it is meant to inform ("Results of a Survey of Student Opinion about Nuclear Power") or to persuade ("Why Nuclear Power Should Be Banned"), should be organized, developed, coherent, and unified. There is, moreover, a special body of terms that are commonly used to discuss the techniques and problems of persuasive writing. They will help you distinguish between logical thinking and errors in reasoning (logical fallacies). These terms are discussed below.

INFERENCES AND FAULTY INFERENCES. An inference is a statement about the unknown arrived at on the basis of what is known through observation. We can observe someone's behavior (*The professor is drumming his fingers*). We infer his state of mind (*He is impatient*). Inferences are never 100 percent sure. There is always an element of guesswork. We make faulty inferences when we jump to conclusions (*A man doesn't answer my question; not knowing that he is deaf, I conclude that he is rude*). Here are some examples.

Observation: Footprints in the sand, clothes at the water's edge, no swimmer in sight
Inference: Someone has gone into the water and not come out (although he could have come out somewhere else and be running around naked).
Faulty inference: Someone has committed suicide. (This conclusion is too big a jump from the evidence. There are too many other possibilities. The person might still be swimming, might have been picked up in a boat, or might have drowned accidentally, etc.)

GENERALIZATIONS AND OVERGENERALIZATIONS. A common kind of inference is the generalization. We observe that something is true of certain individuals or things (the known), and then infer that the same thing is true of all members of the class to which the individual or thing belongs (the unknown). "My Ford stalls at every light; all Fords must be lemons." Generalizations are necessary for good thinking; overgeneralizations like the example of the Ford cause trouble.

Observation: Three carloads of teenagers race down the road, honking and screeching.
Generalization: You seem to have some wild teenagers in this town.
Overgeneralization: All the teenagers in this town are crazy drivers.

Observation: A scientist tries a new serum on 2,000 breast cancer victims and finds that in 79 percent of the cases there is a marked improvement.

Generalization: It looks like we may have a breakthrough in the treatment of breast cancer.

Overgeneralization: A new miracle cure for breast cancer has been discovered.

NOTE: When you make inferences or generalizations, be aware that you are going beyond the evidence. Both inferences and generalizations are fully acceptable, good thinking. Most advances in science are made when one goes beyond the evidence and then attempts to prove one's guess. The intelligent person, however, uses language to indicate that he or she is inferring or generalizing and has not absolutely proved the case. Words like *seem, appear, perhaps, may, according to the evidence,* and *as of now* can avoid a lot of headaches, embarrassment, and law suits.

ANALOGIES AND FALSE ANALOGIES.   An analogy points to similarities between two things which may be quite dissimilar in other ways. It is often helpful to compare the heart to a pump, the circulatory system to plumbing, and students to products of an assembly line. To a degree such comparisons help readers to better "see" the object being described, but it is important that both writers and readers realize that hearts, circulatory systems, and students are much more complicated than pumps, plumbing, and merchandise. The writer should be careful not to carry the analogy too far, and the reader should be wary of writers who do so.

BEGGING THE QUESTION AND ARGUING IN A CIRCLE.   In begging the question one states the arguable point as if it were already proved. In arguing in a circle one restates the questionable point in different words: "Wars will always be with us because wars are inevitable."

ATTACKING THE PERSON INSTEAD OF THE IDEA.   This is best explained by an example: "Don't vote for the levy because George Flatt favors it, and George Flatt is a known drunkard."

AFTER THIS—BECAUSE OF THIS.   You break a mirror and later fall into an uncovered manhole. You blame the accident on the broken mirror, failing to consider that you are worried about flunking out of school, you have been taking tranquilizers, and you were walking down a very dark street. Putting blame on what appears to be the most immediate cause can lead you to ignore other possible causes.

THE EITHER/OR SYNDROME.   Some people pose issues as if there were only two possible alternatives, when often there are more. You are weak in physics and dislike the professor. You decide that if you fail physics this quarter you will quit college. You may not consider the possibility of getting tutorial help, of dropping the course this quarter and taking it later, or of changing your major.

AVOIDING THE POINT.   Even the best writers sometimes stray from the point. That's why it is good to have a clearly stated thesis and a sound outline. Some people, however, stray on purpose. Asked what her record on tax reduction is, a politician might say, "We all hate taxes. I am concerned with your pocket book. I want to see you get the most for your money. Services to this city must be improved." You still don't know what her record on tax reduction is. Listen carefully and judge accordingly.

CARD STACKING. Card stacking occurs when one looks only at the weaknesses or mistakes of another and at none of the positive traits or accomplishments. Example: A newspaper reports only the faults of a candidate and none of her worthwhile acts.

NOTE: For a lighter approach to errors in reasoning read "Love Is a Fallacy" in Chapter 5.

STYLE

Style expresses a writer's individuality. It includes word choice, voice, tone, and sentence structure.

WORD CHOICE. Many words have two kinds of meaning, denotative and connotative.

Denotative words convey direct, explicit, "dictionary" meanings: *carburetor, ball bearing, tooth.*

Connotative words derive their meanings from being used in certain ways over a period of time and being associated with certain ideas. *Mother* brings to mind warmth, gentleness, love; *dog* makes many people think of faithfulness, protection, something to cuddle. Consider the differences in the connotative meanings of the following words: *pater, father, male parent, dad, pop; house, home, shack, pad; beautiful, pretty, chic, sexy.*

The good writer is always aware of the context in which his or her words are placed. The experiences we have make us react to certain words in a special way. If, for example, you were bitten by a dog and had to take painful anti-rabies shots, your reaction to the word *dog* would be quite different from that of a person who was recently rescued by a dog. If you have been beaten regularly by your mother, the word *mother* might not connote good things to you. You cannot, therefore, be sure that your reader will interpret your words as you mean them unless your context helps to make their meanings clear.

Words are also classified as abstract and concrete.

Abstract words represent ideas, emotions, qualities, and the like: *friendship, love, patriotism, loyalty.* Such words are good and necessary, but they often tend to mean different things to different people. Some people, for example, believe that it is patriotic to criticize the government in order to improve it. Others believe that any criticism is unAmerican. "Love it or leave it!" they shout. Some people feel that love involves total commitment with one other person; others believe that you can love more than one person at a time. The best way to be sure that your meaning is clear is to define it fully. Examples usually help a great deal.

Concrete words are specific. The more specific a word you use, the more likely it is that your reader will get the same picture you wish to convey: *dachshund* is more specific than *dog; six-room brick bungalow* is much clearer than *house.*

"Allness" words such as *all, every, always,* and *never* are words that may be difficult or impossible to support. A statement beginning with "We *all* know" implies that you have taken a poll and are sure of what is in the minds of everyone present. *"Everyone* knows" indicates that you have the wherewithal to know what all the people on earth know at a particular point in time. "People have *always* acted this way and *always* will" says that you know everything about all people in the past as well as in the future. Even the word *most* in "Most people agree that . . ." implies that you have taken an opinion poll and are sure about the opinions of more than half. Being careful to use only words that say what you *really* know will help you avoid these pitfalls. Your words will carry greater weight, and you will appear to others as a more mature, responsible person.

VOICE. There are two voices, active and passive. In the active voice, the subject *does* the acting, possessing, feeling: "Miss Tote fired Kempert." "Carl owns the lot." "Lena admires Steve." In the passive voice the subject, in a sense, *receives* the action of the verb: "Kempert was fired by Miss Tote." "The lot is owned by Carl." "Steve is admired by Lena."

Because the passive voice is wordier and less direct than the active, the latter is considered more effective for most writing situations.

TONE. Each writer conveys an attitude: aloof, friendly, cold, dispassionate, respectful. Connotation, sentence structure, and voice are factors that contribute to tone. The tone should be appropriate to the material and the audience. One doesn't, for example, treat a tragic situation lightly. In turn, some readers resent a tone that is too friendly, preachy, or condescending, and some don't understand humor.

SENTENCE STRUCTURE. Simplicity and directness in sentence structure are effective in most situations. Too many short, simple sentences can make writing seem childish or choppy and repetitive, but sentences should not be made long and convoluted simply to create the appearance of erudition. In some situations short sentences can provide drama and "punch."

READING FOCUS

Evaluating other people's writing is a serious responsibility that requires skill and thoughtfulness, but first it is important to read the material carefully. This means that you may often have to read the selections more than once and use the dictionary when necessary. But it also requires that you reach out to the writers, be sensitive to their meaning, get on their "wave length." Before you criticize someone's message, be sure that you have received it as fully and accurately as possible; otherwise your criticism won't hold up.

WRITING FOCUS

Good writing requires the realization that your reader can receive only what you place on paper, not your unstated thoughts. If your thesis is clear in your own mind, you will more likely state it clearly on paper. If you fully support that thesis with interesting, apt, and logical information that is well organized, fully developed, coherent, and unified, your reader has a far better chance to receive your message in the way you intend it. If, in addition, your writing indicates an awareness of good word choice, voice, and tone, you have done about as much as you can do.

Language is a powerful tool; it pays to wield it well.

Narration

CHAPTER 2

READING FOCUS

❖ Sharpen your awareness of how writers manipulate events in time to achieve various effects.

❖ Use your knowledge of where the main idea, lesson, or moral of narrative writing is usually found to help you read narration more quickly and effectively.

WRITING FOCUS

❖ Use the narrative form to prove a point, to share an experience, or to entertain.

❖ Edit and order the events you have selected to make your narration more effective.

Although many students think of narrative writing primarily as fiction, narration is actually used for a wide range of nonfiction: biography and autobiography, journalistic and legal writing, scientific and travel journals, social work and psychiatric case histories, and in historical and anthropological works. Conversely, expository techniques like definition, classification, and comparison/contrast can be found in narrative writing.

When narrating, the writer relates events as they move from one point in time to another, usually chronologically. However, he or she can, and often does, manipulate events back and forth. News story writers, for example, turn the pattern on its head, putting the latest and most important information first. In case histories, journals, and other narrative forms, instead of unnecessarily repeating incidents that reoccur at intervals, the writer often summarizes them. In some narrative forms, the author interrupts the events with commentary. In the interview the writer can influence the narrative by the way he asks questions.

section 2a

Read the seven selections in this section first as a unit, paying special attention to the endings. Reread for content; then answer the questions.

CURBING ONE'S CURIOSITY

The man was lying in the gutter listening to a curb. A policeman walked over and asked him what he was listening to. The man said, "Come on down here and listen."

The policeman got on his hands and knees, then got right back up and said, "I can't hear anything!"

"That's the way it's been all day," replied the man.

THE ORIGIN OF DEATH

A HOTTENTOT FOLK TALE

The Moon, it is said, once sent an insect to men, saying, "Go to men and tell them, 'As I die, and dying live, so you shall also die, and dying live.'"

The insect started with the message, but, while on his way, was overtaken by the hare, who asked, "On what errand are you bound?"

The insect answered, "I am sent by the moon to men to tell them that as she dies and dying lives, so shall they also die and dying live."

The hare said, "As you are an awkward runner, let me go." With these words he ran off, and when he reached men he said, "I am sent by the Moon to tell you, 'As I die and dying perish, in the same manner you also shall die and come wholly to an end.'"

The hare then returned to the Moon and told her what he had said to

From *An African Treasury* selected by Langston Hughes. © 1960 by Langston Hughes. Used by permission of Crown Publishers, Inc.

men. The Moon reproached him angrily, saying, "Do you dare tell the people a thing which I have not said?"

With these words the Moon took up a piece of wood and struck the hare on the nose. Since that day the hare's nose has been slit, but men believe what Hare had told them.

THE CONCEPTION OF JESUS

And in the sixth month the angel Gabriel was sent from God unto a city of Galilee, named Nazareth, to a virgin espoused to a man whose name was Joseph, of the house of David; and the virgin's name was Mary. And the angel came in unto her, and said, Hail, thou that art highly favored, the Lord is with thee: blessed art thou among women. And when she saw him, she was troubled at his saying, and cast in her mind what manner of salutation this should be. And the angel said unto her, Fear not, Mary: for thou hast found favor with God. And, behold, thou shalt conceive in thy womb, and bring forth a son, and shalt call his name JESUS. He shall be great, and shall be called the Son of the Highest; and the Lord God shall give unto him the throne of his father David: and he shall reign over the house of Jacob for ever; and of his kingdom there shall be no end. Then said Mary unto the angel, How shall this be, seeing I know not a man? And the angel answered and said unto her, The Holy Ghost shall come upon thee, and the power of the Highest shall overshadow thee: therefore also that holy thing which shall be born of thee shall be called the Son of God. And, behold, thy cousin Elisabeth, she hath also conceived a son in her old age; and this is the sixth month with her, who was called barren. For with God nothing shall be impossible. And Mary said, Behold the handmaid of the Lord; be it unto me according to thy word. And the angel departed from her.

From Luke 1:26–38.

DEFINE: *espoused, know, barren.*

THE BIRTH OF BUDDHA

It is related that at that time the midsummer festival had been proclaimed in the city of Kapilavatthu, and the multitude were enjoying the feast. And queen Maha-Maya, abstaining from strong drink, and brilliant with garlands and perfumes, took part in the festivities for the six days previous to the day of full moon. And when it came to be the day of full moon, she rose early, bathed in perfumed water, and dispensed four hundred thousand pieces of money in great largess. And decked in full gala attire, she ate of the choicest food; after which she took the eight vows, and entered her elegantly furnished chamber of state. And lying down on the royal couch, she fell asleep and dreamed the following dream:

From *Mythology: The Voyage of the Hero* by David Adams Leeming. Copyright © 1973 by J. B. Lippincott Co. By permission of Harper & Row, Publishers, Inc.

The four guardian angels came and lifted her up, together with her couch, and took her away to the Himalaya Mountains. There, in the Manosila table-land, which is sixty leagues in extent, they laid her under a prodigious sal-tree, seven leagues in height, and took up their positions respectfully at one side. Then came the wives of these guardian angels, and conducted her to Anotatta Lake, and bathed her, to remove every human stain. And after clothing her with divine garments, they anointed her with perfumes and decked her with divine flowers. Not far off was Silver Hill, and in it a golden mansion. There they spread a divine couch with its head toward the east, and laid her down upon it. Now the future Buddha had become a superb white elephant, and was wandering about at no great distance, on Gold Hill. Descending thence, he ascended Silver Hill, and approaching from the north, he plucked a white lotus with his silvery trunk, and trumpeting loudly, went into the golden mansion. And three times he walked round his mother's couch, with his right side towards it, and striking her on her right side, he seemed to enter her womb. Thus the conception took place in the midsummer festival.

DEFINE: *largess, prodigious, league.*

THE BURR-HAMILTON DUEL

This is one report of the famous duel between Alexander Hamilton and Aaron Burr in which Hamilton was killed. The Chronicle *was founded by Burr and his friends. The* New York Evening Post, *which Hamilton founded, denied that Hamilton fired at Burr.*

New York Morning Chronicle, July 18, 1804

[1] Colonel Burr arrived first on the ground, as had been previously agreed. When General Hamilton arrived the parties exchanged salutations, and the seconds proceeded to make their arrangements. They measured the distance, ten full paces, and cast lots for the choice of position and also to determine by whom the word should be given, both of which fell to the second of General Hamilton. They then proceeded to load the pistols in each other's presence, after which the parties took their stations. The gentleman who was to give the word then explained to the parties the rules which were to govern them in firing, which were as follows:

[2] "The parties being placed at their stations—the second who gives the word shall ask them whether they are ready; being answered in the affirmative, he shall say 'present,' after this the parties shall present and fire when they please—if one fires before the other, the opposite second shall say one, two, three, fire—and shall then fire or lose his fire."

[3] He then asked if they were prepared, being answered in the affirmative, he gave the word "present," as had been agreed upon, and both parties took aim and fired in succession, the intervening time is not expressed, as the seconds do not precisely agree on that point. The fire of Colonel Burr took effect, and General Hamilton almost instantly fell. Colonel Burr then advanced toward General Hamilton with a manner

and gesture that appeared to General Hamilton's friend to be expressive of regret, but without speaking, turned about and withdrew, being urged from the field by his friend as has been subsequently stated, with a view to prevent his being recognized by the surgeon and bargeman, who were then approaching. No further communication took place between the principals, and the barge that carried Colonel Burr immediately returned to the city. We conceive it proper to add that the conduct of the parties in this interview was perfectly proper, as suited the occasion.

DEFINE: subsequently, conceive.

TIMMS VERSUS ONDEGO ELECTRIC

A legal brief is the formal presentation of an argument for or against a defendant or a plaintiff. The names in this brief have been changed.

In Timms v. Ondego Electric (114OE373-1965), Ondego Electric had been requested to furnish electric service to an airport. In so doing, a transformer enclosed by a fence was placed on the property. Ondego Electric had no easement in the airport property; neither did Ondego Electric have a contract with the property owner; nor did the power company pay rent to the property owner. The original owner requested Ondego Electric to provide service, including the placing of the transformer and any auxiliary equipment. The power company placed its equipment on the premises with the full knowledge and acquiescence of the property owner. The public travelled over the airport property; in fact, there was a path within ten to twenty feet of the enclosure. Decedent, last seen alive walking in the direction of the airport, was later found dead within the enclosure, near the transformer. He had been electrocuted. At that time, the fence which formed the east wall of the enclosure was down flat on the ground, a condition which had existed for at least five weeks. Furthermore, the transformer was negligently maintained; the transformer was upset; the lid was off, some of the wires were broken and oil from within the transformer had spilled out upon the cement base. A jury returned a verdict for plaintiff in his action for wrongful death.

DEFINE: easement, auxiliary, acquiescence, decedent, plaintiff.

Alexander Calandra

ANGELS ON A PIN

Some time ago, I received a call from a colleague who asked if I would be the referee on the grading of an examination question. He was about to give a student a zero for his answer to a physics question, while

© Saturday Review, 1968. All rights reserved. Footnotes added.

the student claimed he should receive a perfect score and would if the system were not set up against the student. The instructor and the student agreed to submit this to an impartial arbiter, and I was selected.

2   I went to my colleague's office and read the examination question: "Show how it is possible to determine the height of a tall building with the aid of a barometer."

3   The student had answered: "Take the barometer to the top of the building, attach a long rope to it, lower the barometer to the street, and then bring it up, measuring the length of the rope. The length of the rope is the height of the building."

4   I pointed out that the student really had a strong case for full credit, since he had answered the question completely and correctly. On the other hand, if full credit were given, it could well contribute to a high grade for the student in his physics course. A high grade is supposed to certify competence in physics, but the answer did not confirm this. I suggested that the student have another try at answering the question. I was not surprised that my colleague agreed, but I was surprised that the student did.

5   I gave the student six minutes to answer the question, with the warning that his answer should show some knowledge of physics. At the end of five minutes, he had not written anything. I asked if he wished to give up, but he said no. He had many answers to this problem; he was just thinking of the best one. I excused myself for interrupting him, and asked him to please go on. In the next minute, he dashed off his answer which read:

6   "Take the barometer to the top of the building and lean over the edge of the roof. Drop the barometer, timing its fall with a stopwatch. Then, using the formula $S = \frac{1}{2}at^2$, calculate the height of the building."

7   At this point, I asked my colleague if he would give up. He conceded, and I gave the student almost full credit.

8   In leaving my colleague's office, I recalled that the student had said he had other answers to the problem, so I asked him what they were. "Oh, yes," said the student. "There are many ways of getting the height of a tall building with the aid of a barometer. For example, you could take the barometer out on a sunny day and measure the height of the barometer, the length of its shadow, and the length of the shadow of the building, and by the use of a simple proportion, determine the height of the building."

9   "Fine," I said. "And the others?"

10   "Yes," said the student. "There is a very basic measurement method that you will like. In this method, you take the barometer and begin to walk up the stairs. As you climb the stairs, you mark off the length of the barometer along the wall. You then count the number of marks, and this will give you the height of the building in barometer units. A very direct method.

11   "Of course, if you want a more sophisticated method, you can tie the barometer to the end of a string, swing it as a pendulum, and determine the value of 'g' at the street level and at the top of the building. From the difference between the two values of 'g,' the height of the building can, in principle, be calculated."

12   Finally he concluded, there are many other ways of solving the problem. "Probably the best," he said, "is to take the barometer to the basement and knock on the superintendent's door. When the superintendent answers, you speak to him as follows: 'Mr. Superintendent, here I have a fine barometer. If you will tell me the height of this building, I will give you this barometer.' "

13   At this point, I asked the student if he really did not know the conventional answer to this question. He admitted that he did, but said that he was fed up with high school and college instructors trying to teach him how to think, to use the "scientific method,"[1] and to explore the deep inner logic of the subject in a pedantic way, as is often done in the new mathematics, rather than teaching him the structure of the subject. With this in mind, he decided to revive scholasticism[2] as an academic lark to challenge the Sputnik-panicked[3] classrooms of America.

DEFINE: *barometer* (2); *pedantic* (13).

ANALYSIS

structure   1. List the different kinds of endings in all selections except the excerpts about Jesus and Buddha. One ending, for example, provides a moral; another gives the result of a series of incidents.

2. What are some of the advantages of placing the main idea, the "lesson," or moral at the end of the narrative? What are some of the disadvantages?

meaning   3. What is the similarity between the conception of Buddha and the conception of Christ?

4. In "Angels on a Pin," why is the student upset?

opinion   5. Do you agree with the student's criticism of the teacher?

6. Was the professor right in changing the student's grade?

WRITING SUGGESTIONS

1. Tell a joke.

2. Tell a brief story in your own words.

3. Tell about a problem you had with a teacher or someone else in authority and how it was resolved.

[1] The scientific method involves the formulation of hypotheses based on carefully collected data, then the testing of the hypotheses experimentally.

[2] Scholasticism refers to the theological and philosophical systems of the Middle Ages, which attempted to correlate faith with reason. They dealt almost entirely in abstractions, and some would pose questions like "How many angels can dance on the head of a pin?"

[3] When the Russians in 1957 launched the first man-made satellite, many Americans began to be concerned about the quality of the teaching of science and mathematics in the U.S.

Section 2b

Two News Stories, Two Assassinations

In modern news stories the most important information comes first, regardless of the order in which events happened. Thus, narrative order is turned upside down. Note how events are reported in the following stories; then answer the questions.

Washington, April 14, 1865

Washington was thrown into an intense excitement a few minutes before eleven o'clock this evening, by the announcement that the President and Secretary Seward had been assassinated and were dead.

The wildest excitement prevailed in all parts of the city. Men, women and children, old and young, rushed to and fro, and the rumors were magnified until we had nearly every member of the Cabinet killed. Some time elapsed before authentic data could be ascertained in regard to the affair.

The President and Mrs. Lincoln were at Ford's theatre, listening to the performance of *The American Cousin,* occupying a box in the second tier. At the close of the third act a person entered the box occupied by the President, and shot Mr. Lincoln in the head. The shot entered the back of his head, and came out above the temple.

The assassin then jumped from the box upon the stage and ran across to the other side, exhibiting a dagger in his hand, flourishing it in a tragical manner, shouting the same words repeated by the desperado at Mr. Seward's house, adding to it, "The South is avenged," and then escaped from the back entrance to the stage, but in his passage dropped his pistol and his hat.

5 Mr. Lincoln fell forward from his seat, and Mrs. Lincoln fainted.

The moment the astonished audience could realize what had happened, the President was taken and carried to Mr. Peterson's house, in Tenth street, opposite to the theatre. Medical aid was immediately sent for, and the wound was at first supposed to be fatal, and it was announced that he could not live, but at half-past twelve he is still alive, though in a precarious condition.

New York Herald, April 15, 1865

DEFINE: *ascertained, precarious.*

Dallas, November 22, 1963

President John Fitzgerald Kennedy was shot and killed by an assassin today.

He died of a wound in the brain caused by a rifle bullet that was fired at him as he was riding through downtown Dallas in a motorcade.

Vice President Lyndon Baines Johnson, who was riding in the third car behind Mr. Kennedy's, was sworn in as the 36th President of the United States 99 minutes after Mr. Kennedy's death.

Mr. Johnson is 55 years old; Mr. Kennedy was 46.

⁵ Shortly after the assassination, Lee H. Oswald, who once defected to the Soviet Union and who has been active in the Fair Play for Cuba Committee, was arrested by the Dallas police. Tonight he was accused of the killing.

© 1963 by The New York Times Company. Reprinted by permission.

ANALYSIS

structure 1. If the Lincoln assassination story were written chronologically, with what paragraph would it begin?

2. What one word in the first sentence of the Kennedy story keeps the story from being strictly chronological?

3. Write news headlines for the two assassination stories. Remember that a modern news headline gives the most important information.

4. Write a headline and an introduction for the Burr-Hamilton story (in Section 2A) as a modern newspaper might handle it.

5. Criticize all three news stories from the point of view that news stories are usually expected to present the most important facts first.

WRITING SUGGESTIONS

1. Take an interesting news story from your daily newspaper and change it into a chronological narrative.

2. Write a news story about a school, neighborhood, or civic event.

Three Case Histories

The following excerpts from case histories[1] are written in narrative form, but instead of reporting similar behavioral problems separately, the writers summarize a series of such episodes. They also comment freely.

[1] Reprinted with permission of Macmillan Publishing Co., Inc. from *Children Who Hate* by Fritz Redl and David Wineman. Copyright © 1951 by The Free Press, a corporation.

ANDY

Andy, who had spent most of his first years in a chain of foster homes, was episodically taken in by his grandmother, a professional prostitute. Here he visualized open sexual relations between adults, including various perversions. The grandmother, perhaps in keeping with her own instinct-dominated pattern and also as a means of avoiding any responsibility for real ego training, was extremely permissive with him, granting him many exorbitant gratifications unless he displeased her, at which times he was severely beaten. When he was six, he was taken to live with his father and stepmother. Here there was as little basic acceptance as had existed in his former life but in addition an increased quality of rejection in that the stepmother was completely ungratifying and critical. His father, a passive, insecure man, completely dominated by the stepmother, added to this chain of trauma through his inability to protect Andy against the stepmother, thus completing the sense of disillusion and feeling of unwantedness that Andy may have hoped to overcome when he came to his own home with his "very own" father.

DEFINE: *episodically, exorbitant, trauma.*

LARRY

Larry, born out of wedlock in a charitable institution, remained here for the first two years of his life. His mother visited him only occasionally. Between the ages of two to five he was shuttled about from foster home to foster home. Occasionally he lived with his mother in the home of maternal grandparents. When Larry was six, his mother came to Detroit and married a man much older than she. Shortly thereafter Larry came to live with them. He was six and one-half at this time. The mother was weak, passive, detached. Her tie to Larry appeared to be on a very tenuous level. The stepfather was a short, squat, powerfully built man. He was severely alcoholic, profane, brutal. From the very beginning of Larry's entrance into the home, he became the butt for the stepfather's primitive bullying. The degree of sadism that the stepfather expressed toward Larry is almost unbelievable. He was beaten severely, threatened with a shotgun, booted, thrown into a drainage ditch in front of their home, and locked in a woodshed for long hours without food. Many times the stepfather threatened, shotgun in hand, to kill him. The stepfather's motivation for this treatment of Larry, aside from an apparently frank and obvious sadistic temperament, was accentuated by the fact that Larry was slow, forgetful, clumsy in performance of heavy chores, and extremely infantile. In addition the stepfather, who had a thirty-eight year old son from a previous marriage from whom he was estranged, expressed an open hatred for all boys, saying they were "no good, dumb, can't be trusted, etc."

DEFINE: *tenuous, sadism, estranged.*

MIKE

Practically the whole first year he was with us at Pioneer House, Mike had almost nightly attacks of excitement and aggressiveness at bedtime which would reach a climax when the counselor would leave the sleeping room after the story reading. His antics were very disturbing to the rest of the group. He would make high banshee wails, striking out at his pillow like an imaginary attacker, muttering fierce counterthreats against it (I'll kill you, bastard, bitch, mother fucker). Or he might branch out into vicious aggression against one of the other children mixed with teasing erotic seduction of the other into his wild mood pattern, with occasional sex play thrown in. Inevitably, every evening, we would have to take him out and sit with him for sometimes thirty to forty-five minutes. He would usually start out on a high plane of hysteric euphorics with whoever was holding him, again repeating with the adult some of the erotic aggressiveness he had displayed toward the children, wriggling and wanting to dart through the house so that he would have to be physically restrained by light holding until he reinstituted some controls. All along the only verbalization that was possible at all was gently soothing reassurance like "O.K., Mike, let's quiet down, everything's going to be O.K., you know it's like this every night. When you quiet down a little, you can go back to bed." Should we make any attempt to probe, to ask him what was bothering him, we got absolutely nowhere; as a matter of fact, it only increased his upset. Gradually, after about a year at the Home, Mike began to show definite indications of some new abilities to conceptualize some of his fantasies through words as well as through acting them out and thus, in connection with bedtime behavior, we were slowly able to get him to talk. Finally, he was able to actually say that every night he was "real scared" that someone was going to "get him" and that this was worse after the counselor left and he was alone with the "guys." In this way, we were able to make the connection clear to him: "When you're scared, you get wild." It took a year before this point was reached with Mike.

DEFINE: *hysteric, euphoric, conceptualize.*

ANALYSIS

structure

1. These case histories do not, for the most part, record detailed day-to-day acts of the children in the exact order in which the acts occurred. What acts are reported and in what manner?

2. Discuss the advantages of this kind of writing.

3. Rewrite either "Andy" or "Larry" to include only narration. Omit interpretation.

meaning

4. In the "Andy" case, explain "chain of trauma."

5. Discuss the grandmother's "instinct-dominated pattern."

6. Why did the counselors want Mike to talk?

style 7. Is the sexually explicit language necessary?

8. What kinds of information would have to be added to the case histories to change them into more fully developed narratives?

9. "Her tie to Larry appeared to be on a very tenuous level." This sentence can be improved by eliminating unnecessary words: "Her tie to Larry was tenuous." Find other examples of wordiness or imprecision and suggest improvements.

WRITING SUGGESTION

Write a case history of a child with behavioral problems. (Disguise the identity.)

Memories of Childhood and Youth

Piri Thomas

IN BUSINESS

1   Living in number 109 was snap breeze. I knew practically everybody on the block and, if I didn't, they knew me. When I went to the barbershop, José the barber would ask me, "Shape up or trim?" He liked to trim because in three hot minutes he could earn fifty cents. But I always gave him a hard way to shovel and said, "Give me the works with a square back." "*Ay coño,*" he groaned and started to cut hair and breathe bad breath on me, on spite, while I ignored him on spite.

2   Just being a kid, nothing different from all the other kids, was good. Even when you slept over at some other kid's house, it was almost like being in your own house. They all had kids, rats, and roaches in common. And life was full of happy moments—spitting out of tenement windows at unsuspecting people below, popping off with sling shots, or even better, with Red Ryder BB rifles, watching the neighbors fight through their open windows or make love under half-drawn shades.

3   The good kick in the hot summer was to sleep on the fire escape. Sometimes I lay awake all night and thought about all the things I would do when I grew up, about the nice duds I'd have like a champ uptown and come back around the block and treat all the kids to *cuchifritos* and pour tons of nickels into the jukebox and help anybody that was in trouble, from a junkie to a priest. I dreamed big; it didn't cost anything.

4   In the morning I stood on Lexington Avenue in Spanish Harlem, one finger poked through my pants pocket, scratching myself, while I droned, "Shine, mister—good shine, only fifteen cents. Shine, mister . . ." It was hard to shine shoes and harder to keep my corner from getting copped by an early-rising shine boy. I had to be prepared to mess a guy

From *Down These Mean Streets* by Piri Thomas. Copyright © 1967 by Piri Thomas. Reprinted by permission of Alfred A. Knopf, Inc.

up; that corner spot wasn't mine alone. I had to earn it every time I shined shoes there.

5 When I got a customer, we both played our roles. The customer, tall and aloof, smiled, "Gimme a shine, kid," and I replied, "*Sí, señor,* sir, I'll give you one that you'll have to put sunglasses on to eat the bright down."

6 My knees grinding against the gritty sidewalk, I adopted a serious, businesslike air. Carefully, but confidently, I snaked out my rags, polish, and brushes. I gave my cool breeze customer the treatment. I rolled his pants cuff up—"That'll keep shoe polish off"—straightened his socks, patted his shoe, assured him he was in good hands, and loosened and re-tied his shoes. Then I wiped my nose with a delicate finger, picked up my shoe brush, and scrunched away the first hard crust of dirt. I opened my bottle of black shoe cleaner—dab, rub in, wipe off, pat the shoe down. Then I opened my can of polish—dab on with three fingers, pat-a-pid, pat-a-pid. He's not looking—spit on the shoe, more polish, let it dry, tap the bottom of his sole, smile up at Mr. Big Tip (you hope), "Next, sir."

7 I repeated the process on the other shoe, then picked up my brush and rubbed the bristles very hard against the palm of my hand, scien-tific-like, to warm the brush hairs up so they would melt the black shoe wax and give a cool unlumpy shine. I peeked out of the corner of my eye to see if Mr. Big Tip was watching my modern shoeshine methods. The bum *was* looking. I hadn't touched his shoe, forcing him to look.

8 The shoe began to gleam dully—more spit, more polish, more brush, little more spit, little more polish, and a lotta rag. I repeated on the other shoe. As Mr. Big Tip started digging in his pocket, I prepared for the climax of my performance. Just as he finished saying, "Damn nice shine, kid," I said, "Oh, I ain't finished, sir. I got a special service," and I plunged my wax-covered fingers into a dark corner of my shoe box and brought out a bottle of "Special shoe lanolin cream for better preserva-tion of leather."

9 I applied a dab, a tiny dab, pausing long enough to say very confi-dently, "You can't put on too much or it'll spoil the shine. It gotta be just right." Then I grabbed the shoe rag firmly, like a maestro with a baton, and hummed a rhythm with it, slapping out a beat on the shoes. A final swish here and there, and *mira!*—finished. Sweating from the effort of my creation, I slowly rose from my knees, bent from the strain, my hand cas-ually extended, palm flat up, and murmured, "Fifteen cents, sir," with a look that said, "But it's worth much more, don't you think?" Mr. Big Tip dropped a quarter and a nickel into the offering plate, and I said, "Thanks a mil, sir," thinking, *Take it cool,* as I cast a watchful eye at his retreating back.

10 But wasn't it great to work for a living? I calculated how long it would take to make my first million shining shoes. Too long. I would be something like 987 years old. Maybe I could steal it faster.

Shirley Chisholm

FROM THE BARBADOS TO BROOKLYN

1   Crop failures caused famines in the Caribbean islands in the early 1920s. Many West Indians fled to the United States, and most of them went to some neighborhood in New York City where they knew a relative or a friend from home was living. As a result, little colonies of islanders grew up all over the city—a Haitian neighborhood in Manhattan, a Trinidadian one on Long Island, and so on.

2   There was a large colony of Barbadians in Brooklyn, and it was there that my father, Charles St. Hill, and my mother, Ruby Seale, went—separately. He was a native of British Guiana who had grown up in Cuba and Barbados. She was a teen-aged Barbadian girl. They had known each other in Barbados, but not well; in Brooklyn they got better acquainted, fell in love, and married. I was born in 1924. My sister Odessa came about a year later, and two years later my sister Muriel.

3   Mother was still only a girl herself and had trouble coping with three babies, especially her oldest. I learned to walk and talk very early. By the time I was two and a half, no bigger than a mite (I have never weighed much more than 100 pounds), I was already dominating other children around me—with my mouth. I lectured them and ordered them around. Even Mother was almost afraid of me.

4   Once, when I was still not yet three, she left me with the two younger girls. "Look out for Dess and Mu," she instructed me. When she came back, I was walking up and down with five-month-old Muriel in my arms. Mother wanted to shout, but she caught herself; she might have frightened me into dropping the baby. First she took Muriel out of my arms. Then she screamed at me.

5   Mother was a seamstress; she had probably gone to Belmont Market, a five-block-long confusion of pushcarts selling anything that could be loaded on a pushcart, to buy cloth. Her sewing machine fascinated me. I would go to it and turn and turn its wheels. When Mother went out, she tried to put the machine up where I couldn't reach it, but I piled up chairs and climbed until I could.

6   "It might be a good thing to take her to a farm," Mother began to suggest to Father. "She could run and play there." Mother was thinking of my grandmother's farm in Barbados. Her idea made a lot of sense economically. The middle 1920s may have been a time of legendary prosperity for some Americans, but not enough of it was rubbing off on young black immigrant couples in the big city. My father was unskilled. He worked as a baker's helper and later as a factory hand. His pay, even supplemented by what Mother could earn by sewing, was not much for a family of five. How could they ever save to buy a house and provide educations for their girls?

From *Unbought and Unbossed* by Shirley Chisholm. Copyright © 1970 by Shirley Chisholm. Reprinted by permission of Houghton Mifflin Company.

Merle Miller

HARRY TRUMAN GOES TO WORK

Mr. President, tell me about your first job.

"Well, when I was ten, maybe eleven years old, I got a job at Jim Clinton's drugstore on the northeast corner of the square in Independence. I had to get there at six thirty in the morning and set up the place so that when Mr. Clinton came down, he would find everything in order. I'd mop the floor and dust off the bottles and wipe off the counters, and then I'd wake Jim Clinton at seven."

Did you ever have any early-morning customers?

"Oh, yes, a great many. The people who were church members, the high hats in town, the ones who were afraid to go into a saloon and buy a drink, they'd come in, and I'd have to set out a bottle of whiskey, and they'd pay a dime for a drink before most people were up and around to see them. They'd put their dimes on the counter, and I'd leave all those dimes there until Mr. Clinton came in, and he'd put them in the cash register.

5   "All those fancy high hats, they'd say, 'Harry, give me a drink,' and I'd do it. And that's where I got my idea of what prohibitionists and high hats are. That's the reason some of them didn't like me. Because they knew I knew their background and their history.

"There were saloons all around the square, and the tough old birds who didn't give a damn about what people think, they'd go into the saloons and buy a drink when they wanted it. But as I say, the so-called *good* people, the fancy ones, they'd come in and buy a drink behind the prescription counter from a boy who didn't have any right to sell it to them.

"But that's the way I got to . . . well, feel a lack of respect for the counterfeits, and I don't care where they are. In Washington or wherever. There's a story they tell about this high hat that got to be Postmaster General of the United States. I think Mark Twain told it on him.

"He got to be Postmaster General, and he came back to his hometown to visit, and there wasn't anybody at the station to meet him but the village idiot. And the high hat wanted to know what people in the town had said when they found out he was Postmaster General.

"And the village idiot said, 'They didn't say anything. They just laughed.'

10   "That's what happens if you're a high hat and start taking yourself too seriously."

Do you think you ever did that, Mr. President?

"I tried not to. I did my level best not to, and if I had, the Boss and Margaret wouldn't ever have let me get away with it."

Mr. President, I understand that when you were still a boy, you got a job working as timekeeper for the Santa Fe Railroad.

From *Plain Speaking* by Merle Miller. Copyright © 1973, 1974 by Merle Miller. Reprinted by permission of Berkley Publishing Corporation, New York.

"I worked for an old fellow named Smith. L. J. Smith his name was, and he was head of the construction company that was building the double track for the Santa Fe Railroad down here from Eaton Falls to where the Missouri Pacific comes into the Santa Fe down at Sheffield.

15   "I was eighteen years old, and I'd just finished high school and knew I wasn't going to get to go to West Point. So I took this job as a timekeeper. I took it to help out at home, to keep my brother, Vivian, and my sister, Mary, in school. My father was having a hard time with finances just then.

"Old man Smith had three camps, and there were about a hundred hoboes in each camp, and I got very well acquainted with them. My job was to keep tabs on them, to keep track of how much time they put in, and then I'd write out their paychecks for them. I'd usually write those checks in a saloon on the north side of the square in Independence here, a saloon called Pogunpo's or in old man Schmidt's saloon in Sheffield. I used to sit there and pay off those hoboes. And they weren't bad fellows. They'd work for two weeks. They'd get discounted if they drew their checks before that time. So they'd work two weeks, and then they'd spend all their money for whiskey in the saloon and come back to work the next Monday morning. I'd pay them off on Saturday night.

"But they weren't bad fellows. Not in any way. Most of them had backgrounds that caused them to be hoboes. Either they'd had family troubles or they'd been in jail for some damn fool thing that wasn't a penitentiary offense. But they weren't bad citizens at all. I remember one time I told the old man that ran the saloon, he was an old Dutchman and wore whiskers, I told him, I said, 'This old bastard is the blacksmith out there on the railroad, and we need him. So try to cut out on his whiskey.'

"Well, damn old Schmidt went out and told this blacksmith what I'd said, and I never got a better cussing in my life than I did for interfering with the freedom of an American citizen. And he was right. And that taught me something.

"But after that I guess the blacksmith was grateful for it because he took a file, a regular ordinary file about that long and made a butcher knife out of it and tempered it so that the edge would never come off. He made two of them for me, and I think one of them is still around the house somewhere. . . . So he didn't hold it against me that I was trying to keep him from getting drunk."

20   *When you said camps, what were they, houses or tents?*

"Tents mostly. There were tents, and I had a tricycle car on the railroad that I went up and down on. I had to make a list of the men that were working every morning at seven thirty, and then I had to go back at one thirty in the afternoon to be sure that they were still there. So when the time came for their being paid, I had the records. No one ever doubted the records I kept."

How much did those men make?

"They made eleven dollars for two weeks' work, and as I say, they'd get paid on Saturday, and by Monday morning most of them had drunk it all up. But it was one of the best experiences that I ever had because that was when I began to understand who the underdog was and what he thought about the people who were the high hats. They felt just like I did about them. They didn't have any time for them. And neither did I. I always liked the underdogs better than the high hats. I still do."

Weren't you ever uneasy? I mean, you were a reader of books and wore glasses and, as you say, you'd been called a sissy.

25 "No. No. I never had any trouble with those birds. They were just as nice as they could be, and when I left, the foreman down there in Sheffield said, 'Harry's all right from the navel out in every direction.' Which when you come to think of it is just about the highest compliment I ever have been paid.

"Some of those hoboes had better educations than the president of Ha-vud University, and they weren't stuck up about it either. The average of them was just as smart as the smartest people in the country, and they'd had experiences, and a lot of them told me about their experiences. I hope I profited from it, and I think I did. I had to quit at the end of the summer, but my goodness, that was a great experience for me."

I understand you learned a few cuss words that summer.

"I did. The words some of those men knew I'd never heard before, but later when I was in the Army, there was an occasion or two when those words came in handy, and I used them.

"That experience also taught me that the lower classes so called are better than the high hats and the counterfeits, and they can be trusted more, too.

30 "About this counterfeit business. My Grandfather Young felt the same way. We had a church in the front yard where the cemetery is now. And the Baptists and the Methodists and all of them used it. And Grandfather Young when I was six years old, he died when I was eight, he told me that whenever the customers in any of those denominations prayed too loud in the Amen corner, you'd better go home and lock your smokehouse.

"And I found that to be true. I've never cared much for the loud prayers or for people who do that much going on about religion."

DEFINE: *prohibitionist* (paragraph 5); *counterfeits* (7); *denominations* (30).

ANALYSIS

NOTE: As you proceed through this book, you will frequently be asked to summarize or outline a selection. Your ability to write good summaries and outlines indicates that you recognize main ideas, that you can separate the important from the unimportant. The summary of "In Business" and the outline of "Harry Truman Goes to Work" below are examples of what you will be expected to write.

SAMPLE SUMMARY

"In Business" is a brief excerpt from the book, *Down These Mean Streets,* by Piri Thomas. It gives a glimpse of his life in Spanish Harlem, especially his experiences as a shoeshine boy.

"Harry Truman Goes to Work" is an excerpt from *Plain Speaking,* a book by Merle Miller, based on a series of interviews with former President Harry S. Truman. The selection is divided into two parts, the first telling of Truman's first job when he was ten or eleven, the second telling of his work as paymaster of hobo workers when he was 18.

I. Drug Store Helper
  A. Cleaning up
  B. Serving liquor
  C. Views on high hats
  D. Story about postmaster general

II. Paymaster at Hobo Camps
  A. Helped support family
  B. Description of job
  C. Views on hoboes
  D. Comments on cuss words
  E. Comments on counterfeits

structure

1. Provide one example of a statement summarizing events from each of the selections.

2. Provide one example of interpretation or commentary from each selection.

3. What time periods are covered in each selection?

4. Why is it important to be aware of the time in which something is written?

5. In "In Business" is the shoeshine incident specific or typical? Explain.

6. What information does Shirley Chisholm provide in her first paragraph that is not provided in the other selections in this section?

7. Explain how Merle Miller controls the narration in his interview.

meaning

8. What personality traits does each storyteller reveal about herself or himself?

9. Why is it unnecessary for Thomas to define the Spanish terms he uses?

10. Why does Truman look down on high hats and Prohibitionists?

11. Who is the Boss? (The answer is not given directly in the text.)

12. What did Grandfather Young say about people who pray too loud? Explain his comment and add your own.

13. Aside from the pay he got, why did Truman find his paymaster job valuable?

style

14. The last sentence in paragraph 2 of "In Business" is an example of irony. Explain.

15. Discuss the terms in "In Business" like *copped, mess a guy up, Mr. Big Tip,* and *Take it cool* in relation to the tone of the selection.

16. Whose writing is more polished, Chisholm's or Thomas's? Support your view.

[1] Notice that the outline does not follow the interview in exact order. All of Truman's views on hoboes, for example, are not stated in one place, but the outline places them together.

1. Write a brief narration about a period in your childhood or early youth.
2. Interview a friend or a family member about his childhood.
3. Interview yourself.

James Ansara

THE EDUCATED MAN

My father was a man steeped in the aphorisms and parables of his race, with which he spiced even his everyday conversation. Best of all I liked the stories he often resorted to to illustrate truisms. I remember the first time he told the one about the education of Sheikh Yusif's son. I had finished college, and my problem was whether to continue my intellectual pursuits or to launch myself into the practical activities of the world. One evening I sought to discuss the matter with him, but instead of giving me his advice he offered to tell me a story that his father had once told him. It was after dinner and we were having black coffee flavored with the essence of roses. Between long, satisfying sips, this was the story he told:—

Once there was a sheikh, Yusif al-Hamadi, who was determined that some day his only son, Ali, should become a learned man.

When Ali completed his elementary studies under his tutors, the Sheikh called together his advisers and asked them where his son could acquire the best possible education. With one voice, they answered, "The University of El-Azhar, in Cairo."

So at El-Azhar, then the most renowned university in the whole world, the son of Sheikh Yusif studied with great energy and soon proved himself a true scholar. After eight years of study, the Ulama of the university pronounced Ali an educated man, and the son wrote that he was returning home.

5 As a scholar, Ali scorned the vanities of life and departed from Cairo riding a jackass and wearing the coarse raiment of an ascetic. Jogging along with his books behind him and his diploma fastened to his side, Ali lost himself in meditating upon the writings of the poets and philosophers.

When he was only a day's journey from his home, the young scholar entered a village mosque to rest for a while. It was Friday and the place was full of worshipers. A Khatib was preaching on the miraculous deeds of the Prophet.

Now Ali, as a result of his profound study of the teachings of the Prophet, had become an uncompromising puritan of the Faith. There-

Copyright © 1937 R 1965 by The Atlantic Monthly Company, Boston, Mass. Reprinted with permission.

fore, when the Khatib told his credulous congregation that Mohammed caused springs to flow in the desert, moved mountains, and flew on his horse to heaven, Ali was outraged.

"Stop! cried Ali. "Believe not this false man. All that he has told you are lies, not the true faith. Our teacher, Mohammed, was not a supernatural being, but a man who saw the light, the truth—"

The Khatib interrupted to ask the young man upon what authority he contradicted him. Ali proudly informed him that he was a scholar, a graduate of the great University of El-Azhar. The preacher, with a sneer on his face, turned toward his congregation.

10 "This man, who calls himself a scholar, is a heretic, an atheist who dares come among you, the Faithful, and throw doubt upon the greatness of our Prophet Mohammed, blessed be his name. Cast him out of the mosque; he contaminates its sanctity."

The people seized Ali and dragged him to the street, beating and kicking him and tearing his clothes. Outside, his books and diploma were destroyed, and the unconscious Ali was tied to his jackass backward and stoned out of the village.

When word came of the approach of Ali, Sheikh Yusif and the neighboring sheikhs, whom the proud father had invited to join him to receive and honor his scholarly son, rode forth to meet the learned graduate of El-Azhar. But lo, the scholar was dangling from the back of a jackass, his learned head bouncing against its haunches. Bruised, half naked, he was muttering like an idiot.

Not for several days was Ali well enough to tell his father what had befallen him. When he finished, Sheikh Yusif sighed deeply and said, "Ali, you have come back to me only half educated. You must return to Cairo." The young man protested that there was nothing more the university could teach him, and Sheikh Yusif agreed. The rest of his education was to be outside of El-Azhar.

Back in Cairo, Ali was to discover a new world. According to his father's instructions, he spent the first six months in the shop of a merchant, bartering and wrangling in the busiest bazaar of Cairo. Following that, the chief of police took him in hand and introduced him to the life of the city in all its varied aspects. For a time he was a beggar outside one of the great mosques, a disciple of a magician, a waiter in a low café. Ali also came to know the life of a sailor, a wandering trader, and a laborer.

15 At the end of the fifth year, Ali informed his father that his education was completed and he was again returning home.

This time, the son of Sheikh Yusif left Cairo riding a spirited Arabian, dressed in silks and satins, and attended by a train of servants. His stops during the journey were brief, until he reached the village of the Khatib. It was again Friday and the same Khatib was declaiming the same miracles to the credulous peasants. Ali joined the congregation and listened to the words of the preacher with a rapture equal to that of his neighbors. His "Ah" and "Great is our Prophet" were even more fervent than those about him.

When the Khatib concluded his sermon, Ali humbly begged to be heard.

"In spite of my youth," said Ali, "I have studied much and traveled wide, seeking the truth and wisdom of our great Prophet, blessed be his name. But never have I heard or read a sermon equal in truth and piety to that of your reverend Khatib. Not only is he a learned man, but a holy one, for his knowledge of the life of the Prophet comes only from the deepest source of faith and piety, a knowledge denied to ordinary men. Fortunate are you in having such a saint. Fortunate am I too, for here ends my search for the holiest man of our age.

"O holy Khatib, fit companion of Caliphs, I beg of you a boon!"

20   The bewildered Khatib could only ask the nature of that boon.

"It is written in the Holy Koran that a relic from a saint brings endless blessings to the Faithful. A hair from thy beard, O Saintly One!"

Still perplexed, the Khatib could not, before his whole congregation, deny such a pious request. The young man with bowed head slowly mounted the *mumbar* and, in sight of all the people, with two extended fingers pulled a hair from the outthrust, flowing beard. Ali kissed it with deep reverence, folded it meticulously in a white silk kerchief, and placed it inside his shirt next to his heart.

A murmur arose from the congregation—their Khatib was a holy man! Even before Ali left the *mumbar,* the stampede toward the preacher had begun. By the time the son of Sheikh Yusif had forced his way through the mad crowd to the street, not a hair was left on the Khatib's face or head, not a shred of clothing on his body, and he lay behind the *mumbar* writhing and gasping like a plucked rooster.

That evening, Ali arrived home and there was great rejoicing in his father's house. His wit and dignity, his profound store of knowledge, his tact and manners, charmed all the guests and swelled the heart of his father with pride.

25   When at last the guests departed and Ali was alone with his father, he recounted to him his second visit to the village of the Khatib. The old Sheikh nodded his head approvingly and said:—

"Now, my son, I can die in peace. You have tempered book learning with worldly wisdom and returned a truly educated man."

DEFINE: aphorisms (1); *Khatib* (6); heretic (10); credulous (16).

ANALYSIS

structure   1. Summarize the selection in three or four sentences.

2. What is the date of the story's publication?

3. What are the time periods involved in the story?

4. What is the main idea of the parable? If it is stated, copy the exact words. If it is not stated, state it.

meaning   5. Does the Sheikh's story answer the question raised by his son? Explain.

6. Briefly explain the two encounters that Ali has with the Khatib. In each case tell what influence his education has on his actions.

opinion   7. What do you think is the best kind of education? (Before answering the question, you might find it helpful to read Unit 10, "How Should We Teach Our Young?" in the Idea Bank, Chapter 10.)

WRITING SUGGESTIONS

1. Tell about one of your most effective learning experiences outside of school.
2. Tell how a story, a movie, a play, or a poem helped to solve one of your problems.

ꝛection 2c

In the following selections we see narration at work in a long article written for a magazine and in two excerpts from books. While the first selection is a cross between narration and exposition, the other two are thoroughly narrative.

Patrick Fenton

CONFESSIONS OF A WORKING STIFF

1   The Big Ben is hammering out its 5:45 alarm in the half-dark of another Tuesday morning. If I'm lucky, my car down in the street will kick over for me. I don't want to think about that now; all I want to do is roll over into the warm covers that hug my wife. I can hear the wind as it whistles up and down the sides of the building. Tuesday is always the worst day—it's the day the drudgery, boredom, and fatigue start all over again. I'm off from work on Sunday and Monday, so Tuesday is my blue Monday.

2   I make my living humping cargo for Seaboard World Airlines, one of the big international airlines at Kennedy Airport. They handle strictly all cargo. I was once told that one of the Rockerfellers is the major stockholder for the airline, but I don't really think about that too much. I don't get paid to think. The big thing is to beat that race with the time clock every morning of your life so the airline will be happy. The worst thing a man could ever do is to make suggestions about building a better airline. They pay people $40,000 a year to come up with better ideas. It doesn't matter that these ideas never work, it's just that they get nervous when a guy from South Brooklyn or Ozone Park acts like he actually has a brain.

From Patrick Fenton, "Confessions of a Working Stiff." Copyright © 1975 by NYM Corporation. Reprinted with the permission of *New York* Magazine.

3   I throw a Myadec high-potency vitamin into my mouth to ward off one of the ten colds I get every year from humping mailbags out in the cold rain at Kennedy. A huge DC-8 stretch jet waits impatiently for the 8,000 pounds of mail that I will soon feed its empty belly. I wash the Myadec down with some orange juice and grab a brown bag filled with bologna and cheese. Inside the lunch bag there is sometimes a silly note from my wife that says, "I Love You—Guess Who?" It is all that keeps me going to a job that I hate.

4   I've been going there for seven years now and my job is still the same. It's weary work that makes a man feel used up and worn out. You push and you pull all day long with your back. You tie down pallets loaded with thousands of pounds of freight. You fill igloo-shaped containers with hundreds of boxes that all look the same. If you're assigned to work the warehouse, it's really your hard luck. This is the job all the men hate most. You stack box upon box until the pallet resembles the exact shape of the inside of the plane. You get the same monotonous feeling an adult gets when he plays with a child's blocks. When you finish one pallet, you find another and start the whole dull process over again.

5   The airline pays me $192 a week for this. After they take out taxes and $5.81 for the pension, I go home with $142. Once a month they take out $10 for term life insurance, and $5.50 for union dues. The week they take out the life insurance is always the worst: I go home with $132. My job will never change. I will fill up the same igloos with the same boxes for the next 34 years of my life, I will hump the same mailbags into the belly of the plane, and push the same 8,000-pound pallets with my back. I will have to do this until I'm 65 years old. Then I'll be free, if I don't die of a heart attack before that, and the airline will let me retire.

6   In winter the warehouse is cold and damp. There is no heat. The large steel doors that line the warehouse walls stay open most of the day. In the cold months, wind, rain and snow blow across the floor. In the summer the warehouse becomes an oven. Dust and sand from the runways mix with the toxic fumes of fork lifts, leaving a dry, stale taste in your mouth. The high windows above the doors are covered with a thick, black dirt that kills the sun. The men work in shadows with the constant roar of jet engines blowing dangerously in their ears.

7   Working the warehouse is a tedious job that leaves a man's mind empty. If he's smart he will spend his days wool-gathering. He will think about pretty girls that he once knew, or some other daydream of warm, dry places where you never had a chill. The worst thing he can do is to think about his problems. If he starts to think about how he is going to pay the mortgage on the $30,000 home that he can't afford, it will bring him down. He will wonder why he comes to the cargo airline every morning of his life, and even on Christmas Day. He will start to wonder why he has to listen to the deafening sound of the jets as they rev up their engines. He will wonder why he crawls on his hands and knees, breaking his back a little bit more every day.

8   To keep his kids in that great place in the country in the summer, that great place far away from Brooklyn and the South Bronx, he must work every hour of overtime that the airline offers him. If he never turns down an hour, if he works some 600 hours over, he can make about $15,000.

To do this he must turn against himself, he must pray that the phone rings in the middle of the night, even though it's snowing out and he doesn't feel like working. He must hump cargo late into the night, eat meatball heroes for supper, drink coffee that starts to taste like oil, and then hope that his car starts when it's time to go home. If he gets sick—well, he better not think about that.

9   All over Long Island, Ozone Park, Brooklyn, and as far away as the Bronx, men stir in the early morning hours as a new day begins. Every morning is the same as the last. Some of the men drink beer for breakfast instead of coffee. Way out in Bay Shore a cargoman snaps open a can of Budweiser. It's 6 A.M., and he covers the top of the can with his thumb in order to keep down the loud hiss as the beer escapes. He doesn't want to awaken his children as they dream away the morning in the next room. Soon he will swing his Pinto wagon up onto the crowded Long Island Expressway and start the long ride to the job. As he slips the car out of the driveway he tucks another can of beer between his legs.

10   All the men have something in common: they hate the work they are doing and they drink a little too much. They come to work only to punch a timecard that has their last name on it. At the end of the week they will pick up a paycheck with their last name on it. They will never receive a bonus for a job well done, or even a party. At Christmastime a card from the president of the airline will arrive at each one of their houses. It will say Merry Christmas and have the president's name printed at the bottom of it. They know that the airline will be there long after they are dead. Nothing stops it. It runs non-stop, without sleep, through Christmas Day, New Year's Eve, Martin Luther King's birthday, even the deaths of Presidents.

11   It's seven in the morning and the day shift is starting to drift in. Huge tractors are backing up to the big-mouth doors of the warehouse. Cattle trucks bring tons of beef to feed its insatiable appetite for cargo. Smoke-covered trailers with refrigerated units packed deep with green peppers sit with their diesel engines idling. Names like White, Mack, and Kenworth are welded to the front of their radiators, which hiss and moan from the overload. The men walk through the factory-type gates of the parking lot with their heads bowed, oblivious of the shuddering diesels that await them.

12   Once inside the warehouse they gather in groups of threes and fours like prisoners in an exercise yard. They stand in front of the two time clocks that hang below a window in the manager's office. They smoke and cough in the early morning hour as they await their work assignments. The manager, a nervous-looking man with a stomach that is starting to push out at his belt, walks out with the pink work sheets in his hand. [. . .]

13   A brutal rain has started to beat down on the oil-covered concrete of the ramp as the 306 screeches in off the runway. Its engines scream as they spit off sheets of rain and oil. Two of the men cover their ears as they run to put up a ladder to the front of the plane. The airline will give them ear covers only if they pay for half of them. A lot of the men never buy them. If they want, the airline will give them two little plugs free. The plugs don't work and hurt the inside of the ears.

14   The men will spend the rest of the day in the rain. Some of them will set up conveyor belts and trucks to unload the thousands of pounds of cargo that sit in the deep belly of the plane. Then they will feed the awkward bird until it is full and ready to fly again. They will crawl on their hands and knees in its belly, counting and humping hundreds of mailbags. The rest of the men will work up topside on the plane, pushing 8,000-pound pallets with their backs. Like Egyptians building a pyramid, they will pull and push until the pallet finally gives in and moves like a massive stone sliding through sand. They don't complain too much: they know that when the airline comes up with a better system some of them will go.

15   The old-timers at the airline can't understand why the younger men stay on. They know what the cargo airline can do to a man. It can work him hard but make him lazy at the same time. The work comes in spurts. Sometimes a man will be pushed for three hours of sweat, other times he will just stand around bored. It's not the hard work that breaks a man at the airline, it's the boredom of doing the same job over and over again.

16   At the end of the day the men start to move in off the ramp. The rain is still beating down at their backs but they move slowly. Their faces are red and raw from the rain-soaked wind that has been snapping at them for eight hours. The harsh wind moves in from the direction of the city. From the ramp you can see the Manhattan skyline, gray- and blue-looking, as it peeks up from the west wall of the warehouse. There is nothing to block the winter weather as it rolls in like a storm across a prairie. They head down to the locker room, heads bowed, like a football team that never wins. [. . .]

DEFINE: *humping* (2); *insatiable, oblivious* (11).

ANALYSIS

structure

1. State the main idea of the selection in one sentence. Include the title and author.

2. Is the main idea stated in the article or is it implied?

3. Does the selection deal primarily with specific situations or typical situations? Explain.

4. Is the article more effective or less effective because it first focuses on one individual rather than on the whole group?

5. In what paragraph does it begin to shift its focus to the group?

meaning

6. Why don't the men leave the job if they hate it so much?

7. What is the worst aspect of the job?

style

8. List four or five words from the article which describe the author's feeling about his job and his life.

9. How does Fenton set the tone for the article in paragraph 1?

10. Discuss the effectiveness or lack of effectiveness of the simile used in the last sentence.

11. List three to five words which most effectively describe your present job or a class that you either like or hate.

opinion 12. Compare your job with Fenton's. Is yours equally distasteful or do you enjoy your work?

13. From what kinds of jobs do people usually get more pleasure?

14. Is it unusual or typical for Americans to tie themselves to certain jobs in order to achieve a certain standard of living?

WRITING SUGGESTIONS

1. Tell how you go about doing a job or task you hate.
2. Tell how you go about doing a job or task you enjoy doing.

Desmond Morris

INSECTIVORE TO CULTURAL APE

1   The primate group, to which our naked ape belongs, arose originally from primitive insectivore stock. These early mammals were small, insignificant creatures, scuttling nervously around in the safety of the forests, while the reptile overlords were dominating the animal scene. Between eighty and fifty million years ago, following the collapse of the great age of reptiles, these little insect-eaters began to venture out into new territories. There they spread and grew into many strange shapes. Some became plant-eaters and burrowed under the ground for safety, or grew long, stilt-like legs with which to flee from their enemies. Others became long-clawed, sharp-toothed killers. Although the major reptiles had abdicated and left the scene, the open country was once again a battlefield.

2   Meanwhile, in the undergrowth, small feet were still clinging to the security of the forest vegetation. Progress was being made here, too. The early insect-eaters began to broaden their diet and conquer the digestive problems of devouring fruits, nuts, berries, buds and leaves. As they evolved into the lowliest forms of primates, their vision improved, the eyes coming forward to the front of the face and the hands developing as food-graspers. With three-dimensional vision, manipulating limbs and slowly enlarging brains, they came more and more to dominate their arboreal world.

3   Somewhere between twenty-five and thirty-five million years ago, these pre-monkeys had already started to evolve into monkeys proper. They were beginning to develop long, balancing tails and were increasing considerably in body size. Some were on their way to becoming leaf-eating specialists, but most were keeping to a broad, mixed diet. As time

From *The Naked Ape* by Desmond Morris. Copyright © 1967 by Desmond Morris. Reprinted with permission of McGraw-Hill Book Company.

passed, some of these monkey-like creatures became bigger and heavier. Instead of scampering and leaping they switched to brachiating—swinging hand over hand along the underside of the branches. Their tails became obsolete. Their size, although making them more cumbersome in the trees, made them less wary of ground-level sorties.

4   Even so, at this stage—the ape phase—there was much to be said for keeping to the lush comfort and easy pickings of their forest of Eden. Only if the environment gave them a rude shove into the great open spaces would they be likely to move. Unlike the early mammalian explorers, they had become specialized in forest existence. Millions of years of development had gone into perfecting this forest aristocracy, and if they left now they would have to compete with the (by this time) highly advanced ground-living herbivores and killers. And so there they stayed, munching their fruit and quietly minding their own business.

5   It should be stressed that this ape trend was for some reason taking place only in the Old World. Monkeys had evolved separately as advanced tree-dwellers in both the Old and the New World, but the American branch of the primates never made the ape grade. In the Old World, on the other hand, ancestral apes were spreading over a wide forest area from western Africa, at one extreme, to southeastern Asia at the other. Today the remnants of this development can be seen in the African chimpanzees and gorillas and the Asian gibbons and orang-utans. Between these two extremities the world is now devoid of hairy apes. The lush forests have gone.

6   What happened to the early apes? We know that the climate began to work against them and that, by a point somewhere around fifteen million years ago, their forest strongholds had become seriously reduced in size. The ancestral apes were forced to do one of two things: either they had to cling on to what was left of their old forest homes, or, in an almost biblical sense, they had to face expulsion from the Garden. The ancestors of the chimpanzees, gorillas, gibbons and orangs stayed put, and their numbers have been slowly dwindling ever since. The ancestors of the only other surviving ape—the naked ape—struck out, left the forests, and threw themselves into competition with the already efficiently adapted ground-dwellers. It was a risky business, but in terms of evolutionary success it paid dividends.

7   The naked ape's success story from this point on is well known, but a brief summary will help, because it is vital to keep in mind the events which followed if we are to gain an objective understanding of the present-day behaviour of the species.

8   Faced with a new environment, our ancestors encountered a bleak prospect. They had to become either better killers than the old-time carnivores, or better grazers than the old-time herbivores. We know today that, in a sense, success has been won on both scores; but agriculture is only a few thousand years old, and we are dealing in millions of years. Specialized exploitation of the plant life of the open country was beyond the capacity of our early ancestors and had to await the development of advanced techniques of modern times. The digestive system necessary for a direct conquest of the grassland food supply was lacking. The fruit and nut diet of the forest could be adapted to a root and bulb diet at ground

level, but the limitations were severe. Instead of lazily reaching out to the end of the branch for a luscious ripe fruit, the vegetable-seeking ground ape would be forced to scratch and scrape painstakingly in the hard earth for his precious food.

9   His old forest diet, however, was not all fruit and nut. Animal proteins were undoubtedly of great importance to him. He came originally, after all, from basic insectivore stock, and his ancient arboreal home had always been rich in insect life. Juicy bugs, eggs, young helpless nestlings, tree-frogs and small reptiles were all grist to his mill. What is more, they posed no great problems for his rather generalized digestive system. Down on the ground this source of food supply was by no means absent and there was nothing to stop him increasing this part of his diet. At first, he was no match for the professional killer of the carnivore world. Even a small mongoose, not to mention a big cat, could beat him to the kill. But young animals of all kinds, helpless ones or sick ones, were there for the taking, and the first step on the road to major meat-eating was an easy one. The really big prizes, however, were poised on long, stilt-like legs, ready to flee at a moment's notice at quite impossible speeds. The protein-laden ungulates were beyond his grasp.

10 This brings us to the last million or so years of the naked ape's ancestral history, and to a series of shattering and increasingly dramatic developments. Several things happened together, and it is important to realize this. All too often, when the story is told, the separate parts of it are spread out as if one major advance led to another, but this is misleading. The ancestral ground-apes already had large and high-quality brains. They had good eyes and efficient grasping hands. They inevitably, as primates, had some degree of social organization. With strong pressure on them to increase their prey-killing prowess, vital changes began to take place. They became more upright—fast, better runners. Their hands became freed from locomotion duties—strong, efficient weapon-holders. Their brains became more complex—brighter, quicker decision-makers. These things did not follow one another in a major, set sequence; they blossomed together, minute advances being made first in one quality and then in another, each urging the other on. A hunting ape, a killer ape, was in the making.

11 It could be argued that evolution might have favored the less drastic step of developing a more typical cat- or dog-like killer, a kind of cat-ape or dog-ape, by the simple process of enlarging the teeth and nails into savage fang-like and claw-like weapons. But this would have put the ancestral ground-ape into direct competition with the already highly specialized cat and dog killers. It would have meant competing with them on their own terms. and the outcome would no doubt have been disastrous for the primates in question. (For all we know, this may actually have been tried and failed so badly that the evidence has not been found.) Instead, an entirely new approach was made, using artificial weapons instead of natural ones, and it worked.

12 From tool-using to tool-making was the next step, and alongside this development went improved hunting techniques, not only in terms of weapons, but also in terms of social cooperation. The hunting apes were pack-hunters, and as their techniques of killing were improved, so

were their methods of social organization. Wolves in a pack deploy themselves, but the hunting ape already had a much better brain than a wolf and could turn it to such problems as group communication and cooperation. Increasingly complex manoeuvres could be developed. The growth of the brain surged on.

13   Essentially this was a hunting-group of males. The females were too busy rearing the young to be able to play a major role in chasing and catching prey. As the complexity of the hunt increased and the forays became more prolonged, it became essential for the hunting ape to abandon the meandering, nomadic ways of its ancestors. A home base was necessary, a place to come back to with the spoils, where the females and young would be waiting and could share the food. This step, as we shall see in later chapters, has had profound effects on many aspects of the behavior of even the most sophisticated naked apes of today.

14   So the hunting ape became a territorial ape. His whole sexual, parental and social pattern began to be affected. His old wandering, fruit-plucking way of life was fading rapidly. He had now really left his forest of Eden. He was an ape with responsibilities. He began to worry about the prehistoric equivalent of washing machines and refrigerators. He began to develop the home comforts—fire, food storage, artificial shelters. But this is where we must stop for the moment, for we are moving out of the realms of biology and into the realms of culture. The biological basis of these advanced steps lies in the development of a brain large and complex enough to enable the hunting ape to take them, but the exact form they assume is no longer a matter of specific genetic control. The forest ape that became a ground ape that became a hunting ape that became a territorial ape has become a cultural ape, and we must call a temporary halt.

DEFINE: *insectivore* (1); *mammalian* (4); *exploitation* (8); *arboreal, carnivore* (9); *primate* (10).

ANALYSIS

structure   1. Develop an outline or chronological list of the main time periods in the development of the naked ape and the most important changes that occurred to him during those time periods. Introduce your outline or list with a thesis statement.

2. Using your outline or list, write a summary of the excerpt.

3. Find and copy the summary statement (one sentence) in the article.

4. Why does Morris cover 30 million years in one section and only one million years in another?

meaning   5. In what part of the world did the ape trend fail to occur?

6. What two choices were left for the early apes?

7. List two of the problems that faced the apes which descended from the trees.

8. List three dramatic improvements that took place in the naked ape's last million years of development.

9. What hunting advantage did the hunting ape have over wolves?

10. How did having a home base affect the naked ape's life?

Louis Fischer

FREEDOM MARCH

In 1928 India was on the verge of a popular uprising against the British. When a series of appeals for independence were turned down by the British government, the Congress Party of India adopted a resolution for unabridged independence and secession from the Empire. All eyes now turned to Mahatma Gandhi, the spiritual leader of the country.

1 The country was tense with suspense. Rabindranath Tagore, for whom Gandhi had the deepest veneration, was in the neighborhood of Sabarmati Ashram and came for a visit on January 18. Piqued by curiosity, he inquired what the Mahatma had in store for India in 1930. "I am furiously thinking day and night," Gandhi replied, "and I do not see any light coming out of the surrounding darkness."

2 "There is a lot of violence in the air," Gandhi stated. In these circumstances civil disobedience, the only alternative to "armed rebellion," involved "undoubted risks," and he was therefore searching for a form of civil disobedience which could not explode into nation-wide violence. For six weeks he searched while the country waited impatiently. India's eyes were on Gandhi's hut.

3 Presently he knew what he would do.

4 Before proceeding with his plan he communicated it to the Viceroy, for he always held that "any secrecy hinders the real spirit of democracy." The letter to Irwin was surely the strangest ever received by the head of a government. "Dear Friend," it began. "Before embarking on Civil Disobedience and taking the risk I have dreaded to take all these years, I would fain approach you and find a way out." He believed in negotiation which might give the adversary an alternative. "I cannot intentionally hurt anything that lives, much less human beings, even though they may do the greatest wrong to me and mine," the letter continued. "Whilst, therefore, I hold the British rule to be a curse, I do not intend harm to a single Englishman or to any legitimate interest he may have in India. . . . And why do I regard the British rule as a curse? It has impoverished the dumb millions by a system of progressive exploitation and by a ruinous expensive military and civil administration which the country can never afford. It has reduced us politically to serfdom. It has sapped the foundations of our culture. . . . I fear . . . there has never been any intention of granting . . . Dominion status to India in the immediate future. . . ."

5 Then Gandhi particularized. In an independent India, he wrote,

From "The Salt of Freedom" in *Gandhi, His Life and Message for the World* by Louis Fischer. Copyright © 1954 by Louis Fischer. Reprinted by arrangement with The New American Library, New York.

the whole revenue system would have to be "revised so as to make the peasant's good its primary concern. But the British system seems to be designed to crush the very life out of him. Even the salt he must use to live is so taxed as to make the burden fall heaviest on him. . . . The tax shows itself still more burdensome on the poor man when it is remembered that salt is the one thing he must eat more than the rich man." Elsewhere he explained that the peasant's salt tax amounted to three days' income a year. The peasant used more salt than the rich because he perspired more while working in the fields under the scorching tropical sun of India. Gandhi's letter complained further that "The drink and drug revenue, too, is derived from the poor. It saps the foundations both of their health and morals.

6   "The iniquities sampled above," the Mahatma charged, "are being maintained in order to carry on a foreign administration demonstrably the most expensive in the world. Take your own salary," he said to the Viceroy. "It is over 21,000 rupees [about $7,000] a month, besides many other indirect additions. . . . You are getting over 700 rupees a day [approximately $233] against India's average income of less than two annas [four cents] a day. Thus you are getting much over five thousand times India's average income. The British Prime Minister is getting only ninety times Britain's average income. On bended knee I ask you to ponder this phenomenon. I have taken a personal illustration to drive home a painful truth. I have too great a regard for you as a man to wish to hurt your feelings. I know that you do not need the salary you get. Probably the whole of your salary goes to charity. But a system that provides such an arrangement deserves to be summarily scrapped. What is true of the Viceregal salary is true generally of the whole administration. . . .

7   "Nothing but organized nonviolence," Gandhi wrote further, "can check the organized violence of the British government. . . . This nonviolence will be expressed through civil disobedience. . . . My ambition is no less than to convert the British people through nonviolence, and thus make them see the wrong they have done to India."

8   Then he pleaded for negotiations. "I respectfully invite you to pave the way for the immediate removal of these evils, and thus open a way for a real conference between equals."

9   "But"—and this was Gandhi's plan—"if you cannot see your way to deal with these evils and if my letter makes no appeal to your heart, on the eleventh day of this month I shall proceed with such co-workers of the Ashram as I can take, to disregard the provisions of the Salt Laws. . . . It is, I know, open to you to frustrate my design by arresting me. I hope that there will be tens of thousands ready, in a disciplined manner, to take up the work after me."

10   Lord Irwin did not reply; his secretary sent an acknowledgment. He refused to see Gandhi, nor did he arrest him.

11   As March 11th neared, India bubbled with excitement. Scores of foreign and domestic newspapermen dogged Gandhi's footsteps in the ashram; what exactly would he do? Thousands camped around the village to witness the spectacle. Cables from the world kept the Ahmedabad post office humming. "God guard you," the Reverend Dr. John Haynes Holmes telegraphed from New York.

[12] On March 12, prayers having been sung, the Mahatma and seventy-eight male members of the ashram, whose names and personal particulars were published in *Young India* for the convenience of the police, left the village on foot. "We are marching in the name of God," Gandhi said.

[13] They headed due south toward the sea. For twenty-four days they walked. Gandhi leaned on a lacquered bamboo staff an inch thick and 54 inches long with an iron tip. A horse was available for Gandhi but he never used it. "Less than twelve miles a day in two stages with not much luggage! Child's play!" he declared. Some days they did fifteen miles. He was sixty-one. Several ashramites became fatigued and footsore. "The modern generation is delicate, weak and much pampered," he commented. He spun an hour every day and kept a diary.

[14] Gandhi and his moving congregation followed winding dirt roads from village to village. Peasants sprinkled the roads and strewed leaves on them. Every settlement on the line of march was festooned with the national colors. As the pilgrims passed, peasants who had gathered from the countryside sank to their knees. Two or three times a day the marchers halted for meetings where the Mahatma and others exhorted the population to wear and make homespun, abjure alcohol and opium, abandon child marriage, and live pure lives.

[15] In the area traversed, over three hundred village headmen gave up their government jobs. The inhabitants of a village would usually accompany the marchers to the next, as a sort of honor guard. From all over India young men and women arrived to attach themselves to the advancing column of ashramites. When Gandhi reached the sea at Dandi on April 5th, his small band had grown into a nonviolent army several thousand strong.

[16] The entire night of April 5th, the ashramites did not sleep but prayed, and early in the morning they accompanied the Mahatma to the sea. He dipped into the water, returned to the beach, and there picked up some salt left by the waves. Mrs. Sarojini Naidu, standing by his side, cried, "Hail, Deliverer."

[17] Gandhi thus broke the British law which made it a punishable crime to possess salt not purchased from the government salt monopoly. He himself had not used salt for six years.

[18] Had Gandhi gone by train or automobile to make salt, the effect would have been considerable. But to walk two hundred and forty-one miles in twenty-four days and rivet the attention of all India, to trek across the countryside saying, "Watch, I will give a signal to the nation," and then to pick up a palmful of salt in publicized defiance of a mighty government, that required imagination, dignity, and the sense of showmanship of a great artist. It appealed to illiterate peasants and it fascinated sophisticated critics like Subhas Chandra Bose who compared the Salt March to "Napoleon's march to Paris after his return from Elba."

[19] The act performed, Gandhi withdrew from the scene. India had its cue; he had communicated with it by stealing some salt from a beach.

[20] Along India's long seacoast and in her numerous bays and inlets, peasants waded into the water with pans and produced salt illegally. The police made mass arrests. Congress volunteers sold contraband salt in the

cities. Many received short prison terms. The police raided the Congress party headquarters in Bombay where salt was being made in pans on the roof. A protesting crowd of sixty thousand assembled; hundreds were handcuffed or their arms fastened with ropes and led off to jail. The salt lifted by Gandhi from the beach at Dandi was sold to the highest bidder for 1600 rupees, over $500, which went to a public fund. Jawaharlal Nehru was sentenced to six months for infringing the Salt Act. The Mayor of Calcutta received a similar sentence for reading seditious literature to a public meeting and urging a boycott of foreign textiles. Kishorlal Mashruwala, one of the Mahatma's most faithful disciples, was incarcerated for two years. Many towns observed hartals when Congress leaders were arrested. Whole provinces were deprived of their nationalist leaders. Vithalbhai Patel, the speaker of the federal Legislative Assembly, resigned and advised Indians to boycott the government. At Peshawar, on the northwest frontier, the police and military were driven from the city; subsequently, troops retook the town and killed seventy and wounded one hundred. The government placed all nationalist newspapers under censorship. The Viceroy, writes Lord Irwin's biographer, "had filled the jails with no less than sixty thousand political offenders." A month after Gandhi had bathed in the sea at Dandi, India seethed in angry yet peaceful revolt. Eager to continue the movement and knowing, from experience, that Gandhi would cancel it if they were violent, Indians remained nonviolent despite beatings, kicks, and arrests.

[21]   On May 4th, less than a month after he had become a salt criminal, Gandhi was arrested in the night while sleeping in a tent a few miles from the scene of his crime. The prison authorities measured him and noted his height: five feet, five inches. To be sure they could identify him again for subsequent arrests, apparently, they recorded his birthmarks: a little scar on the right thigh, a small mole on the lower right eyelid, and a scar the size of a pea below the left elbow. Gandhi loved it in jail. "I have been quite happy and making up for arrears in sleep," he wrote Miss Slade. The prison goat was milked in his presence. (He drank no cow or buffalo milk but his wife Kasturbai had persuaded him, during a near-fatal illness, to take goat's milk. It helped, and he remained an addict for the rest of his life.)

[22]   Several days before his arrest, Gandhi had informed the Viceroy that, "God willing," he would, with some companions, raid the Dharsana Salt Works, 150 miles north of Bombay. God, it developed, was not willing. Mrs. Sarojini Naidu, the poet, substituted as leader of the raid. Twenty-five hundred volunteers participated. Before proceeding Mrs. Naidu warned them that they would be beaten "but," she said, "you must not resist; you must not even raise a hand or ward off a blow."

[23]   Webb Miller, the well-known correspondent of the United Press, who died in England during the second world war, was on the scene and described the event first in dispatches and then in his book, *I Found No Peace*. Manilal Gandhi, second son of the Mahatma, advanced at the head of the marchers and approached the great salt pans which were surrounded by ditches and barbed wire and guarded by four hundred Surat policemen under the command of six British officers. "In complete silence," Miller writes, "the Gandhi men drew up and halted a hundred

yards from the stockade. A picked column advanced from the crowd, waded the ditches, and approached the barbed-wire stockade." The officers ordered them to retreat but they continued to step forward. "Suddenly," the report reads, "at a word of command, scores of native policemen rushed upon the advancing marchers and rained blows on their heads with their steel-shod lathis [staves]. Not one of the marchers even raised an arm to fend off the blows. They went down like ten-pins. From where I stood I heard the sickening whack of the clubs on unprotected skulls. The waiting crowd of marchers groaned and sucked in their breath in sympathetic pain at every blow. Those struck down fell sprawling, unconscious or writhing with fractured skulls or broken shoulders. . . . The survivors, without breaking ranks, silently and doggedly marched on until struck down." When the first column was laid low, another advanced. "Although everyone knew," Webb Miller writes, "that within a few minutes he would be beaten down, perhaps killed, I could detect no sign of wavering or fear. They marched steadily, with heads up, without the encouragement of music or cheering or any possibility that they might escape injury or death. The police rushed out and methodically and mechanically beat down the second column. There was no fight, no struggle, the marchers simply walked forward until struck down." Another group of twenty-five advanced and sat down. "The police," Miller testifies, "commenced savagely kicking the seated men in the abdomen and testicles." Another column presented itself. Enraged, the police dragged them by their arms and feet and threw them into the ditches. "One was dragged to a ditch where I stood," Miller recorded; "the splash of his body doused me with muddy water. Another policeman dragged a Gandhi man to the ditch, threw him in, and belabored him over the head with his lathi. Hour after hour stretcher-bearers carried back a stream of inert, bleeding men."

[24] A British officer took Mrs. Naidu's arm and said, "Sarojini Naidu, you are under arrest." She shook off his hand. "I will come," she said, "but don't touch me." Manilal Gandhi likewise submitted to arrest.

[25] The raids and beatings continued for several days.

[26] India was now free. Legally, technically, nothing had changed. India was still a British colony. But there was a difference and Rabindranath Tagore explained it. He told the *Manchester Guardian* of May 17, 1930, that "Eruope has completely lost her former moral prestige in Asia. She is no longer regarded as the champion throughout the world of fair dealing and the exponent of high principle, but as the upholder of Western race supremacy and the exploiter of those outside her own borders. For Europe this is, in actual fact, a great moral defeat that has happened. Even though Asia is physically weak and unable to protect herself from aggression where her vital interests are menaced, nevertheless she can now afford to look down on Europe where before she looked up." Tagore attributed the achievement in India to Gandhi.

[27] The Salt March and its aftermath did two things: it gave the Indians the conviction that they could lift the foreign yoke from their shoulders; it made the British aware that they were subjugating India. It was inevitable, after 1930, that India would some day refuse to be ruled, and, more important, that England would some day refuse to rule.

28   When the Indians allowed themselves to be beaten with batons and rifle butts and did not cringe they showed that England was powerless and India invincible. The rest was merely a matter of time.

DEFINE: iniquities, phenomenon (6); *ashram,* (12); *abjure* (14); *seditious* (20).

ANALYSIS

structure   1. Write a brief summary of the excerpt (about 200 to 250 words).

meaning   2. Why did Gandhi have to be particularly careful about the method of civil disobedience that he chose?

3. Why did he choose to oppose the salt tax in particular?

4. Why did he write to the Viceroy in advance of his march and also publish a list of his fellow marchers?

5. Why does Fischer believe that Gandhi's choice of actions was such a stroke of genius?

6. The British didn't leave India until many years after the Salt March. Why did many of the Hindus consider it such a great victory?

Review of Chapter 2

Narration is used to entertain, to make a point, to record events, to depict behavior, and to seek the common ground of mutual experience. It is used in material ranging from jokes and myths to legal briefs and scientific studies. It is used in history, biography, journalism, and in story telling.

Although time and events are sometimes rearranged[1] by the writer to achieve his purpose, narration is most often structured chronologically, and the resolution, the weight of the evidence, the moral is placed at the end. In the news story, however, this structure is turned on its head—the most important information being presented at the beginning.

Being aware of narrative structure, the reader can look to the end for answers. If the answers do not seem clear or logical, he can trace his way back to see what he missed, or to decide whether the author failed to build a sound foundation for the conclusion. In reading news stories the reader can expect to find the main ideas at the beginning and details at the end.

The writer of narration is aware of the values that the narrative form provides in allowing the reader to think along and "see" along with the writer. He is aware of time and tense. He selects from many events those that are most pertinent to his purpose and orders them in a meaningful way. He learns to shift tenses only if necessary and to be sure that he makes his shifts clear to the reader. He is also sure that his ending evolves logically out of the material that precedes it.

[1] In fiction the writer sometimes does this to build suspense. In nonfiction narrative writing it is used to make a point or to make the material more interesting. It should not, of course, be used to distort facts.

WRITING SUGGESTION

Write a narrative of a significant period in your life which culminated in some achievement, such as making a team, mastering a skill, being accepted into a group, or graduating from school.

EVALUATION

Consider the longer selections in Section 2B and all of those in Section 2C. Choose two that use narration most effectively, holding your interest and making their points. Evaluate them by using the criteria suggested in Chapter 1 but giving special consideration to the narrative qualities of the selections you chose.

Description

CHAPTER 3

READING FOCUS

❖ Be receptive to the sights, sounds, smells, tastes, and touch sensations that the author provides.

❖ See the relationship between these details and the total mood, atmosphere, or picture that the writer is trying to create.

❖ Distinguish between objective and subjective description.

❖ Distinguish description that is fresh, imaginative, and vivid from that which is trite and superficial.

WRITING FOCUS

❖ Be sufficiently observant (if you aren't already) to know that a leaf is not just green and a blackboard is not just black; that eyes aren't only blue or brown, and that most people aren't entirely ugly or entirely beautiful.

❖ Decide on the overall effect you wish to achieve; then supply sufficient detail to create that effect in the minds of your readers.

❖ Organize your descriptions in such a manner that it is possible for your reader to visualize the pictures you create.

The uses of descriptive writing, as in the case of narration, are underestimated by many students who think of description mostly in terms of poetry and fiction. They tend to overlook the need for people such as scientists, engineers, sportswriters, naturalists, explorers, and advertising copy writers to carefully describe what they see and do. Very little writing is so bare that it contains no description at all.

Description flavors writing, providing the sights, sounds, tastes, odors, and the feel. More, it can probe beneath surfaces and provide insights that cameras cannot capture.

Because readers cannot receive pictures that are poorly focused, description must be handled in a carefully planned sequence so that the reader can more easily reassemble it in his or her mind. It may move from far to near, from top to bottom, from large to small, from left to right. Most often, however, writers tend to move from general to specific or vice versa.

Description can be either objective or subjective. The former attempts to be exact and devoid of personal feeling. The latter usually focuses less on exact detail and more on general impressions and feelings. In "Houses Are Like Sentinels" in Section 3B, the author does not give the number, sizes, or dimensions of the houses, nor even their shapes. To him they are "like sentinels in the plain, old keepers of the weather watch." Compare that approach to the objective descriptions of the fuel pump and the heart in the same section. These provide precise descriptions, devoid of feeling.

section 3a

"Wanted" Poster

BANK ROBBERY; INTERSTATE FLIGHT - ARMED ROBBERY

Entered NCIC
I.O. 4740
3-30-77

WANTED BY FBI
MILLARD OSCAR HUBBARD

FBI No. 168,172 A

ALIASES: Dick Bedillion, Bill Campbell, Harry Cox, Jim Lovelace, John Lovelace, Wayne Lycans, Ralph Moore, "Dillinger", "Hubb"

NCIC: POAA0415171203121516

4 0 1 A 10 17
M 17 U 100

Photograph taken 1974

Date photograph taken unknown

DESCRIPTION
AGE: 48, born August 15, 1928, Whitley County, Kentucky
HEIGHT: 5'8" to 5'9"   EYES: brown
WEIGHT: 145 to 150 pounds   COMPLEXION: medium
BUILD: medium   RACE: white
HAIR: black, graying   NATIONALITY: American
OCCUPATIONS: carpenter, construction worker, concrete worker, truck driver
REMARKS: reportedly an avid fisherman and hunter, may wear wig and glasses, lower teeth false
SOCIAL SECURITY NUMBER USED: 403-34-6678

CRIMINAL RECORD
Hubbard has been convicted of armed robbery, housebreaking, robbery, and transporting stolen motor vehicle interstate.

CAUTION
HUBBARD HAS USED A PISTOL AND AN M-16 RIFLE IN THE BANK ROBBERIES FOR WHICH HE IS BEING SOUGHT. HE SHOULD BE CONSIDERED ARMED, DANGEROUS, AND AN ESCAPE RISK.

Federal warrants were issued April 3, 1975, at Lexington, Kentucky, charging Hubbard with unlawful flight to avoid prosecution for operating motor vehicle without owner's consent, possession of stolen license plate, and armed robbery (Title 18, U. S. Code, Section 1073); August 17, 1976, at Knoxville, Tennessee, September 1, 1976, and September 15, 1976, at Columbus, Ohio, charging Hubbard with bank robbery (Title 18, U. S. Code, Sections 2113a, 2113d, and 2).

Matrimonial Ads

Some people associate matrimonial ads only with promiscuous youth. Most of the following ads were written by people in their late twenties or older. They were placed in a conservative magazine, a literary gazette, a New England newspaper, and a newspaper in Bombay, India.

ATTRACTIVE MALE, 43, divorced 3 years, desires nice looking woman, 28-38, who wants to share warm, fulfilling relationship leading to marriage. I'm 6'3", strong and healthy, and would be very loving and gentle to that "special person." My interests include travel, music, the arts and a steady dose of the great outdoors: running, skiing, tennis, fishing, scuba diving, etc. I'm a successful businessman, financially secure, who enjoys living and challenges. You're probably a college graduate, have similar interests, enjoy being a woman, and feel comfortable and happy in a one to one relationship. Send letter and photo.

NYC WOMAN, 37, attractive, professional, spiritual seeker, loves early music, hiking, skiing, the ocean, Yoga, health foods, and the arts, wishes to meet man who is warm, in touch with his feelings, expressive, nurturing yet masculine, physically fit, has broad intellectual and aesthetic interests, is reasonably financially successful, values personal growth and the spiritual path. No marrieds.

I'M LOOKING for a man 30's-40's with a zest for living yet who is tender and in touch with his spiritual self. I appreciate nature—especially enjoy hiking and gardening. Like to dance and to philosophize. I'm looking for a genuine friendship with the possibility of permanence.

A GOAN CATHOLIC GIRL, 27, tall, slim, attractive double graduate, Bank-officer, qualified in music, well accomplished in domestic duties, with exceptionally high family background, invites matrimonial correspondence from well placed Catholic bachelors in the age group 28–35, minimum graduate, having decent accommodation and with top family background. Advertisement for wider selection only. Apply with full particulars to Box —, Times of India, Bombay.

SUNNI MUSLIM GIRL, 22, VERY beautiful, fair, slim, S.S.C. D. Ed. from respectable family, working as teacher, earning Rs. 500 per month, well versed in household activities requires Sunni Muslim boy who should be from respectable family holding a good post, drawing a handsome salary and having his own accommodation. Write Box —, Bombay.

A RARE BIRD has landed in southern Maine to mend a broken wing. Bird is 44, tall, lean, excellent plumage, lightly grizzled. Flew many directions and now seeks rest from multifarious projects and deciduous loves to finish novel. Poet, carpenter, romanticist, pragmatist, business exec, humanist, entertainer, father, doer, dreamer, marathoner, gardener, restaurateur, giver, joyful but lonely builder of good nests. Bird seeks financial partner, preferably lady of means for real estate restoration or other venture. Romance not necessary. Loyalty a must. A pooling of strengths and needs. A partnership. Write . . . Don't be bashful.

GOOD LOOKING, warm, sensitive Bangor male, early 30's/with 6 yr. old daughter, seeks sensitive, caring, Bangor area woman to share the joys and pain of growing, and to support each other's growth, which comes from mutual sharing. Am looking for someone who enjoys walks in the snow, fireplaces, mellow music, quiet talks together and an honest and open sharing of each other's thoughts and feelings and who is willing to risk reaching out for a truly meaningful relationship.

ITALIAN LAWYER, 48 YEARS BUT really young looking, rich wealthy gentleman, owning land estates and international trading enterprises, slim, athletic, height mt. 1.80, weight kg. 75, wishing to settle partly in India, loving Indian culture, seriously interested marriage beautiful young Indian girl, virgin, highest morality, good general culture, equivalent rich family, preferable correspondence through family, addressing Doctor ——, via Stella, Roma, Italy.

CONSERVATIVE PENSIONER (also has small job) 37. Walks with cane, non-smoker, country intellectual, loves good wine. Would like to correspond with lonely single girl of Buddhist, Shinto, Jewish, or Unitarian religion.

SOMEWHERE IN THIS WORLD there must be an intelligent, sensitive, conservative young woman who can believe in, understand, and respect a man who receives more pleasure from giving than receiving. Never-married male, 31, a conservative, sensitive, hard-core romantic who enjoys warm, quiet conversations and secluded country living, wants to know if you exist and dare to care enough to reach out and touch.

NYC MAN, WASP, in his fifties, not handsome but aristocratic, not presently wealthy but with considerable expectations, interested in literature, the arts, and word games, among other things, seeks companionable, gentle woman, in her forties or so, with similar interests, who likes to cook (I will help). If compatible, marriage a possibility. Please send photograph.

Real Estate and "Situation Wanted" Ads

BEAUTIFUL LOT! LOTS OF ROOM!
BAY VILLAGE!

Lots of room in this 3-bedrm., 1½ bath bungalow in Bay Village. Near schools, parks and fantastic wood environment on private 100x145 lot. Enter foyer to its 20x18 living rm. with wood-burning fireplace, dining rm. has chair rail, French door and beautiful hardwood floors, 14x10. Plus large 20x13 family rm. with hard pegwood floors, paneled walls and plenty of windows letting the outdoors in! Bedrms on 1st, 14x12 and 12x9 with large double door closets, two closets in master bedrm. 2d floor has 22x12 bedrm. with expansion space! Plenty of room in its 13x9 kitchen with wood cabinets, built-in range, stove and dishwasher, off to ½ lav. and 2½-car attached garage. Central air, marble fireplace, louvre doors and charm make this a must home to see! Basement is huge, 33x13, finished rec. rm. plus 16x14 utility rm. plus 17x12 workrm. Large home, excellent location and August possession! Low 70s.

DELIVERY with own 2-ton van. Nights after 3 p.m. Prefer permanent position. $5-$6 hourly + mileage. Very experienced. Healthy 27 yr. old male.

ADMINISTRATIVE ASST. returning to work full time. 5 yrs. recent community service exp. Prior full time in television, airline, and utility fields. Strong organizing and problem-solving skills. Editing exp., usable S/H, typing, bookkeeping. Mature. Dependable. References.

EXCEPTIONAL SALT BOX with center chimney, three bedrooms, two baths, large living room with fireplace and sliding glass doors, den with sliding glass doors, sewing alcove, all electric kitchen. 100' of water frontage on Sheepscot River. Beautifully landscaped. Many extras added at time of construction such as insulation of inside walls to cut down on interior sounds. Decorated with gracious living in mind. This property must be seen to be appreciated for its beauty. $89,500.

BAY VILLAGE RANCH
beautiful, excellent condition
By owner. By appointment
3 bedrooms 24x12, 13x10, 13x12. Living rm. 21x13 has floor-to-ceiling, wood-burning fireplace. Dining rm. 12x10. Cheerful kitchen with separate dinette, all appliances included. Clay tile bath with glass-doored shower over tub. Hardwood floors and plastered walls throughout. Upstairs and down completely carpeted. Screen enclosed porch. 2-car attached garage with 2 electric door openers. Professionally decorated very tastefully throughout. A true picture—picture window view, other windows look out on the yard's 12 magnificent trees. "Lot size" rear yard enclosed with concealed fencing, front and rear yard professionally landscaped; 2 small patios. Air conditioning and smoke detectors throughout. Lot size 85x145
GREAT LOCATION • SERIOUS BUYERS
ONLY
PRICE FIRM $71,300

BEAUTIFUL SPLIT LEVEL HOME—70's Fabulous buy, immaculate 4-bedroom home with a full 2½ baths. Only 6 years old with a full basement and 2½-car garage. Lots of space throughout this home with a large eat-in kitchen with built-ins. Very formal separate dining room. Elegant living room to entertain and a warm, cheery family room with woodburning fireplace. Lots of extras in this very special home. Gas heat, patio, large lot, and plenty of features you would expect in a much more expensive home. Call now for your showing.

ELEGANT 1938 CAPE with 8 spacious rooms. Your comfort is assured as you enjoy the paneled living/dining room, sun porch, 2 fireplaces, and 2½ baths. The attached 2-car garage is also joined with a garden shed, wood shed, and workshop. Enjoy the spectacular ocean view with 10 islands from this very private 10 acres on a hill top. The tastefully landscaped grounds include blueberry fields and 2 great gardens. Good harbors nearby. $150,000.

PRESENTLY employed sales manager is looking to switch sales career. Have peaked my earnings. I am looking for a professional sales career that offers minimum salary of $18-$21K plus incentive. Have 7 yrs. sales background, 5 in management. Have done big ticket sales, and 2 yrs. professional sales trainer. Please only career sales with salary plus incentive.

Product Advertisements

TO A LEGENDARY WATER GOBLET BY WATERFORD

In February you'll hold snowdrops gathered from melting snows. In March you'll have daffodils, intrepid tassels on March's bugle-horn. By April you'll find lilies of the valley, slender beauties, or maybe colored Easter eggs within your crystal depths. And in May you'll feel cool water taken from a lively spring where a rainbow's foot once met fragrant fields, yielding not diamonds piled, but refreshing draughts in which blended colors play.

Perhaps in June, I'll pluck you rosebuds, flush-white with tips yet moist from dew. In July I'll bring you wine, remembering a Genevan slope and hours without end. And when the sun is set to its August moon, I'll give you iced lemon or homemade cream and think on lands beyond the Reeks of Cork where summer smells be rising and a shiny moon sinking behind the hills . . .

Advertisement written by Adelaide Curtis. © Waterford Co.

INNER SHALIMAR . . . OUTER SHALIMAR

Like every woman, every great perfume has both an outer expression and a deeper, inner mood.

How many bold smiles reveal an inner shyness? How many accidental touches are meant as an inner embrace, warm and loving?

Outwardly, Shalimar expresses elegance, calm ... a serene femininity.

But stay with the magnificent scent long enough and you will discover its inner mood ... a clipper ship slicing through the seas, the power of a storm about to break, a deep sensuality waiting to be released.

You don't just dab on a perfume like Shalimar. You wear it body and soul.

Reprinted by permission of Primauté Advertising Inc.

MGB—THE WELL COORDINATED ATHLETE

The MGB is designed to perform on that narrow band where first place is separated from second place by fractions of seconds and tenths of inches.

And like all great athletes who strive to excel in their class, MGB has faced the test of competition and has emerged victorious. It is the reigning National Champion in SCCAE Production for the third year in a row.

Experience its stamina and reflexes on the road: Any road. The curvy, scenic kind or the wide, fast kind. The "B" excels at both.

The MGB puts it all together with its gas-saving four cylinder 1798 c.c. engine and short-throw, four-speed gearbox. Combined, you get maximum response with good gas mileage—from 18 to 23 mpg depending on where and how you drive.

The rack and pinion steering, race seasoned suspension and front disc brakes function with such balance and harmony that the result is truly that of a champion.

Other standard "B" features: Complete instrumentation, including tachometer, trip odometer and gauges for fuel, water, oil and battery. Also reclining bucket seats, wrapped steering wheel, carpeting, oil cooler, mag-style wheels and radial-ply tires.

So go down and meet the athletic MGB at your MG dealer. For dealer's name, call (800) 447-4700. In Illinois, call (800) 322-4400. Calls are toll free.

Reprinted by permission of British Leyland Motors Inc., Leonia, N.J.

DEFINE: *tachometer, odometer, rack and pinion.*

ANALYSIS

style 1. Which of the selections is the most objective? Explain.

2. Why does the MGB ad seem to be more objective than the other ads? Is it? Explain.

3. Why aren't the real estate ads even more subjective than they are?

4. Why does the writer describe not the Waterford goblet but rather what the goblet holds?

1. Write a "wanted" poster for yourself or a classmate, based on a fictitious crime.

2. Write a matrimonial ad. Since you don't have to pay for its publication, make the description of yourself and the mate you desire longer and more detailed than those in the sample ads.

3. "Sell" yourself to an employer via a "situation wanted" ad. Develop your ad much more thoroughly than the sample ads.

4. Write a real estate ad offering your house (real or imaginary) for sale.

5. Write two brief product ads: a "mood" ad like the Shalimar one, and a more "fact-filled" one like the MGB ad.

Section 3b

Places and Things

HOUSES ARE LIKE SENTINELS

Houses are like sentinels in the plain, old keepers of the weather watch. There, in a very little while, wood takes on the appearance of great age. All colors wear soon away in the wind and rain, and then the wood is burned gray and the grain appears and the nails turn red with rust. The windowpanes are black and opaque; you imagine there is nothing within, and indeed there are many ghosts, bones given up to the land. They stand here and there against the sky, and you approach them for a longer time than you expect. They belong in the distance; it is their domain.

From *The Way to Rainy Mountain* by N. Scott Momaday. © 1969, by The University of New Mexico Press. First published in *The Reporter,* January 26, 1967.

THE UNIVERSAL WAITING ROOM

The room intimidates us. It is a dreary place, done in thirties Bureaucratic, too dull to sustain more than a few minutes of mental effort. On the subconscious level, however, it exerts a strong and uncanny hold. It is the universal waiting room. It is the induction center and the clinic; it is the

From *The Lunacy Room* by William K. Zinsser. © 1968, 1970 by William K. Zinsser. Reprinted by permission.

assembly hall and the office where forms are filled out. Thoughts come unbidden there, sneaking back from all the other moments—in the army, at camp, on the first day of school—when we were part of a crowd and therefore lonely.

THE SEWING ROOM

Whenever we children came to stay at my grandmother's house, we were put to sleep in the sewing room, a bleak, shabby, utilitarian rectangle, more office than bedroom, more attic than office, that played to the hierarchy of chambers the role of a poor relation. It was a room seldom entered by the other members of the family, seldom swept by the maid, a room without pride; the old sewing machine, some cast-off chairs, a shadeless lamp, rolls of wrapping paper, piles of cardboard boxes that might someday come in handy, papers of pins, and remnants of material united with the iron folding cots put out for our use and the bare floor boards to give an impression of intense and ruthless temporality. Thin white spreads, of the kind used in hospitals and charity institutions, and naked blinds at the windows reminded us of our orphaned condition and of the ephemeral character of our visit; there was nothing here to encourage us to consider this our home.

From *Memories of a Catholic Girlhood* by Mary McCarthy. Copyright 1948 by Mary McCarthy. Reprinted by permission of Harcourt Brace Jovanovich, Inc. First published in *The New Yorker*.

A SORROWFUL ROOM

The room in which I found myself was very large and lofty. The windows were long, narrow, and pointed, and at so vast a distance from the black oaken floor as to be altogether inaccessible from within. Feeble gleams of encrimsoned light made their way through the trellised panes, and served to render sufficiently distinct the more prominent objects around; the eye, however, struggled in vain to reach the remoter angles of the chamber, or the recesses of the vaulted and fretted ceiling. Dark draperies hung upon the walls. The general furniture was profuse, comfortless, antique, and tattered. Many books and musical instruments lay scattered about, but failed to give any vitality to the scene. I felt that I breathed an atmosphere of sorrow. An air of stern, deep, and irredeemable gloom hung over and pervaded all.

From *The Fall of the House of Usher* by Edgar Allan Poe.

THE COTTAGE

There was a special smell to the cottage at Beach Haven, indigenous, I think, to the Jersey shore. The minute one opened the front door one met it—a combination of dampness, beach sand, old wicker furniture, oil from the guns that stood racked with the fishing rods in the little west room off the hall. Whatever the mixture, to my nostrils it was very sweet. This whiff, this musty breath meant running barefoot on the beach, bathing in the foam of the breakers. It meant sailing on the bay, crabbing from the dock, riding one's bicycle on the wide yellow-pebbled streets, easy and free.

Yet there was more to these summer months than a vacation. We worked hard at what we did. Both parents saw to that, whether it was learning to shoot or swim or manage a sailboat or even to clean fish before we brought them to Bridget at the back door. It was here also that the family came together and stayed together; when my brothers were in college and graduate school they spent much time at Beach Haven, studying, working on a thesis or a projected book such as Harry's volumes on the Interstate Commerce Act.

As years passed the cottage became for us a kind of homestead. Our parents might move from Philadelphia to Haverford to Bethlehem and back again. But always that creaky cottage door with the painted glass panels opened to home. . . . The stuffed curlew over the mantel spread its gray-brown wings, the mounted drumfish stared blindly from its board above the sofa. Upstairs the painted iron beds waited with their hard hair mattresses, and in a corner of the dining room the wooden water cooler dribbled from its spigot.

From *Family Portrait* by Catherine Drinker Bowen. Copyright © 1970 by Catherine Drinker Bowen. Reprinted by permission of Little, Brown and Co. in association with The Atlantic Monthly Press.

THE KITCHEN

The kitchen held our lives together. My mother worked in it all day long, we ate in it almost all meals except the Passover *seder,* I did my homework and first writing at the kitchen table, and in winter I often had a bed made up for me on three kitchen chairs near the stove. On the wall just over the table hung a long horizontal mirror that sloped to a ship's prow at each end and was lined in cherry wood. It took up the whole wall, and drew every object in the kitchen to itself. The walls were a fiercely stippled whitewash, so often rewhitened by my father in slack seasons that the paint looked as if it had been squeezed and cracked into the walls. A large electric bulb hung down the center of the kitchen at the end of a chain that had been hooked into the ceiling; the old gas ring and key still jutted out of the wall like antlers. In the corner next to the toilet was the sink at which we

From *A Walker in the City,* copyright 1951 by Alfred Kazin. Reprinted by permission of Harcourt Brace Jovanovich, Inc.

washed, and the square tub in which my mother did our clothes. Above it, tacked to the shelf on which were pleasantly ranged square, blue-bordered white sugar and spice jars, hung calendars from the Public National Bank on Pitkin Avenue and the Minsker Progressive Branch of the Workman's Circle; receipts for the payment of insurance premiums, and household bills on a spindle; two little boxes engraved with Hebrew letters. One of these was for the poor, the other to buy back the Land of Israel. Each spring a bearded little man would suddenly appear in our kitchen, salute us with a hurried Hebrew blessing, empty the boxes (sometimes with a side-long look of disdain if they were not full), hurriedly bless us again for remembering our less fortunate Jewish brothers and sisters, and so take his departure until the next spring, after vainly trying to persuade my mother to take still another box. We did occasionally remember to drop coins in the boxes, but this was usually only on the dreaded morning of "midterms" and final examinations, because my mother thought it would bring me luck. She was extremely superstitious, but embarrassed about it, and always laughed at herself whenever, on the morning of an examination, she counseled me to leave the house on my right foot. "I know it's silly," her smile seemed to say, "but what harm can it do? It may calm God down."

A FUEL PUMP

A fuel pump is a round metal object about four inches in diameter and three inches high with a lever sticking out of its side. Older models have a small glass bowl on the bottom.

The major parts of a fuel pump are the bottom plate and diaphragm, the middle section, and the operating-lever assembly. The bottom plate is a round, cup-shaped plate about three inches in diameter with bolt holes along the perimeter. The diaphragm, which is made of tough, flexible, elastic material and is cut to match the bottom plate, is the container for the fuel. The bottom plate holds and seals the diaphragm and allows the diaphragm to stretch back and forth. The middle section is a round metal plate about two inches high and three inches in diameter with bolt holes along the perimeter to match those in the bottom plate. The middle section contains two valves that control the direction of the fuel flow. The operating-lever assembly has a shaped lever about five inches long, a pushrod, and a return spring. The assembly drains the fuel into and out of the fuel pump. The lever is attached to the middle section by a pin that acts as a pivot.

When the engine is running, the camshaft in the engine pushes the operating lever down. This action pushes the pushrod up and pulls the diaphragm up. This draws fuel into the fuel pump. When the operating lever returns to normal, it closes the valves in the middle section and pushes the fuel from the pump into the carburetor.

From *Writing and Reading in Technical English* by Nell Ann Pickett and Ann A. Laster. Copyright © 1970 by Nell Ann Pickett and Ann A. Laster. Reprinted by permission of Harper & Row, Publishers.

THE HEART

The heart is a muscular organ located in the chest (*thoracic*) cavity and covered by a fibrous sac, the *pericardium*. Its walls are composed primarily of muscle (*myocardium*), the structure of which is different from either skeletal or smooth muscle. The inner surface of the myocardium, i.e., the surface in contact with the blood within the heart chambers, is lined by a thin layer of cells (*endothelium*).

The human heart is divided longitudinally into right and left halves (Fig. 9-3), each consisting of two chambers, an *atrium* and a *ventricle*. The cavities of the atrium and ventricle on each side of the heart communicate with each other, but the right chambers do not communicate directly with those on the left. Thus, right and left atria and right and left ventricles are distinct.

Perhaps the easiest way to picture the architecture of the heart is to begin with its fibrous skeleton, which comprises four rings of dense connective tissue joined together (Fig. 9-4). To the tops of these rings are anchored the muscle masses of the atria, pulmonary artery, and aorta. To the bottom are attached the muscle masses of the ventricles. The connective-tissue rings form the openings between the atria and ventricles and between the great arteries and ventricles. To these rings are attached four sets of valves (Figs. 9-4 and 9-5).

Between the cavities of the atrium and ventricle in each half of the heart are the *atrioventricular valves* (*AV valves*), which permit blood to flow from atrium to ventricle but not from ventricle to atrium. The right and left AV valves are called, respectively, the *tricuspid* and *mitral* valves. When the blood is moving from atrium to ventricle, the valves lie open against the ventricular wall, but when the ventricles contract, the valves are brought together by the increasing pressure of the ventricular blood and the atrioventricular opening is closed. Blood is therefore forced into the pulmonary artery (from the right ventricle) and into the aorta (from the left ventricle) instead of back into the atria. To prevent the valves themselves from being forced upward into the atrium, they are fastened by fibrous strands to muscular projections of the ventricular walls. These muscular projections do *not* open or close the valves: they act only to limit the valves' movements and prevent them from being everted. . . .

From *Human Physiology: The Mechanisms of Body Function* by Vander, Sherman, and Luciano. Copyright © 1970, 1975 by McGraw Hill, Inc. Used by permission.

ANALYSIS

structure

1. Copy the topic sentences in "Houses Are Like Sentinels," "The Universal Waiting Room," and "The Cottage." (There are three topic sentences in the latter.)

2. List words and phrases that support the topic sentences you selected.

3. Write a thesis statement for "The Cottage."

4. Combine the ideas in two of Poe's sentences to write a thesis statement which introduces you to the room and its atmosphere at the same time.

5. Examine the order in which detail is presented in the following: "A Fuel Pump," "The Heart," and "A Sorrowful Room."

meaning

6. Discuss "They belong in the distance. It is their domain" ("Houses Are Like Sentinels").

7. What common theme do "The Cottage" and "The Kitchen" share?

8. Discuss "part of a crowd and therefore lonely" ("The Universal Waiting Room") and "It may calm God down" ("The Kitchen").

style

9. Indicate the words and phrases which support McCarthy's contention that the sewing room is to the house what the McCarthy children are to the grandmother.

10. Classify the descriptions in this section into three groups according to *tone:* (a) those in which the author expresses a dislike for her subject; (b) those in which she expresses a liking; (c) those in which her position is neutral.

11. "The Universal Waiting Room" doesn't appeal directly to any of the senses. It gives no colors, shapes, sounds, smells, tastes, or textures. Is it a successful description? Explain.

12. *Guard* and *watchman* are synonyms for *sentinel.* Does *sentinel* as used in "Houses Are Like Sentinels" have connotations that make it a more appropriate choice?

13. Comment on Momaday's choice of *domain* rather than *territory, realm,* or *property.*

14. Comment on Poe's use of *encrimsoned* rather than *reddened.*

WRITING SUGGESTIONS

1. Write two brief descriptions of a room, a subjective one and an objective one.

2. Try the preceding exercise with a vase, a key, or a locket.

3. Describe a tool or a kitchen gadget objectively.

4. Rewrite "The Universal Waiting Room," describing the room as fully as you can.

section 3c

People

DINTY MOORE

In memory, the old man is a wobble of chins, an aroma of bay rum, a shirt front of creamy pongee, a fine London suit with a cuff of long underwear peeking out, a pink, just-barbered face and a few long strands of hair plastered on gleaming scalp.

From "Dinty Moore's Restaurant" by Shana Alexander, *Newsweek,* August 20, 1973. Reprinted by permission.

GEORGE FOREMAN

Taken directly, Foreman was no small representative of vital force. He came out from the elevator dressed in embroidered bib overalls and dungaree jacket and entered the lobby of the Inter-Continental flanked by a Black on either side. He did not look like a man so much as a lion standing just as erectly as a man. He appeared sleepy but in the way of a lion digesting a carcass. His broad handsome face (not unreminiscent of a mask of Clark Gable somewhat flattened) was neither friendly nor unfriendly, rather, it was alert in the way a boxer is in some part of him alert no matter how sleepy he looks, a heightening common, perhaps, to all good athletes, so that they can pick an insect out of the air with their fingers but as easily notice the expression on some friend in the thirtieth row from ringside.

From *The Fight* by Norman Mailer. © 1975 by Norman Mailer. Used by permission of Little, Brown and Co.

JOSEPH STALIN

His was a low-slung, smallish figure, neither markedly stout nor thin, inclining, if anything, to the latter. The square-cut tunic seemed always a bit too large for him; one sensed an effort to compensate for the slightness of stature. Yet there was also a composed, collected strength, and a certain rough handsomeness, in his features. The teeth were discolored, the mustache scrawny, coarse, and streaked. This, together with the pocked face and yellow eyes, gave him the aspect of an old battle-scarred tiger. In manner—with us, at least—he was simple, quiet, unassuming. There was no striving for effect. His words were few. They generally sounded reasonable and sensible; indeed, they often were. An unforewarned visitor would never have guessed what depths of calculation, ambition, love of power, jealousy, cruelty, and sly vindictiveness lurked behind this unpretentious façade.

From *Memoirs 1925–1950* by George F. Kennan. Copyright © 1967 by George F. Kennan. Used by permission of Little, Brown and Co. in association with The Atlantic Monthly Press.

DEFINE: pongee, unreminiscent, vindictiveness, unpretentious.

A KIOWA GRANDMOTHER

Now that I can have her only in memory, I see my grandmother in the several postures that were peculiar to her: standing at the wood stove

From *The Way to Rainy Mountain* by N. Scott Momaday. Copyright 1969 by The University of New Mexico Press. First published in *The Reporter,* January 26, 1967. Reprinted by permission of The University of New Mexico Press.

on a winter morning and turning meat in a great iron skillet; sitting at the south window, bent above her beadwork, and afterwards, when her vision failed, looking down for a long time into the fold of her hands; going out upon a cane, very slowly as she did when the weight of age came upon her; praying. I remember her most often at prayer. She made long, rambling prayers out of suffering and hope, having seen many things. I was never sure that I had the right to hear, so exclusive were they of all mere custom and company. The last time I saw her she prayed standing by the side of her bed at night, naked to the waist, the light of a kerosene lamp moving upon her dark skin. Her long, black hair, always drawn and braided in the day, lay upon her shoulders and against her breasts like a shawl. I do not speak Kiowa, and I never understood her prayers, but there was something inherently sad in the sound, some merest hesitation upon the syllables of sorrow. She began in a high and descending pitch, exhausting her breath to silence; then again and again—and always the same intensity of effort, of something that is, and is not, like urgency in the human voice. Transported so in the dancing light among the shadows of her room, she seemed beyond the reach of time. But that was illusion; I think I knew then that I should not see her again.

W. Somerset Maugham

DR. AUDLIN

[1] There was in Dr. Audlin's appearance nothing to attract attention. He was tall and spare, with narrow shoulders and something of a stoop; his hair was grey and thin; his long, sallow face deeply lined. He was not more than fifty, but he looked older. His eyes, pale-blue and rather large, were weary. When you had been with him for a while you noticed that they moved very little; they remained fixed on your face, but so empty of expression were they that it was no discomfort. They seldom lit up. They gave no clue to his thoughts nor changed with the words he spoke. If you were of an observant turn it might have struck you that he blinked much less often than most of us. His hands were on the large side, with long, tapering fingers; they were soft, but firm, cool but not clammy. You could never have said what Dr. Audlin wore unless you had made a point of looking. His clothes were dark. His tie was black. His dress made his sallow lined face paler, and his pale eyes more wan. He gave you the impression of a very sick man.

[2] Dr. Audlin was a psycho-analyst. He had adopted the profession by accident and practised it with misgiving. When the war broke out he had not been long qualified and was getting experience at various hospitals; he offered his services to the authorities, and after a time was sent out to France. It was then that he discovered his singular gift. He could allay

From *The Mixture as Before* by W. Somerset Maugham. Copyright 1940 by W. Somerset Maugham. Reprinted by permission of Doubleday & Company, Inc.; and A. P. Watt & Son.

certain pains by the touch of his cool, firm hands, and by talking to them often induce sleep in men who were suffering from sleeplessness. He spoke slowly. His voice had no particular colour, and its tone did not alter with the words he uttered, but it was musical, soft, and lulling.

John Steinbeck

JUAN CHICOY

1   The electric lantern, with a flat downward reflector, lighted sharply only legs and feet and tires and tree trunks near to the ground. It bobbed and swung, and the little incandescent bulb was blindingly blue-white. Juan Chicoy carried his lantern to the garage, took a bunch of keys from his overalls pocket, found the one that unlocked the padlock, and opened the wide doors. He switched on the overhead light and turned off his lantern.

2   Juan picked a striped mechanic's cap from his workbench. He wore Headlight overalls with big brass buttons on bib and side latches, and over this he wore a black horsehide jacket with black knitted wristlets and neck. His shoes were round-toed and hard, with soles so thick that they seemed swollen. An old scar on his cheek beside his large nose showed as a shadow in the overhead light. He ran fingers through his thick, black hair to get it all in the mechanic's cap. His hands were short and wide and strong, with square fingers and nails flattened by work and grooved and twisted from having been hammered and hurt. The third finger of his left hand had lost the first joint, and the flesh was slightly mushroomed where the finger had been amputated. This little overhanging ball was shiny and of a different texture from the rest of the finger, as though the joint were trying to become a fingertip, and on this finger he wore a wide gold wedding ring, as though this finger was no good for work any more and might as well be used for ornament.

3   A pencil and a ruler and a tire pressure gauge protruded from a slot in his overalls bib. Juan was clean-shaven, but not since yesterday, and along the corners of his chin and on his neck the coming whiskers were grizzled and white like those of an old Airedale. This was the more apparent because the rest of his beard was so intensely black. His black eyes were squinting and humorous, the way a man's eyes squint when he is smoking and cannot take the cigarette from his mouth. And Juan's mouth was full and good, a relaxed mouth, the underlip slightly protruding—not in petulance but in humor and self-confidence—the upper lip well formed except left of center where a deep scar was almost white against the pink tissue. The lip must have been cut clear through at one time, and now this thin taut band of white was a strain on the fullness of

From *The Wayward Bus* by John Steinbeck. Copyright 1947 by John Steinbeck; renewed © 1975 by Elaine Steinbeck, John Steinbeck IV, Thomas Steinbeck. Reprinted by permission of Viking Penguin Inc.

the lip and made it bunch in tiny tucks on either side. His ears were not very large, but they stood out sharply from his head like seashells, or in the position a man would hold them with his hands if he wanted to hear more clearly. Juan seemed to be listening intently all the time, while his squinting eyes seemed to laugh at what he heard, and half of his mouth disapproved. His movements were sure even when he was not doing anything that required sureness. He walked as though he were going to some exact spot. His hands moved with speed and precision and never fiddled with matches or with nails. His teeth were long and the edges were framed with gold, which gave his smile a little fierceness.

Charles Dickens

THOMAS GRADGRIND

1   "Now, what I want is, Facts. Teach these boys and girls nothing but Facts. Facts alone are wanted in life. Plant nothing else, and root out everything else. You can only form the minds of reasoning animals upon Facts; nothing else will ever be of any service to them. This is the principle on which I bring up my own children, and this is the principle on which I bring up these children. Stick to Facts, sir!"

2   The scene was a plain, bare, monotonous vault of a schoolroom, and the speaker's square forefinger emphasized his observations by underscoring every sentence with a line on the schoolmaster's sleeve. The emphasis was helped by the speaker's square wall of a forehead, which had his eyebrows for its base, while his eyes found commodious cellarage in two dark caves, overshadowed by the wall. The emphasis was helped by the speaker's mouth, which was wide, thin, and hard set. The emphasis was helped by the speaker's voice, which was inflexible, dry, and dictatorial. The emphasis was helped by the speaker's hair, which bristled on the skirts of his bald head, a plantation of firs to keep the wind from its shining surface, all covered with knobs, like the crust of a plum pie, as if the head had scarcely warehouse-room for the hard facts stored inside. The speaker's obstinate carriage, square coat, square legs, square shoulders—nay, his very neckcloth, trained to take him by the throat with an unaccommodating grasp, like a stubborn fact, as it was—all helped the emphasis.

3   "In this life, we want nothing but Facts, sir; nothing but Facts!"

4   The speaker, and the schoolmaster, and the third grown person present, all backed a little, and swept with their eyes the inclined plane of little vessels then and there arranged in order, ready to have imperial gallons of facts poured into them until they were full to the brim.

From *Hard Times* by Charles Dickens.

Michael Swift

DINOSAUR

1   He is between 45 and 65. He is white. He is male. He is determinedly heterosexual. He suffers from hypertension. He is trying to quit smoking.

2   He makes between $25,000 and $50,000 a year. He has $20,000 in savings and $10,000 in stocks. He has many debts. He works for a large corporation or owns a small business. He dreams of making it to the top of the heap, but in the middle of the night he sadly realizes he's gone about as far as he's going to go.

3   He graduated from an undistinguished college where he majored in business administration or economics. He had to take courses in English in college that gave him a lot of trouble. He misspells words in the business letters he writes in longhand and is annoyed when his secretary points out the errors. He is basically inarticulate. He reads three or four novels a year. The novels are by Jacqueline Susann or Harold Robbins. He likes novels with a good "story."

4   Modern painting and modern poetry make him angry. He doesn't understand why art critics put down Andrew Wyeth. He doesn't go to the movies much anymore, but he saw "Jaws" and "All the President's Men." Marlon Brando and Jane Fonda make him sick. His wife is interested in the arts and encourages him to attend concerts and plays with her, but he is reluctant to go. He thinks the arts are basically sissy stuff.

5   He watches every football game on television in the fall but isn't keen on baseball anymore. He belongs to a country club and shoots in the high 80s. He makes small bets on his golf game.

6   He drinks gin or scotch. He has three drinks before dinner, two at lunch. He gets tipsy on Saturday afternoons in the grill room at the club where he plays poker for small stakes with other men his age. He would die if a black were ever admitted to the club, but he doesn't mind the token Jews who belong, though he's afraid they might get "pushy" if too many of them were let in. He says, "He's Jewish, but a real nice boy." He never says "nigger" or "jig" but wouldn't like to see his good neighborhood integrated. Not that he really hates blacks, but he's worried about property values. At least that's what he says. His $60,000 home is one of his biggest assets, after all.

7   He doesn't sleep with his wife much anymore. His wife cheats on her golf score and suspects he's cheating on her. After having lived with his wife for 20 years he has come to the sorry conclusion that he doesn't really like her. His wife is on Valium and gets drunk after one drink, which embarrasses him. She goes to a psychiatrist whom he doesn't trust. In fact, he thinks most psychiatrists are "witch doctors." He wishes his wife would go back to the bouffant hairdo she used to wear, instead of that awful Afro. He buys his wife an expensive robe at Christmas and a bottle of Arpege by Lanvin. He is basically stingy.

Reprinted with permission from *The Plain Dealer,* Cleveland, Ohio, March 10, 1977.

8   He loves his two children very much, but is baffled by them. His son is a closet gay or a silversmith in Santa Fe. He wishes his son would marry a "nice girl," settle down and take up golf. His daughter is divorced, had a nervous breakdown and is very promiscuous.

9   He picks up lonely divorcees in their late 40s at the cocktail lounges of the good hotels he stays at on business trips. He likes to fly. He thinks it would be neat to be an airline pilot. It bothers him that there are mature and married stewardesses today and male stewards. He kids with the young, unmarried stewardesses.

10   He rarely goes to church anymore, maybe on Christmas and Easter, but he doesn't consider himself an atheist, though he wonders if there is a God after all.

11   He voted for John Kennedy in 1960 because Kennedy was virile, rich and good-looking. He was horrified by George McGovern and the freaky people at the 1972 Democratic convention. He supported the Vietnam War. He thinks we could have won the war if we had really tried. He thinks Ronald Reagan is an attractive personality, but he feels the governor is too far to the right and he doesn't like anything too far out.

12   He is mildly interested in politics and makes small contributions to the Republican party. He defended Richard Nixon and Spiro Agnew to the bitter end. He feels he was personally betrayed by Nixon. He thinks Jerry Ford is "decent" and "honest" and he voted for him. He thinks Jimmy Carter's obsession with religion is corny, but he doesn't really come out and say it.

13   He finds women's liberation ridiculous. He likes his women to be baby dolls. He would go into cardiac arrest if a homosexual ever propositioned him. He thinks the chains and bracelets young men wear are in bad taste. Young men give him the shakes. He is jealous of them and all the good sex he thinks they're getting. He is afraid young men might steal his job or his wife.

14   He wears single-breasted blue blazers and gray, cuffed trousers that expose his ankles. He makes sure his wing-tip shoes are always shined. His hair is neither short nor long. He doesn't like cities; he lives in a suburb or a small town. He would rather go to Delray Beach than Deauville. He bad mouths New York; the prices there are ridiculous, but he gets a secret charge from the city he visits three or four times a year on business. He stays at the Americana when he's there.

15   He is fond of words like "chief honcho" and "input." He is afraid to die and tries to blot death out of his mind because he's pretty damn sure there's no afterlife. He reads Time magazine and Playboy. He loved his mother very much, but wasn't close to his father. He's moved up the social scale a notch. He doesn't care for exotic food. When he goes to a restaurant he orders steak well done or filet of sole. He likes to do yard work. He lives in a colonial home decorated with traditional furniture. He likes a good-sized car; compacts are for bohemians.

He runs America.

ANALYSIS

structure

1. List some of the words and phrases that support the idea of "vital force" in Mailer's description of George Foreman.

2. Copy the topic sentence of the Stalin paragraph.

3. Write thesis statements for "Thomas Gradgrind" and "Dinosaur."

4. Would the physical description of Juan Chicoy have been clearer if Steinbeck had organized it more tightly? See, for example, how he refers to Juan's mouth in the fifth sentence of paragraph 3, but he doesn't get to Juan's teeth until about five sentences later. Find other such examples.

5. Which selections are narrative as well as descriptive?

meaning

6. What insight into Juan Chicoy's character does Steinbeck provide by his description of the amputated finger and the wedding ring? Look for additional clues to Juan's character.

7. In how many postures does Momaday remember his grandmother? Which posture does he focus on most? Why?

8. What are the "vessels," and why does Dickens use that term?

9. Why does Swift title his work "Dinosaur"?

10. How does Dr. Audlin's appearance seem to help his relationship with his patients?

style

11. Identify the writer's attitude toward the person being described in the first four selections.

12. Examine the use of repetition in the selections by Dickens and Swift. Which words and structures are repeated? What effect is achieved?

13. How does the description of "Dinosaur" differ from the other selections in this section? Why?

WRITING SUGGESTIONS

1. Write a three or four sentence description of someone you love, hate, disdain, or admire.

2. Write a brief description of a very old woman or a newborn baby.

3. Describe a type of person, such as a glamorous actor or actress, alcoholic, bully, or snob.

section 3d

❖❖❖

Memories of Childhood

Dylan Thomas

REMINISCENCES OF CHILDHOOD

1   I like very much people telling me about their childhood, but they'll have to be quick or else I'll be telling them about mine.

2   I was born in a large Welsh town at the beginning of the Great War—an ugly, lovely town (or so it was and is to me), crawling, sprawling by a long and splendid curving shore where truant boys and sandfield boys and old men from nowhere, beachcombed, idled and paddled, watched the dock-bound ships or the ships steaming away into wonder and India, magic and China, countries bright with oranges and loud with lions; threw stones into the sea for the barking outcast dogs; made castles and forts and harbours and race tracks in the sand; and on Saturday summer afternoons listened to the brass band, watched the Punch and Judy, or hung about on the fringes of the crowd to hear the fierce religious speakers who shouted at the sea, as though it were wicked and wrong to roll in and out like that, white-horsed and full of fishes.

3   One man, I remember, used to take off his hat and set fire to his hair every now and then, but I do not remember what it proved, if it proved anything at all, except that he was a very interesting man.

4   This sea-town was my world; outside a strange Wales, coal-pitted, mountained, river-run, full, so far as I knew, of choirs and football teams and sheep and storybook tall hats and red flannel petticoats, moved about its business which was none of mine.

5   Beyond that unknown Wales with its wild names like peals of bells in the darkness, and its mountain men clothed in the skins of animals perhaps and always singing, lay England which was London and the country called the Front, from which many of our neighbours never came back. It was a country to which only young men travelled.

6   At the beginning, the only "front" I knew was the little lobby before our front door. I could not understand how so many people never returned from there, but later I grew to know more, though still without understanding, and carried a wooden rifle in the park and shot down the invisible unknown enemy like a flock of wild birds. And the park itself was a world within the world of the sea-town. Quite near where I lived, so

From "Reminiscences of Childhood" in *Quite Early One Morning* by Dylan Thomas. Copyright 1954 by New Directions Publishing Corporation. Reprinted by permission of New Directions and the Trustees for the Copyrights of the late Dylan Thomas.

near that on summer evenings I could listen in my bed to the voices of older children playing ball on the sloping paper-littered bank, the park was full of terrors and treasures. Though it was only a little park, it held within its borders of old tall trees, notched with our names and shabby from our climbing, as many secret places, caverns and forests, prairies and deserts, as a country somewhere at the end of the sea.

7 And though we would explore it one day, armed and desperate, from end to end, from the robbers' den to the pirates' cabin, the highwayman's inn to the cattle ranch, or the hidden room in the undergrowth, where we held beetle races, and lit the wood fires and roasted potatoes and talked about Africa, and the makes of motor cars, yet still the next day, it remained as unexplored as the Poles—a country just born and always changing.[. . .]

8 The lane was always the place to tell your secrets; if you did not have any, you invented them. Occasionally now I dream that I am turning out of school into the lane of confidences when I say to the boys of my class, "At last, I have a real secret."

"What is it—what is it?"

"I can fly."

9 And when they do not believe me, I flap my arms and slowly leave the ground only a few inches at first, then gaining air until I fly waving my cap level with the upper windows of the school, peering in until the mistress at the piano screams and the metronome falls to the ground and stops, and there is no more time.

10 And I fly over the trees and chimneys of my town, over the dockyards skimming the masts and funnels, over Inkerman Street, Sebastopol Street, and the street where all the women wear men's caps, over the trees of the everlasting park, where a brass band shakes the leaves and sends them showering down on to the nurses and the children, the cripples and the idlers, and the gardeners, and the shouting boys: over the yellow seashore, and the stone-chasing dogs, and the old men, and the singing sea.

The memories of childhood have no order and no end.

ANALYSIS

structure 1. Copy Thomas's thesis statement.

2. What kind of order do Thomas's memories follow? Quote him on this.

style 3. Through whose eyes does Thomas see his childhood? Explain.

4. Thomas paints his pictures mostly with a very broad brush. An example of this is "wonder and India, magic and China, countries bright with oranges and loud with lions." What does he expect his readers to see? Find other examples of his use of the broad brush.

meaning 5. What is the "Front"? Why is it described as "a country to which only young men travelled"?

6. Explain how the small park can have "caverns and forests, prairies and deserts."

WRITING SUGGESTION

Using Thomas's reminiscences as a model, write very broadly about events in your childhood.

James Agee

KNOXVILLE: SUMMER 1915

It is not of the games children play in the evening that I want to speak now, it is of the contemporaneous atmosphere that has little to do with them: that of the fathers of families, each in his space of lawn, his shirt fishlike pale in the unnatural light and his face nearly anonymous, hosing their lawns. The hoses were attached at spiggots that stood out of the brick foundations of the houses. The nozzles were variously set but usually so there was a long sweet stream of spray, the nozzle wet in the hand, the water trickling the right forearm and the peeled-back cuff, and the water whishing out a long loose and low-curved cone, and so gentle a sound. First an insane noise of violence in the nozzle, then the still irregular sound of adjustment, then the smoothing into steadiness and a pitch as accurately turned to the size and style of stream as any violin. So many qualities of sound out of one hose: so many choral differences out of those several hoses that were in earshot. Out of any one hose, the almost dead silence of the release, and the short still arch of the separate big drops, silent as a held breath, and the only noise the flattering noise on leaves and the slapped grass at the fall of each big drop. That, and the intense hiss with the intense stream; that and that same intensity not growing less but growing more quiet and delicate with the turn of whisper when the water was just a wide ball of film. Chiefly, though, the hoses were set much alike, in a compromise between distance and tenderness of spray (and quite surely a sense of art behind this compromise, and a quiet deep joy, too real to recognize itself), and the sounds therefore were pitched much alike; pointed by the snorting start of a new hose; decorated by some man playful with the nozzle; left empty, like God by the sparrows's fall, when any single one of them desists: and all, though near alike, of various pitch; and in this unison. These sweet pale streamings in the light lift out their pallor and their voices all together, mothers hushing their children, the hushing unnaturally prolonged, the men gentle and silent and each snail-like withdrawn into the quietude of what he singly is doing, the urination of huge children stood loosely military against an invisible wall, and gently happy and peaceful, tasting the mean goodness of their living like the last of their suppers in their mouths; while the locusts carry on this noise of hoses on their much higher and sharper key. The noise of the locust is dry, and it seems not to be rasped or vibrated but urged from him as if through a small orifice by a

"Knoxville: Summer 1915" from *A Death in the Family* by James Agee. Copyright © 1957 by The James Agee Trust. Used by permission of Grosset & Dunlap, Inc.

breath that can never give out. Also there is never one locust but an illusion of at least a thousand. The noise of each locust is pitched in some classic locust range out of which none of them varies more than two full tones: and yet you seem to hear each locust discrete from all the rest, and there is a long, slow, pulse in their noise, like the scarcely defined arch of a long and high set bridge. They are all around in every tree, so that the noise seems to come from nowhere and everywhere at once, from the whole shell heaven, shivering in your flesh and teasing your eardrums, the boldest of all the sounds of night. And yet it is habitual to summer nights, and is of the great order of noises, like the noises of the sea and of the blood her precocious grandchild, which you realize you are hearing only when you catch yourself listening. Meantime from low in the dark, just outside the swaying horizons of the hoses, conveying always grass in the damp of dew and its strong green-black smear of smell, the regular yet spaced noises of the crickets, each a sweet cold silver noise three-noted, like the slipping each time of three matched links of a small chain.

ANALYSIS

structure   1. How are Agee's ideas organized in this selection?

2. Is he describing a particular or a typical summer evening?

meaning   3. Explain "his face nearly anonymous."

style   4. Find four similes in the selection.

opinion   5. Does Agee's meticulous attention to detail interest or bore you?

WRITING SUGGESTION

Focusing on a sense or several senses other than sight, describe something in a highly detailed manner.

Samuel L. Clemens

UNCLE JOHN'S FARM

1   As I have said, I spent some part of every year at the farm until I was twelve or thirteen years old. The life which I led there with my cousins was full of charm, and so is the memory of it yet. I can call back the solemn twilight and mystery of the deep woods, the earthy smells, the faint odors of the wild flowers, the sheen of rain-washed foliage, the rattling clatter of drops when the wind shook the trees, the far-off hammering of woodpeckers and the muffled drumming of wood pheasants in the

From *The Autobiography of Mark Twain*.

remoteness of the forest, the snapshot glimpses of disturbed wild creatures scurrying through the grass—I can call it all back and make it as
real as it ever was, and as blessed. I can call back the prairie, and its loneliness and peace, and a vast hawk hanging motionless in the sky, with his
wings spread wide and the blue of the vault showing through the fringe
of their end feathers. I can see the woods in their autumn dress, the oaks
purple, the hickories washed with gold, the maples and the sumachs lu-
minous with crimson fires, and I can hear the rustle made by the fallen
leaves as we plowed through them. I can see the blue clusters of wild
grapes hanging among the foliage of the saplings, and I remember the
taste of them and the smell. I know how the wild blackberries looked, and
how they tasted, and the same with the pawpaws, the hazelnuts, and the
persimmons; and I can feel the thumping rain, upon my head, of hickory
nuts and walnuts when we were out in the frosty dawn to scramble for
them with the pigs, and the gusts of wind loosed them and sent them
down. I know the stain of blackberries, and how pretty it is, and I know
the stain of walnut hulls, and how little it minds soap and water, also
what grudged experience it had of either of them. I know the taste of
maple sap, and when to gather it, and how to arrange the troughs and
the delivery tubes, and how to boil down the juice, and how to hook the
sugar after it is made, also how much better hooked sugar tastes than any
that is honestly come by, let bigots say what they will. I know how a prize
watermelon looks when it is sunning its fat rotundity among pumpkin
vines and "simblins;" I know how to tell when it is ripe without "plug-
ging" it; I know how inviting it looks when it is cooling itself in a tub of
water under the bed, waiting; I know how it looks when it lies on the
table in the sheltered great floor space between house and kitchen, and
the children gathered for the sacrifice and their mouths watering; I know
the crackling sound it makes when the carving knife enters its end, and I
can see the split fly along in front of the blade as the knife cleaves its way
to the other end; I can see its halves fall apart and display the rich red
meat and the black seeds, and the heart standing up, a luxury fit for the
elect; I know how a boy looks behind a yard-long slice of that melon, and
I know how he feels; for I have been there. I know the taste of the watermelon which has been honestly come by, and I know the taste of the watermelon which has been acquired by art. Both taste good, but the
experienced know which tastes best. I know the look of green apples and
peaches and pears on the trees, and I know how entertaining they are when
they are inside of a person. I know how ripe ones look when they are piled
in pyramids under the trees, and how pretty they are and how vivid their
colors. I know how a frozen apple looks, in a barrel down cellar in the win-
tertime, and how hard it is to bite, and how the frost makes the teeth
ache, and yet how good it is, notwithstanding. I know the disposition of
elderly people to select the specked apples for the children, and I once
knew ways to beat the game. I know the look of an apple that is roasting
and sizzling on a hearth on a winter's evening, and I know the comfort
that comes of eating it hot, along with some sugar and a drench of cream. I
know the delicate art and mystery of so cracking hickory nuts and walnuts
on a flatiron with a hammer that the kernels will be delivered whole, and
I know how the nuts, taken in conjunction with winter apples, cider, and

doughnuts, make old people's old tales and old jokes sound fresh and crisp and enchanting, and juggle an evening away before you know what went with the time. I know the look of Uncle Dan'l's kitchen as it was on the privileged nights, when I was a child, and I can see the white and black children grouped on the hearth, with the firelight playing on their faces and the shadows flickering upon the walls, clear back toward the cavernous gloom of the rear, and I can hear Uncle Dan'l telling the immortal tales which Uncle Remus Harris was to gather into his book and charm the world with, by and by; and I can feel again the creepy joy which quivered through me when the time for the ghost story was reached—and the sense of regret, too, which came over me, for it was always the last story of the evening and there was nothing between it and the unwelcome bed.

2   I can remember the bare wooden stairway in my uncle's house, and the turn to the left above the landing, and the rafters and the slanting roof over my bed, and the squares of moonlight on the floor, and the white cold world of snow outside, seen through the curtainless window. I can remember the howling of the wind and the quaking of the house on stormy nights, and how snug and cozy one felt, under the blankets, listening; and how the powdery snow used to sift in, around the sashes, and lie in little ridges on the floor and make the place look chilly in the morning and curb the wild desire to get up—in case there was any. I can remember how very dark that room was, in the dark of the moon, and how packed it was with ghostly stillness when one woke up by accident away in the night, and forgotten sins came flocking out of the secret chambers of the memory and wanted a hearing; and how ill chosen the time seemed for this kind of business; and how dismal was the hoo-hooing of the owl and the wailing of the wolf, sent mourning by on the night wind.

3   I remember the raging of the rain on that roof, summer nights, and how pleasant it was to lie and listen to it, and enjoy the white splendor of the lightning and the majestic booming and crashing of the thunder. It was a very satisfactory room, and there was a lightning rod which was reachable from the window, an adorable and skittish thing to climb up and down, summer nights, when there were duties on hand of a sort to make privacy desirable.

4   I remember the 'coon and 'possum hunts, nights, with the Negroes, and the long marches through the black gloom of the woods, and the excitement which fired everybody when the distant bay of an experienced dog announced that the game was treed; then the wild scramblings and stumblings through briers and bushes and over roots to get to the spot; then the lighting of a fire and the felling of the tree, the joyful frenzy of the dogs and the Negroes, and the weird picture it all made in the red glare—I remember it all well, and the delight that everyone got out of it, except the 'coon.

5   I remember the pigeon seasons, when the birds would come in millions and cover the trees and by their weight break down the branches. They were clubbed to death with sticks; guns were not necessary and were not used. I remember the squirrel hunts, and prairie-chicken hunts, and wild-turkey hunts, and all that; and how we turned out, mornings,

while it was still dark, to go on these expeditions, and how chilly and dismal it was, and how often I regretted that I was well enough to go. A toot on a tin horn brought twice as many dogs as were needed, and in their happiness they raced and scampered about, and knocked small people down, and made no end of unnecessary noise. At the word, they vanished away toward the woods, and we drifted silently after them in the melancholy gloom. But presently the gray dawn stole over the world, the birds piped up, then the sun rose and poured light and comfort all around, everything was fresh and dewy and fragrant, and life was a boon again. After three hours of tramping we arrived back wholesomely tired, overladen with game, very hungry, and just in time for breakfast.

ANALYSIS

structure
1. How is "Uncle John's Farm" organized—by subject, by season, or in some other way? Write the thesis.

meaning
2. What does "acquired by art" mean? Find one of his synonyms for that phrase.

3. What "game" does he play with the old folks?

4. What makes "old people's old tales and old jokes sound fresh and crisp and enchanting"?

5. For what personal purpose did Twain use the lightning rod?

style
6. Twain presents graphic snapshots of his life on the farm. One of them is "I can call back the prairie, and its loneliness and peace, and a vast hawk hanging motionless in the sky . . ." Find two other snapshots.

7. Twain also brings warmth and humor to his descriptions: "I know the stain of blackberries, and how pretty it is, and I know the stain of walnut hulls, and how little it minds soap and water, also what grudged experience it had of either of them." Find one more example.

WRITING SUGGESTION

Try to make something look and taste as good as Mark Twain's watermelon.

Colleen McCullogh

MEGGIE CLEARY'S BIRTHDAY

On December 8th, 1915, Meggie Cleary had her fourth birthday. After the breakfast dishes were put away her mother silently thrust a brown paper parcel into her arms and ordered her outside. So Meggie

From *The Thorn Birds* by Colleen McCullogh. Copyright © 1977 by Colleen McCullogh. Reprinted by permission of Harper & Row, Publishers, Inc.

squatted down behind the gorse bush next to the front gate and tugged impatiently. Her fingers were clumsy, the wrapping heavy; it smelled faintly of the Wahine general store, which told her that whatever lay inside the parcel had miraculously been *bought,* not homemade or donated.

Something fine and mistily gold began to poke through a corner; she attacked the paper faster, peeling it away in long, ragged strips.

"Agnes! Oh, Agnes!" she said lovingly, blinking at the doll lying there in a tattered nest.

A miracle indeed. Only once in her life had Meggie been into Wahine; all the way back in May, because she had been a very good girl. So perched in the buggy beside her mother, on her best behavior, she had been too excited to see or remember much. Except for Agnes, the beautiful doll sitting on the store counter, dressed in a crinoline of pink satin with cream lace frills all over it. Right then and there in her mind she had christened it Agnes, the only name she knew elegant enough for such a peerless creature. Yet over the ensuing months her yearning after Agnes contained nothing of hope; Meggie didn't own a doll and had no idea little girls and dolls belonged together. She played happily with the whistles and slingshots and battered soldiers her brothers discarded, got her hands dirty and her boots muddy.

5   It never occurred to her that Agnes was to play with. Stroking the bright pink folds of the dress, grander than any she had ever seen on a human woman, she picked Agnes up tenderly. The doll had jointed arms and legs which could be moved anywhere; even her neck and tiny, shapely waist were jointed. Her golden hair was exquisitely dressed in a high pompadour studded with pearls, her pale bosom peeped out of a foaming fichu of cream lace fastened with a pearl pin. The finely painted bone china face was beautiful, left unglazed to give the delicately tinted skin a natural matte texture. Astonishingly lifelike blue eyes shone between lashes of real hair, their irises streaked and circled with a darker blue; fascinated, Meggie discovered that when Agnes lay back far enough, her eyes closed. High on one faintly flushed cheek she had a black beauty mark, and her dusky mouth was parted slightly to show tiny white teeth. Meggie put the doll gently on her lap, crossed her feet under her comfortably, and sat just looking.

She was still sitting behind the gorse bush when Jack and Hughie came rustling through the grass where it was too close to the fence to feel a scythe. Her hair was the typical Cleary beacon, all the Cleary children save Frank being martyred by a thatch some shade of red; Jack nudged his brother and pointed gleefully. They separated, grinning at each other, and pretended they were troopers after a Maori renegade. Meggie would not have heard them anyway, so engrossed was she in Agnes, humming softly to herself.

"What's that you've got, Meggie?" Jack shouted, pouncing. "Show us!"

"Yes, show us!" Hughie giggled, outflanking her.

She clasped the doll against her chest and shook her head. "No, she's mine! I got her for my birthday!"

10   "Show us, go on! We just want to have a look."

Pride and joy won out. She held the doll so her brothers could see. "Look, isn't she beautiful? Her name is Agnes."

"Agnes? *Agnes?*" Jack gagged realistically. "What a soppy name! Why don't you call her Margaret or Betty?"

"Because she's Agnes!"

Hughie noticed the joint in the doll's wrist, and whistled. "Hey, Jack, look! It can move its hand!"

15 "Where? Let's see."

"No!" Meggie hugged the doll close again, tears forming. "No, you'll break her! Oh, Jack, don't take her away—you'll break her!"

"Pooh!" His dirty brown hands locked about her wrists, closing tightly. "Want a Chinese burn? And don't be such a crybaby, or I'll tell Bob." He squeezed her skin in opposite directions until it stretched whitely, as Hughie got hold of the doll's skirts and pulled. "Gimme, or I'll do it really hard!"

"No! Don't, Jack, please don't! You'll break her, I know you will! Oh, please leave her alone! Don't take her, please!" In spite of the cruel grip on her wrists she clung to the doll, sobbing and kicking.

"Got it!" Hughie whooped, as the doll slid under Meggie's crossed forearms.

20 Jack and Hughie found her just as fascinating as Meggie had; off came the dress, the petticoats and long, frilly drawers. Agnes lay naked while the boys pushed and pulled at her, forcing one foot round the back of her head, making her look down her spine, every possible contortion they could think of. They took no notice of Meggie as she stood crying; it did not occur to her to seek help, for in the Cleary family those who could not fight their own battles got scant aid or sympathy, and that went for girls, too.

The doll's golden hair tumbled down, the pearls flew winking into the long grass and disappeared. A dusty boot came down thoughtlessly on the abandoned dress, smearing grease from the smithy across its satin. Meggie dropped to her knees, scrabbling frantically to collect the miniature clothes before more damage was done them, then she began picking among the grass blades where she thought the pearls might have fallen. Her tears were blinding her, the grief in her heart new, for until now she had never owned anything worth grieving for.

ANALYSIS

structure   1. What writing techniques other than description are used in the selection?

2. What time period does "Meggie Cleary's Birthday" cover?

3. What is the one reference to an earlier period?

meaning   4. Why did it never occur to Meggie that Agnes was made to play with?

5. Why was the attack on Agnes especially tragic for Meggie?

6. Why is it necessary to describe Agnes in great detail?

Using narrative and description, write about the destruction of something you loved as a child.

section 3e

Prelude to a Murder

Feodor Dostoyevsky

CRIME AND PUNISHMENT

In this excerpt from Chapter 1, narration, description, and dialogue blend together to build the suspense necessary to take the reader to the brink of a murder.

1   Towards the end of a sultry afternoon early in July a young man came out of his little room in Stolyarny Lane and turned slowly and somewhat irresolutely in the direction of Kamenny Bridge.[1]

2   He had been lucky enough to escape an encounter with his landlady on the stairs. His little room, more like a cupboard than a place to live in, was tucked away under the roof of the high five-storied building. The landlady, who let him the room and provided him with dinners and service, occupied a flat on the floor below, and every time he went out he was forced to pass the door of her kitchen, which nearly always stood wide open. He went past each time with an uneasy, almost frightened, feeling that made him frown with shame. He was heavily in debt to his landlady and shrank from meeting her.

3   It was not that he was a cowed or naturally timorous person, far from it; but he had been for some time in an almost morbid state of irritability and tension. He had cut himself off from everybody and withdrawn so completely into himself that he now shrank from every kind of contact. He was crushingly poor, but he no longer felt the oppression of his poverty. For some time he had ceased to concern himself with everyday affairs. He was not really afraid of any landlady, whatever plots he might think she was hatching against him, but to have to stop on the stairs and listen to all her chatter about trivialities in which he refused to take any interest, all her complaints, threats, and insistent demands for payment, and then to have to extricate himself, lying and making excuses—no, better to creep downstairs as softly as a cat and slip out unnoticed.

From *Crime and Punishment* by Feodor Dostoyevsky, translated by Jessie Coulson (World's Classics Edition, 1963). Reprinted by permission of Oxford University Press.
[1] Raskolnikov lives in the slums, in a poor section of Petersburg near the Haymarket.

4   This time, however, he reached the street feeling astonished at the intensity of his fear of his landlady.

5   "To think that I can contemplate such a terrible act and yet be afraid of such trifles," he thought, and he smiled strangely. "Hm . . . yes . . . a man holds the fate of the world in his two hands, and yet, simply because he is afraid, he just lets things drift—that is a truism . . . I wonder what men are most afraid of . . . Any new departure, and especially a new word—that is what they fear most of all . . . But I am talking too much. That's why I don't act, because I am always talking. Or perhaps I talk so much just because I can't act. I have got into a habit of babbling to my-self during this last month, while I have been lying in a corner for days on end, thinking . . . fantastic nonsense. And why have I come out now? Can I really be capable of *that?* Am I really serious? No, of course I'm not seri-ous. So I am just amusing myself with fancies, children's games? Yes, perhaps I am only playing a game."

6   The heat in the streets was stifling. The stuffiness, the jostling crowds, the bricks and mortar, scaffolding and dust everywhere, and that peculiar summer stench so familiar to everyone who cannot get away from St. Petersburg into the country, all combined to aggravate the dis-turbance of the young man's nerves. The intolerable reek from the public houses, so numerous in that part of the city, and the sight of the drunken men encountered at every turn, even though this was not a holiday, com-pleted the mournfully repellent picture. An expression of the deepest loathing passed across the young man's delicate features. (He was, by the way, a strikingly handsome young man, with fine dark eyes, brown hair, and a slender well-knit figure, taller than the average.) Soon, however, he relapsed again into profound thought, or rather into a sort of abstraction, and continued on his way in complete and wilful unconsciousness of his surroundings. Once or twice he muttered something to himself in a man-ner that, as he had just confessed, had grown habitual with him. He himself realized that at times his thoughts were confused and that he was very weak; he had eaten practically nothing for two days.

7   He was so wretchedly dressed that anybody else, however used to them, might have hesitated to go out in daylight in such rags. It is true that it would have been difficult to attract attention by one's dress in this part of central St. Petersburg. In these streets and alleys near the Haymar-ket, with their numerous houses of ill fame and their swarming population of artisans and labourers, such queer figures sometimes appeared on the scene that even the oddest of them could hardly arouse any surprise. Be-sides, the young man's heart was so full of bitter scorn that, in spite of his often very youthful sensitiveness, wearing his rags in the street caused him no embarrassment. It would have been different had he come across any of his acquaintances or former friends, whom he wished in any case to avoid . . . All the same, when a drunken man, who was being carted off some-where in an enormous dray drawn by an equally enormous cart-horse, sud-denly yelled as he went by "Hi, you in the German hat!"[2] and went on pointing at him and bawling at the top of his voice, the young man stopped

---

[2] All Western (i.e., not of native Russian style) clothes were popularly called German.

dead and clutched feverishly at his hat. It was a high, round hat, which had come from Zimmermann's famous hat-shop,[3] but was now all rubbed and rusty with age, stained and full of slits; what remained of its battered brim was cocked up grotesquely at one side. But it was not shame but an entirely different emotion, more like terror, that had seized him.

8   "I knew it!" he muttered in confusion. "I foresaw something like this, but this is worse than anything I thought of. A piece of stupidity like this, an insignificant trifle, might wreck the whole affair. Yes, the hat is too noticeable. It is ridiculous, and that means that it attracts attention. I must get a cap, any sort of old cap, to go with my rags, not this monstrosity. Nobody wears this sort of thing. It would be noticed a mile off, and remembered . . . that's the point: it would be remembered afterwards, and it would be evidence . . . I must be as inconspicuous as possible . . . Trifles are important! . . . Trifles like this can bring disaster."

9   He had not far to go; he even knew how many paces it was from his own door—exactly seven hundred and thirty.[4] He had counted them once, when he had first begun to give his imagination free rein. At that time he did not believe in the reality of his imaginings, and their audacity, which both repelled and fascinated him at the same time, was merely irritating. Now, a month later, he saw them in a different light, and had somehow grown used to regarding the "ugly" dream as a real project, although he still did not trust himself to carry it out, and reproached himself for his own weakness and lack of resolution. He was now engaged in *rehearsing* his project, and his agitation increased with every step he took.

10   With a fainting heart and shuddering nerves he approached an enormous building which fronted the canal on one side, and Sadovaya Street on the other. The building was split up into small tenements, which housed all kinds of tradespeople—tailors, locksmiths, cooks, various German craftsmen, prostitutes, clerks, and so on. People were hurrying in and out of its two gates and across its two courtyards. The building had three or four porters, and the young man thought himself lucky not to meet any of them as he slipped from the gate to the first staircase on the right. It was narrow and dark, but he already knew that, and the circumstance pleased him; in such obscurity there was no danger from prying eyes. 'If I feel so afraid at this moment, what would it be like if I had really brought myself to the point of doing *the thing itself?*' he thought involuntarily, as he came up to the fourth floor. Here his way was blocked by two porters, old soldiers, who were removing furniture from one of the flats. He knew that a German clerk lived here with his family. "The German must be removing, and that means that the old woman's will be the only flat occupied on the fourth floor on this staircase, at any rate for some time. That's fine . . . in case I . . ." he thought, as he rang the old woman's bell. The bell tinkled feebly, as though it were made of tin, not copper. Small

[3] Zimmermann was an actual—and expensive—Petersburg hatmaker.
[4] In most of his references to Petersburg streets and landmarks, Dostoyevsky uses real names. The distance between the actually existing buildings which he had in mind, from Raskolnikov's room to the pawnbroker's, was indeed about 730 paces.

flats in that kind of house nearly all have such bells, but he had forgotten what it sounded like and its peculiar tinkle seemed to startle him, as if it brought back something to his memory with great clearness ... He shuddered; evidently his nerves were too weak *this time.* After a short interval the door opened the merest crack, and a woman peered suspiciously out at her visitor; only her glittering little eyes were visible in the gloom. She seemed reassured, however, when she saw that there were several people on the landing, and opened the door wider. The young man stepped across the threshold into a dark hall divided by a partition from the tiny kitchen. The old woman stood silently before him, looking at him with a question in her eyes. She was a tiny dried-up scrap of a creature, about sixty years old, with sharp, malicious little eyes and a small sharp nose. She was bare-headed and her fair hair, just beginning to go grey, was thick with grease. A strip of flannel was twisted round her long thin neck, which was wrinkled and yellow like a hen's legs, and in spite of the heat a short jacket of worn fur, yellow with age, hung from her shoulders. She coughed and groaned continually. The young man must have been looking at her rather oddly, for distrust flashed into her eyes again.

11 Reminding himself that he must be as polite as possible, the young man made a hurried half-bow and muttered: "Raskolnikov, a student. I was here a month ago."[5]

12 "I remember you were, my friend, I remember very well," the old woman answered drily, still without taking her eyes from his face.

13 "Well ... I've come again on the same business," continued Raskolnikov, rather disconcerted by her suspicion. "Perhaps, though," he thought uneasily, "she was always like this, only I didn't notice it before."

14 The old woman remained silent, apparently still doubtful, and then stood aside and pointed to a door, saying, as she let her visitor pass: "Go in, my friend."

ANALYSIS

structure

1. Write a three or four sentence summary of the excerpt.

meaning

2. Is Dostoyevsky more interested in the physical looks or the mental state of his hero? Explain.

3. What does Raskolnikov say to himself about his tendency to talk too much?

4. Does his fear of his landlady seem rational? Discuss.

5. Why does he become so terrified when the drunken man mentions his German hat?

6. Consider why Dostoyevsky focuses more attention on the description of the intended victim, the money lender, than he does on that of the potential murderer.

[5] The old woman is a moneylender.

Write a detailed account of someone's thoughts as he or she goes to one of the following:

to a dentist to have a tooth pulled
to the funeral of a loved one
to the home of a girl or boyfriend to propose marriage or break an engagement
to a ball park to play in a game that will decide a championship
to a dangerous neighborhood at night
to your home at 2 a.m. after promising to return by midnight

Review of Chapter 3

All but the most bare writing contains some description. In this chapter you have read humorous ·and serious descriptions of people, places, and things. Some descriptions depict pictures with photographic detail; others create general impressions—moods, atmosphere, the broad brush stroke.

Description can be objective, written with no emotion, or subjective, written with feeling. Writers not only transmit pictures of what they see; they often probe beneath the surface, providing insights into character and motivation.

Students who practice writing description learn to see things in increasingly greater detail; they become more skillful at finding just the right words to depict what they see. They also learn to organize their words more effectively. Finally, they learn that both objects and people (especially people) are more complex than they appear at first glance or on first meeting.

Readers, on the other hand, learn to tune in to the writer's wave length and recreate in their minds the pictures that the writer depicts.

EVALUATION

In considering the selections in Sections 3C and 3E, which characters do you recall most vividly? Why? In Sections 3B, 3D, and 3E, which scene is painted in clearest detail? Which do you *feel* most? Which selection provides the best overall description? In each answer try to pinpoint the method or methods the writer uses to elicit your response.

Examples

CHAPTER 4

READING FOCUS

- ❖ Be aware of the function of the examples.
- ❖ Be sure to relate the examples to the generalizations they support.
- ❖ Refrain from dwelling unnecessarily on each example once you clearly understand the generalization it illustrates. (Writers often use more examples than are necessary.)
- ❖ Be aware of examples that don't truly support the point that the writer is trying to make.

WRITING FOCUS

- ❖ Choose apt examples that truly support your thesis.
- ❖ Organize the examples in the most effective manner for your purpose.
- ❖ Use examples not only to clarify your ideas but to make your writing more interesting.

"The climate on Earth seems to be tending toward various extremes," commented the eminent climatologist as he sipped his protein drink.

"What's that?" muttered his wife as she carefully unfolded the *Wall Street Journal.*

"Well, for example, 1977 began with one of the coldest winters in history in the East and one of the driest winters in the West; Florida had snow and Alaska was warm."

* * *

"George is terribly irritable. I'm worried," said George's wife Emily to her mother-in-law, Agatha.

"I haven't noticed it," replied Mrs. Quatro absentmindedly. "He complained about your cooking last night on the phone, but there's nothing unusual about that."

"He's been yellin' at th' kids for nothin' at all, he fired his secretary for comin' late just once, and last night he come home half drunk. And you know he's not a drinker."

* * *

Some of the most startling assassinations of the last hundred years were carried out by individuals without the help or knowledge of any organized body—the murders of Stolypin and President McKinley; the killing of President Carnot, of Gandhi and President Kennedy.

From *Terrorism* by Walter Laqueur.

Using examples is one of the best ways of making an idea convincing. The ideas that the climate of Earth seems to be moving toward extremes, that George is terribly irritable, and that some assassins work independently are made clearer by the examples that follow. Giving examples of what examples are, in fact, has made it virtually unnecessary to define what an example is: *a specific instance in which a generalization proves true; an illustration, a sample.*

Examples can be used in various ways: at the beginning of a paper to catch the reader's attention; at the end to provide a dramatic, humorous, or thoughtful conclusion; in the body of the paper; or in a combination of these methods. In any case, it is wise to be aware of their function and to know which generalization or generalizations each supports.

Divided into three sections, the balance of this chapter will take you from short paragraphs and articles developed by examples, through selections that group examples according to various criteria, and finally to more complicated selections.

JUST A TAD DIFFERENT

"Pull 'er up a tad, please, mister," said the nonchalant teen-ager pumping gas in a Union 76 service station off Interstate 75 near Vienna, Ga.

"What'd you say, son?" asked the driver with Pennsylvania plates.

"Pull 'er up a tad."

"Pull 'er what?"

5 "Would you please move your car closer to the pump?"

The Pennsylvania driver laughed, moved his car closer and thereby ended another skirmish in the word between the states. Along the interstates, and more often away from them, old Southern expressions like "a tad"—an indefinable little bit—survive.

For the moment at least, the South continues to cherish its language. In the South, as in no other American region, people use language as it surely was meant to be employed: a lush, personal, emphatic treasure of coins to be spent slowly and for value. Thus, in Southern idiom, no lady is merely pregnant; she is "in bloom" or "her bees are aswarming." Girls are variously "ugly as homemade soap" or "pretty as a speckled pup." It does not rain in the South; it "comes up a cloud." For young children, the mystery of the belly button is easy to explain: it is "where the Yankee shot you." Acquaintanceship? "We've howdied but we haven't shook." Crowding? "There's not room enough in here to skin a cat without getting hair in your mouth." If things are going well, "life's just a slide on a doughnut." There is also the Southern man who lies so much that he needs someone else to call his dog. Similes fall like raindrops: slow as a pond, high as a pine, sorry as gully dirt.

Much of this expressiveness, like everything else in the region, has black influences. "I'm always behead or behind," complains a black cook in Georgia over the fact that she could never get caught up in her work. In a Mississippi court, recalls TIME's Margaret Boeth, Southern-born, a black defendant explained his relationship to the common-law wife he had murdered. She was his "much-right" woman, he said. "I figured I had as much right to her as anybody else."

From *Time*, The Weekly Newsmagazine, September 27, 1976. Copyright Time, Inc. 1976. Reprinted by permission.

DEFINE: *nonchalant, idiom.*

E. B. White

HERE IS NEW YORK

It is a miracle that New York works at all. The whole thing is implausible. Every time the residents brush their teeth, millions of gallons of water must be drawn from the Catskills and the hills of Westchester. When a young man in Manhattan writes a letter to his girl in Brooklyn, the love message gets blown to her through a pneumatic tube—*pfft*—just like that. The subterranean system of telephone cables, power lines, steam pipes, gas mains and sewer pipes is reason enough to abandon the island to the gods and the weevils. Every time an incision is made in the pavement, the noisy surgeons expose ganglia that are tangled beyond belief. By rights New York should have destroyed itself long ago, from panic or fire or rioting or failure of some vital supply line in its circulatory system or from some deep labyrinthine short circuit. Long ago the city should have experienced an insoluble traffic snarl at some impossible bottleneck. It should have perished of hunger when food lines failed for a few days. It should have been wiped out by a plague starting in its slums or carried in by ships' rats. It should have been overwhelmed by the sea that licks at it on every side. The workers in its myriad cells should have succumbed to nerves, from the fearful pall of smoke-fog that drifts over every few days from Jersey, blotting out all light at noon and leaving the high offices suspended, men groping and depressed, and the sense of world's end. It should have been touched in the head by the August heat and gone off its rocker.

From *Here Is New York* by E. B. White. Copyright 1949 by E. B. White. Reprinted by permission of Harper & Row, Publishers, Inc.

DEFINE: *implausible, labyrinthine.*

Alan Moorehead

THE SOVIET COUNCIL AT WORK

For six hours every day the Soviet Council of People's Commissars met under Lenin's chairmanship, and a fantastic stream of decrees began to pour out of Smolny. Nothing like it had been seen in the world before; it was a program that uprooted every institution and tradition in Russian life. The abolition of private ownership in land was followed by the nationalization of the banks, of the merchant marine, and of all industrial enterprises. The stock market was swept away, and so were the rights of inheritance. All state debts were annulled, and gold was declared a government monopoly. Wages of the People's Commissars were pegged at 500

From *The Russian Revolution* by Alan Moorehead. Copyright © 1958 by Time, Inc. Reprinted by permission of Harper & Row, Publishers, Inc.

rubles a month for single people with additional payments for families. The old criminal courts were supplemented or replaced by "revolutionary tribunals" made up of a president and six peasants, workers and soldiers, and any citizen could appear as a lawyer. Men and women were declared equal in law, and the strict Czarist code governing marriage and divorce was abolished; a civil marriage now took the place of the church ceremony, and divorce could be obtained by either party of the marriage merely asking for it. All titles were submerged into the universal "Citizen" or "Comrade." The church was permitted to continue but in a drastically truncated form; its lands—and they were enormous—were confiscated and religious teaching was forbidden in the schools. The state religion was now Leninism. The Western calendar, which was now thirteen days ahead of the old Russian calendar, was declared law, and even the alphabet was pruned of various letters and signs. Later on, strikes were declared to be treason.

DEFINE: *commissar, confiscated, truncated.*

Ovid

THE ART OF LOVE

I make no pretense of justifying the laxity of my morals; I never resort to untruthful pretexts to excuse my wanderings from the path of virtue. I freely confess my faults, if such avowals can serve any useful purpose. Now I have acknowledged my guilt in general terms, I mean to make a clean breast of all my follies. I curse my failings, yet I cannot help finding pleasure in the very faults that I deplore. How burdensome is the yoke that one would fain cast off. I have not the strength nor the will-power to govern my passions; they bear me along with them, even as the swift tide hurries away the slender bark.

It is not any particular type of beauty that sets my heart on fire. A hundred motives compel me to be always in love. Here is a girl that drops her gaze demurely. That is enough, my heart catches fire and her modesty is the lure that ensnares me. And here is one that is out for booty. To her I fall a willing victim because she is no novice and because she bids fair to be keen and enterprising on a downy couch. And then, if I see one with an expression that recalls to me the Sabine dames, I forthwith tell myself that she has longings but knows how to conceal them. Are you a learned lady? I fall in love with your rare accomplishments. Unlearned? Your *naïveté* enthralls me. This one finds Callimachus a sorry poet compared with me. I please her, and lo, straightway she pleases me. This one finds fault with my verses and tells me I am no poet. Despite her strictures I fain would have her in my arms. This one walks languorously. Her gait enchants me. This one is prim. Peradventure, if she had a lover 'twould soften her. This one

From Elegy IV in *The Art of Love* by Ovid. Translation copyright © 1959 by Grosset & Dunlap, Inc.

sings delightfully, and breathes from her soft throat the most melodious strains. I long to steal a kiss from her parted lips. Another lightly fingers the trembling chords of her lyre; where is he who could help adoring such skillful fingers? Here is one that wins me with her dancing. I feast my eyes on her seductive poses, on the rhythmic movements of her arms, on the swaying of her whole body as she moves in time to the music. But never mind me, whom any one can set on fire. Let Hippolytus see her; even he would become a Priapus. You, my tall beauty, recall the heroines of olden days and the bed is not a whit too long for you. And you, my dainty little treasure; I love you, too, just as much. Both are enchanting. Tall and short, I love them both. Here is one that wears no finery; I muse how jewels would enhance her beauty. Here is one tricked out with gems; how dazzling are her charms. Of fair and dark I am alike the slave; white-skinned or sun-burnt, I adore them all. Black tresses flutter on a snowy neck? Leda's loveliness lay in her raven hair. Is she fair, the girl I see yonder? Why, 'twas to her golden hair Aurora owed her beauty. Everywhere history helps me to justify my love. A young woman delights me, an older one enthralls me. The one has the beauty of her body, the other experience and richness of mind, to recommend her. In a word, of all the beauties they rave about in Rome, there's none whose lover I am not fain to be.

DEFINE: *fain, naïveté.*

Gordon Parks

POSSESSED BY A FEAR OF DEATH

1   When I was eleven, I became possessed of an exaggerated fear of death. It started one quiet summer afternoon with an explosion in the alley behind our house. I jumped up from under a shade tree and tailed Poppa toward the scene. Black smoke billowed skyward, a large hole gaped in the wall of our barn and several maimed chickens and a head-less turkey flopped about on the ground. Then Poppa stopped and mut-tered, "Good Lord." I clutched his overalls and looked. A man, or what was left of him, was strewn about in three parts. A gas main he had been repairing had somehow ignited and blown everything around it to bits.

2   Then once, with two friends, I had swum along the bottom of the muddy Marmaton River, trying to locate the body of a Negro man. We had been promised fifty cents apiece by the same white policeman who had shot him while he was in the water trying to escape arrest. The dead man had been in a crap game with several others who had managed to get away. My buddy, Johnny Young, was swimming beside me; we swam

From "My Mother's Dream for Me" in *A Choice of Weapons* by Gordon Parks. Copyright © 1965, 1966 by Gordon Parks. Reprinted by permission of Harper & Row, Publishers, Inc.

with ice hooks which we were to use for grappling. The two of us touched the corpse at the same instant. Fear streaked through me and the memory of his bloated body haunted my dreams for nights.

3   One night at the Empress Theater, I sat alone in the peanut gallery watching a motion picture, *The Phantom of the Opera*. When the curious heroine, against Lon Chaney's warning, snatched away his mask, and the skull of death filled the screen, I screamed out loud and ran out of the theater. I didn't stop until I reached home, crying to Momma, "I'm going to die! I'm going to die."

4   Momma, after several months of cajoling, had all but destroyed this fear when another cruel thing happened. A Negro gambler called Captain Tuck was mysteriously killed on the Frisco tracks. Elmer Kinard, a buddy, and I had gone to the Cheney Mortuary out of youthful, and perhaps morbid, curiosity. Two white men, standing at the back door where bodies were received, smiled mischievously and beckoned to us. Elmer was wise and ran, but they caught me. "Come on in, boy. You want to see Captain Tuck, don't you?"

5   "No, no," I pleaded. "No, no, let me go."

6   The two men lifted me through the door and shoved me into a dark room. "Cap'n Tuck's in here, boy. You can say hello to him." The stench of embalming fluid mixed with fright. I started vomiting, screaming and pounding the door. Then a smeared light bulb flicked on and, there before me, his broken body covering the slab, was Captain Tuck. My body froze and I collapsed beside the door.

7   After they revived me and put me on the street, I ran home with the old fear again running the distance beside me. My brother Clem evened the score with his fists the next day, but from then on Poppa proclaimed that no Parks would ever be caught dead in Cheney's. "The Koonantz boys will do all our burying from now on," he told Orlando Cheney.

8   Another time, I saw a woman cut another woman to death. There were men around, but they didn't stop it. They all stood there as if they were watching a horror movie. Months later, I would shudder at the sight of Johnny Young, one of my closest buddies, lying, shot to death, at the feet of his father and the girl he loved. His murderer had been in love with the same girl. And not long after, Emphry Hawkins, who had helped us bear Johnny's coffin, was also shot to death.

9   As the train whistled through the evening, I realized that only hours before, during what seemed like a bottomless night, I had left my bed to sleep on the floor beside my mother's coffin. It was, I knew now, a final attempt to destroy this fear of death.

ANALYSIS

structure   1. For each selection in Section 4A except "Here Is New York," state what idea the examples support. To illustrate: In "Here Is New York," the examples support the idea that New York is implausible.

2. "Possessed by a Fear of Death" is an excerpt, not originally written as a unit to be read by itself. Broaden the thesis by adding to Parks's first sentence so that it ties the beginning and ending of the selection more closely together.

3. Why did Parks include so many examples? Would one or two have sufficed?

4. The selection is comprised almost entirely of brief narratives. Why, then, is it considered to be developed by examples?

meaning   5. Does the author of "Just a Tad Different" approve or disapprove of Southern speech? Support your view.

6. What is E. B. White's attitude toward New York?

style   7. Is "The Soviet Council at Work" objective or subjective?

8. Do you think that Ovid's views are serious or funny? Explain.

WRITING SUGGESTIONS

Write example paragraphs about one or more of the following topics:

a. defects, oddities, or positive aspects of your city or town
b. special "in" words or phrases used by your particular age group, by people in your part of the city, state, or country, or by your racial or religious group
c. the individuals to whom you've been most attracted and the reason for your attraction
d. experiences that you've had with death and their effect on your attitude toward death

SPECIAL ASSIGNMENT

Study the two versions of "The Newtonian Relativity Principle" that follow, paying special attention to the use of examples and the placement of the generalizations; then answer the questions.

Lincoln Barnett

THE NEWTONIAN RELATIVITY PRINCIPLE

Anyone who has ever ridden on a railroad train knows how rapidly another train flashes by when it is traveling in the opposite direction, and conversely how it may look almost motionless when it is moving in the same direction. A variation of this effect can be very deceptive in an enclosed station like Grand Central Terminal in New York. Once in a while a train gets under way so gently that passengers feel no recoil whatever. Then if they happen to look out of the window and see another train slide past on the next track, they have no way of knowing which train is in motion and which is at rest; nor can they tell how fast either one is moving or in what

From *The Universe and Dr. Einstein,* by Lincoln Barnett. Copyright © 1948 by Harper & Brothers. Copyright 1950, 1957 by Lincoln Barnett. Reprinted by permission of William Morrow & Company.

direction. The only way they can judge their situation is by looking out the other side of the car for some fixed body of reference like the station platform or a signal light. Sir Isaac Newton was aware of these tricks of motion, only he thought in terms of ships. He knew that on a calm day at sea a sailor can shave himself or drink soup as comfortably as when his ship is lying motionless in harbor. The water in his basin, the soup in his bowl, will remain unruffled whether the ship is making five knots, 15 knots, or 25 knots. So unless he peers out at the sea it will be impossible for him to know how fast his ship is moving or indeed if it is moving at all. Of course if the sea should get rough or the ship change course abruptly, then he will sense his state of motion. But granted the idealized conditions of a glass-calm sea and a silent ship, nothing that happens below decks—no amount of observation or mechanical experiment performed *inside* the ship—will disclose its velocity through the sea. The physical principle suggested by these considerations was formulated by Newton in 1687. "The motions of bodies included in a given space," he wrote, "are the same among themselves, whether that space is at rest or moves uniformly forward in a straight line." This is known as the Newtonian or Galilean Relativity Principle. It can also be phrased in more general terms: mechanical laws which are valid in one place are equally valid in any other place which moves uniformly relative to the first.

DEFINE: *conversely.*

REVISED VERSION:
THE NEWTONIAN RELATIVITY PRINCIPLE

The Newtonian or Galilean Relativity Principle formulated by Newton in 1687 declares that "the motions of bodies included in a given space are the same among themselves, whether that space is at rest or moves uniformly forward in a straight line." Anyone, for example, who has ever ridden on a railroad train knows how rapidly another train flashes by when it is traveling in the opposite direction, and conversely how it may look almost motionless when it is moving in the same direction. A variation of this effect can be very deceptive in an enclosed station like Grand Central Terminal in New York. Once in a while a train gets under way so gently that passengers feel no recoil whatever. Then if they happen to look out of the window and see another train slide past on the next track, they have no way of knowing which train is in motion and which is at rest; nor can they tell how fast either one is moving or in what direction. The only way they can judge their situation is by looking out the other side of the car for some fixed body of reference like the station platform or a signal light. Sir Isaac Newton was aware of these tricks of motion; only he thought in terms of ships. He knew that on a calm day at sea a sailor can shave himself or drink soup as comfortably as when his ship is lying motionless in harbor. The water in his basin, the soup in his bowl, will remain unruffled whether the ship is making five knots, 15 knots, or 25 knots. So unless he peers out at the sea it will be impossible for him to know how fast his ship is moving or indeed if it is moving at all. Of course if the sea should get rough or the ship change course abruptly, then he will sense his state of motion. But granted the idealized conditions of a glass-calm sea and a silent ship, nothing that happens below decks—no amount of observation or mechanical experiment performed inside the ship—will disclose its velocity through the sea. *The physical principle suggested by these considerations, to state Newton's law in more general terms, is that mechanical laws which are valid in one place are equally valid in any other place which moves uniformly relative to the first.*

ANALYSIS

structure

1. How do the two versions differ in structure?

2. Which version is easier to understand? Why?

style

3. What is significant about the kinds of examples used and the vocabulary the author selected to explain an important scientific theory?

WRITING SUGGESTIONS

1. Explain the Newtonian Relativity Principle in your own words. Try to support it with examples of your own.

2. State a different scientific principle and explain it with the help of examples.

section 4b

Alvin Toffler

THE PAPER WEDDING GOWN

That man-thing relationships are growing more and more temporary may be illustrated by examining the culture surrounding the little girl who trades in her doll. This child soon learns that Barbie dolls are by no means the only physical objects that pass into and out of her young life at a rapid clip. Diapers, bibs, paper napkins, Kleenex, towels, non-returnable soda bottles—all are used up quickly in her home and ruthlessly eliminated. Corn muffins come in baking tins that are thrown away after one use. Spinach is encased in plastic sacks that can be dropped into a

From *Future Shock,* by Alvin Toffler. Copyright © 1970 by Alvin Toffler. Reprinted by permission of Random House, Inc.

pan of boiling water for heating, and then thrown away. TV dinners are cooked and often served on throw-away trays. Her home is a large processing machine through which objects flow, entering and leaving, at a faster and faster rate of speed. From birth on, she is inextricably embedded in a throw-away culture.

2   The idea of using a product once or for a brief period, and then replacing it, runs counter to the grain of societies or individuals steeped in a heritage of poverty. Not long ago Uriel Rone, a market researcher for the French advertising agency Publicis, told me: "The French housewife is not used to disposable products. She likes to keep things, even old things, rather than throw them away. We represented one company that wanted to introduce a kind of plastic throw-away curtain. We did a marketing study for them and found the resistance too strong." This resistance, however, is dying all over the developed world.

3   Thus a writer, Edward Maze, has pointed out that many Americans visiting Sweden in the early 1950's were astounded by its cleanliness. "We were almost awed by the fact that there were no beer and soft drink bottles by the roadsides, as, much to our shame, there were in America. But by the 1960's, lo and behold, bottles were suddenly blooming along Swedish highways . . . What happened? Sweden had become a buy, use and throw-away society, following the American pattern." In Japan today throw-away tissues are so universal that cloth handkerchiefs are regarded as old fashioned, not to say unsanitary. In England for sixpence one may buy a "Dentamatic throw-away toothbrush" which comes already coated with toothpaste for its one-time use. And even in France, disposable cigarette lighters are commonplace. From cardboard milk containers to the rockets that power space vehicles, products created for short-term or one-time use are becoming more numerous and crucial to our way of life.

4   The recent introduction of paper and quasi-paper clothing carried the trend toward disposability a step further. Fashionable boutiques and working-class clothing stores have sprouted whole departments devoted to gaily colored and imaginatively designed paper apparel. Fashion magazines display breathtakingly sumptuous gowns, coats, pajamas, even wedding dresses made of paper. The bride pictured in one of these wears a long white train of lace-like paper that, the caption writer notes, will make "great kitchen curtains" after the ceremony.

5   Paper clothes are particularly suitable for children. Writes one fashion expert: "Little girls will soon be able to spill ice cream, draw pictures and make cutouts on their clothes while their mothers smile benignly at their creativity." And for adults who want to express their own creativity, there is even a "paint-yourself-dress" complete with brushes. Price: $2.00.

6   Price, of course, is a critical factor behind the paper explosion. Thus a department store features simple A-line dresses made of what it calls "devil-may-care cellulose fiber and nylon." At $1.29 each, it is almost cheaper for the consumer to buy and discard a new one than to send an ordinary dress to the cleaners. Soon it will be. But more than economics is involved, for the extension of the throw-away culture has important psychological consequences.

⁷ We develop a throw-away mentality to match our throw-away products. This mentality produces, among other things, a set of radically altered values with respect to property. But the spread of disposability through the society also implies decreased durations in man-thing relationships. Instead of being linked with a single object over a relatively long span of time, we are linked for brief periods with the succession of objects that supplant it.

DEFINE: inextricably (1); quasi-paper (4); supplant (7).

ANALYSIS

structure 1. List some of the evidence that Toffler uses to support his contention that man-thing relationships are growing more temporary.

2. Does he support the idea in paragraph 7 that we "develop a throw-away mentality to match our throw-away products . . . a set of radically altered values with respect to property"?

style 3. Consider his use of terminology like "ruthlessly eliminated" and "inextricably embedded" (paragraph 1). Are they apt terms, or do they overstate the case?

opinion 4. Is Toffler's argument convincing, or is he generalizing on the basis of too few examples?

5. Can you think of examples that would support a contradictory thesis?

WRITING SUGGESTIONS

1. Write about "waste in our society."
2. Connect our waste problems with ecological problems.

Theodore Sorensen

KENNEDY

¹ John Fitzgerald Kennedy had no fear or premonition of dying. Having narrowly survived death in the war and in the hospital, having tragically suffered the death of a brother and a sister, having been told as a young man that his adrenal deficiency might well cut short his years, he did not need to be reminded that the life he loved was a precious, impermanent gift, not to be wasted for a moment. But neither could he ever again be worried or frightened by the presence of death amidst life. "I know nothing can happen to him," his father once said. "I've stood by his

From *Kennedy* by Theodore C. Sorensen. Copyright © 1965 by Theodore C. Sorensen. Reprinted by permission of Harper & Row, Publishers, Inc.

deathbed four times. Each time I said good-bye to him, and he always came back."

2   John Kennedy could speak of death like all other subjects, candidly, objectively and at times humorously. The possibility of his own assassination he regarded as simply one more way in which his plans for the future might be thwarted. Yet he rarely mentioned death in a personal way and, to my knowledge, never spoke seriously about his own, once he recovered his health. He looked forward to a long life, never talking, for example, about arrangements for his burial or a memorial. He had a will drawn up, to be sure, but that was an act of prudence, not premonition; and asking Ted Reardon and me to witness it on June 18, 1954, he had made it the occasion for a joke: "It's legal for you to do this—because I can assure you there's nothing in here for either of you." Two years later, driving me home one evening at high speed, he humorously speculated on whom the Nebraska headlines would feature if we were killed together in a crash.

3   He had no morbid fascination with the subject of death. When his wife and daughter stopped by his White House desk with a dead bird Caroline wanted to bury, he preferred not to look at it. (Dead animals, in fact, appalled him. He did not like to hunt, was upset about the deer he had shot at the LBJ ranch, and often dangerously swerved his car to avoid running over a rabbit or dog, alive or dead, in the middle of the road.)

4   During the Berlin and Cuban missile crises, he expressed concern not over the possibilities of his death but over the terrible tragedy that might befall his children and all the children of the world. Even then he was not moody or melancholy about the subject; although his own letters to the next-of-kin of those killed in Vietnam, he admitted, constituted one of his most difficult tasks. Perhaps he came closest to revealing his inner thoughts when the Irish Ambassador presented a Wexford cup in honor of little John's christening with a poem:

> . . . When the storms break for him
> May the trees shake for him
> Their blossoms down;
> And in the night that he is troubled
> May a friend wake for him
> So that his time be doubled;
> And at the end of all loving and love
> May the Man above
> Give him a crown.

5   The President, moving toward the microphone for his remarks of acceptance, whispered to the Ambassador: "I wish that was for me."

6   Another poem—one of his favorites, which he often asked Jacqueline to recite—was Alan Seeger's "I Have a Rendezvous with Death." He was moved by the fact that Seeger had been cut down in the brilliance of his youth. "It is," he once said at a war memorial, "against the law of nature for parents to bury their children . . . a son with all of his life before him." "The poignancy of men dying young always moved my husband," said Jacqueline, "possibly because of his brother Joe." And possibly he

lived each day of his own life to the utmost because he did not know when his own rendezvous with death might come.

7   Simply accepting death as an inevitable fact of life, and simply recognizing assassination as an unavoidable hazard of the Presidency, he refused to worry about his personal safety—not with any bravado or braggadocio but with an almost fatalistic unconcern for danger. He had preferred the risks of a dangerous back operation to the frustrations of life on crutches. He had preferred the risks of flying in poor planes and poor weather to the frustrations of holding back his campaign. And he preferred the risks of less protection in the Presidency to the frustrations of cutting off public contact.

8   He mentioned more than once—but almost in passing—that no absolute protection was possible, that a determined assassin could always find a way, and that a sniper from a high window or rooftop seemed to him the least preventable. Occasionally he would read one of the dozens of written threats on his life that he received almost every week in the White House. But he regarded assassination as the Secret Service's worry, not his. "Jim Rowley," he quipped, "is most efficient. He has never lost a President."

DEFINE: premonition, adrenal deficiency (1); *rendezvous, poignancy* (6).

ANALYSIS

structure   1. Write a brief outline of the "Kennedy" selection. Under each of the major supporting points, list the examples used.

2. Using your outline, write a four or five sentence summary of the selection.

style   3. Is this writing objective or subjective? Support your answer.

opinion   4. In recent years the subject of death has been discussed more openly than in the past. Is that good or bad?

5. What is your attitude toward death, and how did you develop that attitude?

WRITING SUGGESTION

Using incidents from your life, show how your attitude toward death was developed.

Russell Baker

BITTER MEDICINE

1   I went to the hospital. The cashier stopped me at the door. "You can't afford to come in here," she said. This was not news. Nobody can

© 1978 by The New York Times Company. Reprinted by permission.

afford to go to a hospital anymore. The cost of medical care is so high that the average patient sent to surgery for a tonsillectomy is bankrupt before the doctor can get around to his second tonsil. This is why so many Americans nowadays have one tonsil out and one tonsil in.

2   I told the cashier I didn't want any medical care, but was just visiting. Visitor's admission was $20, which, as the ticket taker observed, was $5 cheaper than an orchestra seat for Liza Minelli's new musical. The elevator ride was $7, so I used the stairs, which cost only $5.

3   At the top of the climb I was inhaling deeply. Technicians hurried me to an inhalation-testing room where a breath analyzer established that I was inhaling, in addition to air, the odors of floor wax, ether, iodine, toilet disinfectant, gift fruit baskets and adhesive tape.

4   Floor-wax odor cost me $10; ether, $50; iodine, $25; disinfectant, $20; gift fruit baskets, $15, and adhesive tape, $20. The air was free. There was a $100 charge for use of the inhalation-testing room, a $75 charge for use of the breath analyzer, and a $30 charge for the paper on which the bill was written. Naturally, I had to pay by check, having neglected to take out major hospital inhalation coverage.

5   Two guards restrained me in a corner of the corridor while a nurse phoned the bank to make sure I was not a bad-check artist. I was charged $40 for the guards, $25 for use of the corner, $10 for the telephone call, and $50 for the clean bill of financial health.

6   I went along the corridor toward the room occupied by my friend, a wealthy entrepreneur who had swallowed a fishbone during an expense-account lunch. For use of the corridor I was charged $50. Use of the overhead lights in the corridor cost me $20, and use of the heat from the radiators, $30. Since it would have cost $150 to enter my friend's room I stood outside and looked through the open door. Use of the open door for this purpose cost $15.

7   My friend was not there.

8   "Where is the man who swallowed the fishbone?" I asked a nurse. "The charge for information is $130," she said with an apologetic smile. The charge for the smile was $25 and the charge for its apologetic character was $40.

9   By this time, my bank balance was so low I was afraid I wouldn't be able to afford an exit. In fact, I would have made a run for the stairs and taken my chances against the accountant and treasurer if at that moment my wealthy friend had not appeared around a corner, fully dressed and sobbing.

10   His story, like the annals of the poor, was short and simple. He had been wiped out, possibly ruined. The fishbone had proved more elusive than the doctors had anticipated. They had been compelled to go into the esophagus, then into the stomach before they removed it.

11   By that time, however, his bank accounts had been consumed; his insurance exhausted; his airplane, yacht and cars sold at auction; and his estates in Maine, Delaware and Venezuela all lost. Though he had become penniless on the operating table, the hospital had refused to put him out until his incisions had been sewed and had even permitted him to keep the expensive clothes in which he had entered the place.

12   This, the hospital explained, was in line with medical ethics, for

which the charge was $1,500. This friend has always been highly strung and it was not surprising that he broke down and wept in the administration office when told that, though a pauper, he had received the best medical care in the world.

13   The charge for use of the administration office was $100. The charge for weeping was $150. The administrator said he would waive the $300 charge for breaking down and send the rest of the bill to a collection agency. Escorting us to the door, he presented my friend with a gift from the hospital—a tin cup and a dozen pencils—and a piece of advice.

14   "Next time, get a divorce," he said, in a humorous vein. "It's cheaper than swallowing fishbones."

15   The charge for the tin cup was $50; for the pencils, $30; for the advice, $100, and for the humorous vein, which had been transplanted from a patient who had been hounded to death by a collection agency, $15,000.

ANALYSIS

structure   1. The many examples in this selection are set in what kind of (now familiar) rhetorical framework?

style   2. What kind of humor does Baker use to get his message across?

3. His message is loud and clear: "Hospital costs are too high!" Would his article have been more effective if he had started with that statement and then listed actual costs?

4. Find examples of satire in the daily newspapers.

opinion   5. In making a point, what are some of the advantages of using satire?

WRITING SUGGESTION

Using examples, try a humorous approach to a serious problem: too much homework, getting a date, finding a job, dealing with parents, getting the use of the car, dirtying the environment, building nuclear plants.

Norman Cousins

THE ENVIRONMENT OF LANGUAGE

In this selection examples still play an important role, but comments, factual data, and other rhetorical devices are also used.

1   The words men use, Julian Huxley once said, not only express but shape their ideas. Language is an instrument; it is even more an environment. It has as much to do with the philosophical and political condi-

© Saturday Review, 1967. All rights reserved.

tioning of a society as geography or climate. The role of language in contributing to men's problems and their prospects is the subject of an imaginative and valuable study now getting under way at Pro Deo University in Rome, which is winning recognition in world university circles for putting advanced scholarship to work for the concept of a world community.

2   One aspect of the Pro Deo study, as might be expected, has to do with the art of conveying precise meaning from one language to another. Stuart Chase, one of America's leading semanticists, has pointed out that when an English speaker at the United Nations uses the expression "I assume," the French interpreter may say "I deduce" and the Russian interpreter may say "I consider." When Pope Paul VI sent a cable to Prime Minister Alexei Kosygin and Party Chairman Leonid Brezhnev on their accession to office, he expressed the hope that the historic aspirations of the Russian people for a fuller life would be advanced under the new leadership. As translated into Russian by the Vatican's own interpreter, the Pope's expression of hope came out in a way that made it appear that the Pope was making known his endorsement of the new regime. The eventual clarification was inevitably awkward for all concerned.

3   The Pro Deo study, however, will not be confined to problems of precise translation. The major emphasis has to do with something even more fundamental: the dangerous misconceptions and prejudices that take root in language and that undermine human values. The color of a man's skin, for example, is tied to plus-or-minus words that inevitably condition human attitudes. The words "black" and "white," as defined in Western culture, are heavily loaded. "Black" has all sorts of unfavorable connotations; "white" is almost all favorable. One of the more interesting papers being studied by the Pro Deo scholars is by Ossie Davis, the author and actor. Mr. Davis, a Negro, concluded on the basis of a detailed study of dictionaries and *Roget's Thesaurus* that the English language was his enemy. In *Roget's,* he counted 120 synonyms for "blackness," most of them with unpleasant connotations: blot, blotch, blight, smut, smudge, sully, begrime, soot, becloud, obscure, dingy, murky, threatening, frowning, foreboding, forbidden, sinister, baneful, dismal, evil, wicked, malignant, deadly, secretive, unclean, unwashed, foul, blacklist, black book, black-hearted, etc. Incorporated in the same listing were words such as Negro, nigger, and darky.

4   In the same *Roget's,* Mr. Davis found 134 synonyms for the word "white," almost all of them with favorable connotations: purity, cleanness, bright, shining, fair, blonde, stainless, chaste, unblemished, unsullied, innocent, honorable, upright, just, straightforward, genuine, trustworthy, honesty, etc. "White" as a racial designation was, of course, included in this tally of desirable terms.

5   No less invidious than black are some of the words associated with the color yellow: coward, conniver, baseness, fear, effeminacy, funk, soft, spiritless, poltroonery, pusillanimity, timidity, milksop, recreant, sneak, lilylivered, etc. Oriental people are included in the listing.

6   As a matter of factual accuracy, white, black, and yellow as colors are not descriptive of races. The coloration range of so-called white people may run from pale olive to mottled pink. So-called colored people run

from light beige to mahogany. Absolute color designations—white, black, red, yellow—are not merely inaccurate; they have become symbolic rather than descriptive. It will be argued, of course, that definitions of color and the connotations that go with them are independent of sociological implications. There is no getting around the fact, it will be said, that whiteness means cleanliness and blackness means dirtiness. Are we to doctor the dictionary in order to achieve a social good? What this line of argument misses is that people in Western cultures do not realize the extent to which their racial attitudes have been conditioned since early childhood by the power of words to ennoble or condemn, augment or detract, glorify or demean. Negative language infects the subconscious of most Western people from the time they first learn to speak. Prejudice is not merely imparted or superimposed. It is metabolized in the bloodstream of society. What is needed is not so much a change in language as an awareness of the power of words to condition attitudes. If we can at least recognize the underpinnings of prejudice, we may be in a position to deal with the effects.

7   To be sure, Western languages have no monopoly on words with connotations that affect judgment. In Chinese, whiteness means cleanliness, but it can also mean bloodlessness, coldness, frigidity, absence of feeling, weakness, insensitivity. Also in Chinese, yellowness is associated with sunshine, openness, beauty, flowering, etc. Similarly, the word black in many African tongues has connotations of strength, certainty, recognizability, integrity, while white is associated with paleness, anemia, unnaturalness, deviousness, untrustworthiness.

8   The purpose of Pro Deo University in undertaking this study is not just to demonstrate that most cultures tend to be self-serving in their language. The purpose is to give educational substance to the belief that it will take all the adroitness and sensitivity of which the human species is capable if it is to be sustained. Earth-dwellers now have the choice of making their world into a neighborhood or a crematorium. Language is one of the factors in that option. The right words may not automatically produce the right actions but they are an essential part of the process.

DEFINE: *semanticist* (2); *invidious, funk, poltroonery, pusillanimity* (5); *metabolized* (6).

ANALYSIS

structure   1. Outline the Cousins article.

2. Using the outline, write a four or five sentence summary.

meaning   3. How do the meanings of "I assume," "I deduce," and "I consider" differ?

4. What problem arose because of the translation of the Pope's message?

5. Why did Ossie Davis say that the English language is his enemy?

6. According to Cousins, how can Westerners overcome the prejudicial slant of our language?

7. What will happen if we don't make our "world into a neighborhood"?

8. Discuss: "Prejudice is not merely imparted or superimposed. It is metabolized in the bloodstream of society."

9. Are so-called whites the only ones who use racist language? Give examples of anti-white expressions.

style 10. At what audience is this article aimed?

11. What is the tone of the article?

12. Does the vocabulary seem affected, or is it correct, considering the audience?

WRITING SUGGESTION

In light of this article, evaluate the jingle "Sticks and stones can break my bones, but names will never hurt me." Use examples, of course.

section 4c

Merlin Stone

TALES WITH A POINT OF VIEW

1 Though we live amid high-rise steel buildings, formica countertops and electronic television screens, there is something in all of us, women and men alike, that makes us feel deeply connected with the past. Perhaps the sudden dampness of a beach cave or the lines of sunlight piercing through the intricate lace patterns of the leaves in a darkened grove of tall trees will awaken from the hidden recesses of our minds the distant echoes of a remote and ancient time, taking us back to the early stirrings of human life on the planet. For people raised and programmed on the patriarchal religions of today, religions that affect us in even the most secular aspects of our society, perhaps there remains a lingering, almost innate memory of sacred shrines and temples tended by priestesses who served in the religion of the original supreme deity. In the beginning, people prayed to the Creatress of Life, the Mistress of Heaven. At the very dawn of religion, God was a woman. Do you remember?

2 For years something has magnetically lured me into exploring the legends, the temple sites, the statues and the ancient rituals of the female deities, drawing me back in time to an age when the Goddess was omnipotent, and women acted as Her clergy, controlling the form and rites of religion.

"Tales with a Point of View" from *When God Was a Woman* by Merlin Stone. Copyright © 1976 by Merlin Stone. Reprinted by permission of The Dial Press.

3   Perhaps it was my training and work as a sculptor that first exposed me to the sculptures of the Goddess found in the ruins of prehistoric sanctuaries and the earliest dwellings of human beings. Perhaps it was a certain romantic mysticism, which once embarrassed me, but to which I now happily confess, that led me over the years into the habit of collecting infomation about the early female religions and the veneration of female deities. Occasionally I tried to dismiss my fascination with this subject as overly fanciful and certainly disconnected from my work (I was building electronic sculptural environments at the time). Nevertheless, I would find myself continually perusing archaeology journals and poring over texts in museum or university library stacks.

4   As I read, I recalled that somewhere along the pathway of my life I had been told—and accepted the idea—that the sun, great and powerful, was naturally worshiped as male, while the moon, hazy, delicate symbol of sentiment and love, had always been revered as female. Much to my surprise I discovered accounts of Sun Goddesses in the lands of Canaan, Anatolia, Arabia and Australia, while Sun Goddesses among the Eskimos, the Japanese and the Khasis of India were accompanied by subordinate brothers who were symbolized as the moon.

5   I had somewhere assimilated the idea that the earth was invariably identified as female, Mother Earth, the one who passively accepts the seed, while heaven was naturally and inherently male, its intangibility symbolic of the supposedly exclusive male ability to think in abstract concepts. This too I had accepted without question—until I learned that nearly all the female deities of the Near and Middle East were titled Queen of Heaven, and in Egypt not only was the ancient Goddess Nut known as the heavens, but her brother-husband Geb was symbolized as the earth.

6   Most astonishing of all was the discovery of numerous accounts of the female Creators of all existence, divinities who were credited with bringing forth not only the first people but the entire earth and the heavens above. There were records of such Goddesses in Sumer, Babylon, Egypt, Africa, Australia and China.

7   In India the Goddess Sarasvati was honored as the inventor of the original alphabet, while in Celtic Ireland the Goddess Brigit was esteemed as the patron deity of language. Texts revealed that it was the Goddess Nidaba in Sumer who was paid honor as the one who initially invented clay tablets and the art of writing. She appeared in that position earlier than any of the male deities who later replaced Her. The official scribe of the Sumerian heaven was a woman. But most significant was the archaeological evidence of the earliest examples of written language so far discovered; these were also located in Sumer, at the temple of the Queen of Heaven in Erech, written there over five thousand years ago. Though writing is most often said to have been invented by *man*, however that may be defined, the combination of the above factors presents a most convincing argument that it may have actually been woman who pressed those first meaningful marks into wet clay.

8   In agreement with the generally accepted theory that women were responsible for the development of agriculture, as an extension of their food-gathering activities, there were female deities everywhere who were

credited with this gift to civilization. In Mesopotamia, where some of the earliest evidences of agricultural development have been found, the Goddess Ninlil was revered for having provided Her people with an understanding of planting and harvesting methods. In nearly all areas of the world, female deities were extolled as healers, dispensers of curative herbs, roots, plants and other medical aids, casting the priestesses who attended the shrines into the role of physicians of those who worshiped there.

9   Some legends described the Goddess as a powerful, courageous warrior, a leader in battle. The worship of the Goddess as valiant warrior seems to have been responsible for the numerous reports of female soldiers, later referred to by the classical Greeks as the Amazons. More thoroughly examining the accounts of the esteem the Amazons paid to the female deity, it became evident that women who worshiped a warrior Goddess hunted and fought in the lands of Libya, Anatolia, Bulgaria, Greece, Armenia and Russia and were far from the mythical fantasy so many writers of today would have us believe.

10   I could not help noticing how far removed from contemporary images were the prehistoric and most ancient historic attitudes toward the thinking capacities and intellect of woman, for nearly everywhere the Goddess was reversed as wise counselor and prophetess. The Celtic Cerridwen was the Goddess of Intelligence and Knowledge in the pre-Christian legends of Ireland, the priestesses of the Goddess Gaia provided the wisdom of divine revelation at pre-Greek sanctuaries, while the Greek Demeter and the Egyptian Isis were both invoked as law-givers and sage dispensers of righteous wisdom, counsel and justice. The Egyptian Goddess Maat represented the very order, rhythm and truth of the Universe. Ishtar of Mesopotamia was referred to as the Directress of People, the Prophetess, the Lady of Vision, while the archaeological records of the city of Nimrud, where Ishtar was worshiped, revealed that women served as judges and magistrates in the courts of law.

11   The more I read, the more I discovered. The worship of female deities appeared in every area of the world, presenting an image of woman that I had never before encountered. As a result, I began to ponder upon the power of myth and eventually to perceive these legends as more than the innocent childlike fables they first appeared to be. They were tales with a most specific point of view.

12   Myths present ideas that guide perception, conditioning us to think and even perceive in a particular way, especially when we are young and impressionable. Often they portray the actions of people who are rewarded or punished for their behavior, and we are encouraged to view these as examples to emulate or avoid. So many of the stories told to us from the time we are just old enough to understand deeply affect our attitudes and comprehension of the world about us and ourselves. Our ethics, morals, conduct, values, sense of duty and even sense of humor are often developed from simple childhood parables and fables. From them we learn what is socially acceptable in the society from which they come. They define good and bad, right and wrong, what is natural and what is unnatural among the people who hold the myths as meaningful. It was quite apparent that the myths and legends that grew from, and were

propagated by, a religion in which the deity was female, and revered as wise, valiant, powerful and just, provided very different images of womanhood from those which we are offered by the male-oriented religions of today.

DEFINE: *patriarchal* (1); *omnipotent* (2); *inherently* (5); *archaeology* (7); *emulate* (12).

ANALYSIS

structure 1. What is Stone's thesis? (Be sure to read the whole selection carefully before writing this.)

2. In supporting her thesis, Stone groups some of the goddesses. Label the groups.

3. In paragraphs 2, 3, and 4, she writes about herself instead of about the goddesses. Why does she do this?

4. Summarize the selection in three or four sentences.

style 5. What kind of writing does Stone imitate in her first paragraph, especially in the last three sentences? Why?

6. What is the effect of the question, "Do you remember?"

7. Discuss the tone of "For people raised and programmed on the patriarchal religions . . ." (paragraph 1).

opinion 8. Might attitudes toward women be different today if we had been taught about women goddesses in our childhood?

WRITING SUGGESTIONS

1. Women: Give examples of decisions and actions in your life that have been influenced by the Women's Liberation Movement. Give examples of how male chauvinism has hurt you.

2. Men: Give examples of differences in attitudes toward women (if any) that you may have developed because of the Women's Liberation Movement.

Vance Packard

THE EMERGING PLASTIC IMAGE OF MAN

> *We have not yet seen what man can make of man.*
> —B. F. Skinner, behavioral psychologist

1   B. F. Skinner's ringing pronouncement reflects ambition as much as fact. But dramatic efforts are indeed under way to reshape people and their behavior. These efforts obviously have profound implications. In quite a few instances the implications are disquieting.

From *The People Shapers* by Vance Packard. Copyright © 1977 by Vance Packard. By permission of Little, Brown and Co.

2   Human engineers are at work in a variety of fields. They are increasing the capacity of a relatively small number of people to control, modify, manipulate, reshape the lives of a great number of other people. And they are functioning in many countries, especially in the United States, Great Britain, Germany, France, Japan, Canada, Israel, Russia, Australia, the Netherlands, and Scandinavia.

3   These new technologists draw primarily upon discoveries in the behavioral, biological, and computer sciences. Control is being achieved over human actions, moods, wishes, thoughts. As the psychologist Perry London put it: "Never in human history has this occurred before, except in fantasy."

4   The results may force us to alter our concepts of the nature of humanness.

5   Many of the revolutionists are caught up in a fervor not normally seen in scientists, who ordinarily speak cautiously. Columbus wasn't cautious and in substantial numbers they are not. They are now certain that new worlds can be discovered inside the human being. And they are eager to get on with the discovering. They see themselves out on the cutting edge of science.

6   One of the geneticists, Nobel Laureate Joshua Lederberg, called on the U.S. Congress to appropriate at least $10,000,000 to set up a national genetic task force. This force would make a crash effort to broaden knowledge of the genetic code, which would simplify the biological engineering of people.

7   Robert Sinsheimer has exulted that for the first time since the Creation a living creature can undertake to redesign its future. He has been serving as the head of the Biology Division at the California Institute of Technology and is a driving force in the current biological revolution. Sinsheimer asserted: "We can be the agent of transition to a wholly new path of evolution."

8   Among behavioral psychologists there are a host of restless revolutionaries. That most famed of the behaviorists, B. F. Skinner of Harvard University, has called for "a technology of behavior" because "we need to make vast changes in human behavior."

9   A few years ago a group of his disciples, in trying to describe "What Behavioral Engineering Is," explained: "For openers, we can develop a technology for routinely producing superior human beings. . . . We have the technology for installing any behavior we want."

10   James V. McConnell, a wide-ranging psychological explorer from the University of Michigan, was quoted in 1974 as proposing: "We should reshape our society so that we all would be trained from birth to do what society wants us to do." (Knowing him, I suspect he was carried away by his natural exuberance and did not intend to make any ominous call for total conformity.)

11   Some of the revolutionists seem to relish the powers being achieved. José M. R. Delgado, a pioneer in brain probing and a most civil man, has called for physical control of the mind in order to develop a "psychocivilized society." He has urged the U.S. government to make "conquering the mind" a national goal.

12   Other noted scientists, I should add, are cautioning the more out-spoken activists. Leon Kass, a molecular biologist and ethicist, calls it an arrogant presumption that scientists think they are wise enough to re-make Man.*

13   Some of the projects to reshape or control Man are simply intriguing. Many are disturbing. Some may make your skin crawl. By the latter I mean such plans as keeping people under surveillance by locking trans-mitters to their bodies, creating subhumans for menial work and as a source of spare parts for human bodies, transplanting heads, creating humans with four or more parents, and pacifying troublesome people, including children, by cutting into the brain.

14   The strategies being pressed by the human engineers have caused some observers to suggest that we are hurling toward the fictional worlds envisioned by two Englishmen. I refer to George Orwell's *1984* and Aldous Huxley's *Brave New World,* projected for six centuries from now. Actually, Orwell's Big Brother was pretty heavy-handed and simplistic compared with Huxley's World Controller, Mustapha Mond.

15   Orwell, writing in the period of Stalin and Hitler, primarily extrap-olated totalitarian policing techniques. His Big Brother controlled by in-trusion, such as installing a watching TV eye in every home and by set-ting up Thought Police. He ruled by exquisite forms of coercion, and by massive indoctrination.

16   Huxley's Controller, conceived earlier, in 1932, developed his con-trols by far more sophisticated scientific techniques. His Controller saw that total control should start at conception. In hatcheries made possible by reproductive biology, embryos were molded to order by genetic means to become humans of certain types. The level of intelligence was con-trolled in part by manipulating the amount of oxygen given the fetuses. Future sewer workers, who needed few brains, were mass-produced on low levels of oxygen.

17   Once new humans were born, a variety of controls continued, from infancy on. Persons were induced to love their assigned status and the re-gime by the use of "neo-Pavlovian conditioning" techniques, by sleep teaching, and by a wondrous "soma" drug. There is no single soma drug as such today but the states it produced—tranquillity, stimulation, colorful visions, and apparently high suggestibility—all can now be pro-duced by specific drugs or precise techniques.

18   Most of the techniques Huxley fantasized for the distant future are already becoming available or are at least being forecast by reputable sci-entists. One of them is sleep teaching. Modern experiments have shown that a person can learn from messages whispered in his ear as he is falling asleep. Huxley (erroneously as it turned out) had the person deeply asleep

*Throughout this book I capitalize the word *man* when using it in the dictionary sense of the human race, in order to avoid the awkward his-or-her construction. Unfortunately, males seem to have controlled the forming of English words de-scribing the earth's foremost primate. Note the common singular forms hu*man* and *man*kind. Even words referring to persons of the feminine gender have a mas-culine base, as in wo*man* and fe*male*. There is, of course, *Homo sapiens,* but *Homo* means "man" in Latin. Modernization obviously is in order.

when learning from the whispered messages, but his idea was valid in the main.

[19] Today there is no all-powerful Controller in sight in the Western world. The coming crunch on natural resources combined with rampant overbreeding in many areas of the world make it likely that we will be hearing calls for more authoritarian governments within the coming quarter century. At any rate there are already a host of technologists in a variety of fields who qualify as people controllers or people shapers. They are becoming, willingly or not, a new elite. Many work for institutions, including governments, to help those institutions increase their power to control us and to impose their values and views on others. Meanwhile, the ordinary person's sense of power over his life is threatened.

[20] A few years ago I participated in a conference in Wyoming on the topic "Captive Man in a Free Society." One of the other speakers was the late Sidney Jourard, a noted humanistic psychologist. In talking of the technologists of control—and some of them were present—he made a comment that remains etched in my mind:

"The worst thing that can happen is that a person doesn't count."

ANALYSIS

structure 1. Write an outline of the selection. Include in it the major points and a listing of the examples used (when they are) to support those points.

meaning 2. Explain the title.

3. Explain the references to George Orwell and Aldous Huxley.

4. Explain the concluding statement.

5. Discuss "We should reshape our society so that we all would be trained from birth to do what society wants us to do."

style 6. It is obvious that Packard is disturbed by the increasing power of the behaviorists, but he writes of them with obvious restraint. What does he rely on principally to show his attitude?

opinion 7. What is your feeling about the possible dangers created by the work of the human engineers—or do you feel that work to be a panacea?

8. Do you believe that the work of the human engineers should be controlled? If so, who should do the controlling: the government, other scientists, religious leaders?

WRITING SUGGESTION

Write a paragraph or two using Packard's material but changing the tone drastically either in support of the behaviorists or against them.

NOTE: For further material to use in example papers, see the Idea Bank, Chapter 10. There are materials on patent medicines, love, loneliness, sexism, education, and more from which examples can be drawn. Also see "George Orwell's 1984—How Close Are We?" in Chapter 6.

Review of Chapter 4

Survey the chapter to remind yourself about the many ways examples are used to help explain and illustrate various ideas. Consider their uses in introductions, conclusions, and in support of major points. In writing your final papers for this chapter, call on some of these devices to make your writing more interesting and effective.

WRITING SUGGESTIONS

1. Look into your crystal ball and give some examples of how the various sciences and technologies will change man. ("Emerging Plastic Image of Man")
2. Perhaps you want to look further and provide a sampling of what the hereafter holds.
3. Provide a sampling of life in the home of an "engineered" family. ("Emerging . . . ")

EVALUATION

Which article uses examples most effectively? Which uses them least effectively? Support your opinions.

Classification ❖❖❖❖❖❖❖❖

❖❖

❖❖❖❖❖❖❖❖❖❖❖❖❖❖❖❖❖❖❖❖❖ # CHAPTER 5

READING FOCUS

❖ Be aware of the organization of classification papers. Their fairly predictable structure can often make reading easier for those who look for it.

❖ Be aware that arbitrary classifications can be unfair, even dangerous.

WRITING FOCUS

❖ Be observant enough to see distinctions and similarities among various types of people, things, situations, etc.

❖ Be sure to apply only one standard of classification to each system.

❖ Be clear and consistent in setting up your system.

❖ Be aware that there are often exceptions to classifications, and your reader should be warned of this.

❖ Carefully consider how fully you must support your classifications. Depending on their complexity and on the probable knowledge of your audience, you may have to define, describe, and/or provide examples to make your system clear.

We classify subjects as relatively simple as shopping lists and as complicated as the yellow pages of telephone directories or the millions of books in libraries. *To classify is to analyze a subject, breaking it into parts according to a single standard.* The basis (standard) for classification of the "Paperback Best

Seller" list that follows is "places where sold." "I'll Have One of Each" classifies used car buyers according to what they want in a car.

Classification systems are sometimes developed without adequate research and applied rigidly. Serious questions have been raised in recent years about methods of classifying people as having or lacking college aptitudes, being mentally ill, or having criminal tendencies. (For a discussion of the latter classification, read "The Criminal Type" in Section 9B.)

Section 5a

TABLE OF CONTENTS

Reprinted with permission from *Science,* August 18, 1978. Vol. 201, no. 4356. Copyright 1978 by the American Association for the Advancement of Science.

PAPERBACK BEST SELLERS

MASS MARKET

Mass-market paperbacks are softcover books sold at newsstands, variety stores and supermarkets, as well as in bookstores. This listing is based on computer-processed reports from bookstores and representative wholesalers with more than 40,000 outlets across the United States.

1 THE THORN BIRDS, by Colleen McCullough. (Avon, $2.50.) Australian family saga: fiction.

2 JAWS 2, by Hank Searls (Bantam, $2.25.) Female great white shark returns to familiar waters.

3 LOOKING OUT FOR #1, by Robert J. Ringer. (Fawcett/Crest, $2.50.) Getting yours.

4 TWINS, by Bari Wood and Jack Geasland. (NAL/Signet, $2.50.) Twin doctors and their relationship in life and death: fiction.

5 THE LAWLESS, by John Jakes. (Jove/HBJ, $2.25.) The Kent family saga reaches the glittering, corrupt 1890's.

6 FULL DISCLOSURE, by William Safire. (Ballantine, $2.50.) President goes blind: White House intrigue. Fiction.

7 NIGHTWING, by Martin Cruz Smith. (Jove/HBJ, $2.25.) Vampire bats menace America: fiction.

8 DELTA OF VENUS, by Anaïs Nin. (Bantam, $2.50.) Elegant erotica written for a wealthy patron: fiction.

9 THE DRAGONS OF EDEN, by Carl Sagan. (Ballantine, $2.25.) How intelligence evolved.

10 THE INVESTIGATION, by Dorothy Uhnak. (Pocket, $2.50.) Woman accused of murdering her children: fiction.

11 THE SWORD OF SHANNARA, by Terry Brooks. (Ballantine, $2.50.) Fantasy novel.

12 THE BASTARD, by John Jakes. (Jove, $2.25.) First book in the Kent family chronicles: basis of the recent TV series.

13 YOUR ERRONEOUS ZONES, by Wayne W. Dyer. (Avon, $2.25.) Self-help pep talk.

14 MONTY, by Robert La Guardia. (Avon, $2.25.) Life of the actor Montgomery Clift.

15 THE PROMISE, by Danielle Steel. (Dell, $1.95.) Lovers separated by a tragic set of circumstances: fiction.

TRADE

Trade paperbacks are softcover books usually sold in bookstores and at an average price higher than mass-market paperbacks. This listing is based on computer-processed reports from bookstores and wholesalers with more than 2,500 outlets across the United States.

1 THE COMPLETE RUNNER, by the Editors of Runner's World Magazine. (Avon, $4.95.) Advice by professionals.

2 THE DIETER'S GUIDE TO WEIGHT LOSS DURING SEX, by Richard Smith. (Workman, $2.95.) Spoof on diet and sex manuals.

3 THE JOY OF SEX, by Alex Comfort. (Simon & Schuster/Fireside, $6.95.) With illustrations.

4 THE RUNNER'S HANDBOOK, by Bob Glover and Jack Shepherd. (Penguin, $3.95.) Fitness guide for men and women.

5 CROCKETT'S VICTORY GARDEN, by James Underwood Crockett. (Little, Brown, $9.95.) Month-by-month guide.

6 THE AUDUBON SOCIETY FIELD GUIDE TO NORTH AMERICAN BIRDS (Eastern Region), by John Bull and John Farrand Jr. (Knopf, $7.95.) Illustrated.

7 THE PEOPLE'S PHARMACY, by Joe Graedon. (Avon, $3.95.) Guide to prescriptions, over-the-counter drugs and home remedies.

8 TINY FOOTPRINTS, by B. Kliban. (Workman, $2.95.) Cartoons.

9 OUR BODIES, OURSELVES, by the Boston Women's Health Book Collective. (Simon & Schuster/Touchstone, $4.95.) Illustrated guide.

10 MURPHY'S LAW, by Arthur Bloch. (Price/Stern/Sloan, $2.50.) Humorous explanations of why things go wrong.

11 ON DEATH AND DYING, by Dr. Elisabeth Kübler-Ross. (Macmillan, $2.25.) Lessons to be learned from the terminally ill.

12 IRELAND: A TERRIBLE BEAUTY, by Jill and Leon Uris. (Bantam, $7.95.) A "love song" in words and photographs.

13 STALKING THE PERFECT TAN, by G. B. Trudeau. (Holt, Rinehart & Winston, $1.95.) Shifting political winds caught in cartoon form.

14 HOW TO FLATTEN YOUR STOMACH, by Jim Everroad. (Price/Stern/Sloan, $1.75.) Exercises.

15 THE FIRST THREE YEARS OF LIFE, by Burton L. White. (Avon, $4.95.) Guide for parents.

© 1978 by The New York Times Company. Reprinted by permission.

I'LL HAVE ONE OF EACH

A used-car salesman of our acquaintance once told us there are only three kinds of automobile buyers: One wants to own a particular make of car, one wants to pay a certain amount for his car and the other wants to pay so much a month. The first fellow will walk onto the lot looking for a Ford. He might drive out in a Model A or an LTD; it doesn't matter what year, what it costs or how much mileage is on the odometer. The second buyer has $800 to spend, and he wants an $800 automobile, no matter if it is a foreign sports car, a station wagon, a two-door sedan or a pickup truck. The third fellow, even more poorly advised than the other two, wants to make payments of $65 a month, and he'll buy anything the salesman offers him so long as he can get it on those terms.

From *The Complete Motorcycle Book* by Lyle Kenyon Engel and Deke Houlgate. Copyright © 1974 by Lyle Kenyon Engel. Reprinted by permission of Four Winds Press, a Division of Scholastic Magazines, Inc.

Robert J. Ringer

THREE TYPE THEORY

What this theory states is that there are only three types of people who exist in the business world (again, with the one exception being a person who stands to directly benefit as a result of your earning, and receiving, income), as follows:

TYPE NUMBER ONE: This type lets you know from the outset—either through his words or actions, or both—that he's out to get all of your chips. He then follows through by attempting to do just that.

TYPE NUMBER TWO: This type assures you that he's not interested in getting your chips, and he usually infers that he wants to see you get everything "that's coming to you." He then follows through, just like Type Number One, and attempts to grab all of your chips anyway.

TYPE NUMBER THREE: This type also assures you that he's not interested in getting any of your chips, but, unlike Type Number Two, he sincerely means it. That, however, is where the difference ends; due to any one of a number of reasons—ranging from his own bungling to his personal standards for rationalizing what's right and wrong—he, like Types Number One and Two, still ends up trying to grab your chips.

From *Winning through Intimidation* by Robert J. Ringer. Second Edition. Copyright 1974 by Robert J. Ringer.

Kenneth Roberts

THE EVILS OF CONSISTENCY

All the great villains and small villains whom I met so frequently . . . were consistent men—unimaginative men who consistently believed in war as a means of settling disputes between nations; equally misguided men who consistently believed that war must be avoided at all hazards, no matter what the provocation; narrow men who consistently upheld the beliefs and acts of one political party and saw no good in any other; shortsighted men who consistently refused to see that the welfare of their own nation was dependent upon the welfare of every other nation; ignorant men who consistently thought that the policies of their own government should be supported and followed, whether those policies were right or wrong; dangerous men who consistently thought that all people with black skins are inferior to those with white skins; intolerant men who consistently believed that all people with white skins should be forced to accept all people with black skins as equals. And I know that any nation that cannot or will not avoid the dreadful pitfalls of consistency will be one with the dead empires. . . .

From *Lydia Bailey* by Kenneth Roberts. Copyright © 1947 by Kenneth Roberts and Anna M. Roberts. Reprinted by permission of Doubleday & Company, Inc.

ANALYSIS

structure

1. The standards of classification for "Paperback Best Sellers" and "I'll Have One of Each" are cited in the introduction to this chapter. Devise a different classification standard for listing books and another for buyers of used cars.

2. State the standard of classification for "Three Type Theory" and "The Evils of Consistency."

3. Divide the headings in the *Science* table of contents into two groups (clear cut, and less distinct) according to how clearly they describe the subject matter in their areas. It is clear, for example, what letters are, but what is a report?

4. What are the standards of classification for the two tables of contents in this book?

meaning

5. What's wrong with the approaches of the car buyers in "I'll Have One of Each"?

6. If you boil down Ringer's three types of business people, how many types do you really have? Explain.

7. We usually think of consistency as a virtue. Why does Kenneth Roberts consider it an evil?

8. What is the similarity between "The Evils of Consistency" and "I'll Have One of Each"?

style

9. In "I'll Have One of Each," what is the effect of saying, "A used car salesman

of our acquaintance once told us . . ." instead of "There are three kinds of used car buyers"?

10. What is the effect of using contractions and words like *fellow* and *chips* in "I'll Have Once of Each" and "Three Type Theory"?

11. What word is used incorrectly in ":Three Type Theory"?

12. Since Roberts considers consistency evil in the context in which he uses it, could he not have used a stronger word than *consistency*? Suggest one or two.

WRITING SUGGESTION

Base a classification paragraph on the standard of classification you wrote for paperback books or used car buyers.

section 5b

Rachel Carson

TYPES OF WHALES

Eventually the whales, as though to divide the sea's food resources among them, became separated into three groups: the plankton-eaters, the fish-eaters, and the squid-eaters. The plankton-eating whales can exist only where there are dense masses of small shrimp or copepods to supply their enormous food requirements. This limits them, except for scattered areas, to arctic and antarctic waters and the high temperate latitudes. Fish-eating whales may find food over a somewhat wider range of ocean, but they are restricted to places where there are enormous populations of schooling fish. The blue water of the tropics and of the open ocean basins offers little to either of these groups. But that immense, square-headed, formidably toothed whale known as the cachalot or sperm whale discovered long ago what men have known for only a short time—that hundreds of fathoms below the almost untenanted surface waters of these regions there is an abundant animal life. The sperm whale has taken these deep waters for his hunting grounds; his quarry is the deep-water population of squids, including the giant squid Architeuthis, which lives pelagically at depths of 1500 feet or more. The head of the sperm whale is often marked with long stripes, which consist of a great number of circular scars made by the suck-

From *The Sea Around Us* by Rachel L. Carson. Copyright © 1950, 1951, 1961 by Rachel L. Carson. Reprinted by permission of Oxford University Press, Inc.

ers of the squid. From this evidence we can imagine the battles that go on, in the darkness of the deep water, between these two huge creatures—the sperm whale with its 70-ton bulk, the squid with a body as long as 30 feet, and writhing, grasping arms extending the total length of the animal to perhaps 50 feet.

DEFINE: *plankton, copepods, pelagically.*

Walter Laqueur

TERRORISM TODAY

The postwar wave of urban terrorism began in the late 1960s and has now continued, on and off, for about a decade. It has occurred in many countries and taken many different forms but, broadly speaking, it can be divided into three different subspecies. First, there is separatist-nationalist terrorism, such as in Ulster or the Middle East, Canada or Spain, an old acquaintance from past ages. Second, Latin American terrorism, the trendsetter and, in many respects, a phenomenon *sui generis*. The continent has seen more civil wars, coups d'état and assassinations than anywhere else, but systematic urban terror was an innovation. Last, there was the urban terrorism in North America, Western Europe and Japan, which grew out of the New Left or, to be precise, the failure of the New Left in West Germany, Italy, America and Japan, and which on occasion was also practiced by quasi-Fascist groups. The terrorists of the New Left mistakenly assumed that methods used in Latin America would work elsewhere or that Latin American conditions could be created artificially in the more developed countries, and this at a time when these methods had not even been too effective south of the Rio Grande.

From *Terrorism* by Walter Laqueur. © 1977 by Walter Laqueur. Used by permission of Little, Brown and Co. and Weidenfeld (Publishers), Ltd.

F. D. Ommanney

TYPES OF CORAL REEFS

There are three main types of coral reef. The first is the fringing reef which lies just off the main shore, separated from it by a narrow and shallow lagoon. It is this kind of reef which encircles Mauritius like a girdle, leaving between itself and the coast of the island a shallow stretch of water, in places only a few hundred yards wide but in others, as at Grand Port, expanding to a width of two miles or more. Fringing reefs, too, en-

From *The Shoals of Capricorn.* Copyright 1952 by F. D. Ommanney. Reprinted by permission of Curtis Brown Ltd.

circle many of the islands that we visited such as Coëtivy and Agalega and, though irregular and broken in places, lie off parts of the coasts of Mahé and Praslin in the Seychelles. Down the east coast of Africa from Cape Guardafui to the coast of Portuguese East there runs an almost continuous coral reef which is mostly of the fringing type.

2 The second type is the barrier reef, which lies at a much greater distance from the coast than the fringing reef and may be several miles wide with many channels through it, and is separated from the mainland by a wide lagoon. The most famous example of this type is the Great Barrier Reef off the eastern coast of Australia. It is over a thousand miles long. In its northern half the barrier may not be more than 20 or 30 miles from the Queensland coast, but in its southern half it is as much as 50 or 100 miles from the coast and consists of several parallel reefs with channels between them.

3 The third type of reef is the atoll, a ring of growing corals crowned with palm trees, often hundreds of miles from any true land and rising abruptly in the ocean from a depth of thousands of fathoms. In the Chagos Islands we found true atolls at Diego Garcia and Peros Banhos, irregular rings of coral rock and sand on which a lush vegetation has taken root, and on which plantations have long been cultivated by man. In the Aldabra group also, 700 miles south-west of the Seychelles, we found coral reefs of varying degrees of perfection.

Thomas Fuller

FOUR TYPES OF STUDENTS

1 . . . Experienced schoolmasters may quickly make a grammar of boys' natures, and reduce them all, saving some few exceptions, to these general rules:

2 Those that are ingenious and industrious. The conjunction of two such planets in a youth presage much good unto him. To such a lad a frown may be a whipping, and a whipping death; yea, where their master whips them once, shame whips them all the week after. Such natures he useth with all gentleness.

3 Those that are ingenious and idle. These think, with the hare in the fable, that, running with snails (so they count the rest of their schoolfellows), they shall come soon enough to the post, though sleeping a good while before their starting. Oh, a good rod would finely take them napping!

4 Those that are dull and diligent. Wines, the stronger they be, the more lees they have when they are new. Many boys are muddy-headed till they be clarified with age, and such afterwards prove the best. Bristol diamonds[1] are both bright and squared and pointed by nature, and yet are soft and worthless; orient ones in India are rough and rugged natu-

[1]Quartz crystals from Bristol, England.

rally. Hard, rugged, and dull natures of youth acquit themselves afterwards the jewels of the country, and therefore their dullness at first is to be borne with, if they be diligent. The schoolmaster deserves to be beaten himself who beats nature in a boy for a fault. And I question whether all the whippings in the world can make their parts, which are naturally sluggish, rise one minute before the hour nature hath appointed.

5   Those that are invincibly dull and negligent also. Correction may reform the latter, not amend the former. All the whetting in the world can never set a razor's edge on that which hath no steel in it. Such boys he consigneth over to other professions. Shipwrights and boatmakers will choose those crooked pieces of timber which other carpenters refuse. Those may make excellent merchants and mechanics who will not serve for scholars.

DEFINE: *conjunction, consigneth.*

FIVE KINDS OF MORTGAGES

TYPE OF MORTGAGE AND HOW IT WORKS	PROS AND CONS	WHO BENEFITS
Graduated payment mortgage. Monthly payments are arranged to start out low but get bigger later, perhaps in a series of steps at specified intervals. The term of the loan and the interest rate remain unchanged.	The main object is to make buying easier in the beginning. Initial payments have to be balanced by larger payments later. One disadvantage: Possible "negative amortization" in the early years, which means that for a time your debt grows instead of diminishing.	Mainly first-time home buyers, who have a hard time becoming homeowners but can reasonably look forward to higher earnings that will enable them to afford the bigger payments coming later.
Variable rate mortgage. Instead of a fixed interest rate, this loan carries an interest rate that may change within limits—up or down—from time to time during the life of the loan, reflecting changes in market rates for money.	Because the size of the payments you'll have to make in the future is uncertain, this loan is a bit of a gamble. If money rates go down in the future, your payments will go down. But if rates go up, so will your payments.	Helps lenders keep their flow of funds in step with changing conditions, and this in turn could make home loans easier to come by when money is tight. You may get fractionally lower interest at first or other inducements to make future uncertainties more palatable.
Rollover mortgage. The rate of interest is fixed and the size of the monthly payment is fixed, but the whole loan—including principal, rate of interest and term—is renegotiated, or rolled over, at stated intervals, usually every five years.	If interest rates go up, you can expect to be charged more when you renegotiate. But you'll also have opportunity to adjust other aspects of the loan, such as term and principal. Or you can pay off the outstanding balance without penalty. Renegotiation is guaranteed.	Lenders, for the same reason variable rate loans are good for them. Benefits to borrowers are as shown for variable rate loans, with this plus: Periodic renegotiation gives you a chance to rejigger the loan to suit your changing needs without all the expense of refinancing.

TYPE OF MORTGAGE AND HOW IT WORKS	PROS AND CONS	WHO BENEFITS
Price-level adjusted mortgage. The interest rate remains fixed, but the outstanding balance and monthly payments change according to fluctuations in a specified price index.	If interest cost is your big worry, this plan at least ties down the percentage rate. All else remains uncertain, including how much you'll have to pay in toto and each month.	If this plan gets you a loan when you can get one no other way, then it helps you. Otherwise it mainly helps lenders. Not likely to become popular with borrowers.
Reverse annuity mortgage. You take out a loan secured by the accumulated equity in your house. The money is used to purchase an annuity that provides monthly income to you. You continue to live in the house. Its sale pays off the loan.	This is not a plan for putting money *into* a house. It's a plan for taking money *out*. It converts an existing frozen asset into current income that you can use without giving up your house.	Homeowners, principally older and retired people who have paid for or substantially paid for their homes but need additional current income to live on.

Reprinted with permission from *Changing Times* Magazine, © 1978 Kiplinger Washington Editors, Inc., May 1, 1978.

ANALYSIS

structure
1. State the basis for classification of all selections except "Terrorism Today."
2. What is the problem with finding the basis for classification of the "Terrorism" selection?
3. In addition to naming and describing the types of reefs, what other rhetorical method does the "Coral Reefs" selection use?
4. Which of the selections gets off the subject—in an interesting way?
5. Write an outline to cover the information in the first three of the five kinds of mortgages.

meaning
6. Discuss Fuller's approach to discipline.
7. Explain the phrase "shame whips them all week after."
8. Explain "All the whetting in the world can never set a razor's edge on that which hath no steel in it."

style
9. Fuller supports his classification of students with apt comments and comparisons. Find at least two of the comparisons.

opinion
10. Some people explain away terrorism by saying that it is the only way that they can get their rights. Discuss.

WRITING SUGGESTION

Write a classification paper based on your outline of "Five Kinds of Mortgages."

SPECIAL ASSIGNMENT

The following bit of informal classification is taken from the autobiography of a famous Scottish writer. It may give you an idea for a classification paper about teachers—inspiring, cruel, boring, humorous, etc. Or you may, instead, want to classify whips or paddles.

Edwin Muir

A REGIMENT OF TEACHERS

Yet there were times when I enjoyed going to school: it all depended on who was teaching me. I passed under a whole regiment of teachers there, male and female: teachers who shouted at me, who hit me over the head with the pointer, who strapped me (for the tawse was used vigorously), who took an interest in me, who sneered at me (and they were the worst); teachers whose personal habits I came to know as I grew older: who drank, or were infatuated with the pretty girls in their class, or had a curious walk or some curious habit. We studied them with the inquisitiveness of visitors to a zoo; for to us they were really animals behind bars. There were teachers who terrified us, and whose eyes, fixed on us, could assume the hypnotic glare of an animal-tamer. I knew the appearance of all the straps in all the classrooms: there were thick, voluptuous ones, and thin, mean, venomous ones; laid down on the desk after execution, they folded up with ruthless grace like sleepy cats. In some of them the tails had been burned over a fire to make them sting more sharply. Certain boys were punished day after day as part of the routine: a brutal ceremony which we watched in a silent fascination and dread which might easily have implanted in us a taste for sadism and insidiously corrupted us. The punishment varied from three strokes on the hand to twelve. There were teachers who did not use the strap more than three or four times in a year, and others who flogged on monotonously day after day, as if they were pounding some recalcitrant substance, not the hands of living boys. I avoided the strap as well as I could; in some classes I could completely forget it, and then I liked school, for the teachers were invariably good at their work. One teacher, Miss Annan, did not use the strap at all. She had a cheerful, impudent, devoted class who only needed her presence to become inspired. She taught us English, and but for her we might never have realized what the subject meant beyond the drudgery of parsing and analysis. She opened our eyes; we felt we were a sort of aristocracy, for what we did for her we did freely. She must have been a remarkable woman; she seemed to have endless charm, vitality, and patience. She filled us with confidence and a kind of goodness which was quite unlike the goodness asked from us by the other teachers. Yet she never put us on our honour; she simply took us as we were and by some power changed us.

From *Autobiography* by Edwin Muir. Reprinted by permission of Gavin Muir and The Hogarth Press Ltd.

section 5c

William Safire

DOING A NUMBER ON WORDS

1 Now hear this: it is time at last for the second annual Vogue Word Watch.

2 In the closely guarded Citation Room of Webster's New World Dictionary in Cleveland, lexicographer David Guralnik is watching the file thicken on the locution **do a number on.** Is it an evanescent nonce phrase, or will it work its way into dictionaries?

3 "The phrase 'do a number on' first appeared in our files in the late 1960's," says Mr. Guralnik, "with a steady growth to more than 100 citations. Although in its earliest uses it always seemed to mean 'to deceive,' it has been extended, and softened in meaning so that it now often means no more than 'to affect,' but generally in some devious way: 'She stumbled into the bathroom and did a masochistic number on her teeth with an electric toothbrush. . . .' "

4 Meanwhile, in his clipping-cluttered room in San Francisco, Peter Tamony, who watches words for the Oxford Dictionary, is also eyeballing "doing a number on." "To do one's number," word-watcher Tamony suggests, "was to do one's act, one's specialty in the old vaudeville days, taken from the numbered sequence of acts on the bill or program. The meaning evolved from an act, to a general pretense, to a deception."

5 Some words streak across our discourse and soon fade. Last year's **terrific** is this year's **incredible!**; last year's **right?** is this year's wrong; yesterday's **way to go** is gone; **whatsisname** has changed to **whatsisface.** Where do the vogue words come from? In the past, jazz musicians led the way. Black English has also been the source of vogue words, and today, a perfume advertiser who sloganeers "It's ba-a-ad—and that's good!" is using the reverse-twist of black lingo employed to confuse outsiders. Another source has been "Needle Park," land of the narcotics junkies, that lingers on with **It's the pits,** a common derogation, taken from the addict's resort to the armpits when other blood vessels have collapsed from too frequent injection of dope.

6 But other sources of vogue words are taking over. Games and sports, for one: **Square one,** a games term, is what we reluctantly go back to; a basketball phrase, **one-on-one,** is used now to describe any direct confrontation, tête-à-tête or match-up; football has contributed **cheap shot** (a tackle after the whistle, or late hit) and **blind-side,** a verb for dealing an unexpected blow. Because an old-time baseball pitcher never knew which

© 1977 by The New York Times Company. Reprinted by permission.

way his spitball would break, the verb **to spitball** now means "to speculate."

7   The advertising-publishing-news world, which can no longer be called Madison Avenue, is another powerful source. **Media event,** a variant of Daniel Boorstin's "pseudoevent," connotes staginess and manipulation. Publishers looking for a **good read** lean weakly on books they advertise as **page-turners.** To appeal to nostalgia or to associate with newly fashionable Southernism, copywriters use the adjective **down-home** to sweep the countryside—as in "real down-home taste" for a cigarette, or "that down-home quality" of a political figure.

8   The down-home Carter Administration will surely make its linguistic contributions. **Compatibility** is enshrined and **disharmoniousness** abhorred, and **zero-based** is the bottom line of the future (a management term taken from technology's "zero error," sociology's "zero population growth," and a 1969 White House usage, "zero mistakes").

9   "He's behind the **power curve** on this," said a Carter aide of a colleague who was unaware of the latest top-level decisions. Merriam-Webster's associate editor Anne Soukhanov shows a mid-60's use of "power curve" based on a statistics-graph test for alternatives, which has since come to evoke a keening arc of fast decision-making.

10   Political trendsetters have replaced the term for permanent power center that Henry Fairlie named "the Establishment." **Community** has taken its place—as in defense community, intelligence community. It has a friendly air. When attacked as the "power structure," "new-boy network," or one of the "complexes" (military-industrial, academic-media), the group allies itself with **The System,** always capitalized, as in "The System works."

11   Women's-movement politics provides new terms. The flip "lib" has long been set aside, and the exaggerated substitution of "person" for "man" has been ridiculed. However, **queen bee** is a useful characterization of one who benefits from, but contributes little to, the struggle for women's rights. The use of **upfront** is growing, lately as one word, but with Merriam-Webster citations also in hyphenated form and as two words, to mean forthright and disdainful of deviousness. (The word may be rooted in the exploitation of women by antiwar demonstrators of the 60's in the saying "Chicks up front.") Even the meaning of **multiple** is changing; formerly taken to mean the price-earnings ratio of a share of stock, the dull old word is now assumed to refer to a highly desirable form of orgasm.

12   Here's the point: A sound lexicographic case can be made for the theory that our traditional sources of vogue lingo—the argot of musicians, the cant of the underworld, and the inventive richness of black English—are being replaced by the political and communications worlds, acting not merely as disseminators but as originators as well. (Adman Leo Greenland calls this kind of thinking **breaking new snow,** the ski-based vogue term for originality.) How will this change of wellsprings affect the future of American slang?

13   The first effect will be—get this—"stretched-out words." A word lengthened by a redundancy may be an offense to the sharp eye, but it can be an aid to the less attentive ear. That accounts for the vogue of **early on,**

a Britishism, with American television commentators; it adds emphasis to the simple "early," and cachet to the indeterminate long-ago: "Early on, God created Heaven and Earth."

14   Similarly, nobody is selected to "head" an agency, but to **head up** the agency, which adds an intensifier desired by a speaker as in "eat **up** your cereal," or "write **down** your name." (Or "stretch **out**" the word.) "At this point in time" was well derided, but the meaningless intensifiers are increasing: "That's **flat-out** wrong," said press secretary Jody Powell, using an auto-racing word meaning to drive with the accelerator flat against the floorboard, and, by extension, to act without restraint. In Mr. Powell's usage, the word-stretching for emphasis introduces error, or is flat wrong.

15   The mediamania for verbal stretch-out can be seen in the high price of the *prix-fixe* "co-." "Congress will be a **co-equal** branch," says Speaker "Tip" O'Neill. How is co-equal more equal than equal? For the same reason a **judgment call** is more judgmental than a mere judgment, or a **match-up** more evenly matched than a match: With Orwellian evenhandedness, the "co-" stretch gives "equal" a more equal ring, and the sound is more important than the sight.

16   The second effect of the rise of gray flannel English as a new main wellspring for colloquial speech is—are you ready?—the telegraphed punchline. In written English, the writer may add emphasis by <u>underlining</u>, *italicizing,* or punctuating(!!!) (?).

17   Or paragraphing.

18   In spoken English, however, to add emphasis the speaker must shout, glower or gesticulate. Since none of these methods is permissible on television, the question is: How can the speaker cue a listener to pay attention, or remind a sleepy cameraman to roll film?

19   The answer is: with a waker-upper, some oral telegram that the punch is coming. That familiar device has been implanted throughout this piece, unnoticed because its force is in show-news business, not on the printed page.

20   The answer is **The answer is.** Or **Here's the point.** Or **Get this.** Or **ta-dahh!** Or **Would you believe?** Or—and this'll killya, as comedians used to say to dead audiences—**Are you ready?**

21   That verbal jab-in-the-ribs, that telegraphed punchline of co-host hype, is destined to be the voguish speech pattern of the immediate future. That is, unless readers and writers band together to keep the ill-spoken word from—are you ready?—doing a number on the English language.

DEFINE: *lexicographer* (2); *masochistic* (3); *vogue* (5); *argot, cant* (12).

ANALYSIS

structure   1. Find and copy Safire's thesis.

2. There is a subordinate or minor thesis to his article. State it.

3. At one point the article moves from a classification/example structure to a

cause/effect/example structure. Find the transitional sentence that introduces the effects.

meaning

4. List the two major effects.

5. Explain the changes in the meaning of the phrase "to do a number."

6. What is the modern meaning of the term "to spitball"?

7. What is the purpose of "stretched-out-words" and "telegraphed punchlines"?

style

8. What phrase does Safire use as a unifying technique?

9. Find three examples of Safire's use of the "telegraphed punchline."

10. Discuss the sentence introducing paragraph 5, "Some words streak across our discourse . . ." Does it make sense?

WRITING SUGGESTION

Classify words by their sounds instead of their meanings: funny sounding and serious sounding, light and heavy, threatening and friendly.

Shana Alexander

THE FINE ART OF MARITAL FIGHTING

1   When primitive man lived in the jungle, surrounded by real, lethal enemies, the aggressive impulse is what kept him alive. For modern man, the problem gets complicated because he usually encounters only what the psychologist calls "intimate enemies"—wives, husbands, sweethearts, children, parents, friends, and others whom he sometimes would like to kill, but toward whom he nonetheless feels basic, underlying goodwill.

2   When he gets mad at one of these people, modern man tends to go to pieces. His jungle rage embarrasses, betrays, even terrifies him. "He forgets that real intimacy *demands* that there be fighting," Bach[1] says. He fails to realize that "nonfighting is only appropriate between strangers— people who have nothing worth fighting about. When two people begin to really *care* about each other, they become emotionally vulnerable— and the battles start."

3   Listening to Bach enumerate the many destructive, "bad" fight styles is rather like strolling through a vast Stillman's gym of domestic discord. Over there, lolling about on the canvas, watching TV, walking out, sitting in a trancelike state, drinking beer, doing their nails, even falling asleep, are the "Withdrawal-Evaders," people who will not fight. These people, Bach says, are very sick. After counseling thousands of

Shana Alexander, *Life* copyright © 1963 Time Inc. Reprinted with permission.

[1]Dr. George R. Bach is a psychologist with dreams of establishing a marital fight center for embattled husbands and wives. He feels that most American spouses fight dirty.

them, he is convinced that "falling asleep causes more divorces than any other single act."

4   And over *there,* viciously flailing, kicking, and throwing knives at one another, shouting obnoxious abuse, hitting below the belt, deliberately provoking anger, exchanging meaningless insults (You stink! *You* doublestink!)—simply needling or battering one another for the hell of it—are people indulging in "open noxious attack." They are the "Professional Ego-Smashers," and they are almost as sick—but not quite—as the first bunch.

5   An interesting subgroup here are the "Chain-Reactors," specialists in what Bach once characterized as "throwing in the kitchen sink from left field." A chain-reacting husband opens up by remarking, "Well, I see you burned the toast again this morning." When his wife begins to make new toast, he continues, "And another thing . . . that no-good brother of yours hasn't had a job for two years." This sort of fight, says Bach, "usually pyramids to a Valhalla-type of total attack."

6   The third group of people are all smiling blandly and saying, "Yes, dear." But each one drags after him a huge gunnysack. These people are the "Pseudo-Accommodators," the ones who pretend to go along with the partner's point of view for the sake of momentary peace, but who never really mean it. The gunnysacks are full of grievances, reservations, doubts, secret contempt. Eventually the overloaded sacks burst open, making an awful mess.

7   The fourth group are "Carom Fighters," a sinister lot. They use noxious attack not directly against the partner but against some person, idea, activity, value, or object which the partner loves or stands for. They are a whiz at spoiling a good mood or wrecking a party, and when they *really* get mad, they can be extremely dangerous. Bach once made a study of one hundred intimate murders and discovered that two-thirds of the killers did not kill their partner, but instead destroyed someone whom the partner loved.

8   Even more destructive are the "Double Binders," people who set up warm expectations but make no attempt to fulfill them or, worse, deliver a rebuke instead of the promised reward. This nasty technique is known to some psychologists as the "mew phenomenon": "Kitty mews for milk. The mother cat mews back warmly to intimate that kitty should come and get it. But when the kitten nuzzles up for a drink, he gets slashed in the face with a sharp claw instead." In human terms, a wife says, for example, "I have nothing to wear." Her husband says, "Buy yourself a new dress—you deserve it." But when she comes home wearing the prize, he says, "What's that thing supposed to be, a paper bag with sleeves?"—adding, "Boy, do you look fat!"

9   The most irritating bad fighters, according to Bach, are the "Character Analysts," a pompous lot of stuffed shirts who love to explain to the mate what his or her real, subconscious, or hidden feelings are. This accomplishes nothing except to infuriate the mate by putting him on the defensive for being himself. This style of fighting is common among lawyers, members of the professional classes, and especially, psychotherapists. It is presumptuous, highly alienating, and never in the least useful

except in those rare partnerships in which husband and wife are equally addicted to a sick, sick game which Bach calls "Psychoanalytic Archaeology—the earlier, the farther back, the deeper, the better!"

10   In a far corner of Bach's marital gym are the "Gimmes," overdemanding fighters who specialize in "overloading the system." They always want more; nothing is ever enough. New car, new house, more money, more love, more understanding—no matter what the specific demand, the partner never can satisfy it. It is a bottomless well.

11   Across from them are found the "Withholders," stingily restraining affection, approval, recognition, material things, privileges—anything which could be provided with reasonable effort or concern and which would give pleasure or make life easier for the partner.

12   In a dark, scary back corner are the "Underminers," who deliberately arouse or intensify emotional insecurities, reinforce moods of anxiety or depression, try to keep the partner on edge, threaten disaster, or continually harp on something the partner dreads. They may even wish it to happen.

13   The last group are the "Benedict Arnolds," who not only fail to defend their partners against destructive, dangerous, and unfair situations, forces, people, and attacks but actually encourage such assaults from outsiders.

14   Husbands and wives who come to Psychologist Bach for help invariably can identify themselves from the categories he lists. If they do not recognize themselves, at least they recognize their mate. Either way, most are desperate to know what can be done. Somewhere, they feel, there must be another, sunnier, marital gym, a vast Olympic Games perhaps, populated with nothing but agile, happy, bobbing, weaving, superbly muscled, and incredibly sportsmanlike gladiators.

DEFINE: *vulnerable* (2); "Pseudo–Accommodators" (6); *presumptuous* (9).

ANALYSIS

structure   1. Summarize the article in three or four sentences.

meaning   2. How do modern couples' problems with aggression differ from those of primitive people?

3. Does Bach think that marital fighting is wrong? Explain.

4. Explain "falling asleep causes more divorces than any other single act."

5. Explain the last sentence.

WRITING SUGGESTIONS

1. Classify the couples you know according to the way they fight, act toward each other in public, or speak of each other when their mate isn't present.

2. Classify friends according to their personalities.

ERA OF BIONIC PERSON MOVES NEARER TO REALITY

The 6-million-dollar bionic man or woman of fiction, put together with plastic, metal and electronic parts, is getting closer to reality.

Researchers and medical engineers are devising replacements for the human body—from skin to spinal cord—holding out the promise of finding ways to permit the crippled to walk, the deaf to hear, the voiceless to talk, the blind to see. Powers of nonhandicapped people also may be extended.

The advances are taking place in private and government laboratories throughout the United States and around the world.

Many of the experimenters take advantage of the new-found ability to compress what once were large and complicated electrical circuits into small units. A single silicon chip that can fit on a finger tip contains all the computer logic that once went into a roomful of equipment.

5 Some of the most advanced work in bionics is in the duplication of limbs. Hundreds of amputees have been fitted with myoelectric arms, with artificial hands that open and close via brainpower. The secret: Small electrodes pick up nerve impulses, which then are magnified a thousand times by a power pack and transmitted to miniature motors in the mechanical hand.

Early models of these bionic arms are fragile and limited to persons with below-elbow amputations. Sturdier versions are to include mind-operated elbows and wrists.

Artificial skin, a spinoff from plastics used in spacecraft, now is being placed over transducers and integrated-control mechanisms to give a sense of touch to amputees. The aim is to enable a person with a replacement hand to lift a glass without crushing it or dropping it.

Similar sensors in the heels of artificial and paralyzed legs can send feedback messages to the crippled to assure firm footing.

Humanlike voice. For those who cannot speak, hand-held voice synthesizers are available. Users press keys to activate a humanlike voice with any of about 50 commonly used syllables, words or phrases.

10 Battery-operated equipment has been available for decades for those with hearing difficulties, but only if the sensory nerves are functioning. Now, experimenters hope to implant minute sensors in the heads of deaf persons, sending signals to the brain's auditory parts and bypassing diseased nerves.

Meanwhile, scientists are redesigning old-style hearing aids to include microprocessors, empowering users to determine the distance they want to hear and to filter out background noises.

Hope is growing for the blind. Electrical stimulation of visual parts of the brain is being examined at several places, including the Institute for Biomedical Engineering at the University of Utah, Columbia-Presbyterian Medical Center in New York City, the University of Florida at Gainesville, and in Canada. The basic approach is this:

Television cameras direct signals to a computer, which relays them

Reprinted from *U.S. News & World Report,* March 13, 1978. Copyright 1978 U.S. News & World Report, Inc.

through wires to the brain. Blind volunteers using such devices to scan pages in which letters are represented by Braille dots have been able to read much faster than they did with their finger tips.

Scientists now are concentrating on the tough job of locating the proper cells of the brain to which various signals should be sent. They foresee the day years from now when a tiny TV camera can be implanted in an eye socket, with the rest of the system—including a microprocessor, transmitters and receivers—compressed into the stems of spectacles.

15 Scientists in San Francisco are working on a different system, which converts light to impulses that can be interpreted by the blind. A small TV camera positioned on eyeglasses picks up the scene in front of the wearer and sends signals to an elastic garment worn on the back or abdomen. The signals are transmitted as patterns of taps which the wearer feels.

Silent signals. Experimenters say blind people have quickly learned to interpret the taps so as to identify common objects such as telephones, drinking glasses, chairs and tables.

Simpler devices already are being used and refined to allow the blind to detect things by substituting other senses such as hearing and touch. Special canes, caps and spectacles make it possible for the blind to locate objects—curbs, telephone poles, low-hanging branches and cars—much as a bat does. Silent signals sent out by the devices bounce back from the object and create vibrations the user can hear or feel.

By means of various pitches and intensities, some devices indicate how far away an object is, in which direction it lies, its size and its roughness.

For the blind, new reading machines with optical sensors scan pages, converting printed matter into computer-bound pulses. The pulses then are transformed into indentations which a person can feel with his finger tips either as Braille dots or as the actual shapes of letters, charts and pictures.

20 Another reading machine converts printed words into voicelike sounds designed to duplicate the words. Engineers are working to reduce the costs of this equipment and make its voice talk faster and clearer.

A blind person already can balance his accounts—or perform more complex mathematical computations—with the help of a hand-held calculator that speaks back the information.

Extensive research also is going on to create artificial hearts, kidneys, livers, pancreases and other organs, by capitalizing on the reliability, accuracy and compactness of microprocessors.

The Veterans Administration is working on artificial muscle activated by sounds and high-energy magnets, and on a synthetic spinal cord. Within 15 years, it hopes to build electrical bridges over damaged parts of central nervous systems of the paralyzed.

More brainpower. Many devices being developed for the handicapped could be adapted to expand capabilities of the able-bodied. For example, the TV gadget that taps out patterns could enable a person to sense and to some extent identify objects behind him while looking ahead.

25 Researchers in a new science called neuron bionics seek to broaden the brain's power by linking it to a computer. Unraveling the brain's language remains a major problem.

One scientist envisions the day, however, when a computer small enough to fit into a tooth could contain all the information of a full college course. The user would query the "memory" in the tooth for facts and ideas that don't readily come to mind.

Developments in bionics are coming so rapidly and from so many different places around the globe that the Veterans Administration and the Armour Engineering Center of the Illinois Institute of Technology last October opened a center in Chicago to keep track of what's going on and to carry out further research.

Some outsiders already are comparing the center to the fictional laboratory responsible for developing the superhuman 6-million-dollar man, the bionic woman and the bionic dog.

Scientists laugh that off, pointing out that as of now no synthetic spare part—however well engineered—can match the capability of the organ a normal human being is born with. But the gap is rapidly narrowing.

ANALYSIS

NOTE: Some authorities might classify this selection as being developed by *division* rather than classification. In division one separates a subject into its various logical parts without necessarily classifying. In another sense, however, the various instruments discussed in this article are classified according to the parts of the body they serve.

structure
1. List the main types of inventions mentioned.

2. What is the unifying idea of the article?

meaning
3. What mechanical breakthrough has greatly aided the development of human replacement parts?

4. Up to this time, what physical limitation has kept some deaf people from being helped?

5. What hope is being held out for the paralyzed?

6. What promise does this research have for nonhandicapped people?

7. Are the replacement parts as good as the original parts?

8. With what article in Chapter 4 does this selection tie in? Discuss.

WRITING SUGGESTION

Do some research about new inventions in a specialized area such as stereo equipment, photography, kitchen appliances, fuel savers; then write a classification paper about your findings.

Louis Kronenberger

THE CRANK, THE ECCENTRIC, AND THE INDIVIDUALIST

[1] Our well-founded distaste for cranks has . . . rather blurred our ability to tell a crank from a mere eccentric, or even an eccentric from an individual. On a very rough-and-ready basis we might define an eccentric as a man who is a law unto himself, and a crank as one who, having determined what the law is, insists on laying it down to others. An eccentric[1] puts ice cream on steak simply because he likes it; should a crank do so, he would endow the act with moral grandeur and straightway denounce as sinners (or reactionaries) all who failed to follow suit. The crank, however, seldom deals in anything so agreeable as steak or ice cream; the crank prefers the glories of health bread or the splendors of soybeans. Cranks, at their most familiar, are a sort of peevish prophets, and it's not enough that they should be in the right; others must also be in the wrong. They are by definition obsessed, and, by connotation, obsessed with something odd. They mistake the part for the whole, the props for the play, the inconvenience for the efficacy; they are spoil-sport humanitarians, full of the sour milk of human kindness.[2]

[2] The crank is for several reasons a fairly common figure in American life. To begin with, our reaction against cranks has helped breed more of them. A society that worships good-guyism brands the mere dissenter a misfit, and people who are shunned as square pegs will soon find something deeply immoral about round holes. A society, again, that runs to fads and crazes, that has a natural turn for the ingenious and inventive, will encourage some of its members to be cranks and will doom others. There must be, so to speak, lots of factory-damaged human products that, from being looked upon as rejects, come to crankhood rather than true creativity. Careerwise, there is frequently a missed-the-boat quality in cranks, a psychological origin for their moral obsessiveness; and their "flourishing" off failure is tied up with their having failed at the outset. The crank not only increasingly harangues his audience, but the audience increasingly yawns at, and even walks out on, the crank.[3]

[3] Where a crank is either a moral crusader by nature or a man at war

From "The One and The Many" in *Company Manners,* copyright © 1951, 1953, 1954, by Louis Kronenberger. Reprinted by permission of The Bobbs-Merrill Company, Inc. Footnotes are in original.

[1] Many "eccentrics" are, of course, mere poseurs and publicity seekers. But many are real, and I speak here only of such.

[2] They can be useful, at moments even invaluable, goads; but they fail of love no less than of humor, and seem most ready to plow the earth where they can spoil the lawn. They are the sort of people who, in assessing champagne, would give no consideration to the fizz.

[3] Just as many eccentrics are poseurs, so many cranks are charlatans. The charlatan shrewdly exploits human weakness where the true crank rails against it; the charlatan, preaching some form of nudism or trial marriage, some "holy" brand of licentiousness or God-sent type of laxative, may end up a millionaire. But the true crank has only a chip on his shoulder or bee in his bonnet, not a card up his sleeve.

with his surroundings, an eccentric is neither given to crusading nor op-pressed by the world. Perhaps a certain amount of enjoyment is essential to the eccentric—his life is satisfactory *because* it is pleasant—as a certain lack of enjoyment is essential to the crank. The great blessing of eccentricity is that, since it is a law unto itself, one isn't constantly torn between what is expedient on the one side and what is personally desirable on the other. Something of an anarchist (as your crank is something of a bigot), the ec-centric will often display very unsound, or unsocial, habits and beliefs. But there is nothing self-righteous about his wrongheadedness; he doesn't drag God into keeping a pet leopard in his back yard, or Americanism into going in for rifle practice at 2:00 A.M.

4   True eccentrics, I would think, are fairly rare, for they must not only differ from other people but be quite indifferent to other people's ways: they must, in other words, be as well adjusted as they are odd. So soon as maladjustment enters in, they cease to be characters and turn into cases. On the other hand, many people who with a little encourage-ment might emerge as eccentrics are, from childhood on, judged—and hence turned into—misfits. Where their peculiarities are mocked, and certainly where they are penalized, the results can be very unhappy. In America, where even the slightest individualist must resist great pressure, the true eccentric is never free from it. In England there is a proud tradi-tion of eccentricity: the English are far more given than we are to keeping strange pets, collecting strange objects, pursuing strange hobbies, adopt-ing strange careers; even where they most conform, as in their club life, they will behave toward one another with what, to other races, seems a wild and splendid strangeness. This is so true that England's—and some-times New England's—eccentrics have often a great air about them, pos-sess style rather than mere singularity. Consider how Julia Margaret Cameron would walk the two miles from her house to the railway station stirring a cup of tea as she went. In England and New England on the one hand, and in most of America on the other, there may be a quite op-posite basis for eccentricity: in the one case, the law unto oneself born of social privilege; in the other, the self-made born of being left out of things. The English eccentric suggests a grande dame, the American a spinster.

5   The individualist is by no means an eccentric. He is for one thing aware of alternatives; he chooses—for the most part consciously—be-tween the expedient and the self-satisfying; he refuses to play ball rather than doesn't know a game is in progress; and he will seldom seem freakish or even picturesque. Yet, more and more, the individualist is being looked on as an eccentric and perhaps even a crank; though this attitude is scarcely deliberate on the public's part, it yet subconsciously—or by force of repetition—constitutes a gimmick, a pressure to make people conform. The other method of diminishing individualism in America has been to foster and develop "personality." Though the difference between "personality" and individuality is vast, there exists a strong, however thoughtless, tendency to identify the one with the other. So greatly has conformity triumphed that, no matter how orthodox a man's opinions or conventional his behavior, if he happens to express or conduct himself with the slightest vividness or briskness, he is rated and touted a "per-

son"—what might be supposed an individual! Actually, he may not even have an iota of real personality, may just possess a breezy, adaptable, quick-on-the-trigger manner that enables him to be the life of the party or the spark plug of the conference. In the same way, a woman with a gift for dinner-party chatter and a feminine, discreetly flirtatious air will be thought to have enormous personality.

6   And though such mere types must be written off, there yet *are* a great many Americans with true personality—with an easy charm, a distinctive way of doing and saying things, a regional tang, a surviving girlishness or small-boy quality. They have the appeal, at the very least, of not being like everyone else. But that, in the cliché sense, they are "real persons" is to be doubted. One may go a year without hearing them utter an original, not to say controversial, remark, or seeing them perform a striking, not to say truly unorthodox, act. The centrifugal and extrovert charm of personality is in many ways hostile to individualism, which more naturally manifests itself in withdrawal than in contact, in quiet dissent than in eager acquiescence. Personality and individuality are by no means mutually exclusive, nor is genuine personality necessarily engaging nor genuine individuality necessarily difficult. But the fact remains that we regard personality as a decided blessing, as something a man can't have too much of, and individuality as, oftener than not, a handicap. Individuality is almost by definition antisocial; and the sound "social" maneuver—or it were perhaps better called instinct—is to discredit individuality and eventually outlaw it through enabling people to live *colorfully* alike. As for "personality," it has passed from having great social to acquiring great economic importance: it is the prime mark, and prize asset, of the salesman. And ours is the country where, in order to sell your product, you don't so much point out its merits as you first work like hell to sell yourself.

DEFINE: *poseur* (footnote 1); *obsessed* (1); *charlatan* (footnote 3); *centrifugal (6).*

ANALYSIS

structure 1. The structure of this selection is fairly clear cut, but there is some imbalance in dealing with one of the types. Discuss.

2. What methods does Kronenberger use to help his readers recognize the differences among his types?

meaning 3. Explain the last sentence of paragraph 1: "They (the cranks) mistake the part for the whole, the props for the play, the inconvenience for the efficacy; they are spoil-sport humanitarians, full of the sour milk of human kindness."

4. What seems to be the basic difference between cranks and eccentrics?

5. What is the difference between a crank and a charlatan?

6. What was unusual about Julia Margaret Cameron?

7. What is Kronenberger's conception of an individual?

style 8. Kronenberger has a way with pithy phrases. See, for example, the quotation about cranks in question 3. Find other examples of this kind of writing.

opinion   9. Can a sincere reformer sometimes be labeled a crank?

10. Do you agree with Kronenberger that Americans seem to be "forced" into a kind of conformity?

WRITING SUGGESTIONS

1. Develop a standard of classification for discussing other unusual traits of people.
2. Develop a standard of classification for discussing superior traits.

Michael Maccoby

"WINNING" AND "LOSING" AT WORK

What do you want from your work? Money? Promotions? Interesting challenges? Continual learning? Membership in a high powered team at the cutting edge of technology? The opportunity to develop your own ideas?

Have you ever thought about how your work influences the kind of person you are becoming? How possible is it in a highly competitive corporation to develop yourself emotionally and spiritually as well as intellectually while achieving your work goals?

We are all individuals and so our answers will differ. To find out just how they differ, my colleagues and I have been interviewing engineers and managers for the past few years in an attempt to understand them and the nature of their work: what it means to them, how it affects them, and how it may be related to their character.

The psychoanalytic concept of character refers to emotional attitudes that determine what satisfies or annoys an individual—what he finds attractive, exciting, or frustrating—and how he relates to himself and to others. Essentially, what we look for in the context of character is what *energizes* a person, what turns him on, what gets him up in the morning. Among people in electronics, particularly in management, two elements stand out: the desire to win, and an interest in problem-solving, building, and gaining knowledge. Naturally, we find various mixes of these two elements among people.

The relationship between work and character is real as well as com-

Copyright © 1973 by The Institute of Electrical and Electronic Engineers. Reprinted, with permission, from *IEEE Spectrum,* July 19, 1973.

plex. In exploring it, we have learned that the successful individual is the one who does what needs to be done to meet his organization's particular goals, *not* because he has been told to do it but because he *wants* to do it, he *enjoys* doing it, he feels *impelled* to do it. This may seem reasonable, but it is by no means obvious, and I shall consider its implications in the course of this article.

6   Once it is established that a person does his job well when his character is adaptive to his mode of work, the well-known Peter principle can be redefined to say, quite seriously, that people do not merely rise to the level of their intellectual incompetence; they rise only to a level permitted by their character. Successively promoted until their personalities no longer fit the requirements of work, even the most brilliant engineers and scientists are likely to fail. Furthermore, a character type adaptive to a high level in one kind of organization may not fit another. For example, a fast-moving aggressive manager, ideally suited to working at high levels in a computer company, might well fail in a small instrument company; whereas a responsible and respectful craftsman might succeed at a small instrument company, but not in the semiconductor industry.

7   In the course of our study . . . we have identified four major character types among electronics engineers and their managers, and we have learned about the relationship between these character types and different kinds of work environments. . . .

8   *Four character types.* It should be obvious that in considering types of people we must really deal with a concept social scientists call "ideal type." No individual fits an exact type—everybody is a mixture of personality traits. But just as we can speak of one person as stingy and another as generous, so can we speak of types in terms of dominant tendencies. In high-technology electronics we have identified four basic types of people. I call them the craftsman, the company man, the gamesman, and the jungle fighter.

9   THE CRAFTSMAN. Holding all the traditional values—thrift, belief in the work ethic, and respect for people as well as for craftsmanship and quality—the craftsman is rather closed and hard to get close to, but he's a man of his word and a person who can be trusted in the crunch. He is highly independent, and doesn't generally like to compete against others. One highly respected craftsman noted, "The natural stimulation for me is my interest in the work; the competition seems to me unnatural. For others, it might be different." While the craftsman loves work, he also likes to get away from it and tinker with cars or pursue other hobbies.

10   The craftsman is rarely satisfied in large organizations and feels more at home working in a small group or on a project with a defined and understandable structure. He wants to stay with the product from conception to completion. One craftsman remarked that for him "electrical engineering is a great hobby, but I wonder about it as a profession. I'm not strongly motivated by money; I turned down jobs $300 to $400 more per month because I didn't like the work. I wanted a job like this, with the satisfaction of putting something together and seeing it work."

11   When he rises in the organization it is usually not above what I would call an administrative maintenance position—a laboratory or project director, for example—unless he is one of the rare entrepreneurial

craftsmen-builders who create new industries. In any case, the craftsman is absolutely essential to the creation of advanced technology.

12   THE COMPANY MAN. Unlike the craftsman, the company man is much more likely to identify with the large organization and to be satisfied within large, hierarchical projects. He tends to be a submissive bureaucrat in many ways, although he is generally courteous and more concerned with people than is the craftsman. Much of his satisfaction in life comes from belonging to a powerful, important company and, unlike the craftsman, he would not like to be off on his own. He derives a certain security from knowing where he fits in the structure and perceiving that he can rise within that structure by being responsible, and loyal, and doing his job right.

13   A very ambitious company man is also driven by fear of failure. In his dreams, he is typically chased or is in danger of falling from heights. (One manager actually told us he dreamt he was a spinning top.) The successful company man is both modest about himself and energized into compulsive activity by his fear of falling behind or just losing his momentum. Further, he often displays elements of what the psychoanalyst Erich Fromm, who first developed the theory of social character, describes as the marketing character. This is a person who relates to others by making himself an attractive package, who molds himself into what people want of him; he is a kind of centerless person who is very malleable but who also makes a good salesman. The prototypical marketing man is less adaptive to high technology than he is, say, to an advertising agency. Nevertheless, one often finds such people in certain middle management positions where they serve as mediators.

14   THE GAMESMAN. This individual is in some ways uniquely a product of the U.S. He appears at the beginning of the Republic, yet is very much a modern man. Even though the gamesman comprises only 10-15 percent of our sample, certain game attitudes seem to be increasingly characteristic of the younger high-technology managers. For this reason, and because he has not been adequately recognized, the gamesman deserves an extended description.

15   Alexis de Toqueville noted the penchant in the U.S. for treating business competition as play when he wrote in the early 19th century:

16   "The whole life of an American is passed like a game of chance, a revolutionary crisis, or a battle. As the same causes are continually in operation throughout the country, they ultimately impart an irresistible impulse to the national character."

17   Later, in the middle of the 19th century, a group of scientists interested in developing technology in the U.S. called themselves the "Lazzaroni," after a society of Italian workmen whose goal was to make work into play, and that goal continues to be uppermost in the minds of many scientists and engineers.

18   Today, however, most scientific "play" in the corporation is no longer indulged in by individuals, but has been structured into a kind of game, where teams compete against time, other projects, and the market. Consequently, there is a special need for people who can integrate many specialists into a unified team working at a fast pace. Those who do the job best are the ones who experience this kind of work as a game.

19   The gamesman often aspires to be a kind of quarterback; professional football is his favorite game as it is increasingly the favorite spectator sport in the U.S., replacing the slower, less aggressive, less innovative, and more individualistic game of baseball. The gamesman often sees his work in terms of the metaphors of football and its technology—he will speak of the "game plan," of making "the big play" he'll say, "we're going to have to punt now," or "let's try an end around and see if we can corner a few more yards of the market." Indeed, this language has become part of the jargon of the high-technology business world.

20   Like a successful quarterback, the gamesman is innovative, flexible, detached, and aggressive in a controlled way. He likes to take risks and is fascinated by technique and new methods. He sees the developing project (and his career) in terms of options and possibilities, as in a game, and tends to be turned on, energized, by competitive pressures and crises.

21   Often rather bored and passive when deprived of competition, once the game is on, once he can feel he's in the Super Bowl, he comes to life, remains cool, and thinks hard. While others such as the craftsman may find such high-pressure competition enervating, the gamesman's goal in life is to win and to be known as a winner. (Significantly, while many of the people we interviewed tended to repress or deny their interest in personal power, some of the gamesmen admitted that what they liked most about their job was being the boss and what they liked least was having to take orders from someone else. They want to call the plays.)

22   The gamesman and the craftsman often feel frustrated trying to communicate with one another. (You might say that if the gamesman's idea of play is football, for the craftsman it is tinkering, hiking, or sailing—that is, competing against himself and nature with the overriding goal of perfecting his technique.) The gamesman thinks the craftsman is a stick-in-the-mud, is too cautious, is not ambitious enough, and does not understand the real market. A gamesman told me that he managed a group of scientists who were like children, with neither a sense of business nor the motivation to win; he even called his lab "the sandbox." The craftsman, on the other hand, thinks that the gamesman is unsound, grandiose, superficial, pushy, and not respectful of others.

23   Increasingly, these gamesmen fill the top positions of middle management. They are the project leaders and marketing directors, and they like to integrate, direct, and motivate a team of highly talented specialists who are all working interdependently to win, to be number one—goals that for other character types are irrelevant. (After all, why should winning be more important than creating something of the highest quality, asks the craftsman, or, we would add, of making people's lives better?)

24   Significantly, the game character is less prone to suffer from the emotional problems that we found to be especially common among the craftsmen and some company men we interviewed. These problems are rooted in what Fromm calls the hoarding orientation, by which he means a tendency to retreat behind an emotional shell, thus finding it difficult to communicate with others. Practically every engineer we interviewed reports as problems the kinds of symptoms that psychiatrists describe as obsessive-compulsive—keeping his feelings to himself, avoiding other

people, being overly anxious and finicky, being a perfectionist, and even having difficulty making decisions. Although these problems are sometimes encountered in the gamesman, they are generally less significant for him, and that is one reason he is better able to rise to high levels.

25   Seldom, however, do the gamesmen rise to the very top, even though an increasing number of company men have elements of the gamesman's character. Many gamesmen have mixed feelings about authority, and more than a little adolescent rebelliousness. Consequently, they are often considered too free-wheeling for top management positions. While they like to run the team, they also like to circumvent the rules. Furthermore, the gamesman cannot create his own team. He lacks patience and commitment to people, principles, and goals beyond winning. He is not an independent person and tends to lose sight of realities beyond the game he is currently playing. Indeed, he can be looked upon as creating a secondary reality for himself. If life is not interesting enough for him, he makes it a game and enters a semifantasy world.

26   *Some negative consequences.* The character of the gamesman is not easy to evaluate. Besides the importance of his role in advancing technology, he supports some positive social values; he tends to be very fair, to believe that everybody should be allowed to play who is good, and that neither race, sex, nor religion nor anything else besides contributing to the team matters. But we can see a number of elements that inhibit both his self-development and his effect on others. He is excessively competitive and aggressive. Since he makes life a game, he expects everyone else to do the same. For him, it is enough that everyone gets a "fair" chance to play the game, and he ignores the fact that some people, due to their background or temperament, never have a fair chance to compete. He has a tendency to put people into categories of winners and losers, and to be contemptuous of the losers. Beyond this, his detachment and need to win blind him to the effects of his actions on real people, so that he never seriously considers the social values of the products he makes.

27   Nor is he sufficiently concerned about himself. Somebody with such a character may remain happy so long as he's a winner and so long as he is young and vigorous, but once he loses his vigor and his thrill in winning, he becomes depressed and goalless, questioning the purpose of his life because he hasn't sufficiently developed the ability to love and understand and create. This is borne out by the successful gamesman in his forties who admitted he no longer had a goal in life and felt worried and apathetic. Another gamesman whose big project "failed" has become a depressed alcoholic. In contrast, we have met craftsmen aged 70 and older who are still energetic and interested in new ideas.

28   In common with the company man, the gamesman also tends to report another symptom. He often feels that he gives in to others too easily, that he doesn't control his own destiny, that he is too malleable. Even at the highest levels, such personality types may feel a kind of unconscious self-contempt that they've given in, that they are performing for others rather than developing their own goals.

29   The sense of guilt and self-betrayal they feel over having to sacrifice some of their independence is usually not conscious, but it comes out in dreams and projective tests—particularly on the Rorschach test where

they report self-images of humiliation and castration. Their negative self-image tends to be related to a certain suppressed anger and hardening of the heart that occurs when one gives up a part of oneself or betrays one's convictions in order to get ahead.

30 In contrast to this unconscious guilt, I have observed that some of the most creative businessmen–engineers do not repress their guilt, but act to alleviate it. These individuals are deeply concerned with the effects of their actions and recognize that their behavior has sometimes been destructive to themselves or others. But rather than hiding from their conscience, rather than hardening their hearts, their guilt spurs them to better themselves and their organizations. One corporation president told us, "I saw myself as a slave owner, ripping off the work of other people, and I knew I had to do something to change working conditions."

31 THE JUNGLE FIGHTER. This fourth character type is less frequently encountered, but nonetheless often plays a key role in advanced technology. The jungle fighter experiences the corporation as a battleground where survival and advancement depend on crushing enemies both within and outside the company. Like the gamesman he wants to be a winner, but for him the struggle is not a game but a life-and-death contest. The Rorschach images of the jungle fighters are full of lions, tigers, and panthers; sometimes pictures of these animals are hung on their office walls.

32 Many jungle fighters have strong sadistic tendencies, although it is rare that they will admit this. Nevertheless, some do admit they enjoy crushing the opponent, and seeing his ego crack. They are likely to take pride in being feared by others, but rationalize this by claiming such fear stimulates better work.

33 Sometimes a talented and brilliant jungle fighter will be brought into a corporation in trouble and given the task of reorganizing the company and getting rid of the "dead wood." (It is notable that the other types—craftsmen, game characters, and company men—deeply dislike having to fire anyone.) Consequently, in some corporations, jungle fighters rise to high levels, though they often eventually fail because others become disgusted by their hard-hearted and self-serving conduct. Speaking of the fall of a jungle fighter, one of his associates pointed out that he had "left a trail of bodies behind him and he became a victim of revenge."

34 To get ahead in the corporate world of advanced technology, it is necessary to be competitive. But the competitive urge is very different for each of these four character types. [. . .] A key element is that each type is energized differently: the craftsman by his interest and pleasure in his work; the company man by his fear of failure and desire for acceptance; the gamesman by the glory of victory in the "contest"; and the jungle fighter by his need for power over others. Each character has a strong need for achievement, but achievement means something different for each character type.

DEFINE: *entrepreneurial* (11); *prototypical* (13); *circumvent* (25).

ANALYSIS

structure

1. Briefly summarize the chief characteristics of each type of executive.

meaning

2. What is the psychoanalytic concept of character?

3. Who, according to Maccoby, is a successful person?

4. How does Maccoby redefine the Peter Principle?

5. Interpret the dream about the spinning top.

style

6. Discuss the use of sports language in the classification system.

opinion

7. Maccoby's study was centered on engineers and managers in the electronics field. Do you feel that his conclusions apply to people in other areas as well?

WRITING SUGGESTION

After doing some research about the kinds of people who go into fields like law, medicine, or business, develop a classification system and write an in-depth paper.

Max Shulman

LOVE IS A FALLACY

Cool was I and logical. Keen, calculating, perspicacious, acute and astute—I was all of these. My brain was as powerful as a dynamo, as precise as a chemist's scales, as penetrating as a scalpel. And—think of it—I was only eighteen.

It is not often that one so young has such a giant intellect. Take, for example, Petey Burch, my roommate at the University of Minnesota. Same age, same background, but dumb as an ox. A nice enough fellow, you understand, but nothing upstairs. Emotional type. Unstable. Impressionable. Worst of all, a faddist. Fads, I submit, are the very negation of reason. To be swept up in every new craze that comes along, to surrender yourself to idiocy just because everybody else is doing it—this, to me, is the acme of mindlessness. Not, however, to Petey.

One afternoon I found Petey lying on his bed with an expression of such distress on his face that I immediately diagnosed appendicitis. "Don't move," I said, "Don't take a laxative. I'll get a doctor."

"Raccoon," he mumbled thickly.

5

"Raccoon?" I said, pausing in my flight.

"I want a raccoon coat," he wailed.

I perceived that his trouble was not physical, but mental. "Why do you want a raccoon coat?"

"I should have known it," he cried, pounding his temples. "I should have known they'd come back when the Charleston came back. Like a fool I spent all my money for textbooks, and now I can't get a raccoon coat."

Copyright © 1951 renewed 1979. Reprinted by permission of the Harold Matson Company, Inc.

"Can you mean," I said incredulously, "that people are actually wearing raccoon coats again?"

"All the Big Men on Campus are wearing them. Where've you been?"

"In the library," I said, naming a place not frequented by Big Men on Campus.

He leaped from the bed and paced the room. "I've got to have a raccoon coat," he said passionately. "I've got to!"

"Petey, why? Look at it rationally. Raccoon coats are unsanitary. They shed. They smell bad. They weigh too much. They're unsightly. They—"

"You don't understand," he interrupted impatiently. "It's the thing to do. Don't you want to be in the swim?"

"No," I said truthfully.

"Well, I do," he declared. "I'd give anything for a raccoon coat. Anything!"

My brain, that precision instrument, slipped into high gear. "Anything?" I asked, looking at him narrowly.

"Anything," he affirmed in ringing tones.

I stroked my chin thoughtfully. It so happened that I knew where to get my hands on a raccoon coat. My father had had one in his undergraduate days; it lay now in a trunk in the attic back home. It also happened that Petey had something I wanted. He didn't *have* it exactly, but at least he had first rights on it. I refer to his girl, Polly Espy.

I had long coveted Polly Espy. Let me empahsize that my desire for this young woman was not emotional in nature. She was, to be sure, a girl who excited the emotions, but I was not one to let my heart rule my head. I wanted Polly for a shrewdly calculated, entirely cerebral reason.

I was a freshman in law school. In a few years I would be out in practice. I was well aware of the importance of the right kind of wife in furthering a lawyer's career. The successful lawyers I had observed were, almost without exception, married to beautiful, gracious, intelligent women. With one omission, Polly fitted these specifications perfectly.

Beautiful she was. She was not yet of pin-up proportions, but I felt sure that time would supply the lack. She already had the makings.

Gracious she was. By gracious I mean full of graces. She had an erectness of carriage, an ease of bearing, a poise that clearly indicated the best of breeding. At table her manners were exquisite. I had seen her at the Kozy Kampus Korner eating the specialty of the house—a sandwich that contained scraps of pot roast, gravy, chopped nuts, and a dipper of sauerkraut—without even getting her fingers moist.

Intelligent she was not. In fact, she veered in the opposite direction. But I believed that under my guidance she would smarten up. At any rate, it was worth a try. It is, after all, easier to make a beautiful dumb girl smart than to make an ugly smart girl beautiful.

"Petey," I said, "are you in love with Polly Espy?"

"I think she's a keen kid," he replied, "but I don't know if you'd call it love. Why?"

"Do you," I asked, "have any kind of formal arrangement with her? I mean are you going steady or anything like that?"

"No. We see each other quite a bit, but we both have other dates. Why?"

"Is there," I asked, "any other man for whom she has a particular fondness?"

30 "Not that I know of. Why?"

I nodded with satisfaction. "In other words, if you were out of the picture, the field would be open. Is that right?"

"I guess so. What are you getting at?"

"Nothing, nothing," I said innocently, and took my suitcase out of the closet.

"Where are you going?" asked Petey.

35 "Home for the weekend." I threw a few things into the bag.

"Listen," he said, clutching my arm eagerly, "while you're home, you couldn't get some money from your old man, could you, and lend it to me so I can buy a raccoon coat?"

"I may do better than that," I said with a mysterious wink and closed my bag and left.

"Look," I said to Petey when I got back Monday morning. I threw open the suitcase and revealed the huge, hairy, gamy object that my father had worn in his Stutz Bearcat in 1925.

"Holy Toledo!" said Petey reverently. He plunged his hands into the raccoon coat and then his face. "Holy Toledo!" he repeated fifteen or twenty times.

40 "Would you like it?" I asked.

"Oh yes!" he cried, clutching the greasy pelt to him. Then a canny look came into his eyes. "What do you want for it?"

"Your girl," I said, mincing no words.

"Polly?" he said in a horrified whisper. "You want Polly?"

"That's right."

45 He flung the coat from him. "Never," he said stoutly.

I shrugged. "Okay. If you don't want to be in the swim, I guess it's your business."

I sat down in a chair and pretended to read a book, but out of the corner of my eye I kept watching Petey. He was a torn man. First he looked at the coat with the expression of a waif at a bakery window. Then he turned away and set his jaw resolutely. Then he looked back at the coat, with even more longing in his face. Then he turned away, but with not so much resolution this time. Back and forth his head swiveled, desire waxing, resolution waning. Finally he didn't turn away at all; he just stood and stared with mad lust at the coat.

"It isn't as though I was in love with Polly," he said thickly. "Or going steady or anything like that."

"That's right," I murmured.

50 "What's Polly to me, or me to Polly?"

"Not a thing," said I.

"It's just been a casual kick—just a few laughs, that's all."

"Try on the coat," said I.

He complied. The coat bunched high over his ears and dropped all the way down to his shoe tops. He looked like a mound of dead raccoons. "Fits fine," he said happily.

I rose from my chair. "Is it a deal?" I asked, extending my hand. He swallowed. "It's a deal," he said and shook my hand.

I had my first date with Polly the following evening. This was in the nature of a survey; I wanted to find out just how much work I had to do to get her mind up to the standard I required. I took her first to dinner. "Gee, that was a delish dinner," she said as we left the restaurant. Then I took her to a movie. "Gee, that was a marvy movie," she said as we left the theater. And then I took her home. "Gee, I had a sensaysh time," she said as she bade me good night.

I went back to my room with a heavy heart. I had gravely underestimated the size of my task. This girl's lack of information was terrifying. Nor would it be enough merely to supply her with information. First she had to be taught to *think*. This loomed as a project of no small dimensions, and at first I was tempted to give her back to Petey. But then I got to thinking about her abundant physical charms and about the way she entered a room and the way she handled a knife and fork, and I decided to make an effort.

I went about it, as in all things, systematically. I gave her a course in logic. It happened that I, as a law student, was taking a course in logic myself, so I had all the facts at my finger tips. "Polly," I said to her when I picked her up on our next date, "tonight we are going over to the Knoll and talk."

⁶⁰ "Oo, terrif," she replied. One thing I will say for this girl: you would go far to find another so agreeable.

We went to the Knoll, the campus trysting place, and we sat down under an old oak, and she looked at me expectantly. "What are we going to talk about?" she asked.

"Logic."

She thought this over for a minute and decided she liked it. "Magnif," she said.

"Logic," I said, clearing my throat, "is the science of thinking. Before we can think correctly, we must first learn to recognize the common fallacies of logic. These we will take up tonight."

⁶⁵ "Wow-dow!" she cried, clapping her hands delightedly.

I winced, but went bravely on. "First let us examine the fallacy called Dicto Simpliciter."

"By all means," she urged, batting her lashes eagerly.

"Dicto Simpliciter means an argument based on an unqualified generalization. For example: Exercise is good. Therefore everybody should exercise."

"I agree," said Polly earnestly. "I mean exercise is wonderful. I mean it builds the body and everything."

⁷⁰ "Polly," I said gently, "the argument is a fallacy. *Exercise is good* is an unqualified generalization. For instance, if you have heart disease, exercise is bad, not good. Many people are ordered by their doctors *not* to exercise. You must *qualify* the generalization. You must say exercise is *usually* good, or exercise is good *for most people*. Otherwise you have committed a Dicto Simpliciter. Do you see?"

"No," she confessed. "But this is marvy. Do more! Do more!"

"It will be better if you stop tugging at my sleeve," I told her, and when she desisted, I continued. "Next we take up a fallacy called Hasty Generalization. Listen carefully: You can't speak French. I can't speak French. Petey Burch can't speak French. I must therefore conclude that nobody at the University of Minnesota can speak French."

"Really?" said Polly, amazed. *"Nobody?"*

I hid my exasperation. "Polly, it's a fallacy. The generalization is reached too hastily. There are too few instances to support such a conclusion."

75   "Know any more fallacies?" she asked breathlessly. "This is more fun than dancing even."

I fought off a wave of despair. I was getting nowhere with this girl, absolutely nowhere. Still, I am nothing if not persistent. I continued. "Next comes Post Hoc. Listen to this: Let's not take Bill on our picnic. Every time we take him out with us, it rains."

"I know somebody just like that," she exclaimed. "A girl back home—Eula Becker, her name is. It never fails. Every single time we take her on a picnic—"

"Polly," I said sharply, "it's a fallacy. Eula Becker doesn't *cause* the rain. She has no connection with the rain. You are guilty of Post Hoc if you blame Eula Becker."

"I'll never do it again," she promised contritely. "Are you mad at me?"

80   I sighed deeply. "No, Polly, I'm not mad."

"Then tell me some more fallacies."

"All right. Let's try Contradictory Premises."

"Yes, let's," she chirped, blinking her eyes happily.

I frowned, but plunged ahead. "Here's an example of Contradictory Premises: If God can do anything, can He make a stone so heavy that He won't be able to lift it?"

85   "Of course," she replied promptly.

"But if He can do anything, He can lift the stone," I pointed out.

"Yeah," she said thoughtfully. "Well, then I guess He can't make the stone."

"But He can do anything," I reminded her.

She scratched her pretty, empty head. "I'm all confused," she admitted.

90   "Of course you are. Because when the premises of an argument contradict each other, there can be no argument. If there is an irresistible force, there can be no immovable object. If there is an immovable object, there can be no irresistible force. Get it?"

"Tell me some more of this keen stuff," she said eagerly.

I consulted my watch. "I think we'd better call it a night. I'll take you home now, and you go over all the things you've learned. We'll have another session tomorrow night."

I deposited her at the girls' dormitory, where she assured me that she had had a perfectly terrif evening, and I went glumly home to my room. Petey lay snoring in his bed, the raccoon coat huddled like a great hairy beast at his feet. For a moment I considered waking him and telling him that he could have his girl back. It seemed clear that my project was doomed to failure. The girl simply had a logic-proof head.

But then I reconsidered. I had wasted one evening; I might as well waste another. Who knew? Maybe somewhere in the extinct crater of her mind, a few embers still smoldered. Maybe somehow I could fan them into flame. Admittedly it was not a prospect fraught with hope, but I decided to give it one more try.

95 Seated under the oak the next evening I said, "Our first fallacy tonight is called Ad Misericordiam."

She quivered with delight.

"Listen closely," I said. "A man applies for a job. When the boss asks him what his qualifications are, he replies that he has a wife and six children at home, the wife is a helpless cripple, the children have nothing to eat, no clothes to wear, no shoes on their feet, there are no beds in the house, no coal in the cellar, and winter is coming."

A tear rolled down each of Polly's pink cheeks. "Oh, this is awful, awful," she sobbed.

"Yes, it's awful," I agreed, "but it's no argument. The man never answered the boss's question about his qualifications. Instead he appealed to the boss's sympathy. He committed the fallacy of Ad Misericordiam. Do you understand?"

100 "Have you got a handkerchief?" she blubbered.

I handed her a handkerchief and tried to keep from screaming while she wiped her eyes. "Next," I said in a carefully controlled tone, "we will discuss False Analogy. Here is an example: Students should be allowed to look at their textbooks during examinations. After all, surgeons have X-rays to guide them during an operation, lawyers have briefs to guide them during a trial, carpenters have blueprints to guide them when they are building a house. Why, then, shouldn't students be allowed to look at their textbooks during an examination?"

"There now," she said enthusiastically, "is the most marvy idea I've heard in years."

"Polly," I said testily, "the argument is all wrong. Doctors, lawyers, and carpenters aren't taking a test to see how much they have learned, but students are. The situations are altogether different, and you can't make an analogy between them."

"I still think it's a good idea," said Polly.

105 "Nuts," I muttered. Doggedly I pressed on. "Next we'll try Hypothesis Contrary to Fact."

"Sounds yummy," was Polly's reaction.

"Listen: If Madame Curie had not happened to leave a photographic plate in a drawer with a chunk of pitchblende, the world today would not know about radium."

"True, true," said Polly, nodding her head. "Did you see the movie? Oh, it just knocked me out. That Walter Pidgeon is so dreamy. I mean he fractures me."

"If you can forget Mr. Pidgeon for a moment," I said coldly, "I would like to point out that the statement is a fallacy. Maybe Madame Curie would have discovered radium at some later date. Maybe somebody else would have discovered it. Maybe any number of things would have happened. You can't start with a hypothesis that is not true and then draw any supportable conclusions from it."

110   "They ought to put Walter Pidgeon in more pictures," said Polly. "I hardly ever see him any more."

One more chance, I decided. But just one more. There is a limit to what flesh and blood can bear. "The next fallacy is called Poisoning the Well."

"How cute!" she gurgled.

"Two men are having a debate. The first one gets up and says, 'My opponent is a notorious liar. You can't believe a word that he is going to say.' . . . Now, Polly, think. Think hard. What's wrong?"

I watched her closely as she knit her creamy brow in concentration. Suddenly a glimmer of intelligence—the first I had seen—came into her eyes. "It's not fair," she said with indignation. "It's not a bit fair. What chance has the second man got if the first man calls him a liar before he even begins talking?"

115   "Right!" I cried exultantly. "One hundred percent right. It's not fair. The first man has *poisoned the well* before anybody could drink from it. He has hamstrung his opponent before he could even start. . . . Polly, I'm proud of you."

"Pshaw," she murmured, blushing with pleasure.

"You see, my dear, these things aren't so hard. All you have to do is concentrate. Think—examine—evaluate. Come now, let's review everything we have learned."

"Fire away," she said with an airy wave of her hand.

Heartened by the knowledge that Polly was not altogether a cretin, I began a long, patient review of all I had told her. Over and over and over again. I cited instances, pointed out flaws, kept hammering away without let up. It was like digging a tunnel. At first everything was work, sweat, and darkness. I had no idea when I would reach the light, or even *if* I would. But I persisted. I pounded and clawed and scraped, and finally I was rewarded. I saw a chink of light. And then the chink got bigger and the sun came pouring in and all was bright.

120   Five grueling nights this took, but it was worth it. I had made a logician out of Polly; I had taught her to think. My job was done. She was worthy of me at last. She was a fit wife for me, a proper hostess for many mansions, a suitable mother for my well-heeled children.

It must not be thought that I was without love for this girl. Quite the contrary. Just as Pygmalion loved the perfect woman he had fashioned, so I loved mine. I determined to acquaint her with my feelings at our very next meeting. The time had come to change our relationship from academic to romantic.

"Polly," I said when next we sat beneath our oak, "tonight we will not discuss fallacies."

"Aw, gee," she said, disappointed.

"My dear," I said, favoring her with a smile, "we have now spent five evenings together. We have gotten along splendidly. It is clear that we are well matched."

125   "Hasty Generalization," said Polly brightly.

"I beg your pardon," said I.

"Hasty Generalization," she repeated. "How can you say that we are well matched on the basis of only five dates?"

I chuckled with amusement. The dear child had learned her lessons well. "My dear," I said, patting her hand in a tolerant manner, "five dates is plenty. After all, you don't have to eat a whole cake to know that it's good."

"False Analogy," said Polly promptly. "I'm not a cake. I'm a girl."

I chuckled with somewhat less amusement. The dear child had learned her lessons perhaps too well. I decided to change tactics. Obviously the best approach was a simple, strong, direct declaration of love. I paused for a moment while my massive brain chose the proper words. Then I began:

"Polly, I love you. You are the whole world to me, and the moon and the stars and the constellations of outer space. Please, my darling, say that you will go steady with me, for if you will not, life will be meaningless. I will languish. I will refuse my meals. I will wander the face of the earth, a shambling, hollow-eyed hulk."

There, I thought, folding my arms, that ought to do it.

"Ad Misericordiam," said Polly.

I ground my teeth. I was no Pygmalion; I was Frankenstein, and my monster had me by the throat. Frantically I fought back the tide of panic surging through me. At all costs I had to keep cool.

"Well, Polly," I said, forcing a smile, "you certainly have learned your fallacies."

"You're darn right," she said with a vigorous nod.

"And who taught them to you, Polly?"

"You did."

"That's right. So you do owe me something, don't you, my dear? If I hadn't come along you never would have learned about fallacies."

"Hypothesis Contrary to Fact," she said instantly.

I dashed perspiration from my brow. "Polly," I croaked, "you mustn't take all these things so literally. I mean this is just classroom stuff. You know that the things you learn in school don't have anything to do with life."

"Dicto Simpliciter," she said, wagging her finger at me playfully.

That did it. I leaped to my feet, bellowing like a bull. "Will you or will you not go steady with me?"

"I will not," she replied.

"Why not?" I demanded.

"Because this afternoon I promised Petey Burch that I would go steady with him."

I reeled back, overcome with the infamy of it. After he promised, after he made a deal, after he shook my hand! "The rat!" I shrieked, kicking up great chunks of turf. "You can't go with him, Polly. He's a liar. He's a cheat. He's a rat."

"Poisoning the Well," said Polly, "and stop shouting. I think shouting must be a fallacy too."

With an immense effort of will, I modulated my voice. "All right," I said. "You're a logician. Let's look at this thing logically. How could you choose Petey Burch over me? Look at me—a brilliant student, a tremendous intellectual, a man with an assured future. Look at Petey—a knothead, a jitterbug, a guy who'll never know where his next meal is coming from. Can you give me one logical reason why you should go steady with Petey Burch?"

150   "I certainly can," declared Polly. "He's got a raccoon coat."

DEFINE: *perspicacious* (1); *incredulously* (9); *analogy* (103); *cretin* (119).

ANALYSIS

meaning   1. Does the fact that Shulman's story is humorous make his explanation of logical fallacies less valid? Discuss.

style   2. Show how Shulman characterizes the people in his story through the use of their own language.

opinion   3. What makes the story humorous?

4. Do you feel that the narrator is treated justly or unjustly at the end of the story? Explain.

WRITING SUGGESTIONS

Classify one or more of the following: students, parents, life styles, restaurants, car salesmen, car buyers, married couples, single men, single women, family quarrels, kinds of love, nagging, television programs, ten-cent-store gadgets, politicians. For other possibilities see the Idea Bank. You might, for example, classify patent medicine ads, sexist quotations, quotations about love, ways that people are regimented, approaches to education, or terrorists.

NOTE: Avoid the most obvious kinds of classifications. Don't opt, for example, for "smart students," "dull students," and "average students." Try to make your classifications reflect your particular observations and insights.

Review of Chapter 5

Before reviewing this chapter, survey Chapters 2–4. Remind yourself of the value and the effect of each method: *narration* for creating a story, building interest and suspense, and making a point; *description* for adding color, taste, sound, smell, and feeling; *examples* for making difficult concepts clearer.

In reviewing this chapter, consider how classification helps take broad subjects and make them more manageable and understandable. Note how the writers of classification papers create their categories and then use various methods of supporting or explaining them.

EVALUATION

Which selection in the chapter presents the most clear cut, consistent, and apt classification system? Which is the most interesting? Which is the most helpful? Which is most entertaining? Which provides the best insights into the ways that human beings think and act? Which does the best overall job?

Comparison/ Contrast

CHAPTER 6

READING FOCUS

❖ Find the comparison/contrast pattern so that you can quickly see what factors the author is comparing and how he is going about it.

❖ Consider the aptness of the comparison. Is the author fair in his choice of material to compare and in his method of handling it?

WRITING FOCUS

❖ Decide what the purpose of your comparison/contrast is and what ground rules you will follow.

❖ Since comparison/contrast can get very complicated, plan your work very carefully. Outlining is almost always advisable.

❖ Select subjects that are comparable and handle them fairly.

❖ Separate similarities from contrasts to avoid confusion and repetition.

❖ Try various patterns to see which is most effective.

Seeing likenesses and differences is a fundamental thought process, the basis for all kinds of generalizations and judgments. Comparison leans toward similarities. Contrast emphasizes differences. The word "comparison" used alone often encompasses the idea of both.

Comparing something strange with something familiar usually helps the reader visualize more easily than if the writer resorts to long descriptions or explanations. We get some idea of what an aardwolf is, for example, if we are told that it looks like a hyena, but unlike the hyena, eats termites.

The ground rules in writing comparison/contrast papers deal mostly with choosing subjects that are comparable in the first place and then handling them in a balanced, equitable manner. If you had reason to compare an elephant with an ant, you would not dwell on the question of size, but there might be some profit in comparing relative strength, adaptability, social organization, etc. You might even dare compare Mickey Mouse to Shakespeare if you focused on factors such as humor, inventiveness, and the kinds of audiences that each attracts, not on philosophical and poetic values.

Comparison/contrast papers are written in various patterns. Similarities are usually handled with the word "both" to avoid needless repetition. Contrasts are written within sentences (See "Universities and Athletes"), in alternate sentences (See "Big Frog in Small Pond or . . ."), in blocks of sentences within paragraphs, in alternating paragraphs, or in blocks of paragraphs within themes. They are also found in combinations of these patterns.

section 6a

Read all of the selections in the section; then answer the questions.

Peter F. Drucker

BIG FROG IN SMALL POND OR . . .?

There are basic differences between the large and the small enterprise. In the small enterprise you operate primarily through personal contacts. In the large enterprise you have established "policies," "channels" of organization, and fairly rigid procedures. In the small enterprise you have, moreover, immediate effectiveness in a very small area. You can see the effect of your work and of your decisions right away, once you are a little bit above the ground floor. In the large enterprise even the man at the top is only a cog in a big machine. To be sure, his actions affect a much greater area than the actions and decisions of the man in the small organization, but his effectiveness is remote, indirect, and elusive. In a small and even in a middle-sized business, you are normally exposed to all kinds of experi-

From "How to Be an Employee" by Peter F. Drucker, *Fortune*, May 1952.

ences and expected to do a great many things without too much help or guidance. In the large organization you are normally taught one thing thoroughly. In the small one the danger is of becoming a jack-of-all-trades and master of none. In the large it is of becoming the man who knows more and more about less and less.

Harold W. Stoke

UNIVERSITIES AND ATHLETES

The most essential distinction between athletics and education lies in the institution's own interest in the athlete as distinguished from its interest in its other students. Universities attract students in order to teach them what they do not already know; they recruit athletes only when they are already proficient. Students are educated for something which will be useful to them and to society after graduation; athletes are required to spend their time on activities the usefulness of which disappears upon graduation or soon thereafter. Universities exist to do what they can for students; athletes are recruited for what they can do for the universities. This makes the operation of the athletic program in which recruited players are used basically different from any educational interest of colleges and universities.

From "College Athletics—Education or Show Business," in *The Atlantic Monthly*, March, 1954. Copyright © 1954 by Harold W. Stoke. Reprinted with permission of the author.

Gilbert Highet

SOCRATES AND THE SOPHISTS

To some of his contemporaries Socrates looked like a sophist. But *he distrusted and opposed the sophists wherever possible.* They toured the whole Greek world: Socrates stayed in Athens, talking to his fellow-citizens. They made carefully prepared continuous speeches; he only asked questions. They took rich fees for their teaching; he refused regular payment, living and dying poor. They were elegantly dressed, turned out like filmstars on a personal-appearance tour, with secretaries and personal servants and elaborate advertising. Socrates wore the workingman's clothes, bare feet and a smock; in fact, he had been a stonemason and carver by trade, and came from a working-class family. They spoke in specially prepared lecture-halls; he talked to people at streetcorners and in gymnasium (like public baths

From *The Art of Teaching* by Gilbert Highet. Copyright 1950 by Gilbert Highet. Reprinted by permission of Alfred A. Knopf, Inc.

and bathing beaches nowadays), where every afternoon the young men exercised, and the old men talked, while they all sun bathed. He fitted in so well there that he sometimes compared himself to the athletic coach, who does not run or wrestle, but teaches others how to run and wrestle better: Socrates said he trained people to think. Lastly, the sophists said they knew everything and were ready to explain it. Socrates said he knew nothing and was trying to find out.

Luigi Barzini

MACHIAVELLI AND GUICCIARDINI

1   The two men have been compared repeatedly through the centuries. The parallel is almost irresistible. After all, they were both Florentines, born in the same city at about the same time (Machiavelli in 1469 and Guicciardini in 1482); both started young, when the popular republic of Florence employed them as ambassadors; both pursued political careers, and were fascinated by the technique of governing men and achieving power. Both, in the end, were defeated and chose to retire to their country estates, where they studied, wrote historical works and meditated on history's immutable and mysterious laws; both reached the conclusion that men and things were what they were and that all reasonable plans of action had to start from that assumption. The two friends believed that the pursuit of success was an absolute imperative, for individuals as well as states, the only sensible goal for action. "He who has no position in life," Machiavelli wrote, "cannot even get a dog to bark at him."

2   In spite of these superficial similarities they were profoundly different. Machiavelli, the older man, kept some of the youthful illusions of an earlier and happier age. He was an artist, above all, who wrote perhaps the most beautiful, lean and muscular prose in all Italian literature, at times bitter, biting, ironical and light, at other times solemn, grave and sonorous, but always limpid. He lived an irregular, almost bohemian life. He was a brilliant failure, never really managing to achieve his ends: he never made love to the women he wanted, satisfied his ambitions, reached the top in his political career and was never taken seriously as a thinker during his lifetime. . . .

3   Guicciardini was no light-minded artist. He led no bohemian life. He entertained no illusions. Born a wealthy patrician, he was well brought up and educated. His virtuous youth had been spent, as he himself wrote, "without corruption, levity, or waste of time." His only known vice was women, for whom he had a long and persistent, though secret, weakness, women of all conditions and ages. . . .

4   He occupied some of the highest offices in the country with dignity,

Reprinted from *The Italians* by Luigi Barzini, by permission of Atheneum Publishers. Copyright © 1964 by Luigi Barzini.

reaching almost regal powers. He acquired a solid reputation, seriously cultivated historical and political studies, and enlarged his private fortune. He got everything he wanted by honest means, not courting powerful personages, or courting them so discreetly as to be undetected.

Norbert Wiener

ANTS AND MEN

In the ant community, each worker performs its proper functions. There may be a separate caste of soldiers. Certain highly specialized individuals perform the functions of king and queen. If man were to adopt this community as a pattern, he would live in a fascist state, in which ideally each individual is conditioned from birth for his proper occupation: in which rulers are perpetually rulers, soldiers perpetually soldiers, the peasant is never more than a peasant, and the worker is doomed to be a worker.

It is a thesis of this chapter that this aspiration of the fascist for a human state based on the model of the ant results from a profound misapprehension both of the nature of the ant and of the nature of man. I wish to point out that the very physical development of the insect conditions it to be an essentially stupid and unlearning individual, cast in a mold which cannot be modified to any great extent. I also wish to show how these physiological conditions make it into a cheap mass-produced article, of no more individual value than a paper pie plate to be thrown away after it is once used. On the other hand, I wish to show that the human individual, capable of vast learning and study, which may occupy almost half of his life, is physically equipped, as the ant is not, for this capacity. Variety and possibility are inherent in the human sensorium—and are indeed the key to man's most noble flights—because variety and possibility belong to the very structure of the human organism.

From *The Human Use of Human Beings* by Norbert Wiener. Copyright 1950, 1954 by Norbert Wiener. Reprinted by permission of Houghton Mifflin Company.

Daniel J. Boorstin

THE WASHINGTON AND CROCKETT MYTHS

Never did a more incongruous pair than Davy Crockett and George Washington live together in a national Valhalla. Idolized by the new nation, the legendary Washington was a kind of anti-Crockett. The bluster,

From "The Mythologizing of George Washington" in *The Americans: The National Experience,* by Daniel J. Boorstin. Copyright © 1965 by Daniel J. Boorstin. Reprinted by permission of Random House, Inc.

the crudity, the vulgarity, the monstrous boosterism of Crockett and his fellow supermen of the subliterature were all qualities which Washington most conspicuously lacked. At the same time, the dignity, the reverence for God, the sober judgment, the sense of destiny, and the vision of the distant future, for all of which Washington was proverbial, were unknown to the Ring-tailed Roarers of the West. Yet both Crockett and Washington were popular heroes, and both emerged into legendary fame during the first half of the 19th century.

2   The legendary Washington, no less than the legendary Crockett, was a product of the anachronism and abridgment of American history. Crockett and his kind, however, had first been spawned by spontaneous generation. They began as by-products of American life rather than as artifices of an American literature. The legends of the comic supermen, which had originated in oral anecdote, never entirely lost the sound and accent of the raconteur's voice, even when frozen into their crude literary form.

3   There were elements of spontaneity, of course, in the Washington legend, too, but it was, for the most part, a self-conscious product. The Crockett and Fink legends caught the spoken echoes of campfire and saloon, captured and diffused them in crudely printed almanacs, in sporting magazines, and anonymous wheezes. The Demigod Washington was to be a cumbersome figure of literary contrivance. The contrast between the Crockett subliterature (flimsy, ephemeral scraps which seldom could be dignified as "books") and the Washington literature (heavy, elegantly printed works, copiously illustrated by maps and engravings, the proud personal product of eminent statesmen and famous writers) was as striking as that between the legendary characters of the two men themselves.

4   Although both were peculiar products of America, only Washington became part of the national protocol. How this happened showed how different was the Washington legend from its superficially similar counterparts in the Old World. There, names like Romulus and Remus, Aeneas, Charlemagne, Boadicea, King Alfred, St. Louis, St. Joan, and the Cid, glorified the founding of their nations. Some were more mythical than others, but when the modern nations of Italy, France, England, and Spain became self-conscious, the challenge to national historians was to give these hazy figures some historical reality, to make them more plausible by clothing them in historical fact. These nations, which had attained their nationality gradually over the centuries, already possessed legendary founding heroes when they became nations. The challenging task was to historicize them.

5   Not so in the United States. Here a new nation sprang into being almost before it had time to acquire a history. At the outbreak of the Civil War, there were men alive who could remember the death of Washington; he was still an emphatically real historical person. The national problem was not how to make Washington historical; quite the contrary: how could he be made into a myth? The very brevity of American history made special demands, but Americans of the age proved equal to them.

THREE SUBCOMPACT CARS COMPARED

CHEVROLET CHEVETTE

The smallest American car shows its European ancestry in its dimensions, its relatively small, hard-working, and noisy 4-cylinder engine, and, as equipped in the car we tested, in well above average handling characteristics. For anyone looking for a soundly designed economy car of simple and essentially conventional mechanical configuration and for whom its marked lack of adequate room for adults in the rear seat and its lack of sufficient clearance for big shoes on the accelerator pedal would not be disadvantageous, the *Chevette,* in our opinion, would be well worth considering. Fuel economy and acceleration with the optional larger engine were both reasonable, but hardly good for a car of the *Chevette*'s size. Optional front seats were good, and had novel, convenient seat belts and seat-back releases; the safety of the way the rear-seat belts were fitted was questionable, though. Rear-seat and luggage space are not good in comparison with a more technically advanced competitor such as the *VW Rabbit.*

PONTIAC SUNBIRD

The *Pontiac Sunbird* is quite similar to the *Chevrolet Monza Towne Coupe,* and also closely related to the *Monza 2+2, Oldsmobile Starfire,* and *Buick Skylark* hatchbacks. The optional V-6 engine in the *Sunbird* gave good fuel economy with the optional 5-speed transmission, fair performance for its size, and quiet cruising compared to the other cars reported on in this article, but the V-6 ran roughly at low speeds. Fifth gear, actually an overdrive ratio, was not usable at town speeds, but did help fuel economy and noise levels somewhat when it could be used. The low, stylish car has meager trunk space and unpleasant, hard-to-enter rear seats. Handling was above average, not so good as the *Chevette*'s handling, and ride was fairly soft, though unmistakably small-car.

DODGE COLT

Significantly heavier and larger than the *Chevette,* the Japanese-made *Dodge Colt GT* hardtop with optional engine and 5-speed transmission was less noisy at cruising speeds than the *Chevette* and had more room, except for short rear headroom. Unlike most new cars, the *Colt* has no catalytic converter to control exhaust pollutants and unleaded gasoline is not required. Acceleration and fuel consumption were about the same as with the heavier *Pontiac Sunbird,* which had an engine nearly twice as large as that of the *Colt.* Considerable use of the lower gears was necessary to keep the *Colt* engine turning fast enough to run well, though. Ride, handling, and comfort were judged only average for a small car.

Reprinted by special permission from *Consumers' Research Magazine,* Washington, N.J., February 1976.

ANALYSIS

structure

1. List the kinds of comparison/contrast patterns you find in "Universities and Athletes," "Socrates and the Sophists," and "The Washington and Crockett Myths."
   EXAMPLE: In "Machiavelli and Guicciardini" the similarities are discussed in paragraph 1, and the differences are delineated in paragraph 2 (Machiavelli) and paragraphs 3 and 4 (Guicciardini).

2. List the bases of comparison (the aspects that are being compared) in "Universities and Athletes" and "Ants and Men."

3. Rewrite "Big Frog in Small Pond or . . . ?" to form blocks of sentences so that all the information about small enterprises is in the first group and all the information about large enterprises is in the second.

4. Which method seems more effective, the original paragraph or your rewrite? Discuss.

5. Copy the thesis statement of "Machiavelli and Guicciardini."

6. Make a chart to compare the three makes of cars.

meaning

7. Explain the significance of the last sentence in "Socrates and the Sophists." Apply it to your own attitude toward learning.

8. According to Norbert Wiener, why is a fascist society right for ants and wrong for human beings?

9. In your own words explain the differences in the origin of the Davy Crockett and George Washington myths.

opinion

10. Would you rather work in a small firm or a large firm, go to a small school or a large school, live in a small town or a city?

11. The overemphasis on college athletics has been criticized by educators and others for many years. Discuss the pros and cons. Consider junior and senior high school athletic programs too.

WRITING SUGGESTION

Using the chart you prepared in answer to question 6 above, write a comparison/contrast theme on the three subcompact cars.

Carl T. Rowan

COMIC STRIPS NOW SHOW THE STATE OF OUR SOCIETY

As a comic strip devotee whose early years were influenced by Andy Gump, detective Dan Dunn, Joe Palooka, and Popeye the Sailor Man, I want to state a proposition: Comic strips reflect the mental health of this society.

The strips listed above, plus Blondie, Moon Mullins, the Katzenjammer Kids and Dick Tracy, mirrored a time of old-fashioned morality, when premarital sex, extramarital sex, divorce, gambling, drinking and a host of other vices were frowned upon.

But look at the popular new wave of comics:

Andy Capp becomes the glorified anti-hero. This strip, imported from Britain, gives us a little jerk who detests work, lives off his wife's labors, cheats on her every night and glorifies getting drunk.

Occasionally the Andy Capp comic strip offers some delightfully redeeming merit—as when the pert barmaid notices Andy sleeping on the bar and says to Mrs. Capp that she would never marry a man who snores.

The pudgy, homely, ever-suffering Mrs. Capp merely advises the sweet British bird to be careful how she finds out if a man snores.

Andy Capp is joined by the Lockhorns in impressing upon us Western civilization's struggle with alcohol, its curse of marital conflict, divorce and family breakup.

Lockhorn is always plastered. His wife is the sort of woman the average man would want to divorce if he really could get any of those bosomy babes he keeps running into at cocktail parties.

When I grew up, Dan Dunn and Dick Tracy always got the crook. Crime didn't pay. Justice triumphed. Virtue was its own reward.

© *Chicago Tribune–New York News Syndicate*

Copyright, Field Newspaper Syndicate, 1978.

© King Features Syndicate, Inc., 1978

¹⁰ But today's comics show a brutally lovable ignoramus, Sgt. Snorkle, always beating the simpleton GI, Beetle Bailey, to a pulp. In the Kingdom of Id, a ruthless runt of a king lards on repression after repression, but he never loses power.

It's so much like the real world.

How simple America seemed back in the days when all I had to worry about after finishing my paper route was to see if Skeezix in Gasoline Alley had survived what now seems like an insipid series of crises. But now I get Rex Morgan, M.D., leaving me twisting in the wind wondering when someone will imprison crooks who exploit cancer victims. I get Doonesbury worrying about how to seat at a dinner party a U.S. senator who allegedly uplifted a dinner by putting his hand down the front of the gown of a woman aide to the President.

The temptation is to write that comic strippers don't make me laugh the way they used to. But the truth is that I guffaw over Beetle Bailey, the Lockhorns and . . . Luther.

It also says something about my society that the daily press now features a strip—Luther—which reveals the everyday woes, frustration, hopelessness of children who live in the ghettos of America's cities.

¹⁵ One might conclude that the comic strips have grown up. In doing so, they have come to reflect a national social crisis far more complicated than that of the Depression era when Popeye and a can of spinach could wipe out any evil.

DEFINE: *insipid, allegedly* (12).

ANALYSIS

structure 1. Write a thesis statement for Rowan's article.

2. List the virtues reflected in the old-time comics in one column and the vices reflected in modern comics in another.

meaning 3. Why are modern comics so different from old-time comics?

4. Explain "One might conclude that comic strips have grown up."

5. What's an "anti-hero"?

opinion 6. Cite some modern comics that reflect social problems other than crime and violence. Discuss.

7. Do any modern comics go beyond the mere reflection of society to criticism of it?

8. Does the absence of immorality in old-time comic strips mean that there was less immorality then than there is now?

WRITING SUGGESTION

Compare two or more comic strips or TV programs.

William Safire

CAN MAN SURVIVE?

1 "Is there hope for man?"

2 That stark question is posed by political economist Robert Heilbroner in a short new book, *An Inquiry Into the Human Prospect,* and his answer troubles some of the people in guilt-edged Washington who consider themselves, in Heilbroner's phrase, "the sentries of our society."

3 The author assesses the "civilizational malaise," or dread of the future, that appears to grip us, and finds that such anxiety is well-founded. World population growth and food shortages, in his view, will lead to "iron" governments in have-not nations and ultimately to nuclear war; if this does not obliterate us, environmental pollution is ready to replace the bang with the whimper.

4 In the face of these external challenges to mankind, Heilbroner suggests—"whether we are unable to sustain growth or unable to tolerate it"—both the capitalist and the socialist worlds will have to deny even lip service to individual liberty and humanism. Instead they will have to learn to live with harsh hierarchies of power capable of responding to demands of population control, war control and environmental control.

5 Heilbroner admits with some pain that his prescription "plays directly into the bands of those who applaud the 'orderliness' of authoritarian or dictatorial governments." But the freedom of man must be sacrificed on the altar of the survival of mankind.

6 "If then," he concludes, "by the question 'Is there hope for man?' we ask whether it is possible to meet the challenges of the future without the payment of a fearful price, the answer must be: No, there is no such hope."

7 Unlike previous catastrophists such as Thomas Malthus and Oswald Spengler, Heilbroner writes lucidly. For a mythic symbol he rejects Prometheus, who stole fire from the gods to give to man and who stands for daring and creativity, replacing him with fellow-titan Atlas, who carried the heavens on his shoulders, to suggest that the future spirit of mankind must be one of resignation to the bearing of an intolerable burden.

© 1974 by The New York Times Company. Reprinted by permission.

8   Fortunately for the affirmative Prometheans among us, another human prospector has come on stream at the same time, with a book the same length and price (about 140 pages, $5.95) and a wholly different vision. He is Daniel Boorstin, senior historian at the Smithsonian Institution, who recently was awarded the Pulitzer Prize for the final volume of his monumental trilogy, *The Americans,* and who now offers *Democracy and Its Discontents: Reflections on Everyday America.*

9   "Perhaps it would be more comfortable," writes Boorstin, "to live in an age when the dominant purposes were in full flood, when the hope for fulfillment had not been overshadowed by the frustrations of fulfillment." But today, in the "omnipresent present," Americans are worried and puzzled about "self-liquidating ideals."

10   A self-liquidating ideal is one that crosses itself off the national agenda as it is accomplished but leaves behind more frustration than satisfaction. For example, we have set aside huge areas in national parks to preserve the wilderness for people to enjoy—but as more people trek to the parks to enjoy them, the democratized wilderness loses its virginity.

11   As achievements accrue, Boorstin points out, dissatisfaction is guaranteed. Heilbroner sees this, too, as the explanation why social harmony does not follow economic growth: "Poverty is a relative and not an absolute condition," he writes, "so that despite growth, a feeling of disprivilege remains . . ."

12   Every solution breeds a new problem, Prometheus Boorstin and Atlas Heilbroner would agree, but from this statement they march in opposite directions. Heilbroner envisions such immense problems that the only political solution is anti-democratic.

13   Boorstin thinks a "belief in solutions" is fallacious, caused by the example of technology in solving technical problems. Democracy is not the solution to anything, but is the process of solving the problems its solutions create—as he puts it, "getting there is all the fun."

14   "The most distinctive feature of our system is not a system, but a quest," Boorstin holds, "not a neat arrangement of men and institutions, but a flux. What other society has ever committed itself to so tantalizing, so fulfilling, so frustrating a community enterprise?"

15   The debate is worthwhile: Heilbroner is positive in his negation and Boorstin is profoundly serious in his affirmation. Which one will history prove to be realist?

16   To me, the creativity of Prometheus better symbolizes the human prospect than the resignation of Atlas. As long as the Boorstins can place our discontent in historic perspective, and the Heilbroners can shake us with purposeful foreboding, there is "hope for man."

DEFINE: malaise (3); *hierarchies* (4).

ANALYSIS

structure   1. State Safire's thesis.

2. Describe his comparison/contrast pattern.

3. Not until late in the article does Safire introduce the second book. Write an introduction which introduces both books.

4. Compare your introduction with the original. Discuss the merits of each.

meaning 5. Very briefly state the differences between the views of Heilbroner and Boorstin.

6. Why does Prometheus symbolize hope while Atlas symbolizes despair?

7. Explain "self-liquidating ideal," "poverty is a relative and not an absolute condition," and "getting there is all the fun."

style 8. As in the Kronenberger selection (Section 5C), Safire uses pithy phrases (his own and others') that liven this work. (See some examples in question 7.) Find other examples in this selection.

opinion 9. To make an intelligent choice between the views of Heilbroner and Boorstin, it would of course be best to read their books. However, on the basis of the limited information in this article, whose views do you favor? Why?

WRITING SUGGESTION

Compare the views of two politicians on a local, state, or national issue.

E. Fuller Torrey

WITCHDOCTORS AND THE UNIVERSALITY OF HEALING

1 Witch doctors and psychiatrists perform essentially the same function in their respective cultures. They are both therapists; both treat patients, using similar techniques; and both get similar results. Recognition of this should not downgrade psychiatrists—rather it should upgrade witchdoctors.

2 The term "witchdoctor" is Western in origin, imposed on healers of the Third World by 18th and 19th century explorers. The world was simpler then, and the newly discovered cultures were quickly assigned their proper status in the Order of Things. We were white, they were black. We were civilized, they were primitive. We were Christian, they were pagan. We used science, they used magic. We had doctors, they had witchdoctors.

3 American psychiatrists have much to learn from therapists in other cultures. My own experience observing and working with them includes two years in Ethiopia and briefer periods in Sarawak, Bali, Hong Kong, Colombia, and with Alaskan Indians, Puerto Ricans, and Mexican-Americans in this country. What I learned from these doctor-healers was that I, as a psychiatrist, was using the same mechanisms for curing my patients as they were—and, not surprisingly, I was getting about the same results. The mechanisms can be classified under four categories.

Abridged from *The Mind Game: Witchdoctors and Psychiatrists* by E. Fuller Torrey, M.D. (Washington, D.C., 1979).

4   The first is the naming process. A psychiatrist or witchdoctor can work magic by telling a patient what is wrong with him. It conveys to the patient that someone—usually a man of considerable status—understands. And since his problem can be understood, then, implicitly, it can be cured. A psychiatrist who tells an illiterate African that his phobia is related to a fear of failure, or a witchdoctor who tells an American tourist that his phobia is related to possession by an ancestral spirit will be met by equally blank stares. And as therapists they will be equally ineffective. This is a major reason for the failure of most attempts at cross-cultural psychotherapy. Since a shared world-view is necessary for the naming process to be effective, then it is reasonable to expect that the best therapist-patient relationships will be those where both come from the same culture or subculture. The implications for our mental health programs are obvious.

5   The second healing component used by therapists everywhere is their personality characteristics. An increasing amount of research shows that certain personal qualities of the therapist—accurate empathy, nonpossessive warmth, genuineness—are of crucial importance in producing effective psychotherapy. Clearly, more studies are needed in this area, but if they substantiate the emerging trend, then radical changes in the selection of therapists will be in order. Rather than selecting therapists because they can memorize facts and achieve high grades, we should be selecting them on the basis of their personality. Therapists in other cultures are selected more often for their personality characteristics; the fact that they have not studied biochemistry is not considered important.

6   The third component of the healing process that appears to be universal is the patients' expectations. Healers all over the world use many ways to raise the expectations of their patients. The first way is the trip itself to the healer. It is a common observation that the farther a person goes to be healed, the greater are the chances that he will be healed. This is called the pilgrimage. Thus, sick people in Topeka go to the Leahy Clinic in Boston. The resulting therapeutic effects of the trip are exactly the same as have been operating for centuries at Delphi or Lourdes. The next way to raise patients' expectations is the building used for the healing. The more impressive it is, the greater will be the patients' expectations. This has been called the edifice complex. Therapists in different cultures use certain paraphernalia to increase patient expectations. In Western cultures nonpsychiatric healers have their stethoscope and psychotherapists are supposed to have their couch. Therapists in other cultures have their counterpart trademark, often a special drum, mask or amulet. Another aspect of patients' expectations rests upon the therapist's training. Some sort of training program is found for healers in almost all cultures. Blackfoot Indians, for instance, had to complete a seven-year period of training in order to qualify as medicine men.

7   Finally, the same techniques of therapy are used by healers all over the world. Let me provide a few examples: Drugs are one of the techniques of Western therapy of which we are most proud. However, drugs are used by healers in other cultures as well. Rauwulfia root, for example, which was introduced into Western psychiatry in the 1950s as reserpine,

a major tranquilizer, has been used in India for centuries as a tranquilizer, and has also been in wide use in West Africa for many years. Another example is shock therapy. When electric shock therapy was introduced by Cerletti in the 1930s, he was not aware that it had been used in some cultures for up to 4000 years. The technique of applying electric eels to the head of the patient is referred to in the writings of Aristotle, Pliny, and Plutarch.

8   What kind of results do therapists in other cultures—witchdoctors—achieve? A Canadian psychiatrist, Dr. Raymond Prince, spent 17 months studying 46 Nigerian witchdoctors, and judged that the therapeutic results were about equal to those obtained in North American clinics and hospitals.

9   It would appear, then, that psychiatrists have much to learn from witchdoctors. We can see the components of our own therapy system in relief. We can learn why we are effective—or not effective. And we can learn to be less ethnocentric and arrogant about our own therapy and more tolerant of others. If we can learn all this from witchdoctors, then we will have learned much.

DEFINE: *implicitly, phobia* (4); *edifice, paraphernalia* (6); *ethnocentric* (9).

ANALYSIS

structure   1. How does this article differ in methodology from the preceding selections in this chapter?

2. What method of development other than comparison plays an important part in the selection?

3. List the four kinds of mechanisms used by both witch doctors and psychiatrists.

meaning   4. What is the implication of Torrey's use of these contrastive pairs of words in paragraph 2: *civilized/primitive, Christian/pagan*?

5. Which are more successful as healers, the witchdoctors or the psychiatrists?

6. What is Torrey's "message"?

7. Why does cross-cultural psychotherapy usually fail?

style   8. Discuss the effect of the short sentences in paragraph 2. Would it be wise to use that method throughout the article? In the same paragraph, why does Torrey capitalize "Order of Things"?

WRITING SUGGESTION

Compare the methods of a teacher, doctor, or clergyman you like with those of one that you don't like.

W. T. Williams

BRAINS VERSUS COMPUTERS

[1]   ... In science fiction, which is the literature of extrapolation, there is to be found the recurrent theme of the omniscient computer which ultimately takes over the ordering of human life and affairs. Is this possible? I believe it is not; but I also believe that the arguments commonly advanced to refute this possibility are the wrong ones. First, it is often said that computers "do not really think." This, I submit, is nonsense; if computers do not think, then nor do human beings. For how do I detect the process of thinking? I present data—say, an examination paper—to a student, which he scans with a photoelectric organ we call an "eye"; the computer scans its data with a photoelectric organ we call a "tape-reader." There is then a period when nothing obvious happens, though electrical changes can be demonstrated on the monitor-tube of a computer or on the corresponding device—an electroencephalogram—for the student. Lastly, information based on the data is transcribed by means of a mechanical organ called a "hand" by the student and a "teleprinter" by the computer. In other words, as Gilbert Ryle pointed out, the only evidence we have that people think is what they do, our observations of their actions; and the actions of man and machine differ only in the appliances they use.

[2]   Secondly, it is said that computers "only do what they are told," that they have to be programmed for every computation they undertake. But I do not believe that I was born with an innate ability to solve quadratic equations or to identify common members of the British flora; I, too, had to be programmed for these activities, but I happened to call my programmers by different names, such as "schoolteacher," "lecturer" or "professor."

[3]   Lastly, we are told that computers, unlike human beings, cannot interpret their own results. But interpretation is always of one set of information in the light of another set of information; it consists simply of finding the joint pattern in two sets of data. The mathematics of doing this is cumbersome, but well known; the computer would be perfectly willing to do the job if asked.

[4]   There are, of course, real differences. The memory store of the human brain, though slow and uncertain of access, is vastly larger than that of any computer yet built or conceived; but this is not a fundamental difference, and will become less important as computers get larger. Moreover, computers tend to think in straight lines, like the signal reaching a television tube; they do not immediately apprehend it, as the human brain can, as a two-dimensional pattern of moving images. This is merely because the human brain contains many separate thinking paths, all elaborately cross-connected; whereas even the largest computers have few

Reprinted with permission from *Nature,* March, 16, 1963 ("Computers as Botanists"). Copyright 1963 by Macmillan (Journals) Ltd.

distinct paths, with little cross-connexion. This is purely a matter of computer design, and could be overcome if we so desired.

5   Clearly, then, these well-worn arguments will provide no comfort for those who fear domination by computers. One vital distinction between computers and men, hitherto completely overlooked, does nevertheless remain. It was first pointed out by my colleague Mr. A. R. Manser, to whom I am indebted for permission to reproduce the substance of his argument in this communication. Briefly, human beings *want* to compute; and the reasons for their wanting are unrelated to the things they compute. For human beings are provided with more than brains; they have reproductive systems, digestive systems and the like. These supply them with drives, impulses, needs, wants, desires—and some of these may be satisfied by mental activity. I do not intend any reference to some sort of psychological 'compensation'; I mean only that I may undertake additional mental activity—more work—in order to obtain money to buy a refrigerator, because I enjoy food; or to buy a mink coat, to clothe someone I wish to please. Computers, being only brains, live in a cold world, free from all such desires and free, therefore, from the desire to think; and we shall be safe from their domination so long as we continue to build them solely as brains. If we go further—if we aspire to give them reproductive systems, digestive systems and all the facilities for sensuous enjoyment, then they will no longer be computers but genuine robots; and the world of Karel Capek, Isaac Asimov and Arthur Clarke will be around us at last.

6   But even if we do not make this mistake, one danger remains. Computers, even in the very human field of pattern-making, are so much faster and more reliable than human beings that we may be tempted to delegate to them all our computational activities; computation would then become something that men never do. But something men never do soon becomes something men never teach; and all our knowledge of the manifold skills of computing could be lost within a few generations. So one vital question remains: has the human computer, *qua* computer, any advantages over his electronic counterpart? The answer to this question has long been current in computer circles, though I have been unable to trace its original author.

7   Man has indeed three advantages—advantages which he may well retain even into the far-distant future. First, given his abilities, he weighs less than any computer yet designed or even envisaged: there seems no likelihood that an electronic computer capable of so great a variety of computational facilities can be encompassed within 150 lb., even though the human computer increases somewhat in size and weight after the first fifty years' operation. Secondly, man needs far less energy; his energy requirements, being in the form of food and drink, are intensely inconvenient and clumsy, but they are collectively minute when compared with those of an electronic computer. Thirdly, and lastly, and perhaps most important of all, man is the only computer yet designed which can be produced entirely by unskilled labour.

DEFINE: extrapolation, omniscient, electroencephalogram (1).

ANALYSIS

structure
1. State the thesis in one sentence.
2. What are the three bases for comparison discussed in the first three paragraphs?
3. What are the three bases for comparison used in the last paragraph?

meaning
4. Explain "the literature of extrapolation" and "omniscient computer."
5. Williams indicates that some people believe only computers are programmed. How does he answer this?
6. What is the danger to humans of depending entirely on computers to carry out certain functions?
7. Find the final "advantage" of people over computers that Williams lists. Is it stated seriously or "tongue in cheek"? Explain.
8. What is one of the vital distinctions between men and computers that is generally overlooked?

opinion
9. Do computers pose a danger to humans?

WRITING SUGGESTION

Compare a computer with a human brain.

$ection 6c

Gilbert Highet

PICTURES OF WAR

1 Did you ever try to compare the different ways in which artists, living at different times or in different countries, handle the same subject? It is well worth doing. Usually it tells us something new about each of the artists, and the ages they lived in—something we might have suspected, but never realized with such vividness.

2 Take one powerful subject, which has been much in all our minds in these last years: the sufferings of the civilian population during a war. In wartime—always, from the beginning of history—soldiers and sailors have been able to fight and defend themselves: they can act as well as en-

From *Talents and Geniuses* © 1957 by Gilbert Highet. Reprinted by permission of Curtis Brown, Ltd.

dure. But the noncombatants must only suffer in a world which seems to have gone mad. As soon as I think of this, there leaps into my mind's eye a photograph taken during the Japanese invasion of China. It showed a street, or a highroad, or possibly even a railroad station, partly ruined and apparently still under bombardment. The background contained several dim figures running for shelter. The air was dark with smoke and dust. In the foreground was one human being which epitomized the whole madness and cruelty of war. It was a baby of about two, deserted and alone, its face blackened with earth from shell-bursts, its limbs too small to carry it more than a few yards away, its mind too tormented to understand anything of what was happening, its parents perhaps killed a few moments before. There it sat, with its eyes closed on the universe, weeping bitterly.

3   Now, the same subject—the horrors of war as felt by defenseless civilians—has interested a number of the world's finest painters.

4   The most eminent painter of our generation, Pablo Picasso, made it the subject of his most famous picture: *Guernica*. This was done in 1937, just after the Nazi air force, working for Franco, had carried out, as a tactical experiment, the first saturation bombing raid in history, and had virtually destroyed the ancient Basque city of Guernica. Picasso does not attempt to show us the flaming and exploding city, nor the raiding airplanes. The whole picture, although it is enormous in size, contains only five human beings and two animals.

5   On the extreme right is a man with his mouth gaping in a hideous shriek, and his head thrown back at an angle so impossible that only an ultimate agony could produce it. He stretches two ugly and helpless hands to the black sky; and around him are triangular forms which look like stylized flames. On the extreme left is a woman, also screaming madly in a long endless scream, with a dead baby in her arms. In the foreground are three figures. One is a woman, rushing wildly across the scene—but such a woman as we have never seen except in a nightmare (and such events as this are nightmares, which have become facts). Every one of her limbs is distorted with speed and effort; she seems to be trying to escape from everything, even from her body. Opposite her is the corpse of a man, still clutching the fragment of a weapon, but dead—not only dead, but dismembered. Between the two is a gigantic horse, wounded, and screaming in agony, as though it were calling for death. Near it are the impassive head and forequarter of a fighting bull. (These are the two symbols of death best known to the Spaniards: the helpless horse, and the ruthless bull which attacks and destroys it, long before it is itself sacrificed.) Above this entire picture there is one face, not calm, but at least sane: the idealized face of a spirit, holding a lamp at the center of the scene and gazing on it with grief-stricken amazement. The entire picture is executed in gloomy colors: black, glaring white, many shades of gray. Instead of looking like a normal three-dimensional scene taken from reality and transferred to two-dimensional canvas, it seems to vibrate, to stagger, to jerk abruptly into harsh projections which strike our horrified eyes with something like a physical shock.

6   Look back now for more than a century. Look back to the Napo-

leonic wars. Spain suffered in them also, and a Spanish artist recorded her sufferings then too. This was Goya. His finest painting on this subject is *The Executions of May Third 1808.* Picasso's *Guernica* is all distortion and symbolism. Goya's *Executions of May Third* is all realism.

7   The scene is a little valley outside a Spanish city. There are stately buildings in the background. On the left stand four or five defenseless men in civilian clothes, with expressions of terror in their rough Spanish faces. One of them, all in white, waves his hands as though appealing for mercy. On the right, only a few feet away, is a line of uniformed French soldiers, aiming their muskets at the hearts of the condemned men. In one minute, in one second, they will fire a volley. The line of muskets is steady and efficient, appearing all the more ruthless because all the bayonets are fixed; if the bullets fail, the soldiers will stab the men to death. The soldiers themselves are quite impersonal: resolute efficient figures in uniforms and heavy shakos, their faces almost invisible behind arms raised to fire. (Their steady line, contrasted with the broken group of civilians, reminds us of another essential horror of war—that the forces of destruction always seem to be more efficient and better organized than the forces which build civilization.) In the center of the picture, behind the bayonets, is a group of condemned men waiting for their turn to die; they are kneeling, and hiding their faces, or perhaps weeping. A few corpses are already lying on the ground.

8   Now turn back further yet, another two hundred years, to the age which we know best as the age of the Pilgrim Fathers. Just about the time the Pilgrims were building their earliest settlement, a young man in France was completing a set of pictures which he named *The Miseries and Misfortunes of War.* This was Jacques Callot. He was one of the greatest etchers who ever lived, and probably the first man to turn etching into an independent art. He was born about 1592 (a generation after Shakespeare). His father was (of all things) a herald; and he himself was intended for the church. But he ran away from home twice, because he wanted to be an artist. At last he was sent to Italy for training. It was there that he learned his astounding technique and formed his style. For years he served the Medici in Florence. Then he returned to France, and worked for Louis XIII and other potentates. He himself was not a Frenchman, strictly speaking, but a Burgundian from Lorraine; there is a story that he made a wonderful etching of King Louis's siege of La Rochelle, but refused point-blank to make another picture of the same king's armies besieging his own native city of Nancy.

9   Now, consider one of Callot's etchings of *The Miseries and Misfortunes of War.* When we look at it, our first impression is not of destruction and disintegration, but of order, balance, symmetry, and even grace. It is quite a small picture. Picasso's *Guernica* is an enormous mural, covering many square yards. Goya's *Executions* is eight feet by eleven. Callot's etching is not much bigger than a man's hand. It looks rather like an episode from a picturesque ballet, seen from a distant part of the theater. Then we look more closely into it. We examine the various groups which make up this neat symmetrical composition. We see that, though they are all carefully disposed, and form an over-all pattern which is both pleasing

and intricate, they are not merely posed—like lay figures. There is a good deal of action in their arrangement, and there is a sinister logic.

10 The scene is a small village. In the foreground there is a cottage of two or maybe three rooms, only one story high. There are three or four more cottages visible at the right. Opposite them a large old tree frames the picture gracefully. In the background is a little church, which when full might hold sixty people: the whole population of the village and the surrounding farms. It is an elegiac scene. Immediately in front of us as we look at it, an old cart has stopped, and the horse is hanging its head as though in exhaustion. And then we begin to see that the village has been transformed by a life which is not its own. Figures are climbing all over the cart, figures with gay feathers on their heads, and swords sticking out prominently from their left sides; they are unloading the wine casks and whatever else the cart was carrying. Two groups of what might be dancers, at right and left, prove to contain more of these befeathered and sworded figures. One has grasped a woman by the hair as she runs from him; the other is running rapidly after a terrified girl with his sword in the air. The cottages are smoking, with smoke which does not come from their peaceful hearths. They are burning. And the church itself, the church as we look more closely is seen to be on fire; the steeple is already pouring out smoke which will soon change to flames. On the extreme left a purposeful group of soldiers has discharged a volley of shots from muskets at the church. Apparently the villagers have gathered on its steps and in its churchyard to make a concerted stand. Some of them have guns, and are firing back.

11 But the issue is not in doubt. There is a vicious energy about the organized soldiers which convinces us that they will take this village and loot it as they have taken many more already; they are experienced in this kind of amateur fighting. Some of them have already started looting and raping. Meanwhile, how long will the villagers continue to resist, with the church burning over their heads?

12 This is not a mere atrocity picture. Such events were common during the terrible wars of the seventeenth century—especially in the religious conflicts, when men fought more savagely over religious dogmas than they have ever done over politics. Still, its effect is supremely harrowing. And yet there is a paradox. As an artistic composition, the picture is graceful and harmonious. The lines are deft and delicate, the figures of both murderers and victims are skilfully and not grotesquely posed, the bitter conflicts of emotion are offset by the control and the balance of the design.

13 Powerful, these contrasts between artists—powerful and significant. Working in our own time and using many of the new devices of twentieth-century art, Picasso conveyed the effect of an air raid by using figures which were anatomically (though not spiritually) impossible; which were less real than symbolic. In the early nineteenth century, Goya combined realism with romance; his picture of the execution looks like an eye-witness sketch, but it is in fact a collection of carefully composed and heightened contrasts, meant to play on our emotions. Callot, working in the period when the aim of art was symmetry and control, produced

something comparable to a Bach fugue, combining heart-rending pathos with supreme intellectual and aesthetic detachment. Callot lived in the era of authority. Goya in the era of passion and rebellion; Picasso in—what can we call it?—the era of disintegration?

DEFINE: potentates (8); elegiac (10); aesthetic (13).

ANALYSIS

structure

1. This selection is handled in block paragraph form, each subject being fully discussed before going on to the next. Would it be more, less, or equally effective to use an alternating sentence technique?

2. What are Highet's bases for comparison? (Consider the pictures only, not the artists or historic periods.)

3. Write a short summary of the selection, in which you devote only one or two sentences to each picture.

4. Discuss the overall organization of the selection: introduction, transitions, conclusion.

meaning

5. What, according to Highet, is the advantage of comparing ways in which artists of different periods treat similar subjects?

6. What, to Highet, most epitomized the cruelty of warfare?

7. Why does Highet compare Callot's work with a Bach fugue?

8. Discuss the last three words of the selection.

style

9. Is starting with a question effective?

10. Discuss Highet's use of repetition.

11. Discuss his imperative tone: *"Take," "Look," "Turn," "Consider."*

12. Why does he use a sentence fragment to begin his last paragraph?

13. Analyze one of his descriptive sections carefully. Consider, for example, movement from general to particular, left to right, overall impression.

14. Are his descriptions objective or subjective?

WRITING SUGGESTIONS

1. Compare three pictures on the same subject from three different time periods.

2. Compare three novels about three different wars.

Robert Reginald and James Natal

GEORGE ORWELL'S 1984—HOW CLOSE ARE WE?

Published in 1949, George Orwell's 1984 *is one of the most widely quoted novels of modern times because of its almost omniscient predictions of future events. This selection creates a chilling parallel between Orwell's views and conditions in the world today.*

1. Orwell postulated a future in which the world would be divided among the three superstates of Oceania (the Americas, Great Britain, Australia, and South Africa), Eurasia (Russia, Europe, and Siberia), and Eastasia (China, Japan, Mongolia, and Southeast Asia).

Where We Stand Today: The world of the 1970s is controlled by three great superpowers, the U.S., the U.S.S.R., and the People's Republic of China, either directly, as in Eastern Europe, or indirectly through political and economic weapons. As predicted by Orwell, Eastasia (China) is the weakest of the three powers, with the smallest amount of territory and influence, and has "come of age" as a superpower only within the last decade.

2. In Orwell's dystopian world, the three great nations of the future are locked in a purposely unending war, being fought with conventional arms over the territory of north and central Africa, the Near East, and India. The purpose of this warfare is to gain control of the millions of work slaves living in these regions, thus enabling the controlling state to enlarge its war machine. Also, war consumes vast amounts of resources, without increasing the living standards of the populace, while simultaneously providing citizens with a hate object, something on which they can focus their pent-up emotions and frustrations. Despite the fact that all three powers possess nuclear arms, not one is willing to use them for fear of destroying itself. The alliances between the states are constantly shifting, but no two powers are strong enough to conquer the third, so the stalemate continues indefinitely.

Where We Stand Today: The U.S. fought an 11-year "limited war" in Vietnam, with the Russians and Chinese supporting the Communist side. None of the belligerents used nuclear weapons, although all three had large stocks of atomic bombs. The American loss in Southeast Asia does not appear to have materially affected the balance of world power. The "Big Three" powers are continually vying for the loyalities—and resources—of third-world and undeveloped countries, especially in Africa and the Middle East. These smaller countries use this power struggle to their own advantage; there are at least six nations that receive military aid from China and the U.S.S.R., *and* the U.K. and the U.S. Consequently, alliances shift constantly. Ethiopia, for example, was supplied arms by the U.S. for many years; suddenly, it cut its ties with the Americans and accepted arms from the Soviet Union. Meanwhile, Somalia, Ethiopia's enemy and the Russians' principal base in eastern Africa, is talking about severing ties with

"George Orwell's 1984—How Close Are We?" by Robert Reginald and James Natal in *The People's Almanac No. 2* by David Wallechinsky and Irving Wallace. Copyright © 1978 by David Wallechinsky and Irving Wallace. By permission of William Morrow & Company.

the U.S.S.R. and establishing relations with the Americans. Among the big-power states, China and the Soviet Union were allies until the early 1960s; in the 1970s, China developed closer relations with the U.S. than with the U.S.S.R. and seems to want these ties strengthened.

3. Oceania, as Orwell described it, is made up of three social classes: the proles, the mindless workers comprising 85% of the population; the Inner party, the elite upper 2%, which actually controls the state and lives in luxury; and the remaining 13%, the Outer party, which carries out the directives of the state and serves as a rather impoverished middle class. The members of the party are kept under constant surveillance and are not allowed to deviate from the party line. Individualism is sufficient grounds for execution or brainwashing; the party demands unthinking devotion to its slogans.

Where We Stand Today: In the U.S.S.R., the situation is much as Orwell predicted. Only a small portion of the population actually belongs to the Communist party, and only a minute fraction of party members have any power. The elite maintains all of the privileges of the traditional upper classes: fancy cars (Leonid Brezhnev is a collector of classic automobiles), exclusive living facilities, special stores where "unobtainable" goods can be purchased cheaply. Powerful party members can easily bypass the interminable queues so typical of Russia's economy; the sons and daughters of high officials need not worry about passing the strict entrance exams for law or medical schools. The members of the middle echelon share some of these privileges, but they are relatively few compared to those of their superiors. The price paid for these privileges is unbending conformity to the party line, rigidity of thought, and the suppression of initiative and imagination. China is closer to the communist ideal of shared work and shared profits, but it too has an elite ruling cadre which, though not so hypocritical as its Russian counterpart when it comes to capitalist values, does control much of the power. Of China's estimated 800 million people 70–80% are peasants.

In the U.S., a similar power structure also exists. However, in America the power elite derives its political power more from economic advantage and influence than from government placement. Here, the upper 20% of the population earns over 50% of the nation's income and, further and more significant, controls over 75% of the nation's wealth (real estate, material goods, etc.). According to a 1969 study by the IRS, the top 0.008% (17,500 people) of the American population (those with wealth of over $5 million) own more than the bottom 50% (110 million people) combined.

4. The main instrument of control in Oceania is the telescreen, the two-way television sets stationed in all residences and public places. Telescreens are monitored intermittently by the Thought Police, who are searching for the least sign of deviation. The sets may be turned down, but are never shut off completely.

Where We Stand Today: The cable television systems now covering much of the U.S. provide the nucleus for two-way television communications, and such a network has actually been suggested by government officials, supposedly to provide a means of getting instant citizen response to governmental actions. Present-day TV sets, if hooked into cable systems, can be used as passive receivers even when turned off.

In addition to the potential use of residential television sets for monitoring the population at home, other larger electronic systems have not only been proposed but are already being developed for installation in the near future. For example, in Tampa, Fla., a surveillance system is being developed for the police department that consists of a network of computer-controlled videotape cameras and alarms. These cameras, much like those currently in use by banks, would be placed on top of buildings and overlooking large public areas and would be connected to a central monitor at police headquarters. As explained in the surveillance system development plan: "The video-recording camera is installed overlooking a shopping-center parking lot. The camera surveillance is watched on monitors. When suspicious activity occurs, the operator can utilize the affected camera's zoom lens for a close-up."

Beyond this and other similar camera systems, a more insidious system of specific personal surveillance has been devised, allegedly for use in monitoring the movements of "suspect citizens," known criminals, and parolees. This system involves the use of "transpoders," small computer-connected electronic transmitting units attached to a person in a way that makes it impossible to take them off without alerting the control computer. In almost all cases, such secret surveillance equipment is to be deployed in the name of law enforcement, security, and crime prevention, yet who can guarantee that, once installed, it will not be used for watching the general public "Big Brother"—style?

5. The key to Oceania's control of its population is the manipulation of language. Speech has been deliberately debased to the point where it is meaningless. And, to prevent unorthodox thoughts from entering the minds of party members, a completely new language—Newspeak— is being created to make political heresy impossible due to lack of words to convey nonsanctioned ideas. Inherent in the systematic debasement of language is the principle of "doublethink," the ability to believe two contradictory statements simultaneously, without perceiving the illogic inherent in such a position. The party is the sole arbiter of truth, in all spheres. Hence its slogans: War Is Peace, Freedom Is Slavery, Ignorance Is Strength. The reversibility of these slogans is pointed out to the hero as a graphic illustration of doublethink at work.

Where We Stand Today: The Vietnam War generated prime examples of governmental Newspeak and doublethink. Bombing missions were called "protective reaction strikes," a refugee camp became a "new life hamlet," a "condolence award" was money given to the family of a mistakenly killed civilian, and the American invasion of Cambodia was termed an "incursion." Throughout the conflict, language was used to obfuscate and cover up, and for every other purpose except to convey the true nature of what was really taking place. The Defense Dept. (formerly the War Dept.) told the American public that Vietnam was the key to world peace and security; as Vietnam goes, it said, so goes the Free World. The U.S. lost the war, and very little has changed internationally, except for the loss of over a million lives.

During the Nixon administration, governmental Newspeak and doublethink were rampant. When White House press secretary Ron Ziegler contradicted statements made previously, he termed his former statements "inoperative." Criminal acts were committed under the guise of "national security" and "executive privilege." Lies were told and situations confused at press conferences, often after being preceded by the infamous introduction "Now, let me make this perfectly clear. . . ." Nixon aides abused their power from an "excess of zeal" and not from more ominous ambitions. As in the 1984 slogans, lies were the truth, the truth was a lie.

6. The world of 1984 is puritanical to the extreme, with organized Anti-Sex Leagues (sex is actively discouraged, and is allowed only for the procreation of children; it is anticipated that sex will be dispensed with altogether when test-tube babies are possible).

Where We Stand Today: Chinese society has much the same flavor as Victorian England, with rigid societal controls on sexual mores. Couples are encouraged to remain single until the age of 30, premarital sex is a crime, clothing is purposely unisexual (and generally unattractive), cosmetics are forbidden, and the emphasis of society remains on party loyalty over personal ties. Up until very recently, the Soviet Union was similarly Victorian.

7. In Oceania, history is manipulated continually to reflect current governmental policies, and books and periodicals are rewritten constantly to make them consistent with the latest party line. If Oceania were suddenly to switch its political alliance, then old records must be altered to make it appear that the new alliance had always existed. The party claims credit for inventions of the past, literature, and anything else of value. It was the party, for example, that invented the airplane. With all records changed, and no one alive who knows differently, who can say nay?

Where We Stand Today: The U.S.S.R. maintains that it won W.W. II by defeating the Nazi forces in Eastern Europe. American assistance in the struggle is barely mentioned in the official Soviet histories. The Soviets also have claimed credit in the past for the invention of the first airplane, for television, and for a variety of other modern gadgets. Many of these claims are unsupported. Manipulation of history in the U.S.S.R. is particularly evident in official treatment of former politicos. After his death, Stalin was castigated by Khrushchev and labeled a "monster." Stalin's secret police chief, Lavrenti Beria was also denounced and subsequently executed in December, 1953. Anxious to eradicate any memory of the Stalin era, the editors of the third edition of the *Great Soviet Encyclopedia* mailed a special article on the Bering Straits to encyclopedia owners, who were instructed to paste this article over the existing one on Beria. Current Soviet policy is more lenient, however, and Stalin is once again regarded as a strong leader who helped win W.W. II.

In China, especially during the Cultural Revolution in the late 1960s, people fallen from party grace have been declared "enemies of the people" and sent to undergo "reeducation," and their works, if any, have been withdrawn.

The U.S., too, revises its past. Attitudes toward former enemies change with time; for example, the American Indians, the Japanese, and now Castro in Cuba. Before the Nixon visit, China was considered the "yellow peril." Today it is viewed, though cautiously, as a potential ally against the Soviet Union and as a new partner in international trade.

8. Political orthodoxy in Oceania is maintained by the Thought Police of the Ministry of Love (Miniluv), which uses torture and subtle psychological harassment to force heretics to see the errors of their ways, accept the party without reservation, and learn to love Big Brother, the symbolic head of state whose image is omnipresent and whose godlike image is used to sanction all the actions of the government.

Where We Stand Today: In the U.S.S.R., political dissidents are exiled to Siberia, exiled outside the country, subjected to intensive interrogations and torture by the secret police, or declared insane and confined to mental institutions, where they undergo illegal shock treatments designed to change their personalities. China uses the mass pressure of a conformist society to keep its citizens in line; deviants are forced to confess their sins publicly and promise to mend their ways. The godlike figures of Lenin and Mao Tse-tung, respectively, are hearkened to constantly as the elder sages of Marxist wisdom, through their published writings.

The U.S. government is not above using Oceanic methods to achieve its ends. Both the FBI and the CIA have been involved in domestic spying on American citizens, political leaders, congressmen and senators, and dissident political groups. In the carrying out of these unconstitutional invasions of privacy, these government agencies, as well as branches of the military and local police departments, have resorted to harassment, burglary, wiretapping, opening of personal mail, hiring of provocateurs, and distribution of arrest and tax records of those who were under their surveillance. While no charges of using torture have been leveled, it was reported by the Rockefeller Commission that the CIA provided the faculty for schools set up by the State Department through its Agency for International Development, whose Office of Public Safety trained Latin American police officers. It has been alleged that torture and interrogation techniques were taught in those schools. Further, the countries whose police were trained in the CIA schools—Brazil, Chile, and Uruguay—are high on a list compiled by Amnesty International (a political prisoner relief organization) of countries that officially condone torture as policy.

As Orwell predicted, the differences among the three superpowers are gradually fading. In all three states, national economies are subjected to increasing amounts of governmental control. The government has become the employer of last resort, the provider of welfare for the poor, and the sustainer of health, and it is more and more involved in the private lives of citizens. In all three states, the bureaucracies are expanding, becoming more unwieldy with each passing year. Orwell's *1984* is just around the corner—in more ways than one.

DEFINE: *postulated* (1); *dystopian* (2); *transpoders* (11); *doublethink* (12); *obfuscate* (13).

ANALYSIS

Although Reginald and Natal present an interesting case for an imminent *1984*, it would be worthwhile to examine their material carefully for possible weaknesses. Try some or all of the following methods:

1. Outline the points made in the Orwell sections and see how well each point is countered in the "Where We Stand Today" paragraphs.

2. Look at some of the generalizations very carefully: Is the world situation today really as "simple" as Orwell predicted and Reginald and Natal describe it to be? Are wars, in fact, profitable any longer? Are the workers of the U.S.S.R., China, and the U.S.A. "mindless"? Does TV serve only negative purposes? Add other questions to this list.

3. Consider whether Reginald and Natal might not have strengthened their argument by admitting some differences between this world and Orwell's.

WRITING ASSIGNMENT

Write a comparison/contrast paper in which you show how different today's world is from that which Orwell envisioned.

C. H. Thigpen and H. M. Cleckley

THE THREE FACES OF EVE

These excerpts introduce two of the three personalities of a patient with a split personality. Compare these two personalities; then if you want to meet the third, read the book.

1   She did not at first appear to be an unusual or a particularly interesting patient. This neat, colorless young woman was, she said quietly, twenty-five years of age. In a level, slightly monotonous voice she described the severe headaches from which she had suffered now for several months and for which she had been unable to obtain relief. Unlike some patients to whom the elastic term *neurotic* is applied, she did not say that the pain was "unbearable," or that it was "as if an ax were splitting her skull." Nor did she otherwise take a histrionic role in telling her troubles. Without emphasis she described the attacks.

2   Demure and poised, she sat with her feet close together, speaking clearly but in soft, low tones. Her dark hair and pale blue eyes were distinctly pretty, though she seemed too retiring and inert to utilize, or even to be very clearly aware of, her good features and her potential attractiveness.

3   Her local physician had sent her from her home in a town approximately a hundred miles away for psychiatric consultation. Ordinary physical examinations, X-ray and laboratory studies, had disclosed no cause of the headaches. This superlatively calm, utterly self-controlled little figure of propriety showed no suggestion of anything that the layman might think of as *nervousness*. Her hands lay still on the arms of her chair as she spoke. Her head and shoulders drooped just a little. So thorough was her quality of gentle formality that it was difficult to believe that her eyes might ever flash in merriment, that she could ever have told a joke,

From *The Three Faces of Eve*, chapters 1 and 3. Copyright © 1957 by Corbett H. Thigpen, M.D. and Hervey M. Cleckley, used by permission.

or that even as a child, she could have teased anyone in some spontaneous outburst of feeling.

4   She spoke of serious problems in her life and without evasion discussed a situation that might cause distress, perplexity, worry, and frustration for any person of normal feelings. Six years ago she had married a young man. He was a faithful and serious member of the Catholic Church. As a Baptist, serious too in her own religion, she had had misgivings about the oath she was required to take, an oath promising that her children would be carefully brought up as Catholics. Despite these misgivings she had so committed herself and had intended to carry out the solemn agreement.

5   At the first interview she admitted that she could not bring herself to send her little girl, Bonnie, to her husband's church and to tell her that here was to be found the truth and the only truth, about life's final and deepest problems. She wanted Bonnie to go to Sunday school and to have all the benefits of religion, but she feared that her promise of some years ago would force the little girl into something she might not voluntarily accept if she could be given freedom of choice until she attained sufficient age and experience to consider such matters maturely. She had stubbornly refused to have her child baptized in the Catholic Church. Her mother and father took an active part in the contention between husband and wife, repeatedly urging her not to give in. Her husband had argued that if Bonnie went to the Baptist Sunday school she would be similarly indoctrinated in that faith and hence no better prepared to make a truly impartial decision for herself later in life.

6   Mrs. White discussed this problem not as one who is argumentative or fanatical about religion but with the real perplexity of a meek, conscientious person who is overwhelmed by a distressing dilemma. This young mother's sense of guilt and shame in failing to carry out her vow seemed genuine. Prior to the marriage, despite a deep reluctance, she had been able to promise in all sincerity that any children she might bear would be raised strictly according to the rules of her husband's church. Now, with little Bonnie not a generality but an actual girl of three years, she could not, as she expressed it, turn her only child over to an institution that seemed ever more alien and inhospitable. As time passed she apparently had tended to identify all her husband's faults and all sources of contention between them with his church.

7   Mrs. White did not spontaneously heap blame upon her husband or hold him alone responsible for the sorrows and difficulties of their marriage. In fact, she took pains to defend him and offered magnanimous explanations for some of his attitudes and actions that had made her suffer considerably. With encouragement and unhurried persuasion she reluctantly gave some details of the quarreling that had become habitual. Her husband, she said, had seldom been able to show affection or even friendliness toward her during the last few months. Often he seemed to her irritable or sarcastic. Sometimes she could not tell what had offended him and she found herself puzzled about the nature of his complaints. She finally admitted that on one occasion, quite unlike himself, he had struck her. Though it was apparently only a light slap administered in exasperation, her feelings had been deeply hurt.

8   It was almost impossible to imagine this gentle little woman raising her voice in anger or participating aggressively in a personal argument. Her deep and genuine humility seemed to enforce a meekness upon her that one felt might even prove a serious handicap in what lay ahead. Something about her also suggested a few of the admirable qualities implied in the Christian principle of turning the other cheek. This was a woman, it seemed, not lacking in spirit, but who would not be likely to assert herself actively in opposition to another. Surely it must be an unusual man who would lose his temper with this unprovocative, unvengeful woman. What were the grounds for his anger?

9   "He must have his reasons," she granted thoughtfully. "I am not quite sure what it is I do that aggravates him so." She hesitated, then sadly admitted, "I've never seemed to make him happy."

10   He had apparently lost most of the sexual interest he had once felt for her. Never, she confessed with regret, had she been able to reach an orgasm or any sort of exciting fulfillment in their marriage relations. This regret did not seem to arise from personal disappointment in something she had counted on as exhilarating and important, but from a feeling that she had in this respect given her husband grounds for disillusionment and vexation. She denied any other sexual experience and seemed almost unaware of passionately erotic impulses. Since the general marital status had become so unpleasant, she found physical contact with her husband distasteful.

11   The joy this couple must have felt in each other's presence when they planned to marry had, so far as one could tell, disappeared entirely. Little closeness or sharing of interests and personal feelings had grown between them. It was plain that Mrs. White saw no hope of happiness with her husband. It was equally plain that she did not want a divorce. Though she assumed no air of martyrdom, she admitted that she felt strong obligations to continue her marriage. Her failure to have her little girl baptized in the Catholic Church seemed to augment her determination not to break another vow by seeking relief in divorce. Despite all the unpleasantness that had arisen, Mrs. White in many respects showed a convincing loyalty toward her husband. Serious financial obstacles also stood in the way of any solution through divorce. It seemed evident that little Bonnie was the central focus of this woman's feelings and of her being. Fear of what divorce might do to her child convinced her that, no matter how unhappy the marriage might be, she must continue it.

12   Throughout the long first interview Mrs. White did not raise her voice—nor did she shed a tear. The cadence of her speech varied little. Superficially she seemed at times a dull, colorless person, too bound by propriety and inhibition to manifest herself warmly or adequately. Such an impression was misleading, the examiner soon decided. Behind this restrained expression, this almost stiltedly decorous posture, indications of deeply felt grief, despair and bewilderment, and an almost desperate love for little Bonnie became ever more apparent.

13   Were the emotional conflicts and stresses described by Mrs. White responsible for the attacks of severe headache which had brought her to her local doctor? If so, what could be done to give her relief? In referring to her headaches the patient sometimes spoke of them as "blinding." It was not

easy to tell precisely what she meant by this term. Apparently she did not literally or totally lose her sight, but suffered some of the many visual disturbances often reported in migraine. She also spoke of blackouts which followed the headaches. Though she never seemed deliberately evasive, it was difficult for the examiner to get a clear conception of what occurred during these spells. At times Mrs. White referred to them in such a way as to suggest that she simply fainted; and at times the examiner felt she might be describing more complicated periods of amnesia. Neurologic examination revealed no indication of brain tumor or of any other organic disease that might cause periods of unconsciousness. There was no history of convulsive disorder.

14   So this is how the patient, Eve White, appeared in her first psychiatric interview. She was not undernourished but seemed somehow very delicate, the reticent, meticulous manner suggesting a physical fragility. This manner also tended to make some of the troubles she described seem inevitable. Her clinical symptoms were not unusual. Her personal problems were complicated and serious, but by no means extraordinary. (Both cancer and schizophrenia are, from a statistical point of view, commonplace disorders.)

* * *

15   Having found encouragement in the points just mentioned, the physician emphasized them to the young woman.[1] He was able to assure her, despite what she had told him, that he did not consider her to be psychotic. She spoke of her incessant dread that she would lose her little girl. Relations with her husband seemed to be deteriorating dangerously. No matter what she planned, or intended, or tried to do, events so shaped themselves that instead of progress only retrogression occurred. The headaches had been more frequent and more severe. There had been more blackouts. She could not tell how long they lasted.

16   Eve White was clearly frightened and baffled by something she sought to cope with or to escape. Its dreadful threat was palpable to her, and she braced herself as one who awaits what might prove to be an invisible guillotine. But she spoke softly in her characteristic steady voice. The delicate long-fingered hands remained on the arms of her chair as usual. Their immobility conveyed not relaxation but tensions more acute than she had shown on previous visits.

17   Hoping to avoid a further mobilization of anxiety, the physician endeavored to direct discussion toward the more encouraging features of her situation. She returned, however, to the episode of the clothes. Clerks at the stores where she tried to return them had insisted it *was* she who had bought them. She spoke again of the voice she had heard, apparently wishing to say more and finding herself at a loss for adequate expression. She hesitated. There was perhaps a minute or more of silence.

18   The brooding look in her eyes became almost a stare. Eve seemed momentarily dazed. Suddenly her posture began to change. Her body slowly stiffened until she sat rigidly erect. An alien, inexplicable expression then came over her face. This was suddenly erased into utter blank-

[1] The psychiatrist has just assured Eve that because she heard voices she isn't necessarily psychotic. In fact, she seems to be normal in every way.

ness. The lines of her countenance seemed to shift in a barely visible, slow, rippling transformation. For a moment there was the impression of something arcane. Closing her eyes, she winced as she put her hands to her temples, pressed hard, and twisted them as if to combat sudden pain. A slight shudder passed over her entire body.

19   Then the hands lightly dropped. She relaxed easily into an attitude of comfort the physician had never before seen in this patient. A pair of blue eyes popped open. There was a quick reckless smile. In a bright unfamiliar voice that sparkled, the woman said, "Hi, there, Doc!"

20   With a soft and surprisingly intimate syllable of laughter, she crossed her legs, carelessly swirling her skirt in the process. She unhurriedly smoothed the hem down over her knees in a manner that was playful and somehow just a little provocative. From a corner of his preoccupied awareness the physician had vaguely noted for the first time how attractive those legs were. She settled a little more deeply into the cushions of the chair. The demure and constrained posture of Eve White had melted into buoyant repose. One little foot crossed over the other began a slow, small, rhythmic, rocking motion that seemed to express alert contentment as pervasively as the gentle wagging of a fox terrier's tail.

21   Still busy with his own unassimilated surprise, the doctor heard himself say, "How do you feel now?"

22   "Why just fine—never better! How you doing yourself, Doc?"

23   Eve looked for a moment straight into his eyes. Her expression was that of one who is just barely able to restrain laughter. Her eyes rolled up and to one side for an instant, then the lids flicked softly before opening wide again. She tossed her head lightly with a little gesture that threw the fine dark hair forward onto her shoulder. A five-year-old might have so reacted to some sudden, unforeseen amusement. In the patient's gesture there was something of pert sauciness, something in which the artless play of a child and a scarcely conscious flirtatiousness mingled. The therapist reacted to the new presence with feelings that momentarily recalled some half-remembered quotation about the devil entering the prompter's box. But the patient remained at ease and, apparently, for some reason of her own, quite amused. The silence went unbroken for a minute or more.

24   "She's been having a real rough time. There's no doubt about that," the girl said carelessly. "I feel right sorry for her sometimes. She's such a damn dope though .... What she puts up with from that sorry Ralph White—and all her mooning over the little brat...! To hell with it, I say!"

25   She leaned forward in a little movement that suggested a kitten. With one hand she half-heartedly began to scratch her leg just below the knee. She stretched out the other hand amiably and said, "Would you give me a cigarette, please, Doc?"

26   He handed her a cigarette, and then lighting it, said, "Who is 'she'?"

27   "Why, Eve White, of course. Your long-suffering, saintly, little patient."

28   "But aren't you Eve White?" he asked.

29   "That's for laughs," she exclaimed, a ripple of mirth in her tone. She tossed her head slightly again. "Why, you ought to know better than that, Doc!" She paused and looked at him intently. Her face was fresh and marvelously free from the habitual signs of care, seriousness, and underlying stress so familiar in the face of the girl who had come into the office. Shifting her position in the chair, she raised her hand and rolled a lock of her hair slowly between her fingers. Open-eyed, she looked again directly at him. As an impish smile flickered over her childlike face she said softly:

30   "I know you *real* well, Doc . . . lots better than she knows you . . . . And I kind of like you. I bet you're a good dancer, too."

31   After he had disclaimed any special talents for the dance, they exchanged several inconsequential remarks. Then the physician said, "Can you tell me anything more about those dresses that upset your husband so much?"

32   "I ain't got no husband," she replied promptly and emphatically. "Let's get that straight right now." She grinned broadly.

33   "Well, who *are* you?" he asked incredulously.

34   "Why, I'm Eve Black," she said (giving Mrs. White's maiden name). "I'm me and she's herself," the girl added. "I like to live and she don't . . . . Those dresses—well, I can tell you about them. I got out the other day, and I needed some dresses. I like good clothes. So I just went downtown and bought what I wanted. I charged 'em to her husband, too!" She began to laugh softly. "You ought've seen the look on her silly face when he showed her what was in that closet!"

35   There is little point in attempting to give in detail here the differences between this novel feminine apparition and the vanished Eve White. Instead of the gentleness and restraint of that conventional figure, there sparkled in the newcomer a childishly daredevil air, an erotically mischievous glance, a rippling energy, a greedy appetitite for fun. This new and apparently carefree girl spoke casually of Eve White and her problems, always using *she* or *her* in every reference, always respecting the strict bounds of a separate identity.

36   It was also immediately apparent that this new voice was different, that the basic idiom of her language was plainly not that of Eve White. Eve White regularly gave the impression of a taut fragile slenderness. Perhaps because of the easy laxness of this girl's posture and her more vigorous movements, the lines of her body seemed somehow a little more voluptuously rounded. A thousand minute alterations of manner, gesture, expression, posture, of nuances in reflex or instinctive reaction, of glance, of eyebrow tilting, and eye movements—all argued that this could only be another woman. It is not even possible to say just what all these differences were.

37   It would not be difficult for a man to distinguish his wife (or perhaps even his secretary) if she were placed among a hundred other women carefully chosen from millions because of their close resemblance to her, and all dressed identically. But would one wager, however articulate he might be, that he could tell a stranger, or even a person very slightly acquainted with her, how to accomplish this task? If the husband should try to tell us how he himself recognizes his wife, he might accu-

rately convey something to us. But what he conveyed, no matter how hard he tried, would be only an inconsequential fragment. It would not be enough to help us when we ourselves set out to find the designated woman. So, too, we are not equal to the task of telling adequately what so profoundly distinguished from Eve White the carefree girl who had taken place in this vivid mutation.

DEFINE: *neurotic* (1); *indoctrinated* (5); *unprovocative* (8); *decorous* (12); *psychotic* (15); *arcane* (18); *mutation* (37).

WRITING SUGGESTIONS

1. Very few people suffer the psychological disorder that Eve does; however, we all act differently in different situations. Write a comparison/contrast paper in which you contrast two of your "personalities." Pick two situations from the following list (or devise your own) in which your actions would be quite different: with close friends, with your parents, with your priest or rabbi, at a formal dinner, at a bar, in class, at a ballgame or a fight.
2. Write a comparison/contrast theme about Eve.

Review of Chapter 6

The tight organizational patterns found in most comparison/contrast selections make it reasonably easy for the aware reader to locate the main ideas and quickly see the similarities and differences. Such selections usually lend themselves to outlining for the same reason.

When dealing with poorly organized comparison/contrast articles, readers often have to organize the material themselves, using lists, charts, or outlines to reveal the contrasting elements. If the subject warrants it, they should check the author and his sources for possible bias, judge whether both sides have been presented fairly, and decide whether the most important factors have been considered. In evaluating political candidates, it is best to go to as many sources as possible; in appraising products, not only should one go to competitors but also to consumer magazines that do not accept advertisements.

In writing comparison/contrast papers an outline is advisable for all but the most simple subjects. Although at first glance the task of comparing the subcompacts in Section 6A seems relatively simple, you have to deal with three subjects and four bases of comparison, 12 factors. Should another car and several other factors for comparison be added, the work would become quite complex.

Writers of comparison/contrast papers must be sure to use comparable subjects, be fair, and try to develop a balanced, well-organized piece of work so that the reader can easily discern the similarities and differences. It is often necessary to experiment with several patterns to see which is most effective for your purpose.

WRITING SUGGESTIONS

1. Read the selections "The Monastic Way of Death" and "To Dispel Fears of Live Burial" in Section 7B and compare the two processes.

2. Compare one or both articles with how funerals are conducted in your family.

3. See the Idea Bank for other comparison/contrast possibilities. You might, for example, compare two or more poems or pictures in Unit 8 or ideas about education in Unit 10.

EVALUATION

To make a final appraisal of the selections in this chapter, decide which used the most appropriate patterns to achieve their ends, which could just as easily have used different approaches, and which (if any) were poorly handled.

Process

Analysis ❖❖❖❖❖❖❖❖❖❖❖❖❖❖❖❖❖❖❖❖❖❖❖❖❖

❖❖❖❖❖❖❖❖❖❖❖❖❖❖❖❖❖❖❖❖❖❖❖❖❖❖❖❖❖❖❖❖❖❖❖❖❖

❖❖❖❖❖❖❖❖❖❖❖❖❖❖❖❖❖❖❖❖ CHAPTER 7

READING FOCUS

- ❖ Pay strict attention to every detail and to the exact order of the instructions.
- ❖ Don't follow directions blindly; there should be reasons for each step of a process.

WRITING FOCUS

- ❖ Plan the order of the process analysis carefully, and be sure that every detail in each step is fully explained.
- ❖ Don't take your readers' knowledge of the process for granted. Sometimes your omission of a very small step (which you may perform almost unconsciously) may mean failure for your reader.
- ❖ Warn your readers of any danger inherent in the process.

Process analysis papers are How-to-Do-Something or How-Something-Was-Done papers. They can vary in length and subject matter from recipes telling how to scramble eggs to books or series of books telling how to get to the moon. They can be *directive*, telling the reader how to do something, or *informative*, telling the reader how something was done or might be done in the future. They can be "bare bones" with numbered or lettered directions as in recipes, formulas, and many "how to" books, or they can include a great deal of description and commentary as in "The Monastic Way of Death" and "To Dispel Fears of Live Burial," which you will find in this chapter.

Embellished further, process analysis is sometimes indistinguishable from narration. The excerpt from *The Naked Ape* in Section 2C might well be titled "How Man Evolved," and "Starfolk: A Fable" in Section 7C could be called "How the Universe Evolved." Similarly, "How to Scramble an Egg" can take on narrative form if the writer decides to tell about his adventures in scrambling his first egg (using every pot in the kitchen and leaving the place a shambles); and "How the British Won the Battle of Plassey," usually a historical narrative, can become a bare bones process analysis if the writer wants to pare his work down to numbers, dates, and military tactics.

The importance of accuracy in process writing increases as the importance of the operation increases. The neglect or poor performance of one step in the pouring of concrete has caused dams to collapse; omitting one procedure in a flight take-off system has caused planes to crash; improperly drawn contracts have caused millions of dollars to be lost.

Process analysis papers use other methods of development, too, and we will examine them in the selections ahead. Again, the purpose of such examination is not to play a "naming" game—"When does process analysis become narration or when is classification used?"—but to sharpen your awareness of the various writing techniques available to you.

section 7a

Read all of the selections in this section; then answer the questions.

FRIED BLOWFISH TAILS

INGREDIENTS: 15 blowfish tails, ⅓ cup soy sauce, 3 slices ginger, 1 tablespoon dry sherry, ½ teaspoon Five Spices powder, vegetable oil (about 1 cup) for frying.

PREPARATION: (1) Rinse blowfish tails in cold water and dry with paper towels. (2) Combine soy sauce and seasonings. (3) Marinate tails in sauce for about one hour, stirring occasionally. (4) Drain well in collander before frying.

COOKING INSTRUCTIONS: Deep fry the fish tails in vegetable oil (preheated to 375° F). Serve with your favorite blowfish dip.

HOW WE BREATHE

The human respiratory system functions precisely and reliably without the conscious control of a human being. First the air is drawn into the body through the mouth and nasal passages by the action of muscles contracting and expanding under the lungs. After passing through the bronchial tubes, the oxygen is blown into air sacs which resemble clusters of grapes. The capillaries, tiny blood vessels connecting the arteries with the veins, pick up the oxygen and transport it to the main arteries to the heart, which pumps it to the body cells. While this is taking place, waste gas, carbon dioxide, is transported from the cells to the veins, through the heart, and then to the lungs to be exhaled.

Rachel Carson

FORMATION OF THE EARTH

The new earth, freshly torn from its parent sun, was a ball of whirling gases, intensely hot, rushing through the black spaces of the universe on a path and at a speed controlled by immense forces. Gradually the ball of flaming gases cooled. The gases began to liquefy, and Earth became a molten mass. The materials of this mass eventually became sorted out in a definite pattern: the heaviest in the center, the less heavy surrounding them, and the least heavy forming the outer rim. This is the pattern which persists today—a central sphere of molten iron, very nearly as hot as it was two billion years ago, an intermediate sphere of semiplastic basalt, and a hard outer shell, relatively quite thin and composed of solid basalt and granite.

From *The Sea Around Us* by Rachel L. Carson. Copyright © 1950, 1951, 1961 by Rachel L. Carson. Reprinted by permission of Oxford University Press, Inc.

HOW PLYWOOD IS MADE

1   Plywood is a construction material composed of thin sheets of wood glued together. The process of making plywood involves three major stages: peeling the thin layers of wood from the log, gluing the layers together, and pressing the sheets in large hydraulic presses.

2   Peeling the thin layers of wood from the log is done by a huge lathe. Logs, with the bark removed, are placed in the lathe, which turns them against a long, razor-sharp knife. As the thin, continuous layers of wood are peeled from the log, they slide onto conveyor tables. At this point the layers of wood are inspected for defects, sorted into needed lengths and

From *Writing and Reading in Technical English* by Nell Ann Pickett and Ann A. Laster. Copyright © 1970 by Nell Ann Pickett and Ann A. Laster. Reprinted by permission of Harper & Row, Publishers.

widths, and graded. Then, to reduce the amount of moisture in the layers, they are put through automatic driers.

3   The next major stage in making plywood is gluing together the dried layers of wood. Each layer, as it is placed on another, is turned so that the grain is at right angles with the layer below it. Then the layers are glued together. Each layer, or ply, may be as thin as 1/100 of an inch or as thick as ½ inch. Any number of plies may be glued together.

4   The final stage is pressing the plywood to set the glue. The plywood is put in large hydraulic presses, where heat and pressure are applied. As the plywood comes from the presses, it is sanded and trimmed to specified lengths and widths, depending on the use it will be put to. The finished plywood sheets are now ready to be shipped to the dealer or consumer.

Bernard Gladstone

UNCLOGGING A DRAIN

1   Unstopping a clogged sink drain is an annoying home repair problem that usually occurs on a holiday weekend when a plumber is impossible to reach. (They're not much easier to reach on ordinary weekdays either.)

2   Fortunately, in most cases it is a fairly simple repair the homeowner or apartment dweller can handle—assuming the individual has two or three inexpensive tools needed for the job and is familiar with the basic techniques involved.

3   Widely advertised chemical drain cleaners work on most simple grease and hair stoppages but often fail to penetrate heavy grease, soap, and foreign matter accumulations completely blocking a drain pipe.

4   When using a prepared chemical drain cleaner, it is important to follow carefully the package directions, because some are caustic and harmful to skin and eyes. Generally, they work best when there is only a small amount of cold water in the sink. If the bowl is full, bail most of it before using the cleaner.

5   If the chemical cleaner doesn't work try a "plumber's friend"—a rubber suction cup attached to a wood handle, sometimes called a plunger. This tool is used by placing the bell-shaped rubber cup flat over the drain and by pumping up and down to create pressure and suction. In order for it to work effectively, however, there must be enough water in the bowl to cover the bottom half of the rubber cup when it is in position over the drain opening.

6   If the sink has a stopper, remove it first. A bathroom sink will probably have a built-in metal stopper that is raised by lifting a knob or moving a lever near the spout. To remove the stopper, raise it as high as possible, then twist a half or quarter turn. If this doesn't work you may have to unscrew a nut from the linkage under the sink and get it out.

Copyright © 1978 by Bernard Gladstone. Reprinted by permission.

7 Stuff some rags into the overflow opening at the top of the sink (located under the rim) and place the rubber force cup directly over the drain opening. Press down with a quick, firm shove, then lift with a sharp yank. Push down again, then immediately yank upward. Usually, four or five such up-and-down motions will be adequate to do the job.

8 It is important to place extra emphasis on the upward yank, because in most cases this stroke is more effective in breaking a clog than the downward push. It creates a suction drawing up the clog so it can be removed by the subsequent rushes of water.

9 If repeated use of the plumber's force cup does not free the clog, more drastic action will be required. All sinks have U-shaped traps directly under the drain which is where many clogs develop.

10 Most traps have a clean out plug, as illustrated in the drawing, but those that do not are designed with removable slipnuts at each end of the trap.

11 To clean the trap, remove the clean out plug (if it has one) by unscrewing it carefully with a wrench or a large pair of offset pliers, making sure there is a bucket beneath the plug to catch water and material that will fall. Now use a flexible plumber's "snake" (a springy, steel wire or ribbon) to probe the inside of the trap, and the pipe beyond.

12 Keep twisting the wire or snake as it is pushed into the pipe (some of these snakes have a handle fashioned so the user can keep turning the snake while it is being pushed into the pipe). First, probe into the short vertical length that leads to the sink drain. If nothing is found, probe into the wall or floor where the drain pipe continues.

13 When probing the drain lines with the snake, remember that with steady pushing and twisting, the flexible wire can be maneuvered around bends and through elbows. When an obstruction is encountered, break it by twisting the end and by pulling with a series of short pushes and pulls.

14 If the trap has no drain plug, the trap itself will have to be removed. Loosen the large nuts at each end and slide them up the pipe. The trap can then be slid down and off, but be careful not to lose the rubber washers under each nut.

ANALYSIS

structure 1. Find the thesis statements in "How We Breathe," "How Plywood Is Made," and "Unclogging a Drain."

2. Identify the subject of each major division in Gladstone's article. Can the process be carried out if the order of the three steps is rearranged?

style 3. Which of the selections are not directive?

WRITING SUGGESTIONS

1. Write a simple process paper such as "How to Shop Intelligently," "How to Make Pizza," or "How to Paint a Chair."

2. Rewrite "Formation of the Earth" as a bare bones process using numbered statements. Title it "How to Make an Earth."

George De Leon

THE BALDNESS EXPERIMENT

1 The winos who hung around my Brooklyn neighborhood in 1950 were not funny. With their handout hands, reeking breaths, and weird, ugly injuries, they were so self-rejecting that you could bark them away even while you shoved them a nickel. My friends and I didn't think they were funny, but we observed one thing that always busted us up. Almost without exception, they had all their hair.

2 Seriously: we never saw a bald bum. Have you? When was the last time you remember a street alky stumbler with nothing on top?

3 Black, white, old, young, short, tall, all of them had a full mop. And hair that wouldn't quit. It leaped up as if it were electrified, or shagged down in complete asocial indifference, or zoomed back absurdly neat, gray-black and glued. Inexplicably, it seemed that boozing burned out the guts but grew hair.

4 Fifteen years later, I offered this observation to my undergraduate classes in the psychology of personality. Then, one semester, I decided to get past the laugh, integrate my present self with my past self, and actually test the hypothesis that booze grows hair.

5 I conceived a simple investigation, with the class participating as co-researchers. In the project, we'd get some real data on the density, or rather the incidence, of baldness in a random sample of rummies. The tactic was to beachhead ourselves on the Bowery in New York City, fan out in teams of two, and gradually move up from somewhere around Prince Street to 14th Street, the end of the bum region.

6 On two successive Saturday mornings, the whole research outfit— me, four men, and two women—met on the corner of Bowery and Houston to carry out the plan. Every other derelict who was not unconscious was approached, talked to, and looked at. Since no one usually walks up to a rummy except cops and other rummies, something seemed to happen when two pretty young students of mine would say, "Sir, I'd like to ask you a few questions." The winos would rock a bit and—no kidding— you could almost see a little ego emerging.

7 In planning the research, I decided that we should gather as much information as we could that might be relevant to the experiment. We decided to mark down answers to questions about age, race, ethnicity, marital status, family baldness, drinking life, etc. We even asked our sub-

Reprinted from *Psychology Today* Magazine. Copyright © 1977, Ziff-Davis Publishing Company.

jects where they usually slept (in or out of doors), figuring that, too, might influence their hair growth.

8   While one team member interrogated, the other circled around the subject, studying the head, raised and lowered, to observe the pate. Subjects were evaluated on a four-point baldness scale as hairy, receding, bald pate, or totally bald.

9   Interesting problems developed from the beginning; what appeared to be simple was really complex. When do you call a guy bald? What does "receding" mean? (We dispensed with the use of rulers or vernier calipers, assuming that, bombed or not, the derelict would shuffle off as soon as we pulled out any kind of hardware. We felt grateful that he tolerated the paper, pencils, and questions.) So there was no quantification, no precision. We simply had to make quick judgments.

10   Our teams interviewed over 60 Bowery subjects, paying them a quarter a pop, all of which came out of my pocket. Back at the school, the data were tallied and, sure enough, the results confirmed my intuition. Only about 25 percent could be called receding or totally bald, with the remainder being pated or hirsute. I had been right all along, and we reported the results to the class.

11   But it turns out that the skepticism of annoyed youth may actually be the quintessence of good scientific research. After I enjoyed the laughs and took a few bows, a number of students, not on the teams, were quick to raise some sharp objections.

12   First, and most obvious, was that we needed to study baldness in a group of nonderelicts in order to make proper conclusions. Second, wasn't it possible that the teams had been influenced by my colorful classroom predictions about hairy bums and had tended to judge the subjects as nonbalding?

13   The criticism was first rate. I knew that because it threw me into an immediate depression. I hated the students who offered it. I also knew that we'd have to do the whole study again with new teams and new derelicts. This time, nonderelicts would have to be included, too, and I would offer no advance hypothesis that might bias, in my favor, the way kids looked at heads.

14   I waited a whole academic year, got a new personality class, and this time took no chances. During the lectures, it was necessary to arouse the interest of the class in the broad issue of bums and baldness. So I suggested that derelicts were a special group of people who seemed to lose their hair sooner and more completely than other men. In short, I lied. Morality aside, it was a tough one to tell because I feared that it would shape the kids' perception the other way. They might actually see receding hairlines and shiny heads where there really was only hair. But I had to take the risk of betting against myself to make the win more sure.

15   Out on the turf again, a new and larger research squad of six men and six women worked over five straight Saturdays. They did the Bowery in pairs, interviewing about 80 derelicts.

16   We also went after a comparison group. Any man walking in or out of Bloomingdale's or cruising along 5th Avenue in the 50s was operationally defined as a nonderelict. These fine fellows we decided to call "ster-

lings." "Sterling" male shoppers in tweeds were stopped on a random basis in front of Bloomingdale's revolving doors. They were put through the whole routine of questions about drinking, age, etc., and their heads were carefully checked out. One difference was that we were too embarrassed to hand them quarters, so we didn't. Then, about a month later, to extend our control group, I sent five squads into a faculty meeting at Wagner College and got the same information on 49 college professors in one sweep.

17   Happily, the new set of derelict data turned out the same as the old, and the results of the three comparison groups were more striking than expected. When the information was presented simply as nonbald versus balding (which combined receding plus pated plus total), we found that 71 percent of the college professors were balding, 53 percent of the sterlings, and, of the derelicts (both years), only 36 percent (see Figure 1).

18   There were no ethnic or racial differences, nor were the other factors in the questionnaire very important. Still, age must matter, and it does.

19   Under age 25, we found 17 (21 percent) sterlings, but only one derelict and no professors. In fact, the average age of the sterlings was 37.5, while it was 47.5 for the other two groups. This makes sense, since it takes a lot of years to become either a derelict or a college professor.

20   Figure 2 shows the percentage of balding across several age levels. Naturally, the older men in all groups contain a greater proportion of hair losers. But after age 40, the differences among the groups are fascinating. The sterlings and professors reveal similar rising percentages, with the profs leading. The derelicts, however, in the years 41 to 55, actually show a slight decrease, and of the 50 guys on the Bowery past age 55, only 44 percent showed signs of balding as compared with about 80 percent of the oldies in the other groups. So the stereotype of the balding egghead professor is not contradicted by these data. For the Bowery bum, there's no doubt that he simply keeps his hair.

21   Now comes the hard part: what does it all mean? Though it did not show up in our data, I'm sure that genetics is relevant. Even so, what is the likelihood that only the bums have fewer bald daddies? Not much.

22   These results also rule out ethnic and racial factors. Hair and air didn't go together, since the derelicts who said they usually slept out were no less bald than those who snoozed in the dorms of the flophouse hotels.

23   Are the bums breezier and more carefree? Calm or numbed so that they don't feel the stress that most of us do? Is it the food they eat, or don't eat?

24   No. We concluded that it must be the alcohol and some resulting biochemical activity. It happens, since completing the study, that I've learned that medical literature does point to some interaction between liver damage, alcohol metabolism, the female hormone estrogen, hair growth and retention. Seems reasonable to me.

25   If so, I'm elated that our findings are valid. But, in a way, it doesn't matter. The whole trip started for me back in Brooklyn, as a joke. Later, my students and I really observed, recorded what we saw, and attempted to draw conclusions. Seeking the truth is always an adventure; the scientist is in all of us.

ANALYSIS

structure 1. Draw up two process lists (two columns) to show the differences in De Leon's two research operations.

meaning 2. Was the author's purpose in writing the article to prove that "winos" tend to keep their hair longer than "sterlings," or was there another purpose? Explain.

3. What did the author's students learn from his first experiment?

4. What did you learn about research projects?

5. What interesting reaction did the researchers get when they approached the alcoholics? Discuss.

style 6. What indications are there that the author isn't too serious about his subject?

WRITING SUGGESTIONS

1. Write a process paper about a research project you participated in.

2. Show the process you go through to buy an expensive product.

Read the next two selections as a unit before answering questions.

Matthew Kelty

THE MONASTIC WAY OF DEATH

1   When a monk dies here, unless it is in the middle of the night, the big bell is rung slowly for a longer period, a signal for the monks near the monastery to drop what they are doing and come pray for the Brother that he might have a good trip into eternity. Generally a large number are on hand to gather around the bed and join in the prayers. (We do the sacramental Anointing of the Sick in church for any monk getting on in years or sickly, but long before he is approaching death.)

2   Some moments after his death, all take their leave and the Brother Infirmarian takes over. He first washes the body with care and then clothes it in a fresh habit. There is no embalming, and the only special items are that the anus is stopped up to prevent any draining, and a cloth band is wrapped around the head and under the chin to keep the mouth closed. We call the local hospital for a doctor to come out and remove the eyes for the Eye Bank, to which all the monks are subscribed, or else drive the body to the hospital if the doctor is tied up. We do not paint the face or anything like that, but simply pull his hood up over his head and fold his hands in his sleeves. If he is also a priest, he wears a stole. Then, when

"The Monastic Way of Death," by Matthew Kelty. From *The Last Whole Earth Catalog*, p. 224. Reprinted by permission of Whole Earth Co-Evolution Quarterly, Sausalito, Ca.

all is ready, the body is brought in solemn procession with the community to the monastery church. Since one of the monks is a doctor, the official declaration of his death and all the legal matters are taken care of by him and the local monk notary: the laws are quite detailed.

3   The body is laid out on a pallet or stretcher reserved for the purpose and is placed in the nave between the two rows of choir stalls. Then monks in turns keep watch by the body, two at a time, continuously until the burial. They watch in half-hour turns, reading the Psalms aloud to one another. The Psalms are good poetry and good prayer, and they sit well with the heart in the presence of death when you are alone with it in the deep of night. The Easter Candle is kept burning by the body as witness to our faith in the Resurrection: this is a big candle some four feet tall and as thick as your wrist. This with the large processional cross is used at all death rites. The regular Choir Services continue in the presence of the deceased monk, seven times a day, beginning at three in the morning. At such times the two by the body join the choir. The Choir Services are adapted to the event and are concerned with appropriate themes: time, eternity, death, life, resurrection.

4   The funeral Mass generally takes place the next morning, the Memorial Supper of the Lord. Such a Eucharist is quite filled with hope and with joy, and all eat the bread and drink the cup to faith in the life to come and in prayer for the dead Brother. After the Mass the body is sprinkled with blessed water and a thurible of smoking incense carried around it. Then the procession forms and we carry him out to the graveyard back of the monastery church.

5   There the Brothers have already dug a grave deep into the earth, sometimes with the help of compressed-air shovels, since there is hard clay and shale not far below. We gather around the grave and there are more prayers and readings, the grave is blessed and incensed by the Abbot. Then the Brother Infirmarian goes down into the grave by a ladder to receive the body. Meanwhile the pall-bearers have lifted the body from the pallet on the quilt mat which has three long cloth bands on each side by means of which they lower the monk into the grave. The Brother down below arranges the body, slips the quilt out so they can pull it up, pulls the monk's hood down over his face, covers him with a white sheet, and then comes up the ladder. The ladder is removed and the Abbot steps up and scatters a first handful of earth over him in the form of a cross. The pall-bearers start to fill in the grave quietly and gently, beginning at the feet. When the whole body is well covered they stop and the community leaves, after first kneeling on the earth to ask pardon for themselves and all men. A few remain to finish. Then a cross is erected over the grave and later on the name put on it.

6   For some weeks after his death, a cross stands at the monk's place at table in the refectory to remind all of their Brothers that they may pray for him. During the days after, the monks will be praying their Psalters for him that all may be well with him in the next life.

7   Such a monastic funeral is very simple and beautiful. There is nothing gruesome or morbid about it, nor anything phony or artificial. Death is recognized for what it is: the end of life on earth, and no attempt is made to hide this. The body is treated with reverence and love, but is

not embalmed or falsified in any way. Nor do we use a casket or box, since the Brother is being returned to the mother which bore him and who will keep him in her depths until the last day.

8   Possibly the only one in the cemetery (besides an abbot who died while on a train trip) to be buried in a casket is Father Louis (Thomas Merton). He died in Bangkok and was given a military coffin and flown back to this country by the Armed Forces with other dead. Since there had been a long delay, the Abbot decided not to remove the body from the casket, no embalming having been done. The monks found the large casket in their midst somewhat incongruous, yet noted that it was perhaps fitting that the author of *The Sign of Jonas* should have been buried inside so large a fish. Father Louis was always fond of the genuine character of the monastic funeral, and we wondered that he did not in some way make it known to us that the real Jonas did not stay permanently in the belly of the whale. Other than that he had the regular monk's funeral.

Jessica Mitford

TO DISPEL FEARS OF LIVE BURIAL

1   Embalming is indeed a most extraordinary procedure, and one must wonder at the docility of Americans who each year pay hundreds of millions of dollars for its perpetuation, blissfully ignorant of what it is all about, what is done, how it is done. Not one in ten thousand has any idea of what actually takes place. Books on the subject are extremely hard to come by. They are not to be found in most libraries or bookshops.

2   In an era when huge television audiences watch surgical operations in the comfort of their living rooms, when, thanks to the animated cartoon, the geography of the digestive system has become familiar territory even to the nursery school set, in a land where the satisfaction of curiosity about almost all matters is a national pastime, the secrecy surrounding embalming can, surely, hardly be attributed to the inherent gruesomeness of the subject. Custom in this regard has within this century suffered a complete reversal. In the early days of American embalming, when it was performed in the home of the deceased, it was almost mandatory for some relative to stay by the embalmer's side and witness the procedure. Today, family members who might wish to be in attendance would certainly be dissuaded by the funeral director. All others, except apprentices, are excluded by law from the preparation room.

3   A close look at what does actually take place may explain in large measure the undertaker's intractable reticence concerning a procedure that has become his major *raison d'être*. Is it possible he fears that public information about embalming might lead patrons to wonder if they really want this service? If the funeral men are loath to discuss the subject

From *The American Way of Death.* Copyright © 1963 by Jessica Mitford. Reprinted by permission of Simon and Schuster, a Division of Gulf & Western Corporation.

outside the trade, the reader may, understandably, be equally loath to go on reading at this point. For those who have the stomach for it, let us part the formaldehyde curtain. . . .

4   The body is first laid out in the undertaker's morgue—or rather, Mr. Jones is reposing in the preparation room—to be readied to bid the world farewell.

5   The preparation room in any of the better funeral establishments has the tiled and sterile look of a surgery, and indeed the embalmer–restorative artist who does his chores there is beginning to adopt the term "dermasurgeon" (appropriately corrupted by some mortician-writers as "demisurgeon") to describe his calling. His equipment, consisting of scalpels, scissors, augers, forceps, clamps, needles, pumps, tubes, bowls and basins, is crudely imitative of the surgeon's as is his technique, acquired in a nine- or twelve-month post-high-school course in an embalming school. He is supplied by an advanced chemical industry with a bewildering array of fluids, sprays, pastes, oils, powders, creams, to fix or soften tissue, shrink or distend it as needed, dry it here, restore the moisture there. There are cosmetics, waxes and paints to fill and cover features, even plaster of Paris to replace entire limbs. There are ingenious aids to prop and stabilize the cadaver: a Vari-Pose Head Rest, the Edwards Arm and Hand Positioner, the Repose Block (to support the shoulders during the embalming), and the Throop Foot Positioner, which resembles an old-fashioned stocks.

6   Mr. John H. Eckels, president of the Eckels College of Mortuary Science, thus describes the first part of the embalming procedure: "In the hands of a skilled practitioner, this work may be done in a comparatively short time and without mutilating the body other than by slight incision—so slight that it scarcely would cause serious inconvenience if made upon a living person. It is necessary to remove the blood, and doing this not only helps in the disinfecting, but removes the principal cause of disfigurements due to discoloration."

7   Another textbook discusses the all-important time element: "The earlier this is done, the better, for every hour that elapses between death and embalming will add to the problems and complications encountered. . . ." Just how soon should one get going on the embalming? The author tells us, "On the basis of such scanty information made available to this profession through its rudimentary and haphazard system of technical research, we must conclude that the best results are to be obtained if the subject is embalmed before life is completely extinct—that is, before cellular death has occurred. In the average case, this would mean within an hour after somatic death." For those who feel that there is something a little rudimentary, not to say haphazard, about this advice, a comforting thought is offered by another writer. Speaking of fears entertained in early days of premature burial, he points out, "One of the effects of embalming by chemical injection, however, has been to dispel fears of live burial." How true; once the blood is removed, chances of live burial are indeed remote.

8   To return to Mr. Jones, the blood is drained out through the veins and replaced by embalming fluid pumped in through the arteries. As noted in *The Principles and Practices of Embalming,* "every operator has a favorite in-

jection and drainage point—a fact which becomes a handicap only if he fails or refuses to forsake his favorites when conditions demand it." Typical favorites are the carotid artery, femoral artery, jugular vein, subclavian vein. There are various choices of embalming fluid. If Flextone is used, it will produce a "mild, flexible rigidity. The skin retains a velvety softness, the tissues are rubbery and pliable. Ideal for women and children." It may be blended with B. and G. Products Company's Lyf-Lyk tint, which is guaranteed to reproduce "nature's own skin texture . . . the velvety appearance of living tissue." Suntone comes in three separate tints: Suntan; Special Cosmetic Tint, a pink shade "especially indicated for young female subjects"; and Regular Cosmetic Tint, moderately pink.

9   About three to six gallons of a dyed and perfumed solution of formaldehyde, glycerin, borax, phenol, alcohol and water is soon circulating through Mr. Jones, whose mouth has been sewn together with a "needle directed upward between the upper lip and gum and brought out through the left nostril," with the corners raised slightly "for a more pleasant expression." If he should be bucktoothed, his teeth are cleaned with Bon Ami and coated with colorless nail polish. His eyes, meanwhile, are closed with flesh-tinted eye caps and eye cement.

10   The next step is to have at Mr. Jones with a thing called a trocar. This is a long, hollow needle attached to a tube. It is jabbed into the abdomen, poked around the entrails and chest cavity, the contents of which are pumped out and replaced with "cavity fluid." This done, and the hole in the abdomen sewn up, Mr. Jones's face is heavily creamed (to protect the skin from burns which may be caused by leakage of the chemicals), and he is covered with a sheet and left unmolested for a while. But not for long—there is more, much more, in store for him. He had been embalmed, but not yet restored, and the best time to start the restorative work is eight to ten hours after embalming, when the tissues have become firm and dry.

11   The object of all this attention to the corpse, it must be remembered, is to make it presentable for viewing in an attitude of healthy repose. "Our customs require the presentation of our dead in the semblance of normality . . . unmarred by the ravages of illness, disease or mutilation," says Mr. J. Sheridan Mayer in his *Restorative Art*. This is rather a large order since few people die in the full bloom of health, unravaged by illness and unmarked by some disfigurement. The funeral industry is equal to the challenge: "In some cases the gruesome appearance of a mutilated or disease-ridden subject may be quite discouraging. The task of restoration may seem impossible and shake the confidence of the embalmer. This is the time for intestinal fortitude and determination. Once the formative work is begun and affected tissues are cleaned or removed, all doubts of success vanish. It is surprising and gratifying to discover the results which may be obtained."

12   The embalmer, having allowed an appropriate interval to elapse, returns to the attack, but now he brings into play the skill and equipment of sculptor and cosmetician. Is a hand missing? Casting one in plaster of Paris is a simple matter. "For replacement purposes, only a cast of the back of the hand is necessary; this is within the ability of the average

operator and is quite adequate." If a lip or two, a nose or an ear should be missing, the embalmer has at hand a variety of restorative waxes with which to model replacements. Pores and skin texture are simulated by stippling with a little brush, and over this cosmetics are laid on. Head off? Decapitation cases are rather routinely handled. Ragged edges are trimmed, and head joined to torso with a series of splints, wires and sutures. It is a good idea to have a little something at the neck—a scarf or high collar—when time for viewing comes. Swollen mouth? Cut out tissue as needed from inside the lips. If too much is removed, the surface contour can easily be restored by padding with cotton. Swollen necks and cheeks are reduced by removing tissue through vertical incisions made down each side of the neck. "When the deceased is casketed, the pillow will hide the suture incisions . . . as an extra precaution against leakage, the suture may be painted with liquid sealer."

13   The opposite condition is more likely to present itself—that of emaciation. His hypodermic syringe now loaded with massage cream, the embalmer seeks out and fills the hollowed and sunken areas by injection. In this procedure the backs of the hands and fingers and the under-chin area should not be neglected.

14   Positioning the lips is a problem that recurrently challenges the ingenuity of the embalmer. Closed too tightly, they tend to give a stern, even disapproving expression. Ideally, embalmers feel, the lips should give the impression of being ever so slightly parted, the upper lip protruding slightly for a more youthful appearance. This takes some engineering, however, as the lips tend to drift apart. Lip drift can sometimes be remedied by pushing one or two straight pins through the inner margin of the lower lip and then inserting them between the two front upper teeth. If Mr. Jones happens to have no teeth, the pins can just as easily be anchored in his Armstrong Face Former and Denture Replacer. Another method to maintain lip closure is to dislocate the lower jaw, which is then held in its new position by a wire run through holes which have been drilled through the upper and lower jaws at the midline. As the French are fond of saying, *il faut souffrir pour être belle.*[1]

15   If Mr. Jones has died of jaundice, the embalming fluid will very likely turn him green. Does this deter the embalmer? Not if he has intestinal fortitude. Masking pastes and cosmetics are heavily laid on, burial garments and casket interiors are color-correlated with particular care, and Jones is displayed beneath rose-colored lights. Friends will say, "How *well* he looks." Death by carbon monoxide, on the other hand, can be rather a good thing from the embalmer's viewpoint: "One advantage is the fact that this type of discoloration is an exaggerated form of a natural pink coloration." This is nice because the healthy glow is already present and needs but little attention.

16   The patching and filling completed, Mr. Jones is now shaved, washed and dressed. Cream-based cosmetic, available in pink, flesh, suntan, brunette and blond, is applied to his hands and face, his hair is shampooed and combed (and, in the case of Mrs. Jones, set), his hands manicured. For the horny-handed son of toil special care must be taken;

[1] You have to suffer if you want to be beautiful.

cream should be applied to remove ingrained grime, and the nails cleaned. "If he were not in the habit of having them manicured in life, trimming and shaping is advised for better appearance—never questioned by kin."

17   Jones is now ready for casketing (this is the present participle of the verb "to casket"). In this operation, his right shoulder should be depressed slightly "to turn the body a bit to the right and soften the appearance of lying flat on the back." Positioning the hands is a matter of importance, and special rubber positioning blocks may be used. The hands should be cupped slightly for a more lifelike, relaxed appearance. Proper placement of the body requires a delicate sense of balance. It should lie as high as possible in the casket, yet not so high that the lid, when lowered, will hit the nose. On the other hand, we are cautioned, placing the body too low "creates the impression that the body is in a box."

18   Jones is next wheeled into the appointed slumber room where a few last touches may be added—his favorite pipe placed in his hand or, if he was a great reader, a book propped into position. (In the case of little Master Jones a Teddy bear may be clutched.) Here he will hold open house for a few days, visiting hours 10 A.M. to 9 P.M.

DEFINE: *perpetuation* (1); *formaldehyde* (3); *cadaver* (5); *trocar* (10).

ANALYSIS

structure
1. Outline "The Monastic Way of Death." List only the main steps in the process.

2. At what paragraph in "The Monastic Way of Death" does the process analysis end?

3. What is Mitford's thesis?

style
4. Kelty's style can be characterized as reverent and Mitford's as irreverent, even sarcastic. Give examples of words and phrases that reveal the writers' attitudes toward their subjects.

5. What is Mitford's purpose in using "he" in the last sentence instead of "the funeral home" or "the family"?

opinion
6. What kind of funeral do you think Mitford would prefer? Explain.

7. Now that you know the nature of embalming, would you advocate its use on yourself or one of your loved ones? Discuss.

8. Since many religious people hold that the soul departs the body at death, why do they purchase cushioned, water-proofed caskets for their loved ones?

WRITING SUGGESTIONS

1. With information taken from the Mitford article, write extended directions for embalming a corpse.

2. Write an extended process analysis of a funeral you participated in.

3. Tell how your funeral arrangements should be handled.

William A. Nolen

THE FIRST APPENDECTOMY

The patient, or better, victim, of my first major surgical venture was a man I'll call Mr. Polansky. He was fat, he weighed one hundred and ninety pounds and was five feet eight inches tall. He spoke only broken English. He had had a sore abdomen with all the classical signs and symptoms of appendicitis for twenty-four hours before he came to Bellevue.

After two months of my internship, though I had yet to do anything that could be decently called an "operation," I had had what I thought was a fair amount of operating time. I'd watched the assistant residents work, I'd tied knots, cut sutures and even, in order to remove a skin lesion, made an occasional incision. Frankly, I didn't think that surgery was going to be too damn difficult. I figured I was ready, and I was chomping at the bit to go, so when Mr. Polansky arrived I greeted him like a long-lost friend. He was overwhelmed at the interest I showed in his case. He probably couldn't understand why any doctor should be so fascinated by a case of appendicitis: wasn't it a common disease? It was just as well that he didn't realize my interest in him was so personal. He might have been frightened, and with good reason.

At any rate, I set some sort of record in preparing Mr. Polansky for surgery. He had arrived on the ward at four o'clock. By six I had examined him, checked his blood and urine, taken his chest x-ray and had him ready for the operating room.

George Walters, the senior resident on call that night, was to "assist" me during the operation. George was older than the rest of us. I was twenty-five at this time and he was thirty-two. He had taken his surgical training in Europe and was spending one year as a senior resident in an American hospital to establish eligibility for the American College of Surgeons. He had had more experience than the other residents and it took a lot to disturb his equanimity in the operating room. As it turned out, this made him the ideal assistant for me.

5   It was ten o'clock when we wheeled Mr. Polansky to the operating room. At Bellevue, at night, only two operating rooms were kept open—there were six or more going all day—so we had to wait our turn. In the time I had to myself before the operation I had reread the section on appendectomy in the *Atlas of Operative Technique* in our surgical library, and had spent half an hour tying knots on the bedpost in my room. I was, I felt, "ready."

I delivered Mr. Polansky to the operating room and started an intravenous going in his arm. Then I left him to the care of the anesthetist. I had ordered a sedative prior to surgery, so Mr. Polansky was drowsy. The anesthetist, after checking his chart, soon had him sleeping.

Once he was asleep I scrubbed the enormous expanse of Mr. Polansky's abdomen for ten minutes. Then, while George placed the sterile

From *The Making of a Surgeon,* by William A. Nolen. Copyright © 1968, 1970 by William A. Nolen, M.D. Reprinted by permission of Random House, Inc.

drapes, I scrubbed my own hands for another five, mentally reviewing each step of the operation as I did so. Donning gown and gloves I took my place on the right side of the operating-room table. The nurse handed me the scalpel. I was ready to begin.

Suddenly my entire attitude changed. A split second earlier I had been supremely confident; now, with the knife finally in my hand, I stared down at Mr. Polansky's abdomen and for the life of me could not decide where to make the incision. The "landmarks" had disappeared. There was too much belly.

George waited a few seconds, then looked up at me and said, "Go ahead."

"What?" I asked.

"Make the incision," said George.

"Where?" I asked.

"Where?"

"Yes," I answered, "where?"

"Why, here, of course," said George and drew an imaginary line on the abdomen with his fingers.

I took the scalpel and followed where he had directed. I barely scratched Mr. Polansky.

"Press a little harder," George directed. I did. The blade went through the skin to a depth of perhaps one sixteenth of an inch.

"Deeper," said George.

There are five layers of tissue in the abdominal wall: skin, fat, fascia (a tough membranous tissue), muscle and peritoneum (the smooth, glistening, transparent inner lining of the abdomen). I cut down into the fat. Another sixteenth of an inch.

"Bill," said George, looking up at me, "this patient is big. There's at least three inches of fat to get through before we even reach the fascia. At the rate you're going, we won't be into the abdomen for another four hours. For God's sake, will you cut?"

I made up my mind not to be hesitant. I pressed down hard on the knife, and suddenly we were not only through the fat but through the fascia as well.

"Not that hard," George shouted, grabbing my right wrist with his left hand while with his other hand he plunged a gauze pack into the wound to stop the bleeding. "Start clamping," he told me.

The nurse handed us hemostats and we applied these to the numerous vessels I had so hastily opened. "All right," George said, "start tying."

I took the ligature material from the nurse and began to tie off the vessels. Or rather, I tried to tie off the vessels, because suddenly my knot-tying proficiency had melted away. The casual dexterity I had displayed on the bedpost a short hour ago was nowhere in evidence. My fingers, greasy with fat, simply would not perform. My ties slipped off the vessels, the sutures snapped in my fingers, at one point I even managed to tie the end of my rubber glove into the wound. It was, to put it bluntly, a performance in fumbling that would have made Robert Benchley blush.

Here I must give my first paean of praise to George. His patience during the entire performance was nothing short of miraculous. The temptation to pick up the catgut and do the tying himself must have been strong. He could have tied off all the vessels in two minutes. It took me twenty.

Finally we were ready to proceed. "Now," George directed, "split the muscle. But gently, please."

I reverted to my earlier tack. Fiber by fiber I spread the muscle which was the last layer but one that kept us from the inside of the abdomen. Each time I separated the fibres and withdrew my clamp, the fibers rolled together again. After five minutes I was no nearer the appendix than I had been at the start.

George could stand it no longer. But he was apparently afraid to suggest I take a more aggressive approach, fearing I would stick the clamp into, or possibly through, the entire abdomen. Instead he suggested that he help me by spreading the muscle in one direction while I spread it in the other. I made my usual infinitesimal attack on the muscle. In one fell swoop George spread the rest.

"Very well done," he complimented me. "Now let's get in."

30   We each took a clamp and picked up the tissue-paper-thin peritoneum. After two or three hesitant attacks with the scalpel I finally opened it. We were in the abdomen.

"Now," said George, "put your fingers in, feel the cecum [the portion of the bowel to which the appendix is attached] and bring it into the wound."

I stuck my right hand into the abdomen. I felt around—but what was I feeling? I had no idea.

It had always looked so simple when the senior resident did it. Open the abdomen, reach inside, pull up the appendix. Nothing to it. But apparently there was.

Everything felt the same to me. The small intestine, the large intestine, the cecum—how did one tell them apart without seeing them? I grabbed something and pulled it into the wound. Small intestine. No good. Put it back. I grabbed again. This time it was the sigmoid colon. Put it back. On my third try I had the small intestine again.

35   "The appendix must be in an abnormal position," I said to George. "I can't seem to find it."

"Mind if I try?" he asked.

"Not at all," I answered. "I wish you would."

Two of his fingers disappeared into the wound. Five seconds later they emerged, cecum between them, with the appendix flopping from it.

"Stuck down a little," he said kindly. "That's probably why you didn't feel it. It's a hot one," he added. "Let's get at it."

40   The nurse handed me the hemostats, and one by one I applied them to the mesentery of the appendix—the veil of tissue in which the blood vessels run. With George holding the veil between his fingers I had no trouble; I took the ligatures and tied the vessels without a single error. My confidence was coming back.

"Now," George directed, "put in your purse string." (The cecum is a portion of the bowel which has the shape of half a hemisphere. The appendix projects from its surface like a finger. In an appendectomy the routine procedure is to tie the appendix at its base and cut it off a little beyond the tie. Then the remaining stump is inverted into the cecum and kept there by tying the purse-string stitch. This was the stitch I was now going to sew.)

It went horribly. The wall of the cecum is not very thick—perhaps one eighth of an inch. The suture must be placed deeply enough in the wall so that it won't cut through when tied, but not so deep as to pass all the way through the wall. My sutures were alternately too superficial or too deep, but eventually I got the job done.

"All right," said George, "let's get the appendix out of here. Tie off the base."

45   "Now cut off the appendix."

At least in this, the definitive act of the operation, I would be decisive. I took the knife and with one quick slash cut through the appendix—too close to the ligature.

"Oh oh, watch it," said George. "That tie is going to slip."

It did. The appendiceal stump lay there, open. I felt faint.

"Don't panic," said George. "We've still got the purse string. I'll push the stump in—you pull up the stitch and tie. That will take care of it."

50   I picked up the two ends of the suture and put in the first stitch. George shoved the open stump into the cecum. It disappeared as I snugged my tie. Beautiful.

"Two more knots," said George. "Just to be safe."

I tied the first knot and breathed a sigh of relief. The appendiceal stump remained out of sight. On the third knot—for the sake of security—I pulled a little tighter. The stitch broke; the open stump popped up; the cecum disappeared into the abdomen. I broke out in a cold sweat and my knees started to crumble.

Even George momentarily lost his composure. "For Christ's sake, Bill," he said, grasping desperately for the bowel, "what did you have to do that for?" The low point of the operation had been reached.

By the time we had retrieved the cecum, Mr. Polansky's peritoneal cavity had been contaminated. My self-confidence was shattered. And still George let me continue. True, he all but held my hand as we retied and resutured, but the instruments were in my hand.

55   The closure was anticlimactic. Once I had the peritoneum sutured, things went reasonably smoothly. Two hours after we began, the operation was over. "Nice job," George said, doing his best to sound sincere.

"Thanks," I answered, lamely.

The scrub nurse laughed.

Mr. Polansky recovered, I am happy to report, though not without a long and complicated convalescence. His bowel refused to function normally for two weeks and he became enormously distended. He was referred to at our nightly conferences as "Dr. Nolen's pregnant man." Each time the reference was made, it elicited a shudder from me.

During his convalescence I spent every spare moment I could at Mr. Polansky's bedside. My feelings of guilt and responsibility were overwhelming. If he had died I think I would have given up surgery for good.

structure 1. Outline the steps in performing an appendectomy.

2. What aspects of this selection move it into the narrative category?

3. Why is it also a process analysis?

style 4. Discuss the effect of expressions like "too damn difficult" and "chomping at the bit" (paragraph 2).

5. Is the term "victim" in the first sentence meant to be humorous? Explain.

opinion 6. Seeing how nervous Nolen was, should Dr. Walters have taken over the operation?

7. Does this article alter your attitude toward surgeons?

8. How can patients be better protected without impeding the training of doctors?

WRITING SUGGESTION

Using your outline of the steps followed in performing an appendectomy, write a process analysis paragraph.

section 7c

Anne C. Bernstein

HOW CHILDREN LEARN ABOUT SEX AND BIRTH

> *"To get a baby, go to the store and buy a duck."*
> —Susan, a four year old

Every day, thousands of parents sit down to tell their offspring about the birds and the bees. And the cows. And the chickens. And the ducks. Parental descriptions of sex and birth often sound like morning roll call on Noah's Ark. When it comes to people, the lecture suddenly takes on the clinical precision of an advanced anatomy course, as the anxious parent rushes through enough detail to confuse a medical student.

Children take this information, process it through mental jungle gyms, and create their own versions of who comes from where, and how. The children seem content with their answers, and parents, having pro-

Reprinted from *Psychology Today* Magazine. Copyright © 1975, Ziff-Davis Publishing Company.

vided the answers, are not about to start following up with more questions. Chances are, therefore, that misunderstanding will persist.

The most effective way to tell children about sex is to provide information matched to their level of mental development. But because no one ever asks children what they really believe, as opposed to what they were told, we don't understand how their ability to analyze and assimilate information changes year by year.

As part of my research at the University of California, Berkeley, I decided to find out how children understood the explanations and gossip that form their early sex education. With Philip A. Cowan, I devised an interview plan that amounted to turning back on children their perennial question, "How do people get babies?"

5   It might seem as if the answer to that question will depend on what a child has been told, but that's not the case. Even when adults give children straight facts, the story of human reproduction often gets twisted into a remarkable version of creation.

Jane, aged four, told me: "To get a baby to grow in your tummy, you just make it first. You put some eyes on it. Put the head on, and hair, some hair, all curls. You make it with head stuff you find in the store that makes it for you. Well, the mommy and daddy make the baby and then they put it in the tummy and then it goes quickly out."

Jane had never been told, by parents, peers or sex-education books, that babies were manufactured, using parts purchased from the store. She put together the answer out of information gathered and given, and held together by a thread of childish logic that reflected her understanding of the physical world.

Jane's story comes from my interviews with 60 boys and girls, all of whom had younger brothers and sisters. They were all white, middle- and upper-middle-class children who lived in a university community. One third of the children were either three or four years old; one third were seven or eight; and one third were 11 or 12. The children's ages corresponded to certain developmental levels suggested by Swiss psychologist Jean Piaget.

Piaget regards each child as a philosopher who works at making his universe intelligible. As the child develops, he shapes the world in terms of his own level of understanding and then restructures his understanding when he gets new information that doesn't fit his old view of the universe.

10   Answers to my questions fell into six levels of maturity that show a consistent sequence of development. The differences between any two levels reflect a difference in problem-solving strategies. It's the structure of a child's answer, not its content, that distinguishes one level from another.

LEVEL ONE: GEOGRAPHY. The youngest children answered the question, "How do people get babies?" as if it were a question about geography. These children, usually three to four years old, told me:

"You go to a baby store and buy one."

"From tummies."

"From God's place."

15   "It just grows inside mommy's tummy. It's there all the time.

Mommy doesn't have to do anything. She just waits until she feels it."
Antonia, who will soon be four, carried on the following conversation:

ME: How did your brother start to be in your mommy's tummy?

ANTONIA: Um, my baby just went in my mommy's tummy.

ME: How did he go in?

ANTONIA: He was just in my mommy's tummy.

20 ME: Before you said that he wasn't there when you were there. Was he?

ANTONIA: Yeah, and then he was in the other place . . . in America.

ME: In America?

ANTONIA: Yeah, in somebody else's tummy. And then he went through somebody's vagina, then he went in my mommy's tummy.

ME: In whose tummy was he before?

25 ANTONIA: Um, I don't know who his, her name is. It's a her.

This little girl, typical of level-one children, believes a baby that now exists has always existed. The only real question is where he was before he came to live at her house. She knows that her brother grew inside her mother's body. How and when he happened to grow there is beyond her grasp, but she extrapolates from the information she has: babies grow inside tummies and come out vaginas. Before her brother was in her mother's tummy, he must have been in somebody else's tummy, and that somebody must be female because only big girls can grow babies. Presumably this chain can go on indefinitely, with each mommy getting her baby in turn from another woman.

The level-one child does not understand the laws of cause and effect. His belief that babies have always existed is consistent with his conviction that he and all the people he knows have always existed. He cannot imagine a world without himself in it.

LEVEL TWO: MANUFACTURING. This is a level that Henry Ford would have recognized and admired, for these children believe that babies are manufactured by people as if they were refrigerators, TV sets or automobiles. A level-two child knows that babies have not always existed; they must be built.

According to four-year-old Laura, "When people are already made, they make some other people. They make the bones inside, and blood. They make skin. They make the skin first and then they make blood and bones. They paint the blood, paint the red blood and the blue blood." Asked how babies start to be in mommies' tummies, she replied: "Maybe from people. They just put them in the envelope and fold them up and the mommy puts them in her 'gina and they just stay in there." Asked where the babies were before they were in the envelope, she answered, "They buy them at the store."

30 These children seem undeterred by the fact that they've never seen a baby factory or a rack of diapered infants at the local supermarket. When provoked by curiosity or question, they simply make up answers, fitting what they have been told and what they have seen into their view of the world. Because children at this level believe that everything in the world has been made either by a magicianlike God or by people, they assume that babies are created in a similar way.

These children are still egocentric; they can interpret the world only in terms of events or processes they have experienced themselves. Therefore, they often fall into the "digestive fallacy," and believe that babies are conceived by swallowing and born by elimination. One four-year-old boy uses the digestive process to explain how mommies and daddies get to be parents. He says that God makes mommies and daddies "with a little seed": "He puts it down on the table. Then it grows bigger. The people grow together. He makes them eat the seed and then they grow to be people from skel'tons at God's place. Then they stand up and go someplace else where they could live."

A few children at level two connect a father with the birth process, but fit what they have been told to a mechanical process. One girl said, "he puts his hand in his tummy and gets it [the seed] and puts it on the bottom of the mommy and the mommy gets the egg out of her tummy and puts the egg on top of the seed. And then they close their tummies and the baby is born." The child believes that the seed and the egg can come together only by manual means. She conscientiously tried to fit what she had been told about reproduction into physical processes, but she had a few doubts. She told me that "the daddy can't really open up all his tummies."

LEVEL THREE: TRANSITIONAL. Children at this level explain procreation as a mixture of physiology and technology, but they stick to operations that are technically feasible. A level-three child knows that mommy and daddy can't open and close their tummies, but he may assume that conception is impossible without marriage. He may also take quite literally his parents' explanation of conception as "planting a seed." Jack, aged four, told me: "The daddy plants the seed like a flower, I think, except you don't need dirt."

A child at this level of understanding still believes that the world of nature is alive; he talks about nonliving and living things as if they possessed will and acted purposefully. Jeanne, who is seven, said: "The sperm goes into the mommy to each egg and puts it, makes the egg safe. So if something bump comes along it won't crack the egg. The sperm comes from the daddy. It swims into the penis, and I think it makes a little hole and then it swims into the vagina. It has a little mouth and it bites a hole."

35   Level-three children may know that three major ingredients go into making babies: social relationships such as love and marriage; sexual intercourse; and the union of sperm and ovum. However, their ability to combine these factors into a coherent whole is limited. These children are in a transitional period between the stages of development that Piaget calls preoperational and concrete operational.

A preoperational child builds mental maps based on his own experiences; he solves problems by intuition. He cannot assign objects to categories. Asked to define an apple, he's likely to say, "It's to eat." As he moves into the next stage, which can happen any time between seven and 10 years old, he learns to think systematically and generally about concrete objects. Ask him about an apple now, and he'll say, "It's a fruit."

During this transitional period, children are often aware that their explanations don't quite add up. Ursula, who is eight, describes the father's role in reproduction: "Well, he puts his penis right in the place where the baby comes out and somehow it [sperm] comes out of there. It seems like magic sort of, 'cause it just comes out."

Asked why the male contribution is necessary, Ursula, who has seen cartons of eggs in the refrigerator, replied: "Well, the father puts the shell, I forget what it's called, but he puts something in for the egg. If he didn't, then a baby couldn't come. Because it needs the stuff that the father gives. It helps it grow. I think that the stuff has the food part, maybe, and maybe it helps protect it. I think he gives the shell part, and the shell part, I think, is the skin."

Her description transforms the father's traditional social role as family protector into a literal protector of the growing baby. His genetic contribution is first a protective shell for the egg, and then the outer covering of the baby.

40   LEVEL FOUR: CONCRETE PHYSIOLOGY. At levels four through six, the eight- to 12-year-old children give primarily physiological explanations. They can think logically about objects and people and can consider past and future. They understand the idea of cause and effect.

Although level-four children may know the physical facts of life, they don't understand why genetic material must unite before new life can begin. One child thought that sperm existed primarily to provide an escort service: "The sperm reaches the eggs. It looses 'em and brings 'em down to the forming place, I think that's right, and it grows until it's ready to take out."

Karen, who is eight, explained: "The man and the woman get together, and then they put a speck, then the man has his seed and the woman has an egg. They have to come together or else the baby won't really get hatched very well. The seed makes the egg grow. It's just like plants. If you plant a seed, a flower will grow."

Karen knew that sexual intercourse provides a means for the seed and egg to come together. She knew that both are necessary to create new life, but she had no clear idea of why this was so. Nor did she attempt to reason her way to a solution.

Karen's return to the agricultural metaphor is a reminder that children's thought develops in a spiral, not a straight line. They circle back to the same issues, but deal with old information on a more sophisticated level.

Most of the level-four children I talked to were eight years old. At first, they were embarrassed by questions about sex. A typical response was, "I don't know much about it." Having disclaimed knowledge, these children would go on to say that the union of sperm and egg or sexual intercourse was the cause of procreation.

45   LEVEL FIVE: PREFORMATION. At level five, children at least attempt to explain the necessity for sperm and ovum to join, but most insist that the baby springs preformed from one of the germ cells. These children, usually 11 or 12 years old, seem to repeat the history of the science of embryology. Like 17th-century scientists, they believe that one germ cell carries a fully formed, miniature person who simply grows to full size in the uterus. They see no need for a final cause.

Some of these children believe that the baby is in the sperm, which is given food and shelter by the egg. As Patrick, who is nearly 13, explains it: "The lady has an egg and the man has a sperm and sort of he fertilizes the egg, and then the egg slowly grows. The sperm grows into a baby inside the egg. Fertilize? It means it gets inside the egg, the sperm does. The egg before the sperm goes in it sort of like, well, I guess it doesn't have anything in it to grow. It just has food and I guess a shell on the outside. It's sort of the beginning of the baby. It has to happen, because otherwise the sperm would just die because it has no shelter on the outside to keep it alive, no food, nothing. And then the egg, there's nothing in it to grow. It has no . . . no . . . no living animal in there."

Twelve-year-old William, on the other hand, believes that the miniature person inhabits the ovum. He describes fertilization: "That's when the sperm enters the egg. I guess the egg just has sort of an undeveloped embryo and when the sperm enters it, it makes it come to life. It gives it energy and things like that."

The child's sex plays no part in choosing the key ingredient of a baby. As many boys as girls believed that the egg was fully responsible. Others of both sexes were convinced that the sperm carried the child. Unlike the three- and four-year-olds who believe that babies come preformed, level-five children embed this notion in a complex theory of causation.

All these children mentioned sexual intercourse or fertilizing the egg by their second sentence, but some seemed embarrassed by the whole topic. A few complained that it was hard to talk about the subject because it required unacceptable language. Another said, after mentioning marriage and affection, "Then . . . I guess uh, they uh, I guess they would . . . go to bed and do something there."

50   LEVEL SIX: PHYSICAL CAUSALITY. About the time they are 12, children begin to put it all together. They give exclusively physical explanations of conception and birth, and realize that both parents contribute genetic material to the embryo. They are aware of the moral and social aspects of reproduction, but they do not insist that marriage is necessary for conception.

Eleven-year-old Tina describes fertilization: "Well, it just starts it off, I guess. Mixes the genes or puts particles or something into the egg. Genes are the things from the father and the mother, you know, and they put a little bit of each into the baby so the baby turns out to be a little bit like the mother or father or something."

Children like Tina are beginning to move into what Piaget calls the stage of formal operations. They can develop theories and test them against reality; they can think about thinking. Twelve-year-old Michael's account is scientific: "The sperm encounter one ovum and one sperm breaks into the ovum, which produces like a cell, and the cell separates and divides. And so it's dividing, and the ovum goes through a tube and embeds itself in the wall of the, I think it's the fetus of the woman."

Michael's substitution of fetus for uterus leads to an important point. It is the sophistication of a child's reasoning, not simply whether his explanation is correct, that indicates the level of his understanding. Michael's verbal error is like the error of an algebra student who understands quadratic equations but makes a mistake in multiplication.

Not all level-six children gave as thorough an explanation of fertilization as Michael; some said simply, "the two cells meet and start growing."

When questioned, level-six children referred immediately to fertilization or sexual intercourse. None of them seemed embarrassed when I asked, "How do people get babies?"

Surprised Parents. Few of the parents of the children I questioned had accurate ideas about the extent of their children's sexual knowledge. Parents of children at levels one and six predicted their offsprings' answers with some accuracy; most others expected a greater degree of information than the children possessed. All the parents of level-three children expected that their children knew "the truth," and none anticipated the distortions that turned up. Not a single parent anticipated the level-five child's belief in the existence of a preformed person.

As I talked to children of various ages, it seemed apparent that our present efforts at sex education often confuse children. A four-year-old boy, trying to explain where babies come from, told me, "First they were little, a duck, then they grow older, into a baby." His solution seemed peculiar, but his source became clear when a level-two girl repeated it. This four-year-old was explicit.

ME: How would a lady get a baby to grow in her tummy?

SUSAN: Get a duck. 'Cause one day I saw a book about them, and they just get a duck or a goose and they get a little more growned and then they turn into a baby.

ME: A duck will turn into a baby?

SUSAN: They give them some food, people food, and they grow like a baby. To get a baby, go to a store and buy a duck.

ME: How did you find that out?

SUSAN: I just saw, find out from this book.

One widely distributed book, which is recommended for children as young as three, starts with a pencil dot (to represent an ovum), then proceeds through the sex lives of flowers, bees, rabbits, giraffes, chickens and dogs before it reaches the human level. Few young children can encounter this kind of explanation without complete confusion.

Daddy as Cannibal. Another writer, Selma Fraiberg, encountered a four-year-old boy who knew a sex-education book by heart, but insisted that some of the mother's eggs never become babies because the daddy eats them up. "It says so in my book," he claimed, and indeed, it did—in a discussion of reproduction in fish.

Other research suggests a way out of confusion. Lawrence Kohlberg, of Harvard and Elliot Turiel, of the University of California, have studied the development of morality in children. They have found that children can expand their understanding to include concepts that are one level beyond their own.

Using these findings as a guide, we can reduce sex misinformation to a minimum. The level-one preschooler who thinks that babies just grow in mommy's tummy can move up to the manufacturing stage by learning that mommy and daddy make babies. The level-two child, who thinks that babies are manufactured, is ready to learn about the meeting of sperm and ovum. He is not ready for information about dividing cells and the genetic contribution of both parents.

Parents can use their child's curiosity as a guide to the amount of detail he is ready to absorb. By asking the kinds of questions I used, they can find out the level of their child's understanding and begin to provide information geared to the next level. Specific suggestions are listed in the accompanying box.

Children are not miniature adults, and will not think like adults until they grow up. My talks with children have shown that educators need to find out just how children adopt, adapt, and distort information, and then talk to children about sex in new ways. Until they do, our young philosophers will keep on creating unnecessarily confused accounts of the beginnings of life.

TALKING TO YOUR CHILD ABOUT SEX AND BIRTH

70   Never inundate a child with information but tell him what he wants to know in terms he can understand. The child's own curiosity should be a guide to the explicitness of your explanation. Begin by asking questions that will elicit the child's beliefs without leading his reply. In that way, his level of understanding will become apparent. Some of the questions I asked were: How do people get babies? How do mommies get to be mommies? How did your daddy get to be your daddy?

Children usually are ready to hear explanations of sex in terms that are one level beyond their present understanding. If parents communicate their own comfort, the child will feel he has permission to ask what he wants to know.

Never make a child feel stupid or foolish because he looks at reproduction in a fanciful way. It is important to support the child's problem-solving effort without confirming his erroneous information.

Level-One Child. This child believes that babies have always existed. Speaking in level-two terms, a parent might tell him: "Only people can make other people. To make a baby person, you need two grown-up people, a woman and a man, to be the baby's mommy and daddy. The mommy and daddy make the baby from an egg in the mommy's body and a sperm from the daddy's body."

Level-Two Child. This child believes that babies are manufactured. The parent could say, "That's an interesting way of looking at things. That's the way you'd make a doll. You would buy a head and some hair and put it all together. But making a real live baby is different from making a doll or a cake or an airplane."

75   This child can be led to understand that while a factory may have a wide range of components at its disposal, babymakers have only certain ingredients from their own bodies as materials. The parent might continue: "Mommies and daddies have special things in their bodies that they use to make babies. Mommies have tiny eggs and daddies have tiny sperms. When an egg from a mommy and a sperm from a daddy join together, they grow into a baby. The baby grows inside the mommy's body."

The level-two child who speaks of opening tummies might be told: "Can you put your hand inside your tummy? Then do you think the mommy and daddy can really put their hands in their tummies? There must be another way. Do you want to know how they get the egg and the seed together? The daddy's sperm are in his testicles and they come out through his penis. The mommy's vagina is a tunnel to where her eggs are. So if the daddy put his penis into her vagina, the sperm could go through the tunnel to the egg."

Level-Three Child. This child already restricts himself to reproductive processes that are technically possible. The task of the level-three's parents is to clear up misapprehensions, explain why some of his beliefs are mistaken, and provide other physiological explanations.

The child who described the sperm biting a hole with its little mouth to gain access to the vagina can be led to understand that while sperm move in a way that resembles swimming, the sperm is not a whole animal. Unlike a fish, it has no mouth with which to bite. She can be told why a sperm doesn't need a mouth to get into the vagina, which is like a tunnel.

One level-three child described conception in the following manner: "I guess it's like mothers and fathers are related, and their loving each other forms a baby. I don't know how it really comes just by loving and stuff. I guess the love forms the beans and I guess the beans hatches the egg."

80

This child's parents should agree with him, that loving is an important part of making babies. His statement shows that they have already given him an integral part of their value system. They could say, "It's really important for a baby that mothers and fathers love each other and love the baby, so that when the baby is born they can take good care of it. But loving is a feeling and can't start the baby all by itself. A baby is a living creature and it starts growing from living material. When the mother and the father make love, a sperm from the father goes through his penis into the mother's vagina. When the sperm joins with an egg from the mother, the sperm and the egg form one new thing, which grows into a baby."

Levels Four and Five. In talking to level-four and level-five children, the objective is the same, although the level-four child may take longer to understand why genetic material must unite to produce a baby. The level-five child believes that the whole baby exists in either the sperm or the egg, needing the other only to promote its growth. Children at levels four and five need to learn that the baby has not begun to exist until the sperm and egg meet and fuse. They can learn that the seeds of life come from both parents, from whom the baby inherits its physical characteristics.

A useful way to explain genetic contributions is to talk in terms of information. A parent might say that both sperm and egg contain coded information about the baby they will grow to be. He can go on to talk about facial features, color of eyes, hair and skin. It is important to stress that neither the sperm nor the egg has the entire code until they unite. Together, they complete the message to develop into a baby that is the child of a particular set of parents.

DEFINE: *assimilate* (3); *physiology* (33); *genetic* (67); *inundate* (70); *misapprehensions* (77).

ANALYSIS

structure   1. What is Bernstein's thesis? (Include both parts of the article.)

     2. In addition to process analysis, what other method of development is used prominently?

meaning   3. What's the matter with lecturing children about sex and birth with "the clinical precision of an advanced anatomy course"?

     4. What is Piaget's explanation of how children learn?

     5. Discuss the statement "Children are not miniature adults."

style   6. Compare the tone of this researcher, Bernstein, to that of De Leon ("The Baldness Experiment" in Section 7B).

opinion   7. Do you agree with Bernstein's approach to sex education?

     8. Should sex education be taught in the schools?

WRITING SUGGESTIONS

1. Using information from the article, tell how children gradually develop an understanding of sex and birth.

2. Describe the process (à la Bernstein) that one should use in explaining sex to children.

3. Describe the process by which you learned about sex.

Carl Sagan

STARFOLK: A FABLE

1   Once upon a time, about ten or fifteen billion years ago, the universe was without form. There were no galaxies. There were no stars. There were no planets. And there was no life. Darkness was upon the face of the deep. The universe was hydrogen and helium. The explosion of the Big Bang had passed, and the fires of that titanic event—either the creation of the universe or the ashes of a previous incarnation of the universe—were rumbling feebly down the corridors of space.

2   But the gas of hydrogen and helium was not smoothly distributed. Here and there in the great dark, by accident, somewhat more than the ordinary amount of gas was collected. Such clumps grew imperceptibly at the expense of their surroundings, gravitationally attracting larger and larger amounts of neighboring gas. As such clumps grew in mass, their

From *The Cosmic Connection* by Carl Sagan. Copyright © 1973 by Carl Sagan and Jerome Agel. Reprinted by permission of Doubleday & Company, Inc.

denser parts, governed by the inexorable laws of gravitation and conservation of angular momentum, contracted and compacted, spinning faster and faster. Within these great rotating balls and pinwheels of gas, smaller fragments of greater density condensed out; these shattered into billions of smaller shrinking gas balls.

THE FIRST STAR

3   Compaction led to violent collisions of the atoms at the centers of the gas balls. The temperatures became so great that electrons were stripped from protons in the constituent hydrogen atoms. Because protons have like positive charges, they ordinarily electrically repel one another. But after a while the temperatures at the centers of the gas balls became so great that the protons collided with extraordinary energy—an energy so great that the barrier of electrical repulsion that surrounds the proton was penetrated. Once penetration occurred, nuclear forces—the forces that hold the nuclei of atoms together—came into play. From the simple hydrogen gas the next atom in complexity, helium, was formed. In the synthesis of one helium atom from four hydrogen atoms there is a small amount of excess energy left over. This energy, trickling out through the gas ball, reached the surface and was radiated into space. The gas ball had turned on. The first star was formed. There was light on the face of the heavens.

4   The stars evolved over billions of years, slowly turning hydrogen into helium in their deep interiors, converting the slight mass difference into energy, and flooding the skies with light. There were in these times no planets to receive the light, and no life forms to admire the radiance of the heavens.

5   The conversion of hydrogen into helium could not continue indefinitely. Eventually, in the hot interiors of the stars, where the temperatures were high enough to overcome the forces of electrical repulsion, all the hydrogen was consumed. The fires of the stars were stoked. The pressures in the interiors could no longer support the immense weight of the overlying layers of star. The stars then continued their process of collapse, which had been interrupted by the nuclear fires of a billion years before.

6   In contracting further, higher temperatures were reached, temperatures so high that helium atoms—the ash of the previous epoch of nuclear reaction—became usable as stellar fuel. More complex nuclear reactions occurred in the insides of the stars—now swollen, distended red giant stars. Helium was converted to carbon, carbon to oxygen and magnesium, oxygen to neon, magnesium to silicon, silicon to sulfur, and upward through the litany of the periodic table of the elements—a massive stellar alchemy. Vast and intricate mazes of nuclear reactions built up some nuclei. Others coalesced to form much more complex nuclei. Still others fragmented or combined with protons to build only slightly more complex nuclei.

7   But the gravity on the surfaces of red giants is low, because the surfaces have expanded outward from the interiors. The outer layers of red

giants are slowly dissipated into interstellar space, enriching the space between the stars in carbon and oxygen and magnesium and iron and all the elements heavier than hydrogen and helium. In some cases, the outer layers of the star were slowly stripped off, like the successive skins of an onion. In other cases, a colossal nuclear explosion rocked the star, propelling at immense velocity into interstellar space most of the outside of the star. Either by leakage or explosion, by dissipation slow or dissipation fast, star-stuff was spewed back to the dark, thin gas from which the stars had come.

THE PLANETS EVOLVE

8   But here, later generations of stars were aborning. Again the condensations of gas spun their slow gravitational pirouettes, slowly transmogrifying gas cloud into star. But these new second- and third-generation stars were enriched in heavy elements, the patrimony of their stellar antecedents. Now, as stars were formed, smaller condensations formed near them condensations far too small to produce nuclear fires and become stars. They were little dense, cold clots of matter, slowly forming out of the rotating cloud, later to be illuminated by the nuclear fires that they themselves could not generate. These unprepossessing clots became the planets: Some giant and gaseous, composed mostly of hydrogen and helium, cold and far from their parent star; others, smaller and warmer, losing the bulk of their hydrogen and helium by a slow trickling away to space, formed a different sort of planet—rocky, metallic, hard-surfaced.

9   These smaller cosmic debris, congealing and warming, released small quantities of hydrogen-rich gases, trapped in their interiors during the processes of formation. Some gases condensed on the surface, forming the first oceans; other gases remained above the surface, forming the first atmospheres—atmospheres different from the present atmosphere of Earth, atmospheres composed of methane, ammonia, hydrogen sulfide, water, and hydrogen—an unpleasant and unbreathable atmosphere for humans. But this is not yet a story about humans.

10   Starlight fell on this atmosphere. Storms were driven by the Sun, producing thunder and lightning. Volcanoes erupted, hot lava heating the atmosphere near the surface. These processes broke apart molecules of the primitive atmosphere. But the fragments reassorted into more and more complex molecules, falling by chance upon clays, a dizzying process of breakdown, resynthesis, transformation—slowly moving toward molecules of greater and greater complexity, driven by the laws of physics and chemistry. After a time, the oceans achieved the consistency of a warm dilute broth.

SELF-REPLICATING MOLECULES

11   Among the innumerable species of complex organic molecules forming and dissipating in this broth there one day arose a molecule able

crudely to make copies of itself—a molecule which weakly guided the chemical processes in its vicinity to produce molecules like itself—a template molecule, a blueprint molecule, a self-replicating molecule. This molecule was not very efficient. Its copies were inexact. But soon it gained a significant advantage over the other molecules in the early waters. The molecules that could not copy themselves did not. Those that could did. The number of copying molecules greatly increased.

12   As time passed, the copying process became more exact. Other molecules in the waters were reprocessed to form the jigsaw puzzle pieces to fit the copying molecules. A minute and imperceptible statistical advantage of the molecules that could copy themselves was soon transformed by the arithmetic of geometrical progression into the dominant process in the oceans.

13   More and more elaborate reproductive systems arose. Those systems that copied better produced more copies. Those that copied poorly produced fewer copies. Soon most of the molecules were organized into molecular collectives, into self-replicating systems. It was not that any molecules had the glimmering of an idea or the ghostly passage of a need or want or aspiration; merely, those molecules that copied did, and soon the face of the planet became transformed by the copying process. In time, the seas became full of these molecular collectives, forming, metabolizing, replicating . . . forming, metabolizing, replicating . . . forming, metabolizing, mutating, replicating. . . . Elaborate systems arose, molecular collectives exhibiting behavior, moving to where the replication building blocks were more abundant, avoiding molecular collectives that incorporated their neighbors. Natural selection became a molecular sieve, selecting out those combinations of molecules best suited by chance to further replication.

14   All the while the building blocks, the foodstuffs, the parts for later copies, were being produced, mainly by sunlight and lightning and thunder—all driven by the nearby star. The nuclear processes in the insides of the stars drove the planetary processes, which led to and sustained life.

PLANTS DEVELOP

15   As the supply of foodstuffs gradually was exhausted, a new kind of molecular collective arose, one able to produce molecular building blocks internally out of air and water and sunlight. The first animals were joined by the first plants. The animals became parasites upon the plants, as they had been earlier on the stellar manna falling from the skies. The plants slowly changed the composition of the atmosphere; hydrogen was lost to space, ammonia transformed to nitrogen, methane to carbon dioxide. For the first time, oxygen was produced in significant quantities in the atmosphere—oxygen, a deadly poisonous gas able to convert all the self-replicating organic molecules back into simple gases like carbon dioxide and water.

16   But life met this supreme challenge: In some cases by burrowing into environments where oxygen was absent, but—in the most successful

variants—by evolving not only to survive the oxygen but to use it in the more efficient metabolism of foodstuffs.

17 Sex and death evolved—processes that vastly increased the rate of natural selection. Some organisms evolved hard parts, climbed onto, and survived on the land. The pace of production of more complex forms accelerated. Flight evolved. Enormous four-legged beasts thundered across the steaming jungles. Small beasts emerged, born live, instead of in hardshelled containers filled with replicas of the early oceans. They survived through swiftness and cunning—and increasingly long periods in which their knowledge was not so much preprogrammed in self-replicating molecules as learned from parents and experiences.

18 All the while, the climate was variable. Slight variations in the output of sunlight, the orbital motion of the planet, clouds, oceans, and polar icecaps produced climate changes—wiping out whole groups of organisms and causing the exuberant proliferation of other, once insignificant, groups.

19 And then . . . the Earth grew somewhat cold. The forests retreated. Small arboreal animals climbed down from the trees to seek a livelihood on the savannas. They became upright and tool-using. They communicated by producing compressional waves in the air with their eating and breathing organs. They discovered that organic material would, at a high enough temperature, combine with atmospheric oxygen to produce the stable hot plasma called fire. Postpartum learning was greatly accelerated by social interaction. Communal hunting developed, writing was invented, political structures evolved, superstition and science, religion and technology.

MAN

20 And then one day there came to be a creature whose genetic material was in no major way different from the self-replicating molecular collectives of any of the other organisms on his planet, which he called Earth. But he was able to ponder the mystery of his origins, the strange and tortuous path by which he had emerged from star-stuff. He was the matter of the cosmos, contemplating itself. He considered the problematical and enigmatic question of his future. He called himself Man. He was one of the starfolk. And he longed to return to the stars.

DEFINE: *incarnation* (1); *imperceptibly, inexorable* (2); *compaction* (3); *coalesced* (6); *pirouettes, transmogrifying, unprepossessing* (8); *template, replicating* (11).

ANALYSIS

structure   1. What problem in chronology is there in paragraphs 19 and 20?

style   2. If one were writing a strictly scientific document, how might she phrase the following?

"Either by leakage or explosion, by dissipation slow or dissipation fast, star-stuff was spewed back to the dark, thin gas from which the stars had come." (paragraph 7)

"But here, later generations of stars were aborning. Again the condensations of gas spun their slow gravitational pirouettes, slowly transmogrifying gas cloud into star." (paragraph 8)

Find other lines in which Sagan translates scientific data into almost lyrical language.

3. What is the effect of the words "unprepossessing clots" in describing the formation of the planets, one of which is, of course, Earth?

4. Do you have to understand every word to appreciate this "fable"? Discuss.

5. At what audience is this selection aimed?

meaning 6. What was the Big Bang?

7. What was the effect of the development of a molecule that could replicate itself?

8. In paragraph 17, what are "hard-shelled containers filled with replicas of the early oceans"?

9. Why does Sagan give so little space to the arrival of human beings?

opinion 10. To what extent is this fable true?

Review of Chapter 7

Attention to detail, to the order of the steps in a process, and to possible dangers in performing the process are among the key elements in writing good process papers. Although the most common processes are usually described in the "bare bones" form of recipes, formulas, and lists of instructions, process analyses often become the bases for essays, and they can be found in historical accounts, biographies, novels, and other forms of writing. In essays the bare bones are usually fleshed out with description, examples, commentary, and other rhetorical devices. In narration the process usually becomes an integral part of the story.

Obviously, each type of process has its special function and special audience. Someone wishing to follow a cake recipe would not want to dig out the instructions from a narrative that includes anecdotes about how the family parrot got into the batter and the stomach ache it gave the author's husband. On the other hand Mitford has to provide more than a set of instructions on how to embalm a corpse in order to get across her feelings about the grossness and hypocrisy involved in the embalming process. And although Dr. Nolen describes the steps in the appendectomy as he performs them, his focus is not on the process but on the feelings of the young doctor performing his first operation. Mitford and Nolen probably have the same audience, intelligent members of the general public, not necessarily funeral directors or surgeons.

WRITING SUGGESTIONS

Write an extended process paper about how you survived basic training or became an expert runner, bowler, tennis player, or pitcher. Tell how you reached the top ranks of scouting or achieved some other leadership role. Tell how you mastered a musical instrument or developed another skill. Be sure that the emphasis is on *how*.

EVALUATION

Taking the above comments into consideration, review the selections in this chapter and choose two or three selections that describe the process in the most interesting and effective manner. Support your choices.

Definition

CHAPTER 8

READING FOCUS

❖ Know who is doing the defining—their authority, biases, points of view.

❖ Be aware that definition relies more on context than on the dictionary; thus, be sensitive to connotation as well as denotation.

❖ Be aware that definitions change with the times. They may also be influenced by political, religious, cultural, occupational, and class orientation.

WRITING FOCUS

❖ Avoid explaining your definition too fully and thus talking down to your audience; on the other hand, be sure to explain sufficiently.

❖ Call upon as many rhetorical techniques as necessary to make your meaning clear.

❖ Don't be circular; that is, don't define your words by using the same words.

❖ Don't be too restrictive: To define *poultry* as "domesticated birds that swim" eliminates chickens and turkeys.

❖ Don't be too general: To define *poultry* as "domesticated birds" includes parrots and canaries.

❖ Don't start with a classification that is too broad: not "Candy is a food," but "Candy is a confection."

❖ Be sure to name the classification in the definition: not "Democracy is when ..." but "Democracy is a form of government which ..."

"A rose is a rose is a rose," the famous line by Gertrude Stein, doesn't tell anyone who has never seen a rose what a rose is; and "the Rose is Beauty," a line by Henry Austin Dobson, doesn't define roses for people whose conceptions of beauty might differ from Mr. Dobson's.

Defining is not a simple process. Take the "simple" tomato, for example. Because the plant is related to the poisonous belladonna and mandrake, the tomato was avoided for centuries. A sixteenth century herbalist said, "These apples were eaten by some Italians like melons, but the strong, stinking smell gives one sufficient notice how unhealthful and evil they are to eat."

Is the tomato a fruit or a vegetable? In 1893 the question had to be decided by the Supreme Court because imported vegetables could be taxed while fruits were not taxed. The Court decided that, although tomatoes are a "fruit of the vine," in the common language of the people they are considered vegetables. Therefore, the duty on tomatoes stood. So tomatoes are vegetables legally and fruit botanically. Here is a dictionary definition:

> **tomato** **1.** a red or yellowish fruit with a juicy pulp, used as a vegetable: botanically it is a berry **2.** the annual plant (*Lycopersicon esculentum*) of the nightshade family, on which this berry grows.[1]

The formal definition involves three steps: (1) stating the term to be defined, (2) placing it in a class, and (3) differentiating it from other members of that class.

Term	Class	Differentia
poodle	dog	with solid color, curly coat
orange	citrus fruit	edible, round, reddish-yellow
canoe	small boat	light, narrow, sharp edged at ends, moved by paddles

Dictionaries usually provide the three kinds of information as well as synonyms to help the reader grasp the meaning of a word. However, such bare definitions are often not sufficient. Many words call for explanation and elaboration far beyond what dictionaries provide. Such explanations are called *extended definitions*. For example, *Webster's New World Dictionary* defines *jackhammer* as "a portable type of pneumatic hammer, used for drilling rock, brick, etc." In a tool guide we find this extended definition:

[1] From *Webster's New World Dictionary*, Second College Edition. Copyright © 1978 by William Collins + World Publishing Co., Inc. (Hereafter referred to as *WNWD*.) Used with permission.

"The jackhammer is a hand operated pneumatic tool used to cut through hard surfaces. It is usually about two-and-a-half-feet long and weighs from 60 to 90 pounds. In its functioning position (upright), the double handles are parallel to the surface being cut. Attached to the right handle is the on/off switch. Cutting attachments of various kinds may be fastened to the point."

Extended definition is the subject of the balance of this chapter.

Section 8a

Study the definitions that follow; then answer the questions.

WHAT IS CIVILIZATION?

(*WNWD*): **civilization** **1.** the process of civilizing or becoming civilized **2.** the condition of being civilized; social organization of a high order, marked by the development and use of a written language and by advances in the arts and the sciences, government, etc. **3.** the total culture of a particular people, nation, period, etc. **4.** the countries and peoples considered to have reached a high stage of social and cultural development.

Winston Churchill

There are few words which are used more loosely than the word "Civilization." What does it mean? It means a society based upon the opinion of civilians. It means that violence, the rule of warriors and despotic chiefs, the conditions of camps and warfare, of riot and tyranny, give place to parliaments where laws are made, and independent courts of justice in which over long periods those laws are maintained. That is Civilization—and in its soil grow, continually, freedom, comfort, and culture. When Civilization reigns in any country, a wider and less harassed life is afforded to the masses of people. The traditions of the past are cherished and the inheritance bequeathed to us by former wise or valiant men becomes a rich estate to be enjoyed and used by all.

From *Blood, Sweat, and Tears* by Winston Churchill. Copyright © 1941 by Winston S. Churchill. Reprinted by permission of G. P. Putnam's Sons, New York, and McClelland & Stewart, Toronto.

SOME WATERGATE TERMS DEFINED

[1]   In a now famous phrase, Ron Ziegler and John Ehrlichman have declared White House statements proven false to be "no longer operative." This is a very handy phrase which can mean any of the following:

It wasn't true in the first place.
I'm sorry I said it.
I thought it was true then, but I know now it wasn't.

[2]   While the public was left wondering what the phrase meant, responsibility for the original lies was shifted from the liars to the lies themselves. The responsibility was not in the people, not even in the stars, but in the statements themselves, which were spoken of as if they had lives and energy of their own.

[3]   Among the most infuriating euphemisms used by Watergate witnesses is "surreptitious entry," meaning burglary. Thus a crime becomes a game of hide and seek, or at most a naughty prank. Next time you find a burglar in your home don't shout "police!" Say "Oh, you surreptitious devil, you!"

[4]   What ordinary crooks call "casing the joint" before a burglary is called by the Watergate bunch "a vulnerability and feasibility study." Surely these men were just students and technicians. But criminals? Never.

[5]   Illegal wiretapping is evil. Therefore the Watergate people engaged in "electronic surveillance." Spying on a person's activities is "visual surveillance." Evil people cover up, lie, and bribe. Watergate people "contain situations" like so many protective dams.

Reprinted with permission of author from "Watergate Lingo: A Language of Non-Responsibility" by Richard Gambino. Copyright © 1973 by Richard Gambino. Nov./Dec. 1973 Journal of Freedom House, 20 West 40th Street, New York, N.Y.

WHAT IS DEATH?

(*WNWD*): **death**   **1.** the act or fact of dying; permanent ending of all life in a person, animal, or plant.

[1]   The traditional criteria for death are cessation of respiration and heart action, but modern medical technology can keep a patient breathing and his blood circulating long after his brain has died. Now a special Harvard University committee has recommended that brain death, or irreversible coma, be considered a definition of death and has drawn up a set of guidelines for determining when there is no discernible activity of

From "Science and the Citizen: What Is Death?" Copyright © 1968 by Scientific American, Inc. All rights reserved.

the central nervous system. The 13-man committee, drawn from the faculties of medicine, public health, law, arts and sciences, and divinity, was headed by Henry K. Beecher of the Harvard Medical School. Its report was published in the *Journal of the American Medical Association.*

2   According to the committee a permanently nonfunctioning brain is characterized by certain clinical signs. One is unreceptiveness and unresponsiveness of the patient to any external stimuli or inner needs. Another is lack of any spontaneous muscular movement or any unassisted breathing—or effort to breathe—over a period of at least an hour. Finally, there are no reflexes: the pupil of the eye is fixed and dilated even in the presence of a bright light, there is no swallowing or yawning and usually no stretch reflex. These clinical signs constitute primary evidence of brain death; electroencephalograms should be considered secondary because they may show spurious waves. A "flat" brain-wave pattern, according to the report, constitutes confirmation of brain death.

3   The final determination of death through irreversible coma should be made only when the clinical and encephalographic tests have been repeated at least 24 hours after the initial tests. The determination should be made by the physician in charge; it is "unsound and undesirable" to have the family make the decision. Then the family should be informed. "At this point death is to be declared and *then* the respirator turned off."

Thomas Griffith

POP, WHAT'S A POPULIST?

1   There is no truth-in-labeling act to ensure that the press correctly describes people in public life. Politicians used to be called by riper names than they are now, but even in these more discreet days labels can hurt. Gerald Ford is conservative, yet in his confirmation hearings preferred to style himself conservative fiscally, but "moderate on domestic issues." Jimmy Carter? His acceptance speech, he said, "not inadvertently shifted back and forth between liberal and conservative, but I think it was uniformly populist in tone." Is he a populist? "I think so." But what's a populist? "I'll let you define that."

2   These days most politicians are happy to call themselves conservative, and liberalism has become the sin that dares not speak its name. The September issue of *Commentary* in a symposium called "What Is a Liberal—Who Is a Conservative?" provides a useful guide to the semantic bedlam. Most of the 64 contributing intellectuals were once content to call themselves liberal. Now they fastidiously invoke qualifiers. They speak of early and late liberals, paleoliberals, center extremists, tough-minded liberals, of "rad-libs" and "trad-libs."

From *Time,* The Weekly Newsmagazine, October 4, 1976. Copyright Time, Inc. 1976. Reprinted by permission.

3   The difficulty lies in the two drastic sea changes the word liberal has undergone. In the 19th and early 20th centuries it meant laissez-faire. One of the *Commentary* contributors, William F. Buckley, quotes Woodrow Wilson as saying that the history of liberalism is the history of man's efforts to restrain the growth of government. Franklin Roosevelt, of course, gave liberal its new meaning: the use of what has become Big Government to redress society's inequities. Herbert Hoover objected not only to F.D.R.'s policies but also to his theft of the word liberal. Barry Goldwater was the first presidential candidate to glory in the label conservative.

4   The second sea change came in the 1960s when the angry New Left, convinced that liberals and conservatives were alike in their Viet Nam–cold war complicity, trashed the liberal scene. The *Commentary* crowd, including men like Pat Moynihan, recoiled in shock from leftists who extolled the totalitarian "social justice" of a Cuba or a China. To Irving Kristol, 20th century liberalism has become neo-socialism, a creed "more interested in equality than in liberty." Critic Alfred Kazin concludes that liberal and conservative are "fraudulent and intellectually useless terms." Why not, asks another, declare a moratorium on both words, since both have become dulled, "even as insults"?

5   But more of *Commentary's* intellectuals consider liberal and conservative "necessary shorthand" and, though imprecise, indispensable. Out of their individual contributions emerges a rough consensus:

6   Liberals often seem to think that powerlessness makes right; conservatives, that power makes right. Originally, Philosopher Sidney Hook argues, liberals believed that man was inherently good but had been corrupted by defective social institutions that could and should be changed, while conservatives thought man inherently evil and were more suspicious of change. Liberals are optimistic, pragmatic and, says one *Commentary* intellectual, Editor Walter Goodman, "relatively unburdened by doctrine, can be more open to lessons of experience." Conservatives are less accepting of "progress," more concerned with order. A conservative, writes Lawyer and Educator David T. Bazelon, "relies fundamentally on the better elements of the ruling group" and, adds Yale Law School's Joseph W. Bishop Jr., "is slow to change institutions he doesn't like until he has a pretty clear idea of what will take their place."

7   Such definitions have a sounder ring than Philadelphia Mayor Frank Rizzo's simple view that "a conservative is a liberal who got mugged the night before." As *Commentary* suggests, there is life in the old terms yet. Liberal and conservative still represent valid distinctions between how differing temperaments respond to change. Ford is conservative, even if less so than Reagan. Carter, for all his convoluted cautions, is committed to change. Both candidates prefer to blur their identities to suit a volatile public mood that calls itself more conservative than liberal, yet votes more Democratic than Republican. But in such confusion, editorial writers and commentators are free to discover that the old-fashioned labels are not really all that out of date.

Bergen and Cornelia Evans

THE MEANING OF CLICHÉ

1   *Cliché* is a French word meaning a stereotype block and is used in English to describe those phrases (there are thousands of them), originally idioms, metaphors, proverbs, or brief quotations, which overuse and, sometimes, changing circumstances have rendered meaningless. Many of them just fill out the vacancies of thought and speech. A man goes to say *far* and he says *far and wide.* Speech is a difficult thing. We spend more time learning to talk than anything else we do. It is an effort, an unceasing effort. There is strong resistance in us to it and the inertia which this resistance sets up is probably the chief cause of our use of clichés.

2   Many clichés are alliterative, that is, their words begin with the same sound. We do not say we are *cool,* but *cool as a cucumber.* Unless one is *slow but sure,* things go to *rack and ruin* and he may be thrown out *bag and baggage.*

3   Historical changes have made many clichés utterly meaningless. What does *fell* mean in *one fell swoop?* Or *halcyon* in *halcyon days?* Or *moot* in *moot point?* Yet these and hundreds of other phrases, totally devoid of meaning to those who speak them, are heard every day.

4   Many clichés were once original and clever, but repetition by millions, possibly billions, of people for hundreds and even thousands of years in some instances has worn all originality and cleverness away. They were fresh-minted once, but are now battered beyond acceptability. And their use is doubly bad because it characterizes the user as one who thinks he is witty, or would like to be thought witty, and yet is a mere parroter of musty echoes of long-dead wit. His very attempt to sound clever shows him to be dull.

5   Our speech is probably more crammed with clichés today than ever before. The torrent of printed and recorded matter that is dumped on us every day in newspapers and from radio and television is bound to be repetitious and stereotyped. The brightest day in the world's history never produced one-millionth, in fresh, original, and honest expression, of the bulk of what cascades over us every day. All this stuff is prepared in furious haste. There is neither time nor energy for care or thought and the inevitable result is a fabric woven of stereotyped phrases. Ninety per cent of what the public reads and hears is expressed in fossilized fragments and, naturally, ninety per cent of its own expression, apart from the necessities of life, is also expressed in them.

6   This makes the task of the man who wants to speak and write clearly and honestly a difficult one. He must be on his guard all the time, especially against anything that seems particularly apt. That doesn't mean that he is never to use a current phrase or even a hackneyed one. It may be, for example, that after consideration he really does want to say

From *A Dictionary of Contemporary American Usage,* by Bergen Evans and Cornelia Evans. Copyright © 1975 by Bergen Evans and Cornelia Evans. Reprinted by permission of Random House, Inc.

that the pen is mightier than the sword. And if he does, he'd better say it in the cliché form than in some labored circumlocution. But he mustn't expect to be thought clever for saying it. And, of course, he may deliberately choose to speak in clichés in order that his speech may be common and familiar.

7   Wits often use clichés as the basis of their wit, relying on the seeming familiarity of the phrase and the expectation of its inevitable conclusion to set the trap for the innocent reader—such as Oscar Wilde's "Punctuality is the thief of time" or Samuel Butler's "It's better to have loved and lost than never to have lost at all"—but that is a wholly different thing.

Isaac Asimov

WHAT IS INTELLIGENCE, ANYWAY?

1   What is intelligence, anyway? When I was in the army I received a kind of aptitude test that all soldiers took and, against a normal of 100, scored 160. No one at the base had ever seen a figure like that, and for two hours they made a big fuss over me. (It didn't mean anything. The next day I was still a buck private with KP as my highest duty.)

2   All my life I've been registering scores like that, so that I have the complacent feeling that I'm highly intelligent, and I expect other people to think so, too. Actually, though, don't such scores simply mean that I am very good at answering the type of academic questions that are considered worthy of answers by the people who make up the intelligence tests—people with intellectual bents similar to mine?

3   For instance, I had an auto-repair man once, who, on these intelligence tests, could not possibly have scored more than 80, by my estimate. I always took it for granted that I was far more intelligent than he was. Yet, when anything went wrong with my car I hastened to him with it, watched him anxiously as he explored its vitals, and listened to his pronouncements as though they were divine oracles—and he always fixed my car.

4   Well, then, suppose my auto-repair man devised questions for an intelligence test. Or suppose a carpenter did, or a farmer, or, indeed, almost anyone but an academician. By every one of those tests, I'd prove myself a moron. And I'd *be* a moron, too. In a world where I could not use my academic training and my verbal talents but had to do something intricate or hard, working with my hands, I would do poorly. My intelligence, then, is not absolute but is a function of the society I live in and of the fact that a small subsection of that society has managed to foist itself on the rest as an arbiter of such matters.

5   Consider my auto-repair man, again. He had a habit of telling me jokes whenever he saw me. One time he raised his head from under the

Reprinted by permission of Isaac Asimov.

automobile hood to say: "Doc, a deaf-and-dumb guy went into a hardware store to ask for some nails. He put two fingers together on the counter and made hammering motions with the other hand. The clerk brought him a hammer. He shook his head and pointed to the two fingers he was hammering. The clerk brought him nails. He picked out the sizes he wanted, and left. Well, doc, the next guy who came in was a blind man. He wanted scissors. How do you suppose he asked for them?"

6   Indulgently, I lifted my right hand and made scissoring motions with my first two fingers. Whereupon my auto-repair man laughed raucously and said, "Why, you dumb jerk, he used his *voice* and asked for them." Then he said, smugly, "I've been trying that on all my customers today." "Did you catch many?" I asked. "Quite a few," he said, "but I knew for sure I'd catch *you.*" "Why is that?" I asked. "Because you're so goddamned educated, doc, I *knew* you couldn't be very smart."

7   And I have an uneasy feeling he had something there.

Joseph Heller

CATCH-22

Yossarian looked at him soberly and tried another approach. "Is Orr crazy?"

"He sure is," Doc Daneeka said.

"Can you ground him?"

"I sure can. But first he has to ask me to. That's part of the rule."

5   "Then why doesn't he ask you to?"

"Because he's crazy," Doc Daneeka said. "He has to be crazy to keep flying combat missions after all the close calls he's had. Sure, I can ground Orr. But first he has to ask me to."

"That's all he has to do to be grounded?"

"That's all. Let him ask me."

"And then you can ground him?" Yossarian asked.

10   "No. Then I can't ground him."

"You mean there's a catch?"

"Sure there's a catch," Doc Daneeka replied. "Catch-22. Anyone who wants to get out of combat duty isn't really crazy."

There was only one catch and that was Catch-22, which specified that a concern for one's own safety in the face of dangers that were real and immediate was the process of a rational mind. Orr was crazy and could be grounded. All he had to do was ask; and as soon as he did, he would no longer be crazy and would have to fly more missions. Orr would be crazy to fly more missions and sane if he didn't, but if he was sane he had to fly them. If he flew them he was crazy and didn't have to; but if he didn't want to he was sane and had to. Yossarian was moved very deeply by the absolute simplicity of this clause of Catch-22 and let out a respectful whistle.

From *Catch-22*. Copyright © 1955, 1961 by Joseph Heller. Reprinted by permission of Simon & Schuster, a Division of Gulf & Western Corporation.

William Spooner Donald

WILL SOMEONE PLEASE HICCUP MY PAT?

One afternoon nearly a hundred years ago the October wind gusted merrily down Oxford's High Street. Hatless and helpless, a white-haired clergyman with pink cherubic features uttered his plaintive cry for aid. As an athletic youngster chased the spinning topper, other bystanders smiled delightedly—they had just heard at first hand the latest "Spoonerism."

My revered relative William Achibald Spooner was born in 1844, the son of a Staffordshire county court judge. As a young man, he was handicapped by a poor physique, a stammer, and weak eyesight; at first, his only possible claim to future fame lay in the fact that he was an albino, with very pale blue eyes and white hair tinged slightly yellow.

But nature compensated the weakling by blessing him with a brilliant intellect. By 1868 he had been appointed a lecturer at New College, Oxford. Just then he would have been a caricaturist's dream with his freakish looks, nervous manner, and peculiar mental kink that caused him—in his own words—to "make occasional felicities in verbal diction."

Victorian Oxford was a little world of its own where life drifted gently by; a world where splendid intellectuals lived in their ivory towers of Latin, Euclid, and Philosophy; a world where it was always a sunny summer afternoon in a countryside, where Spooner admitted he loved to "pedal gently round on a well-boiled icicle."

5   As the years passed, Spooner grew, probably without himself being aware of the fact, into a "character." A hard worker himself, he detested idleness and is on record as having rent some lazybones with the gem, "You have hissed all my mystery lessons, and completely tasted two whole worms."

With his kindly outlook on life, it was almost natural for him to take holy orders; he was ordained a deacon in 1872 and a priest in 1875. His unique idiosyncrasy never caused any serious trouble and merely made him more popular. On one occasion, in New College chapel in 1879, he announced smilingly that the next hymn would be "Number one seven five—Kinkering Kongs their Titles Take." Other congregations were treated to such jewels as ". . . Our Lord, we know, is a shoving Leopard . . ." and ". . . All of us have in our hearts a half-warmed fish to lead a better life. . . ."

Spooner often preached in the little village churches around Oxford and once delivered an eloquent address on the subject of Aristotle. No doubt the sermon contained some surprising information for his rustic congregation. For after Spooner had left the pulpit, an idea seemed to occur to him, and he hopped back up the steps again.

"Excuse me, dear brethren," he announced brightly, "I just want to say that in my sermon whenever I mentioned Aristotle, I should have said Saint Paul."

Reprinted by permission of William Spooner Donald, Keswick, Cumbria, England.

By 1885 the word "Spoonerism" was in colloquial use in Oxford circles, and a few years later, in general use all over England. If the dividing line between truth and myth is often only a hairsbreadth, does it really matter? One story that has been told concerns an optician's shop in London. Spooner is reputed to have entered and asked to see a "signifying glass." The optican registered polite bewilderment.

10 "Just an ordinary signifying glass," repeated Spooner, perhaps surprised at the man's obtuseness.

"I'm afraid we haven't one in stock, but I'll make inquiries right away, sir," said the shopkeeper, playing for time.

"Oh, don't bother, it doesn't magnify, it doesn't magnify," said Spooner airily, and walked out.

Fortunately for Spooner, he made the right choice when he met his wife-to-be. He was thirty-four years old when he married Frances Goodwin in 1878. The marriage was a happy one, and they had one son and four daughters. Mrs. Spooner was a tall, good-looking girl, and on one occasion the family went on a short holiday in Switzerland. The "genial Dean," as he was then called, took a keen interest in geology, and in no time at all he had mastered much information and many technical definitions on the subject of glaciers.

One day at lunchtime the younger folk were worried because their parents had not returned from a long walk. When Spooner finally appeared with his wife, his explanation was: "We strolled up a long valley, and when we turned a corner we found ourselves completely surrounded by erotic blacks."

15 He was, of course, referring to "erratic blocks," or large boulders left around after the passage of a glacier.

In 1903 Spooner was appointed Warden of New College, the highest possible post for a Fellow. One day walking across the quadrangle, he met a certain Mr. Casson, who had just been elected a Fellow of New College.

"Do come to dinner tonight," said Spooner, "we are welcoming our new Fellow, Mr. Casson."

"But, my dear Warden, I *am* Casson," was the surprised reply.

"Never mind, never mind, come along all the same," said Spooner tactfully.

20 On another occasion in later years when his eyesight was really very bad, Spooner found himself seated next to a most elegant lady at dinner. In a casual moment the latter put her lily-white hand onto the polished table, and Spooner, in an even more casual manner, pronged her hand with his fork, remarking genially, "My bread, I think."

In 1924 Spooner retired as Warden. He had established an astonishing record of continuous residence at New College for sixty-two years first as undergraduate, then as Fellow, then Dean, and finally as Warden. His death in 1930, at the age of eighty-six, was a blushing crow to collectors of those odd linguistic transpositions known by then throughout the English-speaking world as Spoonerisms.

ANALYSIS

structure

1. Which selection is developed by listing missing functions?

2. Which selection defines two terms in the context of their historical background?

3. Which selection is developed primarily by example?

4. Which selection uses an anecdote to make its point?

meaning

5. Give a brief definition for each of the six following terms, using information derived only from the selections:
   a. intelligence
   b. liberalism, conservatism
   c. insanity, sanity
   d. death

6. William Spooner Donald uses two principal methods of development. Name them.

7. How does the *Scientific American* definition, "What Is Death?" compare with the dictionary definition of *death?*

8. Why do the definitions of political terms keep changing?

9. Correct the two clichés in the last paragraph of "The Meaning of Cliché."

10. Explain the faulty logic of *Catch-22.*

11. What is the connection between Asimov's essay and "The Educated Man" in Section 2B?

12. Define *Spoonerism.*

WRITING SUGGESTIONS

Write brief (but extended) definitions of one of the following terms: *intelligence, happiness, fascism.*

section 8b

Herodotus

"HAPPINESS": ONE GREEK'S DEFINITION

1   Solon left home and, after a visit to the court of Amasis in Egypt, went to Sardis to see Croesus.

2   Croesus entertained him hospitably in the palace, and three or four days after his arrival instructed some servants to take him on a tour of the royal treasuries and point out the richness and magnificence of everything. When Solon had made as thorough an inspection as opportunity allowed, Croesus said: "Well, my Athenian friend, I have heard a great deal about your wisdom, and how widely you have traveled in the pursuit of knowledge. I cannot resist my desire to ask you a question: who is the happiest man you have ever seen?"

3   The point of the question was that Croesus supposed himself to be the happiest of men. Solon, however, refused to flatter, and answered in strict accordance with his view of the truth. "An Athenian," he said, "called Tellus."

4   Croesus was taken aback. "And what," he asked sharply, "is your reason for this choice?"

5   "There are two good reasons," said Solon, "first, his city was prosperous, and he had fine sons, and lived to see children born to each of them, and all these children surviving; and, secondly, after a life which by our standards was a good one, he had a glorious death. In a battle with the neighboring town of Eleusis, he fought for his countrymen, routed the enemy, and died like a soldier; and the Athenians paid him the high honor of a public funeral on the spot where he fell."

6   All these details about the happiness of Tellus, Solon doubtless intended as a moral lesson for the king; Croesus, however, thinking he would at least be awarded second prize, asked who was the next happiest person whom Solon had seen.

7   "Two young men of Argos," was the reply; "Cleobis and Biton. They had enough to live on comfortably; and their physical strength is proved not merely by their success in athletics, but much more by the following incident. The Argives were celebrating the festival of Hera, and it was most important that the mother of the two young men should drive to the temple in her ox-cart; but it so happened that the oxen were late in coming back from the fields. Her two sons therefore, as there was no time to lose, harnessed themselves to the cart and dragged it along, with their

Reprinted by permission of Penguin Books Ltd. from *The Histories* by Herodotus, translated by Aubrey de Sélincourt (Penguin Classics, revised ed. 1972) pp. 51–53. Copyright © the Estate of Aubrey de Sélincourt, 1954; © A. R. Burn, 1974.

mother inside, for a distance of nearly six miles, until they reached the temple. After this exploit, which was witnessed by the assembled crowd, they had a most enviable death—a heaven-sent proof of how much better it is to be dead than alive. Men kept crowding round them and congratulating them on their strength, and women kept telling the mother how lucky she was to have such sons, when, in sheer pleasure at this public recognition of her sons' act, she prayed the goddess Hera, before whose shrine she stood, to grant Cleobis and Biton, who had brought her such honor, the greatest blessing that can fall to mortal man.

8   "After her prayer came the ceremonies of sacrifice and feasting; and the two lads, when all was over, fell asleep in the temple—and that was the end of them, for they never woke again.

9   "The Argives had statues made of them, which they sent to Delphi, as a mark of their particular respect."

10   Croesus was vexed with Solon for giving the second prize for happiness to the two young Argives, and snapped out: "That's all very well, my Athenian friend; but what of my own happiness? Is it so utterly contemptible that you won't even compare me with mere common folk like those you have mentioned?"

11   "My lord," replied Solon, "I know God is envious of human prosperity and likes to trouble us. . . . You can see from that, Croesus, what a chancy thing life is. You are very rich, and you rule a numerous people; but the question you asked me I will not answer, until I know that you have died happily. Great wealth can make a man no happier than moderate means, unless he has the luck to continue in prosperity to the end. Many very rich men have been unfortunate, and many with a modest competence have had good luck. The former are better off than the latter in two respects only, whereas the poor but lucky man has the advantage in many ways; for though the rich have the means to satisfy their appetites and to bear calamities, and the poor have not, the poor, if they are lucky, are more likely to keep clear of trouble, and will have besides the blessings of a sound body, health, freedom from trouble, fine children, and good looks.

12   "Now if a man thus favored dies as he has lived, he will be just the one you are looking for: the only sort of person who deserves to be called happy. But mark this: until he is dead, keep the word 'happy' in reserve. Till then, he is not happy, but only lucky.

13   "Nobody of course can have all these advantages, any more than a country can produce everything it needs: whatever it has, it is bound to lack something. The best country is the one which has most. It is the same with people: no man is ever self-sufficient—there is sure to be something missing. But whoever has the greatest number of the good things I have mentioned, and keeps them to the end, and dies a peaceful death, that man, my lord Croesus, deserves in my opinion to be called happy.

14   "Look to the end, no matter what it is you are considering. Often enough God gives a man a glimpse of happiness, and then utterly ruins him."

ANALYSIS

structure   1. Write a thesis statement for the selection.

2. What qualities enter into Herodotus' definition of the good life?

3. List the methods used by Herodotus to explain his definitions.

meaning
4. How does he distinguish between happiness and luck?

5. What did the mother of Cleobis and Biton pray for? Why?

6. Find a contradiction between one aspect of Herodotus' definition and one of his examples.

opinion
7. Compare your definition of *happiness* with that of Herodotus. Discuss.

Read the next two selections as a unit before answering the questions. They, in addition to the paragraphs in this chapter about the language of Watergate and "The Environment of Language" in Section 4B, give you some conception of the powerful force that language is.

THE EUPHEMISM: TELLING IT LIKE IT ISN'T

1   Modern American speech, while not always clear or correct or turned with much style, is supposed to be uncommonly frank. Witness the current explosion of four-letter words and the explicit discussion of sexual topics. In fact, gobbledygook and nice-Nellyism still extend as far as the ear can hear. Housewives on television may chat about their sex lives in terms that a decade ago would have made gynecologists blush; more often than not, these emancipated women still speak about their children's "going to the potty." Government spokesmen talk about "redeployment" of American troops; they mean withdrawal. When sociologists refer to blacks living in slums, they are likely to mumble about "nonwhites" in a "culturally deprived environment." The CIA may never have used the expression "to terminate with extreme prejudice" when it wanted a spy rubbed out. But in the context of a war in which "pacification of the enemy infrastructure" is the military mode of reference to blasting the Viet Cong out of a village, the phrase sounded so plausible that millions readily accepted it as accurate.

2   The image of a generation blessed with a swinging, liberated language is largely an illusion. Despite its swaggering sexual candor, much contemporary speech still hides behind that traditional enemy of plain talk, the euphemism.

3   From a Greek word meaning "to use words of good omen," euphemism is the substitution of a pleasant term for a blunt one—telling it like it isn't. Euphemism has probably existed since the beginning of language. As long as there have been things of which men thought the less said the better, there have been better ways of saying less. In everyday conversa-

From *Time*, The Weekly Newsmagazine, September 19, 1969. Copyright Time, Inc. 1963. Reprinted by permission.

tion the euphemism is, at worst, a necessary evil; at its best, it is a handy verbal tool to avoid making enemies needlessly, or shocking friends. Language purists and the blunt-spoken may wince when a young woman at a party coyly asks for direction to "the powder room," but to most people this kind of familiar euphemism is probably no more harmful or annoying than, say, a split infinitive.

4   On a larger scale, though, the persistent growth of euphemism in a language represents a danger to thought and action, since its fundamental intent is to deceive. As Linguist Benjamin Lee Whorf has pointed out, the structure of a given language determines, in part, how the society that speaks it views reality. If "substandard housing" makes rotting slums appear more livable or inevitable to some people, then their view of American cities has been distorted and their ability to assess the significance of poverty has been reduced. Perhaps the most chilling example of euphemism's destructive power took place in Hitler's Germany. The wholesale corruption of the language under Nazism, notes Critic George Steiner, is symbolized by the phrase *endgültige Lösung* (final solution), which "came to signify the death of 6,000,000 human beings in gas ovens."

5   No one could argue that American English is under siege from linguistic falsehood, but euphemisms today have the nagging persistence of a headache. Despite the increasing use of nudity and sexual innuendo in advertising, Madison Avenue is still the great exponent of talking to "the average person of good upbringing"—as one TV executive has euphemistically described the ordinary American—in ways that won't offend him. Although this is like fooling half the people none of the time, it has produced a handsome bouquet of roses by other names. Thus there is "facial-quality tissue" that is not intended for use on faces, and "rinses" or "tints" for women who might be unsettled to think they dye their hair. In the world of deodorants, people never sweat or smell; they simply "offend." False teeth sound truer when known as "dentures."

6   Admen and packagers, of course, are not the only euphemizers. Almost any way of earning a salary above the level of ditchdigging is known as a profession rather than a job. Janitors for several years have been elevated by image-conscious unions to the status of "custodians"; nowadays, a teen-age rock guitarist with three chords to his credit can class himself with Horowitz as a "recording artist." Cadillac dealers refer to autos as "preowned" rather than "secondhand." Government researchers concerned with old people call them "senior citizens." Ads for bank credit cards and department stores refer to "convenient terms"—meaning 18% annual interest rates payable at the convenience of the creditor.

7   Jargon, the sublanguage peculiar to any trade, contributes to euphemism when its terms seep into general use. The student New Left, which shares a taste for six-syllable words with Government bureaucracy, has concocted a collection of substitute terms for use in politics. To "liberate," in the context of campus uproars, means to capture and occupy. Four people in agreement form a "coalition." In addition to "participatory democracy," which in practice is often a description of anarchy, the university radicals have half seriously given the world "anticipatory Communism," which means to steal. The New Left, though, still has a

long way to go before it can equal the euphemism-creating ability of Government officials. Who else but a Washington economist would invent the phrase "negative saver" to describe someone who spends more money than he makes?

8   A persistent source of modern euphemisms is the feeling, inspired by the prestige of science, that certain words contain implicit subjective judgments, and thus ought to be replaced with more "objective" terms. To speak of "morals" sounds both superior and arbitrary, as though the speaker were indirectly questioning those of the listener. By substituting "values," the concept is miraculously turned into a condition, like humidity or mass, that can be safely measured from a distance. To call someone "poor," in the modern way of thinking, is to speak pejoratively of his condition, while the substitution of "disadvantaged" or "underprivileged," indicates that poverty wasn't his fault. Indeed, says Linguist Mario Pei, by using "underprivileged," we are "made to feel that it is all our fault." The modern reluctance to judge makes it more offensive than ever before to call a man a liar; thus there is a "credibility gap" instead.

9   The liberalization of language in regard to sex involves the use of perhaps a dozen words. The fact of their currency in what was once known as polite conversation raises some unanswered linguistic questions. Which, really, is the rose, and which the other name? Are the old forbidden obscenities really the crude bedrock on which softer and shyer expressions have been built? Or are they simply coarser ways of expressing physical actions and parts of the human anatomy that are more accurately described in less explicit terms? It remains to be seen whether the so-called forbidden words will contribute anything to the honesty and openness of sexual discussion. Perhaps their real value lies in the power to shock, which is inevitably diminished by overexposure. Perhaps the Victorians, who preferred these words unspoken and unprinted, will prove to have had a point after all.

10   For all their prudery, the Victorians were considerably more willing than modern men to discuss ideas—such as social distinctions, morality and death—that have become almost unmentionable. Nineteenth century gentlewomen whose daughters had "limbs" instead of suggestive "legs" did not find it necessary to call their maids "housekeepers," nor did they bridle at referring to "upper" or "lower" classes within society. Rightly or wrongly, the Victorian could talk without embarrassment about "sin," a word that today few but clerics use with frequency or ease. It is even becoming difficult to find a doctor, clergyman or undertaker (known as a "mortician") who will admit that a man has died rather than "expired" or "passed away." Death has not lost its sting; the words for it have.

11   There is little if any hope that euphemisms will ever be excised from mankind's endless struggle with words that, as T. S. Eliot lamented, bend, break and crack under pressure. For one thing, certain kinds of everyday euphemisms have proved their psychological necessity. The uncertain morale of an awkward teen-ager may be momentarily buoyed if he thinks of himself as being afflicted by facial "blemishes" rather than "pimples." The label "For motion discomfort" that airlines place on paper containers undoubtedly helps the squeamish passenger keep con-

trol of his stomach in bumpy weather better than if they were called "vomit bags." Other forms of self-deception may not be beneficial, but may still be emotionally necessary. A girl may tolerate herself more readily if she thinks of herself as a "swinger" rather than as "promiscuous." Voyeurs can salve their guilt feelings when they buy tickets for certain "adult entertainments" on the ground that they are implicitly supporting "freedom of artistic expression."

12 Lexicographer Bergen Evans of Northwestern University believes that euphemisms persist because "lying is an indispensable part of making life tolerable." It is virtuous, but a bit beside the point, to contend that lies are deplorable. So they are; but they cannot be moralized or legislated away, any more than euphemisms can be. Verbal miasma, when it deliberately obscures truth, is an offense to reason. But the inclination to speak of certain things in uncertain terms is a reminder that there will always be areas of life that humanity considers too private, or too close to feelings of guilt, to speak about directly. Like stammers or tears, euphemisms will be created whenever men doubt, or fear, or do not know. The instinct is not wholly unhealthy; there is a measure of wisdom in the familiar saying that a man who calls a spade a spade is fit only to use one.

Haig Bosmajian

INSTRUMENTS OF POWER: NAMING AND DEFINING

1 "Sticks and stones may break my bones, but words can never hurt me." To accept this adage as valid is sheer folly. "What's in a name? that which we call a rose by any other name would smell as sweet." The answer to Juliet's question is "Plenty!" and to her own response to the question we can only say that this is by no means invariably true. The importance, significance, and ramifications of naming and defining people cannot be over-emphasized. From *Genesis* and beyond, to the present time, the power which comes from naming and defining people has had positive as well as negative effects on entire populations.

2 The magic of words and names has always been an integral part of both "primitive" and "civilized" societies. As Margaret Schlauch has observed, "from time immemorial men have thought there is some mysterious essential connection between a thing and the spoken name for it. You could use the name of your enemy, not only to designate him either passionately or dispassionately, but also to exercise a baleful influence."

3 Biblical passages abound in which names and naming are endowed with great power; from the very outset, in *Genesis,* naming and defining are attributed a significant potency: "And out of the ground the Lord God formed every beast of the field and every fowl of the air; and brought them unto Adam to see what he would call them: and whatsoever Adam

From the introduction to *The Language of Oppression* by Haig Bosmajian. Copyright © 1974 by Public Affairs Press, Washington, D.C.

called every living creature, that was the name thereof." Amidst the admonitions in *Leviticus* against theft, lying, and fraud is the warning: "And ye shall not swear my name falsely, neither shalt thou profane the name of thy God: I am the Lord." So important is the name that it must not be blasphemed; those who curse and blaspheme shall be stoned "and he that blasphemeth the name of the Lord, he shall surely be put to death, and all the congregation shall certainly stone him." So important is the name that the denial of it is considered a form of punishment: "But ye are they that foresake the Lord, that forget my holy mountain. . . . Therefore will I number you to the sword, and ye shall all bow down to the slaughter: because when I called, ye did not answer; when I spake, ye did not hear. . . . Therefore thus saith the Lord God, behold, my servants shall eat, but ye shall be hungry. . . . And ye shall leave your name for a curse unto my chosen: for the Lord God shall slay thee, and call his servants by another name."

4   To be unnamed is to be unknown, to have no identity. William Saroyan has observed that "the word nameless, especially in poetry and in much prose, signifies an alien, unknown, and almost unwelcome condition, as when, for instance, a writer speaks of 'a nameless sorrow.' " "Human beings," continues Saroyan, "are for the fact of being named at all, however meaninglessly, lifted out of an area of mystery, doubt, or undesirability into an area in which belonging to everybody else is taken for granted, so that one of the first questions asked by new people, two-year-olds even, whether they are speaking to other new people or to people who have been around for a great many years, is 'What is your name?' "

5   To receive a name is to be elevated to the status of a human being; without a name one's identity is questionable. In stressing the importance of a name and the significance of having none, Joyce Hertzler has said that "among both primitives and moderns, an individual has no definition, no validity for himself, without a name. His name is his badge of individuality, the means whereby he identifies himself and enters upon a truly subjective existence. My own name, for example, stands for me, a person. Divesting me of it reduces me to a meaningless, even pathological, nonentity."

6   In his book *What Is In A Name?* Farhang Zabeeth reminds us that "the Roman slaves originally were without names. Only after being sold they took their master's praenomen in the genitive case followed by the suffix—'por' (boy), e.g., 'Marcipor,' which indicates that some men, so long as they were regarded by others as cattle, did not need a name. However, as soon as they became servants some designation was called forth." To this day one of the forms of punishment meted out to wrong-doers who are imprisoned is to take away their names and to give them numbers. In an increasingly computerized age people are becoming mere numbers—credit card numbers, insurance numbers, bank account numbers, student numbers, et cetera. Identification of human beings by numbers is a negation of their humanity and their existence.

7   Philologist Max Muller has pointed out that "if we examine the most ancient word for 'name,' we find it is *naman* in Sanskrit, *nomen* in Latin, *namo* in Gothic. This *naman* stands for gnaman and is derived from

the root, *gna,* to know, and meant originally that by which we know a thing." In the course of the evolution of human society, R. P. Masani tells us, the early need for names "appears to have been felt almost simultaneously with the origin of speech . . . personality and the rights and obligations connected with it would not exist without the name." In his classic work *The Golden Bough* James Frazer devotes several pages to tabooed names and words in ancient societies, taboos reflecting the power and magic people saw in names and words. Frazer notes, for example, that "the North American Indian regards his name, not as a mere label, but as a distinct part of his personality, just as much as are his eyes or his teeth, and believes that injury will result as surely from the malicious handling of his name as from a wound inflicted on any part of his physical organism."

8   A name can be used as a curse. A name can be blasphemed. Namecalling is so serious a matter that statutes and court decisions prohibit "fighting words" to be uttered. In 1942 the United States Supreme Court upheld the conviction of a person who had addressed a police officer as "a God damned racketeer" and "a damned Fascist." (*Chaplinsky v. New Hampshire,* 315 U.S. 568). Such namecalling, such epithets, said the Court, are not protected speech. So important is one's "good name" that the law prohibits libel.

9   History abounds with instances in which the mere utterance of a name was prohibited. In ancient Greece, according to Frazer, "the names of the priests and other high officials who had to do with the performance of the Eleusinian mysteries might not be uttered in their lifetime. To pronounce them was a legal offense." Jorgen Ruud reports in *Taboo: A Study of Malagasy Customs and Beliefs* that among the Antandroy people the father has absolute authority in his household and that "children are forbidden to mention the name of their father. They must call him father, daddy. . . . The children may not mention his house or the parts of his body by their ordinary names, but must use other terms, i.e., euphemisms."

10   It was Iago who said in *Othello:*

> *Who steals my purse steals trash; 'tis something nothing;*
> *'Twas mine, 'tis his, and has been slave to thousands;*
> *But he that filches from me my good name*
> *Robs me of that which not enriches him*
> *And makes me poor indeed.*

11   Alice, In Lewis Carroll's *Through the Looking Glass,* had trepidations about entering the woods where things were nameless: "This must be the wood," she said thoughtfully to herself, "where things have no names. I wonder what'll become of *my* name when I go in? I shouldn't like to lose it at all—because they'd have to give me another, and it would almost certain to be an ugly one."

12   A Nazi decree of August 17, 1938 stipulated that "Jews may receive only those first names which are listed in the directives of the Ministry of the Interior concerning the use of first names." Further, the decree provided: "If Jews should bear first names other than those permitted . . .

they must . . . adopt an additional name. For males, that name shall be Israel, for females Sara." Another Nazi decree forbade Jews in Germany "to show themselves in public without a Jew's star. . . . [consisting] of a six-pointed star of yellow cloth with black borders, equivalent in size to the palm of the hand. The inscription is to read 'JEW' in black letters. It is to be sewn to the left breast of the garment, and to be worn visibly."

13   The power which comes from names and naming is related directly to the power to define others—individuals, races, sexes, ethnic groups. Our identities, who and what we are, how others see us, are greatly affected by the names we are called and the words with which we are labelled. The names, labels, and phrases employed to "identify" a people may in the end determine their survival. The word "define" comes from the Latin *definire,* meaning to limit. Through definition we restrict, we set boundaries, we name.

14   "When I use a word," said Humpty Dumpty in *Through the Looking Glass,* "it means just what I choose it to mean—neither more nor less." "The question is," said Alice, "whether you can make words mean so many different things." "The question is," said Humpty Dumpty, "which is to be master—that's all."

15   During his days as a civil rights-black power activist, Stokely Carmichael accurately asserted: "It [definition] is very, very important because I believe that people who can define are masters." Self-determination must include self-definition, the ability and right to name oneself; the master-subject relationship is based partly on the master's power to name and define the subject.

16   While names, words and language can be and are used to inspire us, to motivate us to humane acts, to liberate us, they can also be used to dehumanize human beings and to "justify" their suppression and even their extermination. It is not a great step from the coercive suppression of dissent to the extermination of dissenters (as the United States Supreme Court declared in its 1943 compulsory flag salute opinion in *West Virginia State Board of Education v. Barnette*); nor is it a large step from defining a people as non-human or sub-human to their subjugation or annihilation. One of the first acts of an oppressor is to redefine the "enemy" so they will be looked upon as creatures warranting separation, suppression, and even eradication.

17   The Nazis redefined Jews as "bacilli," "parasites," "disease," "demon," and "plague." In his essay "The Hollow Miracle," George Steiner informs us that the Germans "who poured quicklime down the openings of the sewers in Warsaw to kill the living and stifle the stink of the dead wrote about it. They spoke of having to 'liquidate vermin'. . . . Gradually, words lost their original meaning and acquired nightmarish definitions. *Jude, Pole, Russe* came to mean two-legged lice, putrid vermin which good Aryans must squash, as a [Nazi] Party manual said, 'like roaches on a dirty wall.' 'Final solution,' *endgültige Lösung,* came to signify the death of six million human beings in gas ovens."

18   The language of white racism has for centuries been used to "keep the nigger in his place." Our sexist language has allowed men to define who and what a woman is and must be. Labels like "traitors," "sabo-

teurs," "queers," and "obscene degenerates" were applied indiscriminately to students who protested the war in Vietnam or denounced injustices in the United States. Are such people to be listened to? Consulted? Argued with? Obviously not! One does not listen to, much less talk to, traitors and outlaws, sensualists and queers. One only punishes them or, as Spiro Agnew suggested in one of his 1970 speeches, there are some dissenters who should be separated "from our society with no more regret than we should feel over discarding rotten apples."[. . .]

19   This then is our task—to identify the decadence in our language, the inhumane uses of language, the "silly words and expressions" which have been used to justify the unjustifiable, to make palatable the unpalatable, to make reasonable the unreasonable, to make decent the indecent. Hitler's "Final Solution" appeared reasonable once the Jews were successfully labelled by the Nazis as sub-humans, as "parasites," "vermin," and "bacilli." The segregation and suppression of blacks in the United States were justified once they were considered "chattels" and "inferiors." The subjugation of the "American Indians" was defensible since they were defined as "barbarians" and "savages." As Peter Farb has said, "cannibalism, torture, scalping, mutilation, adultery, incest, sodomy, rape, filth, drunkenness—such a catalogue of accusations against a people is an indication not so much of their depravity as that their land is up for grabs." As long as adult women are "chicks," "girls," "dolls," "babes," and "ladies," their status in society will remain "inferior"; they will go on being treated as subjects in the subject-master relationship as long as the language of the law places them into the same class as children, minors, and the insane.

20   It is my hope that an examination of the language of oppression will result in a conscious effort by the reader to help cure this decadence in our language, especially that language which leads to dehumanization of the human being. One way for us to curtail the use of the language of oppression is for those who find themselves being defined into subjugation to rebel against such linguistic suppression. It isn't strange that those persons who insist on defining themselves, who insist on this elemental privilege of self-naming, self-definition, and self-identity encounter vigorous resistance. Predictably, the resistance usually comes from the oppressor or would-be oppressor and is a result of the fact that he or she does not want to relinquish the power which comes from the ability to define others.

ANALYSIS

structure   1. Write a thesis statement for "The Euphemism" and one for "Instruments of Power."

2. Compare the methods used in their introductions.

3. List the methods of development in each article.

4. List at least three sources (authorities) cited by each.

5. Compare the conclusions: Which moderates its position? Which sustains its position and attempts to motivate the reader?

6. Define *euphemism*.

7. Discuss "good" euphemisms and dangerous euphemisms.

8. Discuss "No one could argue that American English is under siege from linguistic falsehood" (paragraph 5) as it applies to politics, advertising, education, and other major areas of life.

9. Discuss "lying is an indispensable part of making life tolerable" (paragraph 12).

10. Considering the strong statements made in paragraphs 4 and 5 of "The Euphemism," does the "watered down" conclusion indicate some weaknesses in logic in the article? Discuss.

11. In the Bosmajian selection, what importance does the Bible give to names?

12. What happened to the names of Roman slaves?

13. What happens to the names of prisoners?

14. Discuss the quotation from *Othello* (Bosmajian, paragraph 10).

15. Explain: "Through definition we restrict, we set boundaries, we name" (paragraph 12).

16. How is language used to separate people?

17. Discuss the differences in tone of the two selections.

18. In his book *The Second Sin,* psychiatrist Thomas Szasz says: "The struggle for definition is veritably the struggle for life itself . . . he who defines (thus) dominates and lives; he who is defined is subjugated and may be killed." In "Instruments of Power," Bosmajian says: "The importance, significance, and ramifications of defining people cannot be over-emphasized." He also quotes Stokely Carmichael as saying: "It (definition) is very, very important because I believe that people who can define are masters." Discuss. Apply the quotations to situations in politics, education, religion, etc.

section 8c

The two extended definitions that follow are both taken from the introductions to recent full-length books written by veteran writers. One sees the world of sports as a virtual religion; the other sees it as the root of many of the evils of our society. Both see sports as having an influence on our lives far beyond the stadiums and the playfields.

Read both selections, each of which might seem extreme in its own way, before coming to your own conclusions.

Michael Novak

THE JOY OF SPORTS

1   I love sports, and I want to bequeath that love to my children—to that stranger with the mitt who is ten, and the two girls who are eight and three. It seems a precious gift to give. But why? Why do I love sports? How can I explain it to myself, let alone to others, especially to those who are skeptical unbelievers?

2   Sports is, somehow, a religion. You either see or you don't see what the excitement is. I wish wives were not so often unbelievers; but, then, many of the male sex are agnostic, too. Often I feel sorry for them. I smart, as well, under their transmitted belief in their own superiority.

3   James Wechsler expressed on New Year's 1974 my own sentiments: "The country seems divided between those caught up in the frenzy and those who could not care less. In many places, the latter must feel like aliens." Wechsler himself was at a New Year's party, serious and contemplative, and when he asked his hosts if he could slip into the study to watch the end of the Notre Dame–Alabama game, he felt a cold condescension circle out from the others and noticed the "fatalistic expression" on the countenance of his wife. The conversation had been intelligent and somber: the state of the nation, Watergate, etc. Wechsler had felt the contest sliding by, unwatched. Heroically, he had not referred to it, wondering all the while how anybody could be so insensitive as to schedule dinner during the hours of such a game. His secret desire voiced, the others turned on him. A journalist snapped: "It's the most *American* thing you can do!" Wechsler knew what he meant by that: "How could an allegedly mature man squander time watching pros claw at each other for pay, or give a damn whether Notre Dame beats Alabama?"

4   But it *is* so important whether Notre Dame beats Alabama. Can't unbelievers understand?

5   The accusation made against Wechsler is a prejudice all believers live under: "To love sports is to love the lowest common denominator, to be lower-class, adolescent, patriotic in a corny way." The *intellectual* thing, the *liberal* thing, the *mature* thing is to set sports aside.

6   This severe prejudice is not usually fatal, not at least to persons of goodwill; but it *is* evidence of insufficiently developed perception. The basic reality of all human life is play, games, sport; these are the realities from which the basic metaphors for all that is important in the rest of life are drawn. Work, politics, and history are the illusory, misleading, false world. *Being, beauty, truth, excellence, transcendence*—these words, grown in the soil of play, wither in the sand of work. Art, prayer, worship, love, civilization: these thrive in the field of play. Play belongs to the Kingdom of Ends, work to the Kingdom of Means. Barbarians play in order to work; the civilized work in order to play.

7   The severe Puritan bias of America leads us to under-value sports.

From *The Joy of Sports: End Zones, Bases, Baskets, Balls, and the Consecration of the American Spirit*, by Michael Novak. © 1976 by Michael Novak, Basic Books, Inc., Publishers, New York. Reprinted with permission of publisher.

America took root in Protestant culture, and as de Tocqueville noted in 1836, Americans did not play, had no sports, centered their lives in work. As America has grown more Catholic, more Jewish, more various, the world of play has acquired intellectual traditions here. The nation needs a post-Protestant understanding of itself. At the heart of its rejuvenation may lie sports.

8   When John F. Kennedy wished to underline the seriousness of some impending decision, he made certain that the news media showed pictures of him playing touch football or walking on the beach. The most important things are in the hands of God, so to speak, and the appropriate human attitude is to enjoy the combat.

9   When Richard M. Nixon wished to underline the seriousness of some impending decision, he made sure the news media learned that he was staying up all night asking for a fresh supply of yellow legal pads, sending out for cottage cheese and catsup. The most important crises, so to speak, require that God's suffering servants *suffer*. The appropriate human attitude is seriousness, suffering, self-discipline. Nixon talked about sports but played little. Sports were part of his work; he made them lessons in morality, rather than in liberty and joy.

10   To care about the Notre Dame-Alabama game during an evening of discussion is—take your pick—A sign of grace? Machismo? Regression? Humanism?

11   Faith in sports, I have discovered, seeks understanding. I cannot forever split my life in two, half in love with sports, half in love with serious thought. Life seeks unity. This book is an attempt by a believer to explore his belief, to find some useful words for it, to give his head reasons for what his heart already knows. Next New Year's Day, again, I will watch three football games. But why? Why is sports a good love, worthy of the best men have to give it?

12   Other believers know how hard it is to put in words what they so deeply and obscurely know. They have also argued with their wives and friends, and even in their own heads. All around this land there is a faith without an explanation, a love without a rationale. This book is written to fill a void among the faithful.

13   It is also written for unbelievers. Perhaps they will gain a larger, ecumenical understanding of those who partake of religions not their own. Perhaps they will learn, vicariously, even if the gift of faith is not given them, what others feel and love.

14   An unbeliever might think that anyone who has seen one football game has seen them all, and that anyone who has seen a hundred, or a thousand, games has seen everything there is to see in them. I know it isn't true, but I have to ask myself, "What grabs me? *Why* do I keep coming back?"

15   I hope the reader enjoys bringing experience into consciousness. This book is not complete if only the author searches memory; the readers must join the game as well. When a sentence hits the mark, let the reader call a strike; when it misses, let the reader hit the corner I was aiming at. Putting things in words is a sport as difficult as any other. I would be happy if this little essay gets others playing it with excellence.

16   There is not much competition in the field at present. Most books

about sports are hagiography, "lives of the saints," hero worship. Other books debunk sports, exposing their corruptions and pretensions. Still others are social science ideologies and theories. In philosophy, a book by Paul Weiss, *The Philosophy of Sports*, stands virtually alone. Considering the importance of sports to humankind—considering the eminence of stadia and gyms and playing fields on university campuses, comparing the size of the sports section to any other in the paper—our intellectual negligence is inexcusable. Only prejudice, or unbelief, can account for it.

17 What "grabs" so many millions? What is the secret power attraction? How can we care so much?

18 I concentrate on baseball, football, and basketball because these are the three sports I love best, a holy trinity. They are also the three that seem to be most powerful in our nation's consciousness. All three were invented in the last hundred years or so. Despite some debts to other games in other lands, all three were invented in America, for Americans. Of the hundreds of sports that might have grown up here, these are the ones that have captured the imagination, energies, and hard work of many millions. What sort of religions are they?

19 I can't say I follow every game with passion. But I am always aware of the Dodgers' fate; it is on some track parallel to mine. And likewise the fate of Notre Dame, the Knicks, the Jets. When they are up, I am up; when they lose, I must learn to tolerate defeat. Many hours of comfort, peace, wisdom, community, and courage these mythic clubs have given me! A belief in miracles (the Franco Harris catch in the last six seconds of a game given up as lost to Oakland in the playoffs of 1972). A sense of continuity. Respect for the brilliant fairness—and unfairness—of the Fates.

20 Sports is part of my religion, like Christianity, or "Western civilization," or poetry, or politics. Philosophers speak of "language games"; their games do not satisfy parts of the human spirit which football reaches. Not that football satisfies everything. It doesn't offer much guidance in how to understand a woman. The emotions it dramatizes, deeper and more mystical than doubters will ever understand, are not the most complex. They are, however, basic, and often starved for notice. "Of armaments and men I sing," Vergil wrote. If war is the teacher men have turned to in order to learn teamwork, discipline, coolness under fire, respect for contingency and fate, football is my moral equivalent of war.

21 Say, if you like, that men *ought* to be less primitive, less violent, less mesmerized by pain and injury. Say, if you like, that football dramatizes what is worst in the human breast and ought, like pornography, to be refused public benediction. Football makes conscious to me part of what I am. And what football says about me, and about millions of others like me, is not half so ugly as it is beautiful. Seeing myself reflected in the dance, the agony and the ritual of a heated contest, I am at peace.

22 So, sitting there that Monday night in September, three days before my fortieth birthday, I watched what I had watched hundreds of times. What gripped me to the set for three hours of a rapidly passing life? It was not novelty. It was some mythic form, some mystic struggle, which the drama of baseball in a million variations game by game portrays. Like football, baseball is a game of aesthetic form, a ritual elaborating some

music of the human spirit. Done well, it is as satisfying as a symphony, as moving as *Swan Lake* or *Madame Butterfly*. People who respond aesthetically to sports are sane. Those who do not may be teachable.

23   There is no substitute for the squeak of sneakers on the court and the sound of the ball slipping through the cords. No words are as adequate as the cool sheen of a baseball fresh from its paper wrapper, tossed to the pitcher at the height of the last game of the World Series. No analysis does justice to the instantaneous decision of a quarterback, trapped on his goal line in the waning seconds of a game, to snap the pigskin toward a blurred target at his distant 30-yard line. To talk about sports without recreating their drama, feel, and excitement would render one worthy of death by continuous committee meetings, from which fate God spare us all.

24   Sports are bursts of dust, squeaky wood, infield grass, collisions at second base, an explosive tackle—they are vivid, concrete, swift, and fun. If this book is to mirror the reality of sports, it must be vivid and concrete; it must be tense with action, switch from scene to scene as swiftly as a television camera. The sections I have called "Sportsreel" may help to do that.

25   The writer should enjoy it with the reader, and perhaps a little more. In all my life I have loved few things as much as sports, found few as faithful and as satisfying. To linger over a book on sports is, for a philosopher, almost too much pleasure; for a theologian, sinful. But delicious.

Robert Lipsyte

SPORTSWORLD: AN AMERICAN DREAMLAND

1   For the past one hundred years most Americans have believed that playing and watching competitive games are not only healthful activities, but represent a positive force on our national psyche. In sports, they believe, children will learn courage and self-control, old people will find blissful nostalgia, and families will discover new ways to communicate among themselves. Immigrants will find shortcuts to recognition as Americans. Rich and poor, black and white, educated and unskilled, we will all find a unifying language. The melting pot may be a myth, but we will all come together in the ballpark.

2   This faith in sports has been vigorously promoted by industry, the military, government, the media. The values of the arena and the locker room have been imposed upon our national life. Coaches and sportswriters are speaking for generals and businessmen, too, when they tell us that a man must be physically and psychologically "tough" to succeed, that he must be clean and punctual and honest, that he must bear pain, bad

From *SportsWorld: An American Dreamland.* Copyright © 1975 by Robert Lipsyte. Reprinted by permission of *Times Books,* a division of Quadrangle/The New York Times Book Co., Inc.

luck, and defeat without whimpering or making excuses. A man must prove his faith in sports and the American Way by whipping himself into shape, playing by the rules, being part of the team, and putting out all the way. If his faith is strong enough, he will triumph. It's his own fault if he loses, fails, remains poor.

3   Even for ballgames, these values, with their implicit definitions of manhood, courage, and success, are not necessarily in the individual's best interests. But for daily life they tend to create a dangerous and grotesque web of ethics and attitudes, an amorphous infrastructure that acts to contain our energies, divert our passions, and socialize us for work or war or depression.

4   I call this infrastructure SportsWorld. For most of my adult life, as a professional observer, I've explored SportsWorld and marveled at its incredible power and pervasiveness. SportsWorld touches everyone and everything. We elect our politicians, judge our children, fight our wars, plan our vacations, oppress our minorities by SportsWorld standards that somehow justify our foulest and freakiest deeds, or at least camouflage them with jargon. We get stoned on such SportsWorld spectaculars as the Super Bowl, the space shots, the Kentucky Derby, the presidential conventions, the Indianapolis 500, all of whose absurd excesses reassure us that we're okay.

5   SportsWorld is a sweaty Oz you'll never find in a geography book, but since the end of the Civil War it has been promoted and sold to us like Rancho real estate, an ultimate sanctuary, a university for the body, a community for the spirit, a place to hide that glows with that time of innocence when we believed that rules and boundaries were honored, that good triumphed over evil, and that the loose ends of experience could be caught and bound and delivered in an explanation as final and as comforting as a goodnight kiss.

6   Sometime in the last fifty years the sports experience was perverted into a SportsWorld state of mind in which the winner was good because he won; the loser, if not actually bad, was at least reduced, and had to prove himself over again, through competition. As each new immigrant crop was milled through the American system, a pick of the harvest was displayed in the SportsWorld showcase, a male preserve of national athletic entertainment traditionally enacted by the working class for the middle class, much as the performing arts are played by the middle class for the amusement of the upper class.

7   By the 1950s, when SportsWorld was dominated by what are now called "white ethnics," the black American was perceived as a challenging force and was encouraged to find outlets in the national sports arena. Although most specific laws against black participation had already been erased, it took cautious, humiliating experiments with such superstars as Jackie Robinson and Larry Doby to prove that spectator prejudice could be deconditioned by a winning team. Within a few years, pools of cheap, eager black and dark Latin labor were channeled into mainstream clubs.

8   So pervasive are the myths of SportsWorld that the recruitment of blacks has been regarded as a gift of true citizenship bestowed upon the Negro when he was ready. It has been conventional wisdom for twenty years that the black exposure in sports has speeded the integration of

American society, that white Americans, having seen that blacks are beautiful and strong, became "liberalized."

9   This is one of the crueler hoaxes of SportsWorld. Sports success probably has been detrimental to black progress. By publicizing the material success of a few hundred athletes, thousands, perhaps millions, of bright young blacks have been swept toward sports when they should have been guided toward careers in medicine or engineering or business. For every black star celebrated in SportsWorld, a thousand of his little brothers were neutralized, kept busy shooting baskets until it was too late for them to qualify beyond marginal work.

10   The white male spectator who knew few ordinary black men to measure himself against may have had his awareness raised by watching such superior human beings as Frank Robinson, Jim Brown, Bill Russell, O. J. Simpson, and other highly merchandised SportsWorld heroes, but it also doubled his worst fears about blacks: added to the black junkie who would rip out his throat was the black superstud who could replace him as a man—in bed, on the job, as a model for his children.

11   By the middle of the 1970s it seemed as though the black experience in SportsWorld might be recapitulated by women. SportsWorld seemed on the verge of becoming the arena in which women would discover and exploit their new "equality." It would be a complex test of adaptability for SportsWorld. The major sports were created by men for the superior muscles, size, and endurance of the male body. Those sports in which balance, flexibility, and dexterity are the crucial elements have never been mass-promoted in America. When a woman beats a man at a man's game, she has to play like a man.

12   There were signs, however, that women may not embrace Sports-World as eagerly as did the blacks, profiting from that sorry lesson as well as from their own greater leverage in American society. It is no accident that Billie Jean King, while still an active player, became an entrepreneur and an important voice in American cultural consciousness while Jackie Robinson was a Rockefeller courtier almost to the end of his life.

13   A great deal of the angry energy generated in America through the coming apart of the 1960s was absorbed by SportsWorld in its various roles as socializer, pacifier, safety valve; as a concentration camp for adolescents and an emotional Disneyland for their parents; as a laboratory for human engineering and a reflector of current moral postures; and as a running commercial for Our Way of Life. SportsWorld is a buffer, a DMZ, between people and the economic and political systems that direct their lives; women, so long denied this particular playland, may just avoid this trap altogether.

14   But SportsWorld's greatest power has always been its flexibility. Even as we are told of SportsWorld's proud traditions, immutable laws, ultimate security from the capriciousness of "real life," SportsWorld is busy changing its rules, readjusting its alliances, checking the trends. SportsWorld is nothing if not responsive. Hockey interest lagging, how about a little more blood on the ice? Speed up baseball with a designated hitter. Move the football goal posts. A three-point shot in basketball. Women agitating at the college arena gates? Let 'em in. Give 'em athletic

scholarships, "jock" dorms, and Minnie Mouse courses. How about a Professional Women's Power Volleyball League?

15   Stars, teams, leagues, even entire sports may rise or fall or never get off the ground, but SportsWorld as a force in American life orbits on.

16   Ah, baseball. Our National Pastime. An incredibly complex contrivance that seems to have been created by a chauvinistic mathematician intent upon giving America a game so idiosyncratic that it would be at least a century before any other country could beat us at it. And indeed it was. After a century in which baseball was celebrated as a unique product of the American character, Chinese boys began winning Little League championships, and young men from Latin America and the Caribbean began making a significant impact upon the major leagues. The highly organized Japanese, who had taken up the game during the postwar occupation of their country (perhaps as penance for yelling "To Hell with Babe Ruth" during banzai charges) were almost ready to attack again.

17   But SportsWorld had spun on. That other peculiarly American game, football, declared itself the New National Pastime. Baseball and God were announced dead at about the same time, but the decision against baseball apparently is taking longer to reverse, thanks in the main to pro football's colossal public relations machine. The National Football League played its scheduled games on Sunday, November 24, 1963, because its historic television deal was pending and Commissioner Pete Rozelle was determined to prove that nothing, *nothing,* could cancel the show. But that winter, NFL sportscasters infiltrated the banquet circuit with the engaging theory—quintessential SportsWorld—that America had been at the brink of a nervous breakdown after President Kennedy's assassination and that only The Sport of the Sixties' business-as-usual attitude had held the country together until Monday's National Day of Mourning unified us all in public grief.

18   Ten years later, though hopefully still grateful, America had grown bored with the cartoon brutality of pro football. America was boogieing to the magic moves and hip, sly rhythms of basketball, The Sport of the Seventies. We've had enough of pure violence, simulated or otherwise, went the SportsWorld wisdom, now we need something smooooooooth.

19   There is no end to SportsWorld theories—of the past, the present, the future—especially now that a new generation of commentators, athletes, coaches, and fans feel free to reform and recast sports, to knock it off the pedestal and slide it under the microscope, giving it more importance than ever. SportsWorld newspapermen dare to describe to us action that we have seen more clearly on television than they have from the press box, and SportsWorld telecasters, isolated from the world in their glass booths, dare to explain to us what the players are *really* thinking. SportsWorld analysts were once merely "pigskin prognosticators" predicting the weekend football scores; now they may be as heavy as any RAND Corporation futurist. Is hockey an art form or is it a paradigm of anarchy, in which case we are obligated as concerned citizens to watch it? Is tennis more than just a convenient new market for clothes and building materials and nondurable goods? What will be The Sport of the Eighties?

Will no sport ever again have its own decade? Will cable television and government-regulated sports gambling and the institutionalized fragmenting of society balkanize us into dozens of jealous Fandoms?

20 SportsWorld, once determinedly anti-intellectual, has become a hotbed of psychologists, physicians, and sociologists questioning premises as well as specific techniques. Should lacrosse players really be eating steak before games, or pancakes? Why are the lockers of defensive linemen neater than those of offensive linemen? Does athletic participation truly "build character" or does it merely reinforce otherwise unacceptable traits? Should communities rather than corporations own teams?

21 But very few people seem to be questioning SportsWorld itself, exploring the possibility that if sports could be separated from SportsWorld we could take a major step toward liberation from the false values, the stereotypes, the idols of the arena that have burdened us all since childhood.

22 SportsWorld is not a conspiracy in the classic sense, but rather an expression of a community of interest. In the Soviet Union, for example, where world-class athletes are the diplomat-soldiers of ideology, and where factory girls are forced to exercise to reduce fatigue and increase production, the entire athletic apparatus is part of government. Here in America, SportsWorld's insidious power is imposed upon athletics by the banks that decide which arenas and recreational facilities shall be built, by the television networks that decide which sports shall be sponsored and viewed, by the press that decides which individuals and teams shall be celebrated, by the municipal governments that decide which clubs shall be subsidized, and by the federal government, which has, through favorable tax rulings and exemptions from law, allowed sports entertainment to grow until it has become the most influential form of mass culture in America.

23 SportsWorld is a grotesque distortion of sports. It has limited the pleasures of play for most Americans while concentrating on turning our best athletes into clowns. It has made the finish more important than the race, and extolled the game as that William Jamesian absurdity, a moral equivalent to war, and the hero of the game as that Henry Jamesian absurdity, a "muscular Christian." It has surpassed patriotism and piety as a currency of communication, while exploiting them both. By the end of the 1960s, SportsWorld wisdom had it that religion was a spectator sport while professional and college athletic contests were the only events Americans held sacred.

24 SportsWorld is neither an American nor a modern phenomenon. Those glorified Olympics of ancient Greece were manipulated for political and commercial purposes; at the end, they held a cracked mirror to a decaying civilization. The modern Olympics were revived at the end of the nineteenth century in an attempt to whip French youth into shape for a battlefield rematch with Germany. Each country of Europe, then the United States, the Soviet Union, the "emerging" nations of Africa and Asia, used the Olympics as political display windows. The 1972 Arab massacre of Israeli athletes was a hideously logical extension of SportsWorld philosophy.

25 SportsWorld begins in elementary school, where the boys are sepa-

rated from the girls. In *Sixties Going on Seventies,* Nora Sayre recounts the poignant confrontation of a gay man and a gay woman at a meeting. She is banging the floor with a baseball bat, and he asks her to stop; the bat symbolizes to him the oppression of sports in his childhood. But to her the bat symbolizes liberation from the restraint that had kept her from aggression, from sports, in her childhood.

26   By puberty, most American children have been classified as failed athletes and assigned to watch and cheer for those who have survived the first of several major "cuts." Those who have been discarded to the grandstands and to the television sets are not necessarily worse off than those tapped for higher levels of competition. SportsWorld heroes exist at sufferance, and the path of glory is often an emotional minefield trapped with pressures to perform and fears of failure. There is no escape from SportsWorld, for player or spectator or even reporter, that watcher in the shadows who pretends to be in the arena but above the fray.

ANALYSIS

structure   1. Write a thesis statement for the introduction to *The Joy of Sports* and another for the introduction to *SportsWorld.*

2. List the major points of each selection.

opinion   3. Whose view of sports do you support? Why?

Review of Chapter 8

Definitions can have very serious consequences. To a large degree, those who decide what intelligence is decide who goes to college; those who decide what crime is decide who goes to jail; and those who decide what death is decide when life-support systems can be removed and when organ transplants can take place.

The more complex or controversial the term is, the more the writer must struggle to make his definition clear. Most extended definitions are structured by introducing the term and then using one or more methods of development to explain the author's meaning. Sometimes, however, the term is introduced later in the selection or not at all.

As a reader, you may find it important to learn of the motives of a definer: Consider the language of Watergate (Section 8A). Sometimes you should know the historical context of a term: Consider the tomato that "went" to the Supreme Court (in the introduction to this chapter), and the definitions of *liberal* and *conservative* ("Pop, What's a Populist?" Section 8A). It's always important to keep an open mind: Consider the amazingly different views of American sports in *The Joy of Sports* and *SportsWorld.*

WRITING SUGGESTIONS

Write an extended definition of an interest or activity that has an important effect on our lives, such as politics, religion, love, philosophy, or entertainment.

Cause/Effect

CHAPTER 9

READING FOCUS

- ❖ Be wary of simplistic reasoning: "Causes" that seem most immediate and apparent often are not the actual causes.
- ❖ Look for the cause/effect pattern so that you can more quickly master the selection.
- ❖ Be aware that causes and effects sometimes chain react—effects becoming causes of other effects. Keep careful track of cause/effect relationships to avoid mistaking the effect of one cause for that of another.
- ❖ Be aware of the point of view of the writer. In seeking the causes of World War II, for example, you will get different answers from the Russians, the Germans, and the Americans, and from economists, psychologists, philosophers, and historians.

WRITING FOCUS

- ❖ Don't jump to conclusions about causes. There is often more than one reason for a given effect.
- ❖ Decide whether you will achieve your purpose more effectively by emphasizing causes, by emphasizing effects, or by discussing both at length.
- ❖ By focusing on a dramatic or tragic effect at the beginning of your paper, you can usually capture your readers' interest, making them want to read on.

❖ Realize that situations change and causes change. We can't solve pollution problems today by getting the horses off the streets.

❖ When there is a chain of causation, be sure to explain the connection between each effect and its cause. Don't take for granted that your reader will follow your line of thinking.

❖ In writing about causal relationships, be as much aware of your own biases as you are of those of your sources.

❖ When you believe that you've found a cause, don't just state it. Support it.

A cause is what makes something happen. An effect is what happens. Cause/effect writing deals with "why," "what makes," "what causes," and their consequences.

Some students run into trouble with cause/effect papers when they neglect to limit their subjects and try to deal with global problems in 500 words. Some reach into the grab bag of "plain," "simple," "evident," "common sense" solutions for highly complex problems. They would, for example, lower taxes while providing more services, blindly trust in a leader, or seek "peace" through bombs. Others may espouse love, but too often they fail to explain how to get people to stop fighting long enough to love each other.

In his book *Why Glass Breaks, Rubber Bends, and Glue Sticks,* Malcolm E. Weiss explains that the differences in the properties of these substances are caused largely by their molecular structure. Although human beings have used these materials for centuries, only in the past hundred years or so have we learned why they do what they do. If it took centuries for us to find why glass breaks and rubber bounces, perhaps we should not feel too frustrated at not yet having solved some of the more complex problems that develop in human relationships.

In "Can Man Survive?" (Section 6B), William Safire says, "Every solution breeds new problems." He quotes historian Daniel Boorstin as declaring that democracy is not the solution to anything but the process of solving problems its solutions create. "Getting there is all the fun," says Boorstin.

To write good cause/effect papers, then, students must have a lot of curiosity, a bit of humility, a touch of cynicism, and a sense of humor. And don't, of course, forget good organization and development.

Read all the selections; then answer the questions.

THE START OF THE NUCLEAR RACE

When the first atomic bomb to be used in warfare ignited the city of Hiroshima at 8:00 a.m. on the morning of August 6, 1945, instantly killing at least 78,000 civilians, the human race took its first terrifying step down the road toward possible self-annihilation. Since that time, the nuclear arms race has continued virtually unchecked until today. The United States possesses 9,000 strategic nuclear weapons, and the Soviet Union 4,500. Due to technological developments, any one of these weapons makes the city-destroying bombs of 1945 look insignificant. Non-nuclear weapons continue to be used to settle political differences, and account for the deaths of 22 million people since the bombing of Hiroshima. At present, over one billion dollars a day is being squandered by the nations of the world to maintain and increase their arsenals.

Richard Malishchak, in a review of the United Nations Special Session on Disarmament, May-June 1978.

THE BIRTH OF LAKE ERIE

Lake Erie, the last of the Great Lakes to be discovered, was the first to take form. In preglacial ages a mighty river flowed eastward through what is now the Lake Erie basin. When the ice sheet formed and moved south, it rammed one lobe along the axis of this stream. It gouged heavily into the soft Devonian shales to the east, and it carved deep grooves in the hard, resistant Devonian limestone at Sandusky Bay to the west. These grooves are conspicuous on the islands, especially on Kelleys Island, where one exposed section of this glacial sculpture has been made into a state park. The southwestern lobe of its basin, where the white pioneers found the Black Swamp, was first uncovered when the last of the ice sheets, known as the Wisconsin, began to melt back from the corner of present Ohio, Indiana, and Michigan. The sun had beat upon the advancing front of this ice sheet, melting it down and releasing from its frozen grip the billions of tons of rock and gravel which were left piled up in terminal moraines 500 feet deep in places. The water filled in between the moraines and the receding ice sheet and discharged out of the Maumee lobe down the Wabash River. And when the water was extensive enough to be called a lake, Lake Erie had begun its metamorphosis to its present shore lines.

Harlan Hatcher, *Lake Erie.*

"GHOSTS" ON TV

"Ghosts" or multiple images on a television screen are caused by re-flected signals. Televison signals travel in a direct path from the transmit-ting antenna to the receiving antenna on the television set. These signals are then converted by the television apparatus into images on its screen. Sometimes, however, the receiving antenna also receives signals that have been transmitted by the television station and then are reflected from something that gets in the way, such as a water tower, mountain or hill, airplane, etc. Since the reflected signals travel a greater distance than the direct signals, they are weaker and arrive later at the receiving antenna. Because these reflected signals arrive later, their timing is different from that of the direct signals. This difference causes the television set to produce a separate image or images. These separate images appear to one side of those produced on the screen by direct signals. They are weaker and give a "ghostlike" appearance; consequently, they are called "ghosts."

Joseph P. Dagher, *Technical Communication.* © 1978. By permission of Prentice-Hall, Inc.

WHAT AMERICANS WANT

Europeans with time-honored experience in the technique of pain-lessly extracting cash from foreigners' pockets have correctly gauged that Americans like to travel abroad provided they don't really have to leave home. They've seen the U.S. armed forces and U.S. oil companies spend mil-lions to give their personnel the illusion of living in a European or African suburbia filled with shopping centers, post exchanges, movie houses, ice-cream parlors, juke boxes, and American-style parking lots. Smart promoters now give the American abroad exactly what he wants. Hotel rooms are fur-nished to please him, meal hours drastically advanced to suit the American habit of eating dinner at 6 P.M., arrangements made to satisfy the Ameri-cans' affection for crowds, action, and noise.

Joseph Wechsberg, "The American Abroad." Copyright © 1957 by The Atlantic Monthly Company, Boston. Reprinted by permission of Paul R. Reynolds, Inc.

"LIFE" ON DEATH ROW

Gary McGivern, who spent 33 months on death row before his con-viction was reversed, tried later to describe the atmosphere there:

"New York's death row at Green Haven State Prison was an ugly, degrading, and dehumanizing place. Sunshine was considered subversive, so the windows were opaque. The condemned men were locked in their cells 23 hours a day. Living conditions on death row were absent of any

Fellowship Magazine. By permission of the Fellowship of Reconciliation.

human values primarily because the death sentence reduces condemned men to pieces of meat. The function of death row was to preserve the meat until it was legally ready for cooking. On death row it was illegal to grow mentally, develop spiritually, and feel emotionally. Execution on these levels of living took place every day. It was a struggle to stay alive. When you sentence a person to death, you aren't treating him like a human being. In fact, the law is saying this human being doesn't belong in our society and we have to kill him. So the confinement on death row is just an extension of that type of thinking. To retain any self-respect and dignity is a daily struggle. It's not the fault of the people working there, the immediate people in charge. It's a matter of the structure itself. It draws what is negative out of human beings. Most of the people on death rows are from that part of our society which is uneducated, poor, from crime-infested areas. Yet they're all people. There's something within us all that's pure and creative."

Karl Menninger

THE CRIME OF PUNISHMENT

1   The great secret, the deeply buried mystery of the apparent public apathy to crime and to proposals for better controlling crime, lies in the persistent, intrusive wish for vengeance.

2   We are ashamed of it; we deny to ourselves and to others that we are influenced by it. Our morals, our religious teachings, even our laws repudiate it. But behind what we do to the offender is the desire for revenge on someone—and the unknown villain proved guilty of wrongdoing is a good scapegoat. We call it a wish to see justice done, i.e., to have him "punished." But in the last analysis this turns out to be a thin cloak for vengeful feelings directed against a legitimized object.

3   It is natural to resent a hurt, and all of us have many unfulfilled wishes to hurt back. But in our civilization that just is not done—openly. Personal revenge we have renounced, but official legalized revenge we can still enjoy. Once someone has been labeled an offender and proved guilty of an offense he is fair game, and our feelings come out in the form of a conviction that a hurt to society should be "repaid."

4   This sentiment of retaliation is, of course, exactly what impels most offenders to do what they do. Except for racketeers, robbers, and professional criminals, the men who are arrested, convicted, and sentenced are usually out to avenge a wrong, assuage a sense of injury, or correct an injustice as they see it. Their victims are individuals whom they believe to be assailants, false friends, rivals, unfaithful spouses, cruel parents—or symbolic figures representing these individuals. . . .

5   Today criminals rather than witches and peasants have become the official wrongdoers, eligible for punitive repayment. Prosecuting attorneys have become *our* agents, if not God's, and often seem to embody the very spirit of revenge and punition. They are expected to be tough, and to strike hard. . . .

From *The Crime of Punishment* by Karl Menninger, M.D. Copyright © 1966, 1968 by Jeannetta Menninger. Reprinted by permission of Viking Penguin, Inc.

Arnold Bennett

WHY A CLASSIC IS A CLASSIC

In earlier paragraphs Bennett suggests that classics are created by a minority of passionate and persistent literary enthusiasts.

What causes the passionate few to make such a fuss about literature? There can be only one reply. They find a keen and lasting pleasure in literature. They enjoy literature as some men enjoy beer. The recurrence of this pleasure naturally keeps their interest in literature very much alive. They are for ever making new researches, for ever practising on themselves. They learn to understand themselves. They learn to know what they want. Their taste becomes surer and surer as their experience lengthens. They do not enjoy to-day what will seem tedious to them to-morrow. When they find a book tedious, no amount of popular clatter will persuade them that it is pleasurable; and when they find it pleasurable no chill silence of the street-crowds will affect their conviction that the book is good and permanent. They have faith in themselves. What are the qualities in a book which give keen and lasting pleasure to the passionate few? This is a question so difficult that it has never yet been completely answered. You may talk lightly about truth, insight, knowledge, wisdom, humour, and beauty. But these comfortable words do not really carry you very far, for each of them has to be defined, especially the first and last. It is all very well for Keats in his airy manner to assert that beauty is truth, truth beauty, and that that is all he knows or needs to know. I, for one, need to know a lot more. And I never shall know. Nobody, not even Hazlitt nor Sainte-Beuve, has ever finally explained why he thought a book beautiful. I take the first fine lines that come to hand—

> The woods of Arcady are dead,
> And over is their antique joy—

and I say that those lines are beautiful because they give me pleasure. But why? No answer! I only know that the passionate few will, broadly, agree with me in deriving this mysterious pleasure from those lines. I am only convinced that the liveliness of our pleasure in those and many other lines by the same author will ultimately cause the majority to believe, by faith, that W. B. Yeats is a genius. The one reassuring aspect of the literary affair is that the passionate few are passionate about the same things. A continuance of interest does, in actual practice, lead ultimately to the same judgments. There is only the difference in width of interest Some of the passionate few lack catholicity, or, rather, the whole of their interest is confined to one narrow channel; they have none left over. These men help specially to vitalise the reputations of the narrower geniuses: such as Crashaw. But their active predilections never contradict the general verdict of the passionate few; rather they reinforce it.

From *Literary Taste: How to Form It,* by Arnold Bennett. Copyright © 1927 by Doubleday & Company, Inc. Reprinted by permission of Doubleday.

Laura Nader

STUDYING UP

1   Look at social science literature in the United States and you will find abundant research on ethnic groups, the poor, and the disadvantaged, but very little on the middle class and scarcely any on the upper classes. There are well over 600 journals in the behavioral sciences alone—psychology, anthropology, and sociology—spewing forth new findings each year, yet over 90 percent of the funding for social science research is allocated for studies of lower economic classes. Social scientists should examine the consequences of this bias, which prefers that the subject of study be socially inferior to the researcher.

2   Studying "up" as well as "down" would force us to rephrase many "common sense" questions. Instead of asking why some people are poor, we would ask why some people are so greedy. We would have to explain the fantastic resistance to change among those whose options are so many—the universities, the auto industry, the professions. We might understand the ghetto better if we examined the people and institutions with which ghetto residents must deal. We could, for example, study the banking and insurance industries that mark out areas of the city to which they will not extend credit or sell insurance—so-called "red-lining." We could study the landlords who in violation of the law pay off municipal officials so that building codes are not enforced.

3   Just look at the consequences of existing social science research on crime. By virtue of our concentration on lower-class crimes, we have aided in the public's definition of the "law-and-order problem" as lower-class or street crime. Yet wasn't it a "law-and-order" problem when 76 workers in Hopewell, Virginia, were infected by the pesticide Kepone and dangerous chemical wastes were pumped into the James River? This kind of white-collar crime, as hazardous to life as the street variety, gets short shrift by justice organizations.

4   A fresh perspective on white-collar crime might change our focus for study. In developing new theories about slum gangs, we might ask whether it is sufficient to see gangs as products of their subculture's value system alone. We would study the marketing or transportation systems that, as in Watts, make virtual islands of some ghetto areas. We would examine the degree to which red-lining, plea bargaining, corrupt judicial appointments, or the often shoddy quality of legal services for the poor contribute to cynicism about the law in the ghetto.

5   We are not dealing with an either/or proposition. We simply need to recognize when it is useful to study up, down, or sideways. By studying a problem across class, we could test whether certain upper- or lower-class problems are due to a particular kind of family pattern or to the context in which that family is operating: how, for example, an executive or blue-collar worker's job affects the entire family's health, safety, and lifestyle. At the least, setting the problems in a comparative frame would

Reprinted from *Psychology Today* Magazine. Copyright © 1977, Ziff-Davis Publishing Company.

help us trace the forces that generate excessive poverty or affluence, and perhaps learn whether they come from the larger society or are transmitted within each group.

6   Studying up as well as down would force us to revise our social science books, whose indexes barely mention the advertising, insurance, banking, realty, or energy industries—institutions and network systems that affect millions of lives. For such work to become central in social science, we need to rethink why it is that social sciences are trained to relate down, while lawyers in general are trained to relate up.

Albert Rosenfeld

"LEARNING" TO GIVE UP

1   We all have an intuitive knowledge—supported by personal experience and common sense, reinforced by religious beliefs and folk wisdom—that our attitudes toward life are of critical importance to our enjoyment of it. Whether we overcome our problems or not (or in some crisis situations, whether we even survive or not) may depend on whether or not we have hope, whether we give up or keep on trying.

2   Over the past few decades, biologists and psychologists have been carrying out some fascinating research that reconfirms how powerfully our mental outlook can affect the outcome of our life situations.

3   You can, for example, do a simple experiment (as Dr. Curt Richter of Johns Hopkins has done repeatedly) with two rats: hold one rat in your hand firmly so that no matter how valiantly he struggles he cannot escape. He will finally give up. Now throw that quiescent rat into a tank of warm water. He will sink, not swim. He has "learned" that there is nothing he can do, that there is no point in struggling. Now throw another rat into the water—one that doesn't "know" that his situation is hopeless and that he is therefore helpless. This rat will swim to safety.

4   Another experiment (done by Dr. Martin E. P. Seligman of the University of Pennsylvania), this time with dogs: suspend a dog in a hammock into which he fits so snugly that he cannot get loose. Give him electric shocks. He will struggle for a while, then just lie there and submit. Later, take the same dog and put him down on one side of a grid that is only half electrified. Though he is perfectly free to get up and move to the unelectrified side, he will sit where he is, enduring the shock, resigned to his fate. Put another dog down in the same spot—a dog that hasn't been taught to be helpless—and he'll move around until he finds an area that doesn't shock him.

5   Okay. Fine for rats and dogs. But what about people?

6   Seligman has been one of the pioneering investigators of the ways in which people's perceptions of themselves as being helpless can in fact render them helpless. His seminal book, *Helplessness: On Depression, Develop-*

© Saturday Review, 1977. All rights reserved.

ment and Death, has influenced many other psychologists to pursue this fruitful area of research. Here is a sample Seligman experiment:

⁷ Take two groups of college students and put them in rooms where they are blasted with noise turned up to almost intolerable levels. In one room there is a button that turns off the noise. The students quickly notice it, push it, and are rewarded with blissful silence. In the other room, however, there is no turn-off button. The students look for one, find nothing, and finally give up. There is no way to escape the noise (except to leave the room before a previously agreed-upon time period has elapsed), so they simply endure.

⁸ Later, the same two groups are put in two other rooms. This time, *both* rooms contain a switch-off mechanism—though not a simple button this time and not as easy to find. Nevertheless, the group that found the button the first time succeeds in finding the "off" switch the second time, too. But the second group, already schooled in the hoplessness of their circumstances, doesn't even search. Its members just sit it out again.

⁹ There is an obvious parallel here. In each of the three cases—rats, dogs, and students—the situation had changed decisively, but because their efforts for alleviation didn't work in the first instance, the "helpless" subjects didn't even try the second time.

¹⁰ Yes, you may say, but the students knew that at a given point the experiment would be over and the noise would stop. Otherwise they would have been more highly motivated to keep on looking. Besides, in the first instance, no matter how motivated they may have been, no matter how hard they may have tried, there simply *was* no way to turn off the noise. Their efforts would have been futile. Aren't many life situations like that—no matter how hard you try, you're doomed to lose?

¹¹ True enough. In at least one of Richter's rat experiments, for example, he wanted to know how long a rat would keep swimming to try to save itself. The rat swam for 50 hours before it drowned. Were some other rat intelligent and articulate, it might observe this and say: See, what was the point? All that effort for nothing. Wasn't that a foolish rat, to try so hard?

¹² No one suggests there is a guarantee that you'll win if you try. But most of the rats in these experiments did, after all, swim to safety. And even in this one instance, the experimenter might have changed his mind in the interim or been influenced by some outside event to stop the experiment. In most human life situations, the outcome is not rigidly preordained. Many studies in clinical medicine, psychology, and anthropology indicate that seriously ill patients who have hope are more likely to survive than those who don't, that those who are highly motivated tend to last longer—and are happier in the knowledge that they are putting up a fight.

¹³ Some population groups are more susceptible to feelings of helplessness than are others: the elderly, for instance; and, as one might suspect, blacks; and women of any color.

¹⁴ In a series of classroom experiments, Dr. Carol Dweck of the University of Illinois found that when girls fail in school, they tend to blame the failure on their inability to master the subject matter. But boys ascribe failure to not trying hard enough. Because girls are considered to be

neater, better-behaved, and harder-working, teachers assume that they are already doing the best they can. Because boys are considered to be sloppier and less diligent by nature, teachers tend to tell them, "You can do better. You're just not trying hard enough." The boys believe it. They do try harder, and do better. Thus, for paradoxical reasons, girls are inadvertently programmed to feel more helpless about improving their situations.

15   Consider another series of classroom experiments being carried out by Dr. Rita Smith, a former student of Seligman's who is now in the African studies program at Temple University in Philadelphia. She has been comparing the helplessness quotients of black and white children. Though the research is incomplete and the results not yet published, it is already quite apparent to Smith that black children, especially those from poor families, give up much more easily than do white children of similar economic status. If you give the two groups a problem that has no solution (as in the case of Seligman's college students in the room with no turn-off button), the black pupils not only quit trying sooner but when given a solvable problem next, they are more likely to be convinced a priori that it can't be done—at least not by them. The white kids tend to stay with the problem longer, and they don't assume they can't solve one problem because they failed to solve the other.

16   Smith attributes these results to the *experience* of black children in a world that does not respond very reliably to their attempts to exercise more control over their lives. The giving-up attitude becomes even more pronounced in the tenth grade than it was in the second grade (the two age groups Smith has been working with). By then, the kids have had eight more years of experience to reconfirm the apparent uselessness of trying.

17   Whether you look at rats, dogs, or people, it's now abundantly clear that those who try harder do better. Intelligent organisms, says Seligman, automatically know how to help themselves: they keep trying; they have hope. Nor does this healthy tendency have to be learned. In fact, it is so built-in, says Seligman, that even special training doesn't enhance it. But *helplessness,* he is convinced, *must be taught.* Most of us, to one extent or another, are guilty of teaching others helplessness and of permitting ourselves to learn it.

18   Science has many uses. Experiments such as those described may not provide us with any technological breakthroughs. They do not "conquer" any diseases. But they do give us scientific validation of, and therefore greater confidence in, the value of traditional virtues such as perseverance and hope—which, in these times, is no small service.

19   Thus through research are our homely truisms doubly confirmed: hope is healthier than despair, perseverance is more sensible than giving up, and helplessness can be self-imposed and therefore self-defeating. The same can be true even in the affairs of nations. One wonders how guilty of defeatism we all, including our statesmen, may be, when we keep saying, There always have been wars, and there always will be wars; people are no damned good, and you can't change human nature; and so on. Whatever the case in point, the fact that "it didn't work last time" has nothing to do with next time. Next time we may swim to safety. Next

time we may find a spot on the grid that doesn't give us a shock. Next time the room may have a turn-off switch.

ANALYSIS

structure 1. List the causes and effects, stated and implied, in the selections on "Ghosts," "What Americans Want," and " 'Life' on Death Row."
Examples:

"The Start of the Nuclear Race"

CAUSE	EFFECT
a. Nuclear bombing of Hiroshima	78,000 civilian deaths
b. Wars with non-nuclear weapons	22 million deaths
c. U.S.–Soviet arms race (implied)	U.S.: 9,000 nuclear weapons, Russians: 4,500 nuclear weapons
d. World arms race	A billion dollars spent per day

"The Birth of Lake Erie"

CAUSE	EFFECT
a. Glacial ice sheet moved south	Gouged deeply into pre-glacial river bed
b. Sun beat down on southern parts of glacial sheet	Released rocks and water which eventually created Lake Erie

2. Of the first five short selections, which one might be considered a process paragraph as well as a cause/effect paragraph?

3. In the same group, which two selections have the "best" conclusions in the sense that they refer back to the thesis and provide a sense of unity?

4. State the thesis of "Studying Up."

5. List three of the advantages (effects) that Nader believes will accrue from studying up as well as down.

6. State the thesis of " 'Learning' to Give Up."

7. Briefly describe three examples of giving up mentioned by Rosenfeld.

8. Outline "Studying Up."

meaning 9. Explain McGivern's use of the terms *meat* and *illegal* (" 'Life' on Death Row").

10. According to Bennett, what brings eventual unity to the struggle of classic lovers to keep classics alive?

11. What qualities in a literary work make it a classic?

12. Discuss the last sentence of "Studying Up."

13. Discuss the implications of "Next time the room may have a switch."

opinion 14. What do Americans miss by going to American-type facilities in various parts of the world ("What Americans Want")?

15. Do we tend to sympathize more with the criminal than with the victim ("The Crime of Punishment")?

Select one of the sentences listed below and write a cause/effect paragraph based on it. You can use the sentence as either the cause or the effect. Make a list of the causes and the effects you intend to include. (Be careful. This can be tricky. For example, if you take the first sentence, you can run into the following kind of problem: If you say, "Stanley beat up his sister, kicked the dog, and set fire to the family car," his actions are the causes, and taking away TV privileges is the effect. If you say, "TV may teach Johnny violence," TV is the cause, and a violent Johnny would be the effect.)

1. Stanley, our seven-year-old, is forbidden to watch TV for a full month.

2. My mother-in-law brought a huge bowl of stuffed cabbage to our house yesterday.

3. The history teacher gave us a surprise test this morning.

4. Mary Lou slapped me sharply across the face.

5. He's in the hospital now with a broken pelvis and three broken ribs.

6. I'll never go to one of those movies again.

section 9b

Jessica Mitford

THE CRIMINAL TYPE

1   Time was when most crimes were laid at the door of the Devil. The English indictment used in the last century took note of Old Nick's complicity by accusing the defendant not only of breaking the law but of "being prompted and instigated by the Devil," and the Supreme Court of North Carolina declared in 1862: "To know the right and still the wrong pursue proceeds from a perverse will brought about by the seductions of the Evil One."

2   With the advent of the new science of criminology toward the end of the nineteenth century, the Devil (possibly to his chagrin) was deposed as primary cause of crime by the hand of an Italian criminologist, one of the first of that calling, Cesare Lombroso. Criminals, Lombroso found, are born that way and bear physical stigmata to show it (which presum-

From *Kind and Usual Punishment: The Prison Business,* by Jessica Mitford. Copyright © 1973 by Jessica Mitford. Reprinted by permission of Alfred A. Knopf, Inc.

ably saddles God with the responsibility, since He created them). They are "not a variation from a norm but practically a special species, a subspecies, having distinct physical and mental characteristics. In general all criminals have long, large, projecting ears, abundant hair, thin beard, prominent frontal sinuses, protruding chin, large cheekbones." Furthermore, his studies, consisting of exhaustive examination of live prisoners and the skulls of dead ones, enabled him to classify born criminals according to their offense: "Thieves have mobile hands and face; small, mobile, restless, frequently oblique eyes; thick and closely set eyebrows; flat or twisted nose; thin beard; hair frequently thin." Rapists may be distinguished by "brilliant eyes, delicate faces" and murderers by "cold, glassy eyes; nose always large and frequently aquiline; jaws strong; cheekbones large; hair curly, dark and abundant." Which caused a contemporary French savant to remark that Lombroso's portraits were very similar to the photographs of his friends.

3   A skeptical Englishman named Charles Goring, physician of His Majesty's Prisons, decided to check up on Lombroso's findings. Around the turn of the century he made a detailed study of the physical characteristics of 3,000 prisoners—but took the precaution of comparing these with a group of English university students, impartially applying his handy measuring tape to noses, ears, eyebrows, chins of convicts and scholars alike over a twelve-year period. His conclusion: "In the present investigation we have exhaustively compared with regard to many physical characteristics different kinds of criminals with each other and criminals as a class with the general population. From these comparisons no evidence has emerged of the existence of a physical criminal type."

4   As the twentieth century progressed, efforts to pinpoint the criminal type followed the gyrations of scientific fashions of the day with bewildering results. Studies published in the thirties by Gustav Aschaffenburg, a distinguished German criminologist, show that the pyknic type (which means stout, squat, with large abdomen) is more prevalent among occasional offenders, while the asthenic type (of slender build and slight muscular development) is more often found among habitual criminals. In the forties came the gland men, Professor William H. Sheldon of Harvard and his colleagues, who divided the human race into three: endomorphs, soft, round, comfort-loving people; ectomorphs, fragile fellows who complain a lot and shrink from crowds; mesomorphs, muscular types with large trunks who walk assertively, talk noisily, and behave aggressively. Watch out for those.

5   Skull shape, glands, IQ, and deviant personality aside, to get a more pragmatic view of the criminal type one merely has to look at the composition of the prison population. Today the prisons are filled with the young, the poor white, the black, the Chicano, the Puerto Rican. Yesterday they were filled with the young, the poor native American, the Irish or Italian immigrant.

6   Most studies of the causes of crime in this decade, whether contained in sociological texts, high-level government commission reports, or best-selling books like Ramsey Clark's *Crime in America,* lament the disproportionately high arrest rate for blacks and poor people and assert with wearing monotony that criminality is a product of slums and pov-

erty. Mr. Clark invites the reader to mark on his city map the areas where health and education are poorest, where unemployment and poverty are highest, where blacks are concentrated—and he will find these areas also have the highest crime rate.

7 Hence the myth that the poor, the young, the black, the Chicano are indeed the criminal type of today is perpetuated, whereas in fact crimes are committed, although not necessarily punished, at all levels of society.

8 There is evidence that a high proportion of people in all walks of life have at some time or other committed what are conventionally called "serious crimes." A study of 1,700 New Yorkers weighted toward the upper income brackets, who had never been arrested for anything, and who were guaranteed anonymity, revealed that 91 percent had committed at least one felony or serious misdemeanor. The mean number of offenses per person was 18. Sixty-four percent of the men and 27 percent of the women had committed at least one felony, for which they could have been sent to the state penitentiary. Thirteen percent of the men admitted to grand larceny, 26 percent to stealing cars, and 17 percent to burglary.

9 If crimes are committed by people of all classes, why the near-universal equation of criminal type and slumdweller, why the vastly unequal representation of poor, black, brown in the nation's jails and prisons? When the "Italian bandit, bloodthirsty Spaniard, bad man from Sicily," and the rest of them climbed their way out of the slums and moved to the suburbs, they ceased to figure as an important factor in crime statistics. Yet as succeeding waves of immigrants, and later blacks, moved into the same slum area the rates of reported crime and delinquency remained high there.

10 No doubt despair and terrible conditions in the slums give rise to one sort of crime, the only kind available to the very poor: theft, robbery, purse-snatching; whereas crimes committed by the former slum-dweller have moved up the scale with his standard of living to those less likely to be detected and punished: embezzlement, sale of fraudulent stock, price-fixing. After all, the bank president is not likely to become a bank robber; nor does the bank robber have the opportunity to embezzle depositors' funds.

11 Professor Theodore Sarbin suggests the further explanation that police are conditioned to perceive some classes of persons (formerly immigrants, now blacks and browns) as being actually or potentially "dangerous," and go about their work accordingly: "The belief that some classes of persons were 'dangerous' guided the search for suspects. . . . Laws are broken by many citizens for many reasons: those suspects who fit the concurrent social type of the criminal are most likely to become objects of police suspicion and of judicial decision-making." The President's Crime Commission comments on the same phenomenon: "A policeman in attempting to solve crimes must employ, in the absence of concrete evidence, circumstantial indicators to link specific crimes with specific people. Thus policemen may stop Negro and Mexican youths in white neighborhoods, may suspect juveniles who act in what the policemen consider an impudent or overly casual manner, and may be influenced by such factors as unusual hair styles or clothes uncommon to

the wearer's group or area. . . . Those who act frightened, penitent, and respectful are more likely to be released, while those who assert their autonomy and act indifferent or resistant run a substantially greater risk of being frisked, interrogated, or even taken into custody."

[12] An experiment conducted in the fall of 1970 by a sociology class at the University of California at Los Angeles bears out these observations. The class undertook to study the differential application of police definitions of criminality by varying one aspect of the "identity" of the prospective criminal subject. They selected a dozen students, black, Chicano, and white, who had blameless driving records free of any moving violations, and asked them to drive to and from school as they normally did, with the addition of a "circumstantial indicator" in the shape of a phosphorescent bumper sticker reading "Black Panther Party." In the first 17 days of the study these students amassed 30 driving citations—failure to signal, improper lane changes, and the like. Two students had to withdraw from the experiment after two days because their licenses were suspended; and the project soon had to be abandoned because the $1,000 appropriation for the experiment had been used up in paying bails and fines of the participants.

[13] As anyone versed in the ways of the criminal justice system will tell you, the screening process begins with the policeman on the beat: the young car thief from a "nice home" will be returned to his family with a warning. If he repeats the offense or gets into more serious trouble, the parents may be called in for a conference with the prosecuting authorities. The well-to-do family has a dozen options: they can send their young delinquent to a boarding school, or to stay with relatives in another part of the country, they can hire the professional services of a psychiatrist or counselor—and the authorities will support them in these efforts. The Juvenile Court judge can see at a glance that this boy does not belong in the toils of the criminal justice system, that given a little tolerance and helpful guidance there is every chance he will straighten out by the time he reaches college age.

[14] For the identical crime the ghetto boy will be arrested, imprisoned in the juvenile detention home, and set on the downward path that ends in the penitentiary. The screening process does not end with arrest, it obtains at every stage of the criminal justice system.

[15] To cite one example that any observer of the crime scene—and particularly the black observer—will doubtless be able to match from his own experience: a few years ago a local newspaper reported horrendous goings-on of high school seniors in Piedmont, a wealthy enclave in Alameda County, California, populated by executives, businessmen, rich politicians. The students had gone on a general rampage that included arson, vandalism, breaking and entering, assault, car theft, rape. Following a conference among parents, their lawyers, and prosecuting authorities, it was decided that no formal action should be taken against the miscreants; they were all released to the custody of their families, who promised to subject them to appropriate discipline. In the very same week, a lawyer of my acquaintance told me with tight-lipped fury of the case of a nine-year-old black ghetto dweller in the same county, arrested for stealing a nickel from a white classmate, charged with "extortion and

robbery," hauled off to juvenile hall, and, despite the urgent pleas of his distraught mother, there imprisoned for six weeks to wait for his court hearing.

16   Thus it seems safe to assert that there is indeed a criminal type—but he is not a biological, anatomical, phrenological, or anthropological type; rather, he is a social creation, etched by the dominant class and ethnic prejudices of a given society.

ANALYSIS

structure   1. Although "The Criminal Type" discusses classification systems, it is not an example of classification. What makes it a cause/effect theme?

2. Copy Mitford's thesis statement.

3. How effective are her introduction and conclusion? Discuss.

4. Does she support her thesis adequately? Support your answer.

meaning   5. According to Mitford, who classifies the criminals in a given society?

6. Does she believe that there is actually an identifiable criminal type?

style   7. Compare the tone of her first four paragraphs with that of her last twelve.

opinion   8. What similarity of ideas is there in "The Criminal Type" and "Studying Up"? Discuss the similarities in "The Criminal Type" and "Instruments of Power" (Section 8B).

9. Do you agree with Mitford's conclusion? Discuss.

WRITING SUGGESTION

Write a brief cause/effect paper about juvenile delinquency, truancy, or pot smoking among teenagers.

Edwin J. Delattre

THE HUMANITIES CAN IRRIGATE DESERTS

"For every one pupil who needs to be guarded from a weak excess of sensibility there are three who need to be awakened from the slumber of cold vulgarity. The task of the modern educator is not to cut down jungles but to irrigate deserts. . . . By starving the sensibility of our pupils we only make them easier prey to the propagandist when he comes. For famished nature will be avenged and a hard heart is no infallible protection against a soft head."

C. S. LEWIS in *The Abolition of Man*

1   Whatever the injustice of the human condition, everyone, regardless of race or sex, enters the world with a full and entirely adequate portion of ignorance. The central questions in all education are how much of this

From the *Chronicle of Higher Education*, Oct. 11, 1977. Copyright 1977 by Editorial Projects for Education, Inc. Reprinted with permission of author and publisher.

ignorance can be overcome, and which domains of ignorance are the most dangerous.

2   When a person studies the mechanics of internal-combustion engines, the intended result is that he should be better able to understand, design, build, or repair such engines, and sometimes that he should be better able to find employment because of his skills—and thus better his life. These are no mean goals.

3   When a person studies the humanities, the intended result is that he should be better able to understand, design, build, or repair a life—for living is a vocation we have in common despite our differences.

4   There are many motives for study, but, as William Arrowsmith insisted in an article called "The Future of Teaching," there is only one "profound motivation for learning, the hope of becoming a better man." The humanities at their best serve, respond to, and encourage this motivation. The humanities provide us with opportunities to become more capable in thought, judgment, communication, appreciation, and action.

5   The humanities are associated with and overlap the fine and especially the liberal arts. Liberal arts were once called liberating arts, not only because "the truth shall make us free," but also because *no one is ever free to do anything that he cannot think of.* Study in humanities—history, literature, poetry, art, comparative religion, languages, philosophy—informs us of ideas that diligence and brilliance have generated; such study thereby enriches what we can think of.

6   Practice in reading, writing, speaking, listening, and evaluating texts likewise enables us to think more rigorously and to imagine more abundantly. These activities free us to possibilities that are new, at least to us, and they unbind us from portions of our ignorance about living well.

7   When, for example, we meet Quentin in *Absalom, Absalom* and sense the destructiveness of his relentless, insatiable urge to know what happened; and when we meet Annie Clark Tanner in *A Mormon Mother* and see the quiet durability that informs her life of disappointment and heartache; and when we then encounter Flaubert's description of Emma Bovary: "Emma insisted on so much happiness that she destroyed all chance of it"—we make discoveries that might otherwise be made only through pain and suffering or that might elude us altogether. Through exposure to such characters and stories we are able to learn *for* ourselves without having to learn all *by* ourselves, or perhaps never to learn.

8   Learning of this kind does not guarantee that we will become better human beings; knowledgeable and informed people often remain malicious and petty. As Hazlitt pointed out, the knowledge gained from reading and understanding Shakespearean tragedy does not free man from evil, but it may free him from being deceived by evil. Texts in the humanities remind us that it is possible to share and appreciate the experiences of others, to learn from their lives and their thoughts. By inviting us to cultivate the human capacity to put ourselves in the place and point of view of another, the texts irrigate deserts.

9   Without exposure to the cultural, intellectual, and moral traditions that are our heritage, we are excluded from a common world that crosses generations. On the one hand, such exclusion tends to compel us to recre-

ate everything, a needless and largely impossible task; on the other, it tends to make us arrogant, to suggest that we are indeed the creators of the world and of all good ideas—when in fact we are only a fragment of the history of man, challenged for a moment with responsibility for the present and the future. Left entirely to ourselves, we could make only the slimmest contributions to wisdom.

10   While the humanities overlap the fine and liberal arts, they are also related of necessity to the sciences and to technology. Some of the disciplines of the humanities raise questions about what ends are worthy to be served, what ideals deserve reverence. But since it is futile to know what is worth doing without having any idea of how to get things done, effective study in the humanities requires respect for and attainment of factual knowledge and technological skill. Similarly, it is pointless to know how to get things done without having any idea what is worth doing, so that informed study in applied science demands reflection in the humanities. Otherwise, we are reduced to the absurd prospect of doing what we are able to do for the inane but popular reason that we are able to do it—whatever it is. The ideals of ethics inform the goals of anesthesiology, just as the achievements of anesthesiology enable us to fulfill the ethical ideal of separating pain and knife.

11   For these reasons, the humanities at their best are the studies that encourage people to become both genuinely realistic and truly idealistic. A realist is not a cynic, but rather a person who respects factual knowledge and its uses and is therefore effective. An idealist is not a fool, but rather a person who recognizes that factual knowledge is not enough to live a life—that such principles as respect for persons and reverence for beauty are required as well. When we achieve both, then knowledge and principle inform our ordinary, commonplace behavior and thought: the way we drive cars, behave in lines, offer ourselves in friendship, spend our money. It is in this sense that the study of the humanities is said to make life good, not only for us as individuals, but also as companions. The quality of individual life and social life depends on the qualities of mind—cultural, intellectual, moral—that we achieve.

12   Anyone who supposes that excellence of mind is achieved by waiting for inspiration has misunderstood the nature of the humanities. They require study and the mastery of skills of thought, judgment, communication, and appreciation. Without such adaptable skills, we become schizophrenic in proficiency—able to repair engines, but inept as parents or friends; able to feel dismay at injustice, but ignorant of the democratic processes of social reform.

13   Educators can do only so much. We work with students a few hours a day, less than 200 days a year; we improve ourselves as time permits; and we get tired. Ignorance has a monumental head start on parents and teachers—it is full-blown at birth, works 24 hours a day every day, and it never wearies. It gets more than occasional support from nearly every segment of the human community. Neither money nor innovation nor imagination are required to sustain it.

14   In the face of this unequal struggle, there is always the temptation to give in: to pressures that humanities and the arts are not as important as jobs; to financial constraints; to the idea that students are not smart

enough or eager enough to make the game worth the candle. Thomas More was right when he told Richard Rich that a person should always take a position whose temptations he can resist. Giving in to ignorance and to the indifference that ignorance breeds amounts to jeopardizing the quality of life in all of its aspects for students now and later. As a teacher, one must be able to resist these temptations.

ANALYSIS

structure

1. Write the thesis statement.

2. Show, paragraph by paragraph, how Delattre presents his argument. Here is a start:
   para. 1:   In the introduction he states the purpose of education.
   para. 2:   He explains the purpose of a technical education.
   para. 3:   He states the purpose of studying the humanities.
   paras. 4-6:   In the next three paragraphs he defines the humanities.

3. List five effects caused by the teaching of the humanities.

4. List two effects of not studying the humanities.

5. Discuss the introduction and conclusion: Are they effective? Do they relate to each other?

meaning

6. Discuss the double meaning of the title.

7. Using the article, define *humanities*.

8. Discuss "The ideals of ethics inform the goals of anesthesiology, just as the achievements of anesthesiology enable us to fulfill the ethical ideal of separating pain and knife" (paragraph 10).

9. What is the advantage of being both an idealist and a realist?

10. Consider this article in relation to "Angels on a Pin" (Section 2A), "The Educated Man" (2B), and "What Is Intelligence, Anyway?" (8A).

Two American writers, one a distinguished editor, the other a famous novelist, react to the brutal death of a young boxer. Read the next two articles as a unit; then answer the questions.

Norman Cousins

WHO KILLED BENNY PARET?

1
Sometime about 1935 or 1936 I had an interview with Mike Jacobs, the prize-fight promoter. I was a fledgling reporter at the time; my beat was education)but during the vacation season I found myself on varied assignments, all the way from ship news to sports reporting. In this way I

© Saturday Review, 1962. All rights reserved.

found myself sitting opposite the most powerful figure in the boxing world.

2   There was nothing spectacular in Mr. Jacobs' manner or appearance; but when he spoke about prize fights, he was no longer a bland little man but a colossus who sounded the way Napoleon must have sounded when he reviewed a battle. You knew you were listening to Number One. His saying something made it true.

3   We discussed what to him was the only important element in successful promoting—how to please the crowd. So far as he was concerned, there was no mystery to it. You put killers in the ring and the people filled your arena. You hire boxing artists—men who are adroit at feinting, parrying, weaving, jabbing, and dancing, but who don't pack dynamite in their fists—and you wind up counting your empty seats. So you searched for the killers and sluggers and maulers—fellows who could hit with the force of a baseball bat.

4   I asked Mr. Jacobs if he was speaking literally when he said people came out to see the killer.

5   "They don't come out to see a tea party," he said evenly. "They come out to see the knockout. They come out to see a man hurt. If they think anything else, they're kidding themselves."

6   Recently, a young man by the name of Benny Paret was killed in the ring. The killing was seen by millions; it was on television. In the twelfth round, he was hit hard in the head several times, went down, was counted out, and never came out of the coma.

7   The Paret fight produced a flurry of investigations. Governor Rockefeller was shocked by what happened and appointed a committee to assess the responsibility. The New York State Boxing Commission decided to find out what was wrong. The District Attorney's office expressed its concern. One question that was solemnly studied in all three probes concerned the action of the referee. Did he act in time to stop the fight? Another question had to do with the role of the examining doctors who certified the physical fitness of the fighters before the bout. Still another question involved Mr. Paret's manager; did he rush his boy into the fight without adequate time to recuperate from the previous one?

8   In short, the investigators looked into every possible cause except the real one. Benny Paret was killed because the human fist delivers enough impact, when directed against the head, to produce a massive hemorrhage in the brain. The human brain is the most delicate and complex mechanism in all creation. It has a lacework of millions of highly fragile nerve connections. Nature attempts to protect this exquisitely intricate machinery by encasing it in a hard shell. Fortunately, the shell is thick enough to withstand a great deal of pounding. Nature, however, can protect man against everything except man himself. Not every blow to the head will kill a man—but there is always the risk of concussion and damage to the brain. A prize fighter may be able to survive even repeated brain concussions and go on fighting, but the damage to his brain may be permanent.

9   In any event, it is futile to investigate the referee's role and seek to determine whether he should have intervened to stop the fight earlier. That is not where the primary responsibility lies. The primary responsi-

bility lies with the people who pay to see a man hurt. The referee who stops a fight too soon from the crowd's viewpoint can expect to be booed. The crowd wants the knockout; it wants to see a man stretched out on the canvas. This is the supreme moment in boxing. It is nonsense to talk about prize fighting as a test of boxing skills. No crowd was ever brought to its feet screaming and cheering at the sight of two men beautifully dodging and weaving out of each other's jabs. The time the crowd comes alive is when a man is hit hard over the heart or the head, when his mouthpiece flies out, when the blood squirts out of his nose or eyes, when he wobbles under the attack and his pursuer continues to smash at him with pole-axe impact.

10   Don't blame it on the referee. Don't even blame it on the fight managers. Put the blame where it belongs—on the prevailing mores that regard prize fighting as a perfectly proper enterprise and vehicle of entertainment. No one doubts that many people enjoy prize fighting and will miss it if it should be thrown out. And that is precisely the point.

Norman Mailer

THE DEATH OF BENNY PARET

1   On the afternoon of the night Emile Griffith and Benny Paret were to fight a third time for the welterweight championship, there was murder in both camps. "I hate that kind of guy," Paret had said earlier to Pete Hamill about Griffith. "A fighter's got to look and talk and act like a man." One of the Broadway gossip columnists had run an item about Griffith a few days before. His girl friend saw it and said to Griffith, "Emile, I didn't know about you being that way." So Griffith hit her. So he said. Now at the weigh-in that morning, Paret had insulted Griffith irrevocably, touching him on the buttocks, while making a few more remarks about his manhood. They almost had their fight on the scales.

2   The accusation of homosexuality arouses a major passion in many men; they spend their lives resisting it with a biological force. There is a kind of man who spends every night of his life getting drunk in a bar, he rants, he brawls, he ends in a small rumble on the street; women say, "For God's sakes, he's homosexual. Why doesn't he just turn queer and get his suffering over with." Yet men protect him. It is because he is choosing not to become homosexual. It was put best by Sartre who said that a homosexual is a man who practices homosexuality. A man who does not, is not homosexual—he is entitled to the dignity of his choice. He is entitled to the fact that he chose not to become homosexual, and is paying presumably his price.

3   The rage in Emile Griffith was extreme. I was at the fight that night, I had never seen a fight like it. It was scheduled for fifteen rounds, but they fought without stopping from the bell which began the round to

Reprinted by permission of G.P. Putnam's Sons from *The Presidential Papers* by Norman Mailer. Copyright © 1960, 1961, 1962, 1963 by Norman Mailer.

the bell which ended it, and then they fought after the bell, sometimes for as much as fifteen seconds before the referee could force them apart.

4 Paret was a Cuban, a proud club fighter who had become welter-weight champion because of his unusual ability to take a punch. His style of fighting was to take three punches to the head in order to give back two. At the end of ten rounds, he would still be bouncing, his opponent would have a headache. But in the last two years, over the fifteen-round fights, he had started to take some bad maulings.

5 This fight had its turns. Griffith won most of the early rounds, but Paret knocked Griffith down in the sixth. Griffith had trouble getting up, but made it, came alive and was dominating Paret again before the round was over. Then Paret began to wilt. In the middle of the eighth round, after a clubbing punch had turned his back to Griffith, Paret walked three disgusted steps away, showing his hindquarters. For a champion, he took much too long to turn back around. It was the first hint of weakness Paret had ever shown, and it must have inspired a particular shame, because he fought the rest of the fight as if he were seeking to demonstrate that he could take more punishment than any man alive. In the twelfth, Griffith caught him. Paret got trapped in a corner. Trying to duck away, his left arm and his head became tangled on the wrong side of the top rope. Griffith was in like a cat ready to rip the life out of a huge boxed rat. He hit him eighteen right hands in a row, an act which took perhaps three or four seconds, Griffith making a pent-up whimpering sound all the while he attacked, the right hand whipping like a piston rod which has broken through the crankcase, or like a baseball bat demolishing a pumpkin. I was sitting in the second row of that corner—they were not ten feet away from me, and like everybody else, I was hypnotized. I had never seen one man hit another so hard and so many times. Over the referee's face came a look of woe as if some spasm had passed its way through him, and then he leaped on Griffith to pull him away. It was the act of a brave man. Griffith was uncontrollable. His trainer leaped into the ring, his manager, his cut man, there were four people holding Griffith, but he was off on an orgy, he had left the Garden, he was back on a hoodlum's street. If he had been able to break loose from his handlers and the referee, he would have jumped Paret to the floor and whaled on him there.

6 And Paret? Paret died on his feet. As he took those eighteen punches something happened to everyone who was in psychic range of the event. Some part of his death reached out to us. One felt it hover in the air. He was still standing in the ropes, trapped as he had been before, he gave some little half-smile of regret, as if he were saying, "I didn't know I was going to die just yet," and then, his head leaning back but still erect, his death came to breathe about him. He began to pass away. As he passed, so his limbs descended beneath him, and he sank slowly to the floor. He went down more slowly than any fighter had ever gone down, he went down like a large ship which turns on end and slides second by second into its grave. As he went down, the sound of Griffith's punches echoed in the mind like a heavy ax in the distance chopping into a wet log.

7 Paret lay on the ground, quivering gently, a small froth on his

mouth. The house doctor jumped into the ring. He knelt. He pried Paret's eyelid open. He looked at the eyeball staring out. He let the lid snap shut. He reached into his satchel, took out a needle, jabbed Paret with a stimulant. Paret's back rose in a high arch. He writhed in real agony. They were calling him back from death. One wanted to cry out, "Leave the man alone. Let him die." But they saved Paret long enough to take him to a hospital where he lingered for days. He was in coma. He never came out of it. If he lived, he would have been a vegetable. His brain was smashed. But they held him in life for a week, they fed him chemicals, and made exploratory operations into his skull, and fed details of his condition to The Goat. And The Goat kicked clods of mud all over the place, and spoke harshly of prohibiting boxing. There was shock in the land. Children had seen the fight on television. There were editorials, gloomy forecasts that the Game was dead. The managers and the prize-fighters got together. Gently, in thick, depressed hypocrisies, they tried to defend their sport. They did not find it easy to explain that they shared an unstated view of life which was religious.

8   It was of course not that religion which is called Judeo-Christian. It was an older religion, a more primitive one—a religion of blood, a murderous and sensitive religion which mocks the effort of the understanding to approach it, and scores the lungs of men like D. H. Lawrence, and burns the brain of men like Ernest Hemingway when they explore out into the mystery, searching to discover some part of the secret. It is the view of life which looks upon death as a condition which is more alive than life or unspeakably more deadening. As such it is not a very attractive notion to the Establishment. But then the Establishment has nothing very much of even the Judeo-Christian tradition. It has a respect for legal and administrative aspects of justice, and it is devoted to the idea of compassion for the poor. But the Establishment has no idea of death, no tolerance for Heaven or Hell, no comprehension of bloodshed. It sees no logic in pain. To the Establishment these notions are a detritus from the past.

9   Like a patient submerged beneath the plastic cover of an oxygen tent, boxing lives on beneath the cool, bored eyes of the doctors in the Establishment. It would not take too much to finish boxing off. Shut down the oxygen, which is to say, turn that switch in the mass media which still gives sanction to organized pugilism, and the fight game would be dead.

10   But the patient is permitted to linger for fear the private detectives of the Establishment, the psychiatrists and psychoanalysts, might not be able to neutralize the problem of gang violence. Not so well as the Game. Of course, the moment some piece of diseased turnip capable of being synthesized cheaply might prove to have the property of tranquilizing a violent young man for a year, the Establishment would wipe out boxing. Every time a punk was arrested, the police would prescribe a pill, and violence would walk the street sheathed and numb. Of course the Mob would lose revenue, but then the Mob is also part of the Establishment, it, and the labor unions and the colleges and the newspapers and the corporations are all part of the Establishment. The Establishment is never simple. It needs the Mob to grease the chassis on its chariot. Therefore,

the Mob would be placated. In a society with strong central government, it is not so difficult to turn up a new source of revenue. What is more difficult is to enter the plea that violence may be an indispensable element of life. This is not the place to have the argument: it is enough to say that if the liberal Establishment is right in its unstated credo that death is a void, and man leads out his life suspended momentarily above that void, why then there is no argument at all. Whatever shortens life is monstrous. We have not the right to shorten life, since life is the only possession of the psyche, and in death we have only nothingness. What then can there be said in defense of sports-car racing, war, or six-ounce gloves?

11   But if we go from life into a death which is larger than our life has been, or into a death which is small, if death comes to nothing for one man because he swallowed his death in his life, and if for another death is alive with dimension, then the certitudes of the Establishment lose power. A drug which offers peace to a pain may dull the nerve which could have taught the mind how to carry that pain into the death which comes on the next day or on the decades that follow. A tranquilizer gives coma to an anxiety which may later smell of the dungeon, beneath the ground. If we are born into life as some living line of intent from an eternity which may have tortured us or nurtured us in death, then we may be obliged to go back to death with more courage and art than we left it. Or face the dim end of going back with less.

12   That is the existential venture, the unstated religious view of boxers trying to beat each other into unconsciousness or, ultimately, into death. It is the culture of the killer who sickens the air about him if he does not find some half-human way to kill a little in order not to deaden all. It is a defense against the plague, against that plague which comes from violence converted into the nausea of all that nonviolence which is void of peace. Paret's death was with horror, but not all the horror was in the beating, much was in the way his death was cheated. Which is to say that his death was twice a nightmare. I knew that something in boxing was spoiled forever for me, that there would be a fear in watching a fight now which was like the fear one felt for any *novillero*[1] when he was having an unhappy day, the bull was dangerous, and the crowd was ugly. You knew he would get hurt. There is fascination in seeing that the first time, but it is not as enjoyable as one expects. It is like watching a novelist who has written a decent book get run over by a car.

13   Something in boxing was spoiled. But not the principle, not the right for one man to try to knock another out in the ring. That was perhaps not a civilized activity, but it belonged to the tradition of the humanist, it was a human activity, it showed a part of what man was like, it belonged to his ability to create art and artful movement on the edge of death or pain or danger or attack, and it had much to say about the subtleties of human style. For there are boxers whose bodies move like a fine brain, and there are others who pound the opposition down with the force of a trade union leader, there are fools and wits and patient craftsmen among boxers, wild men full of a sense of outrage and steady oppressive peasants, clever spoilers, dogged infantrymen who walk forward

[1] *novillero:* a minor bullfighter who fights young bulls; a novice bullfighter.

all night, hypnotists (like Liston), dancers, lovers, mothers giving a scolding, horsemen high on their legs. There is knowledge to be found about our nature, and the nature of animals, of big cats, lions, tigers, gorillas, bears, walruses (Archie Moore), birds, elephants, jackals, bulls. No, I was not down on boxing, but I loved it with freedom no longer. It was more like somebody in your family was fighting now. And the feeling one had for a big fight was no longer clear of terror in its excitement. There was awe in the suspense.

ANALYSIS

structure

1. Discuss the differences in the introductions, bodies, and conclusions of the Cousins and Mailer selections.

2. In considering the chain of causation, what does Mailer attempt to do that Cousins does not attempt?

3. Starting with the last sentence of paragraph 8, the organization of Mailer's writing becomes complicated. He interrupts his discussion of a "religion of blood" to discuss the Establishment's reasons for allowing boxing to continue; then he says, "What is more difficult is to enter the plea that violence may be an indispensable element of life." Then he discusses two different approaches to death. Map his thinking from paragraphs 8 to 13 by making a list. (See example on p. 263, question 2.)

meaning

4. What was the immediate cause of Paret's death?

5. According to both writers, what is the prior and broader cause?

6. According to Mailer, why does the Establishment allow boxing to continue despite all the criticism of it?

7. Did the death of Paret turn Mailer against boxing? Support your view.

8. What does Cousins' opinion of boxing seem to be?

style

9. Discuss the differences in style of the two selections. Which, for example, relies mostly on logic? Which delves deeply into the emotions?

10. Mailer uses many very apt similes. Find five.

WRITING SUGGESTION

Consider the causes and effects of a tragedy you have witnessed or read about, such as the drowning of a child, a fire in a nursing home, or the mugging of an old woman.

Section 9c

Here are three unusual cause/effect selections: a man's terrible struggle with the effects of alcoholism, a vivid discussion of the causes and effects of spanking, and a personal reminiscence, full of odd causes and equally odd effects. Questions follow each of the first two; the third is strictly for fun.

Blair Fuller

MY SEARCH FOR SOBRIETY

1   I was enormous, and my skin was as sensitive as a balloon's. A pin-prick of criticism could have done me in. Meanwhile my bulk threatened to break glasses, lamps, clocks—anything within, or just beyond, ordinary reach.

2   I was a weak Goliath, more threatened than threatening. Stairs and curbs, chair legs—whatever must be maneuvered around, stepped over or away from, anything that might rupture poise—presented danger. Only perfect coordination could mask the secret that I was drunk. I was almost always at least slightly drunk, and if I wasn't, my shakes made me equally dangerous and vulnerable.

3   My hands must be as certain as a locksmith's, since the latches had become increasingly complex and stubborn. My feet must be, if not springy, businesslike—which was very difficult when my heels jolted so hard against a flat sidewalk that my jaw jerked down, or when I landed on the outside edge of the sole of one shoe and had to balance all the way through a stride without staggering. What a long way it would be for Goliath to fall! What an awful sound that impact would make. A heavy squish. What shock and horror those who witnessed it would register.

4   No. How hard they'd laugh.

5   And how unfair and unfeeling their laughter would be! They would assume my downfall followed pleasure, resulted from self-indulgence. They would not understand that in fact they were seeing a knockdown in my battle with the bottle, a battle in which I had long since ceased to find any pleasure except the pleasure of relief at having survived another day of it with the outlines of my life still intact. I still was married, still went to work, followed routines, and went to social events. The outlines still were there, but they enclosed no genuine content. Absorption in work or play or love had become impossible for me, since the battle itself took so much of my energy.

6   There was a period of the day, which had become shorter and quite often did not occur at all, when my inebriation was in balance. I would have a glass in my hand but would not be craving a refill. My humor would be good, my confidence full but not yet overblown. My hands would be steady enough so at least I could believe they were steady. My brain would be working "normally," meaning simply that I was not pre-occupied, during this period, either with finding the next drink or masking the last one. I was free to think of the kinds of things the rest of the

Reprinted by permission of Russell & Volkening, Inc. as agent for the author. Copyright © 1978 by QUEST Magazine, reprinted with permission. Original title (May/June 1978) "Until a Morning Came—My Search for Sobriety."

world thinks about. But after a while I would begin to dream Goliath dreams of fame, fortune, and others' admiration.

7   I would remind myself complacently of how much alcohol Winston Churchill consumed in a day, of W. C. Fields's ad in the *Hollywood Reporter* that said he had never missed a day's shooting or a stage performance because of drink. Four of the six American winners of the Nobel Prize in literature were drunks. Every alcoholic has made such a list for himself. Winston Churchill is on a great many of them, and the other figures vary according to the alcoholic's milieu and profession.

8   Then the beginnings of a hangover would urge me to get another drink in order to feel right again, while my sudden unsteadiness of vision told me that a drink might push me over the line into sloppiness. Propriety was almost lost just sitting there in silence, either alone at home or in a sympathetic bar—one of those quiet, dark bars that morning drinkers favor. And if propriety—dignity at the simplest level—were lost, how could anything serious be accomplished? I had to get up. I had to act out my responsibilities. The day ahead looked like a hundred miles of dusty, hard-bumped dirt road. It seemed idiotically fatiguing that I must reach its end in safety.

9   I looked at the bottles lined up behind the bar. The striding Scot tipping his gray topper, the patriarch peering over his reading glasses— all the cute little symbols on the labels grinned at me. Davids, they were, knowing that Goliath would fall. They could afford to grin. Here it was, perhaps 11 a.m., and they knew that for the rest of the day I'd be fighting them off, and wouldn't succeed. A voice, my own, would be telling me that I needed them just to keep myself together, although I knew and they knew that instead of holding together, I might fall apart, break an object, or one of my bones.

10   Or break down emotionally. That was a deeper fear. I might be unable to make a coherent response to the mailman, say, and go all to pieces before his eyes. Unable to count out the change for a postage-due letter, perhaps. I'd have to ask him if he wouldn't please come back tomorrow when I'd have the correct amount ready for him.

11   No wonder all the Davids were grinning at me. A grown man with such a humiliating imagination. How could I pretend I was still in the battle? I'd been defeated before lunchtime.

12   Behind the bottles lurked another group. Their faces changed in the indistinct light, but I knew them all. They were halfway friends, competitors in some activity, people I saw socially. They would like to see me flat on my ass, so they waited there, a patient theater audience, for the spectacle. Every one of them wanted to see Goliath fall, though none of them had said, "Skip the agonizing. Have another." Or, "Who will it hurt?" My own double said those things to me, and a jaunty and convincing chap he was when he said them. These people, on the contrary, were discreet, but I perceived their hatred, and I wanted to put them to rout.

13   When I addressed them, they vanished and I was left with the startling sound of my voice. The incident shook me and I would look around to see if I'd been heard, even when I knew I was alone. I would stopper the bottle, or pay, and get into motion toward some duty to meticulously, if perhaps wrongly, perform.

14   Sometimes, though, I would have crossed without noticing into a depression deep enough so that my duty or project seemed fruitless to contemplate, and postponement could be justified by a proposed analysis of how I had reached this state. I would declare that today's round was lost and sit on the corner stool, or take a bottle to my office, and try to figure out how I'd got into this battle when I had known, of course, that I must stay out of it. That sounded responsible enough. What could be more important than arriving at an answer to this question? My very life depended on it.

15   When that sort of wisdom was needed, it came right along. Now I could relax. No rush. I was going to devote the next few hours to earnest cerebration. High time I sat down and tried to see the problem clearly, see myself clearly. Let me oil the thinking process with a drink, and get to work on it. Should anyone ask me what I was doing, I'd say I had things to think over.

16   A rumination on my father's alcoholism. Is alcoholism genetically inheritable? No official answer yet. Some evidence pro and con. If not, what are the qualities he and I shared? Why didn't our differences differ us in this respect? My father had died some 12 years before. He had had strokes and was suffering from emphysema. He was 60.

17   Then, in all likelihood, a daydreamed dialogue with a therapist to whom I'd gone with my first wife before we parted 10 years ago. Joint sessions, most of them, and thus generally constrained, yet how he had lingered in my mind, the chiseled lines of his face and his Austrian accent. He had certainly thought that I drank too much. "It so much hurts your *vife.*" But this statement had produced no more insight than I was presently finding.

18   I would go on to more recent events. I had been hospitalized two years before in Algeria where, on a Fulbright professorship, I had been teaching American literature and "Civilization" at the University of Oran. An attack of pancreatitis had produced a nearly fatal knot in my intestines, and my abdomen had been opened to untangle them. The Algerian doctor had told me that I should never have a drink again, not one, on pain of death, and more recently a radium scan of my pancreas done in a San Francisco hospital had shown that the organ was permanently damaged. The radiologist had told me that he had seen such damage only in the pancreases of skid row types brought into Emergency.

19   Since Oran I had teetotaled, sipped wine, drunk wine, become so full of wine that I switched to hard liquor, had an attack of pancreatitis . . . and the cycle would recommence.

20   Of what use was the past? Of not much use to me, apparently, neither the long-ago past that psychiatrists seek nor recent history that convicted me of self-destructive irrationality. Useless, obviously, for here I was, drunk. And if I were that irrational I might as well be drunk and stay drunk. I was of no possible service to anyone or anything.

21   Goliath would by now be very heavy, somber, and I would return to my family, silent. I remembered my days of health. I had done my best today to figure out how to revive them, had failed, and should be treated with hushed consideration.

22   Until a morning came, not very different from many others, when

exhaustion was stronger than any denial and I felt despair. I was the first one downstairs for breakfast and poured my orange juice glass half full of vodka, first taking a swig to steady my hands. Halfway through breakfast, staring dimly at the newspaper, my problem, as it seemed to me, was what to do until I was sober enough to do something.

23   Fix my motorcycle tires. I'd get plenty of fresh air doing that. The rear tire had a slow leak, and I'd fix it with sealant.

24   I could not find the motorcycle shop. Then, in a gas station, I could not remove the top of the sealant's container. My hands were shaking so that I could not remove the valve. I managed, then could not get the sealant spout into the valve. Managed that, but could not get the valve back in. By now my vision was blurred and sweat was pouring off my face. I stood up and nearly fell. I finished the job somehow and rode off, staying in first gear close to the parked cars and gritting my teeth to prevent myself from shouting or crying.

25   I arrived at my office breathing as though I'd run a mile, and grabbed the vodka bottle out of the desk drawer. When it was finished I went across the street for another pint. I no longer had the strength to pretend I was fighting any battle.

26   I wondered if I could telephone. I held the receiver button down with my left fist and practiced dialing. My finger slipped several times and I had to pause to rest, but I finally felt ready. I called my doctor. Telling him that I needed his help, I felt hugely conspicuous but wonderfully lightened. Goliath floating up from the battlefield.

27   "If you feel you need it on the way up, there's a half pint of bourbon in the glove compartment." The recovered alcoholic who was driving me had just reached across my chest to lock my door, the way one does when a child is in the passenger seat.

28   "I won't need it." But I had drunk up the bottle by the time we arrived at Myrtledale in Calistoga, California, where, a sign said, I would share my "strength and hope" with other alcoholics. It was an old resort hotel, then in sore need of paint, with palm trees and rocking-chair veranda in the front.

29   "Don't worry, now," said my driver. "You've come to the right place." I walked unsteadily across the veranda and into a dim convalescent room. Table lamps were burning in the middle of the day. I did not want to see the faces that looked up at me. The collapsed attitudes of the bodies in their chairs told me enough. In a daze I registered at the office and took my place among them, quite deaf and blind and shaken but still feeling lightened by the battle's end.

30   We had all discovered that we were "powerless over alcohol" and that our lives had "become unmanageable"—as good a definition of true alcoholism as any. The addicted are "managed" by their craving for the palliative substance. In the days that followed, one surprise was that this had happened, so to speak, to everyone, to football stars and suburban housewives, to priests, to attractive young women, business executives, policemen and firemen, and to rigidly spic-and-span little old ladies. Excepting alcohol, I could not see any true common denominator among us. I still can't. But we had all hit a point of powerlessness, of loss of control, so that to one degree or another we had fouled what was of value in

our lives. Many had lost far more than I had—their spouses and jobs and freedom. Some had been jailed for serious offenses. One had murdered on the highway. A number of them had been committed to asylums.

31   Myrtledale is four and a half years ago now. In retrospect, those who had most completely lost gained most. I do not mean loss of possessions or positions or relationships, although these things contribute. I mean experienced the feeling that they had lost.

32   A Norwegian ski-jump champion was the most articulate person among us, the readiest to ask questions, apparently the quickest to learn and take advice. He has since been brought back to Myrtledale several times, and I believe now that this very receptivity was a sign that he was struggling to pretend control, to himself at least, to refuse surrender to his situation. By "understanding" everything, he remained slightly superior to it.

33   For the first 48 hours I and other newcomers were given "hummers," shots of bourbon in water, every four or six hours. Hospitals use drugs to lessen the likelihood of DT's and convulsions, but Myrtledale has no medical license. It was founded and is run by Gene Duffy, a streets-of-New York Irishman with no theoretical training but a great deal of experience of treatment programs, much of it from the point of view of a patient. His record of success has made Myrtledale well known to those who direct alcoholics to recovery.

34   The "hummers" were in tall glasses passed on a tray and I found that I could handle mine by using both hands and drinking through a straw. Others had to have the glass held for them, and one man opened his mouth wide and the drink was poured in by the attendant. My first night, a tiny Scots lady with a sweet, shy smile got the DT's in the new-arrival room next to mine—rooms without doors and with heavily screened windows. Her whimpers and shrieks continued until an ambulance came to take her to a hospital.

35   As I gradually sobered up I began to see more clearly, and to hear the others' voices. Ordinary living seemed so distant, its problems so small compared to the one we shared, that there was no small talk. Only alcohol, but in changing moods. Alcoholics make one another laugh a lot. There are hidden-bottle stories: "Then I caught on that the meter reader was drinking it. I talked to him and after that he'd bring a fresh bottle in his briefcase every week. Had some great drunks together." Splendid advice: "I told him my problem and the doctor asked, 'What do you drink?' I told him bourbon and he said, 'Why don't you try switching to Scotch? That's what I'm doing.' " Feats of insane daring: "She said she didn't like the color, so I drove it right off the pier into the bay." And lots of absurd lies. Laughter relieves the pressure of guilt and opens the door a crack to creativity.

36   The fear of death is talked about, too. The therapists talk a lot about death. An alcoholic may not know that a quarter of a million Americans die every year of alcoholism, and that it complicates some 50 other diseases, or that about one-third of our suicides are alcoholics, or that alcohol plays a role in perhaps half our murders and half our highway fatalities. Told these things, alcoholics can share their fears.

37   I listened over cups of hot tea sweetened with honey and over the

plain, good meals. Like the others, I had half forgotten the tastes of food. Tapes of recovered alcoholics telling their stories were played for us, and meetings held at which staff members and sometimes visitors told theirs and to which we all then contributed. Between sessions I began to walk in the surrounding countryside of vineyards and pastures, short walks at first because my legs were weak. Rather than "tree" I began to see branches and buds, the patterns of bark, and to imagine root systems. "Mountain" became live oaks in fields of oats, the evergreens above, and red-tailed hawks in the air. Robert Louis Stevenson spent a winter in a house situated in a pass whose entrance I could see, and I imagined him there and thought of his work. My senses, which alcohol had so enclosed, began once more to show me things and to stimulate thought.

38   Yet I was still quite mad, as I look back on it. Ideas about everything—politics and economics and literary matters and friends and relations—succeeded each other disjointedly. Notions about the whys and wherefores of my life occurred with great intensity, were discarded, and reoccurred with the same intensity. My emotions changed momentarily from depression to exultation to a low, cooling fear. I knew it all one minute, and nothing the next. Had I the stability to accept what I was being given?

39   No moment came, either at Myrtledale or later, when I felt completely secure, but as I sobered I experienced a great and joyful feeling of relief. There was no doubting the incapacitation I had done myself, no doubt that a point had had to be turned. I had come to it after a long period of sterile denial and was truly glad that I had reached it. Potentially there was much of life before me. Thank God!

40   Thank God, for there is no person to thank, certainly not my own wisdom. Addictives have only one another to talk to if they want to talk about themselves, and only by giving and receiving is any sense of proportion, any idea of where one had been and where there is to go, developed. But there is a limit to such help. I am powerless over alcohol, and the sweet smile of the Scots lady, who returned from the hospital before I left Myrtledale, is not going to give me that power.

41   I took a Greyhound bus from Calistoga back home to San Francisco. Director Duffy was suspicious of this choice. It has happened at I should think all recovery places that the patient plays a schizophrenic charade the entire time he is there and rushes out to the first bar he can find. But I was not at all tempted and have been very rarely since.

42   I let myself into my house and stood a minute in the hall, sniffing the floor wax and flowers and Ajax cleanser, familiar smells but from a long time ago. The pictures and furniture were sharply defined. Then my seven-year-old son appeared, running down the stairs and talking away about a marvelous wind-up toy he had just seen in a shop. When I hugged him, I felt that I had not really done so since he had been perhaps three, and when I picked up my three-year-old daughter I wondered if I had ever truly hugged her.

43   It is a different world seen from the eyes of a man of normal stature. For example, the people in it do not judge as they judged Goliath, meaning that their expectations do not concern me as they did. Their expectations are their concern. I must do what I can do, imagine and think what

I can think, and take it on faith that others will thus get my best in work and affection. The figure that I think of as a model of ambition and behavior is the illiterate and poor juggler in the Anatole France story who was discovered alone in the cathedral juggling before the altar. The juggler's instinct was right, and France, who so intensely did what he could do, knew it as well as felt it. Time was when I thought the story merely sweet.

44   Time is needed, much time, for recovery, but the time is a pleasure and I hope it will be endless in my life. Since I drank between the ages of 15 and 45, therefore are habits that must change. What drink do you ask for at a cocktail party? Drinkers sometimes wonder how I can stand parties that go on for hours, and it isn't always easy listening to the same anecdote for the third time from the woman on my left. What do you do when you return home from work? What of your friends whom you never see outside of bars? These simple things produce uneasiness at first, but they now seem very minor.

45   On a somewhat deeper level I have understood that I must take care of myself if I am to give what I have to give, and in order to take that care I must like myself as Goliath never did. What is there to like within me? It is not an intellectual question and not an easy one. I look into my memory at what I have done and what I do, and try simply to feel my reactions. What do I feel good about? There are episodes I considered triumphs at the time about which I do not feel good at all. My reactions do not all correspond to conventional wisdom but, somewhat to my surprise, many do. I want to be responsible, constructive, helpful to those I love.

46   Goliath, and the person I was before him, felt miserably inadequate when I did not succeed at any project undertaken. While these feelings are not unknown to me, they are much diminished. I am not all-powerful. I cannot fix whatever it is I'd like to fix. Being truly helpful to another human, for example, beyond tying the injured man's shoe, is the most difficult task there is. It is the trying to do it that counts. Even if the project succeeds, there follows only a brief satisfaction. It is the trying that lasts.

47   Meetings with other recovering alcoholics have certainly helped form that conclusion. Their destructive deeds have been done, as mine have, and they can't be undone, but if the perpetrator of no matter what crime against the commonweal is trying to do things differently now, he is a valuable person.

48   After leaving Myrtledale I went to many meetings. Every day I would read something related to alcoholism or alcoholics. I prayed. I wanted constantly to remind myself of where I'd been and what I must guard against. What I had just been through made me feel conspicuous, outsized again, although differently. But as time and meetings passed, I shrank to brotherhood. There is no better feeling.

49   I attend fewer meetings now, one a week, usually, and I do not read so much. I have shrunk and feel less need. But I intend to go to meetings forever and to read forever. Alcohol is a baffling, cunning enemy to the addicted. Its temptation produces astonishing rationalizations and, once touched again, self-perpetuating depressions. I must never take it lightly. At moments of stress and fatigue I have noticed that I am suddenly "see-

ing" the liquor billboards and that the saloons' windows are inviting. I must remember and remind myself. That's not hard, so far.

50   Goliaths are of no use to anyone. They only frighten children. Juggling is a skill, perhaps an art. It can be a profession. Some jugglers have achieved fame and fortune.

51   None of that matters very much. I am a juggler, and juggle I will.

ANALYSIS

structure   1. Summarize the two cause/effect sequences in one or two sentences each.

2. What glimpses of the past does Fuller provide?

3. The conclusion (last two paragraphs) refers back to the introduction, but it indicates growth, not a static situation. Discuss.

style   4. Discuss the use of Goliath and the juggler as symbols.

5. In paragraph 9, what is personified? What symbolism is involved?

6. Discuss Fuller's very detailed account of what it feels like to be an alcoholic.

opinion   7. Why do many alcoholics make lists of celebrated alcoholics?

8. Does this article serve as a deterrent to potential alcoholics? Would it have been better if the author had concluded with a warning?

9. Are alcoholics to be blamed for being alcoholic?

10. Is enough being done to discourage people from drinking and to help alcoholics recover?

WRITING SUGGESTION

Consider the causes and effects of a bad habit or addiction that you, a member of your family, or a friend has gotten into.

Brian G. Gilmartin

THE CASE AGAINST SPANKING

1   Since the late 1960s, the childrearing pendulum has been moving back toward the right. School officials and popular psychologists today are counseling parents not to give in to their children's every whim; they emphasize that parents have rights, too. This new emphasis on the perils of permissiveness and on the importance of teaching responsibility is healthy enough, but unfortunately there is evidence that an increasing minority of parents is misconstruing professional counsel to be "firm" with children. The United States is becoming an increasingly violent

"The Case Against Spanking" by Brian G. Gilmartin. Copyright © 1979 *Human Behavior* Magazine. Reprinted by permission.

place to live. Crime statistics tell only a part of the story. Themes of violence continue to pervade television and motion pictures. And violence in the home has become commonplace at all socioeconomic levels. The basic unwritten consensus among the majority of Americans seems to be that it is acceptable and even desirable to use violence as a method of discipline in certain kinds of situations.

2   A recent study conducted by sociologist Murray Straus revealed that 81 percent of American parents employed corporal punishment on their children at some time over the past year. More than 60 percent of the parents surveyed spanked or beat their children on an average of at least once per week. And perhaps most surprisng of all was the finding that 46 percent of all college students had been beaten or physically assaulted by a parent at some time during their senior year of high school.

3   During the past four decades, social scientists have empirically demonstrated numerous serious disadvantages to the use of physical and other severe forms of punishment. Between 1969 and 1972, I conducted a detailed study of 200 suburban Los Angeles area middle-class families. I found that people usually employ severe forms of punishment, sincerely expecting beneficial results. But the violent reactions of a parent almost always resulted in the youngster becoming even less responsive to the needs and wishes of his or her elders. I found that parents became violent when their children's behavior made them feel severely frustrated and exasperated. Feelings of exasperation are an understandable result of being unable to constructively influence how their offspring behaves.

4   The act of disciplining a child can be a frustrating one. However, at the outset it needs to be stressed that discipline means *education.* Discipline is essentially programmed guidance that helps people to develop internal self-control, self-direction and efficiency. If it is to work, discipline requires mutual respect and trust. On the other hand, punishment requires external control over a person by force and coercion. Punishing agents seldom trust or respect the one punished.

5   Children who are frequently spanked tend to become highly resentful and distrustful of authority. Indeed, sometimes their often blind feelings of extreme hostility for, and distrust of, any and all authority figures reach the point of being dangerous to both themselves and others.

6   Moralists have long argued that a major reason for our burgeoning violent crime rate is that allegedly, fewer parents are spanking their offspring. Paradoxically, virtually every study ever made into the backgrounds of violent criminals has shown that they are far more likely than law-abiding citizens to have been subjected to a great many beatings and other forms of cruel physical punishment by their parents and other adult guardians. These same data have also shown that besides a great deal of physical punishment, violent criminals in almost all cases had never received any genuine warmth or respect as human beings from their families. Those in positions of authority had always been cruel, callous and indifferent to them. It was hence very easy for them to turn around and react back toward society in kind.

7   Children who are often spanked tend to be conspicuously quieter, less articulate and more sullen than those who grow up under milder, more democratic forms of discipline. In addition, harshly disciplined off-

spring tend to display a large amount of negativity in their approach to people and to life. Such traits as negativity and sullenness are a good deal more common among boys in our culture than among girls. Since almost all studies on discipline in the home have shown that boys tend to be the target of more physical punishment and psychic humiliation than girls, this is not surprising. And it may partially account for the greater openness of girls to classroom learning, particularly during the years of middle childhood. It may also be one of the factors responsible for the diminished ability of males in this society to express their feelings and emotions.

8   One of the most powerful arguments against the use of painful forms of punishment has emerged from the work of psychologist Richard A. Sternbach. Sternbach was once affiliated with a large hospital clinic in Cleveland, Ohio, that specialized in the treatment of children who had been born without the ability to experience physical pain. This is a rare genetic disorder that afflicts perhaps five or six children out of every one million born. Most of its victims are boys, and most of them do not have anything else wrong with them other than their inability to perceive pain.

9   Through his work, Sternbach had the opportunity to closely observe scores of such boys and their interactions with parents. His most significant observation was that about half the parents of these boys applied a fairly frequent amount of corporal punishment on them. Indeed, the percentage of parents who spanked sons who were incapable of feeling pain was essentially the same as the percentage who spanked sons of the same age who had a normal ability to perceive pain. As a matter of fact, some of the boys who could not feel pain were spanked a good deal more frequently than were the normal boys. This was because their behavior was far more closely supervised.

10   Sternbach's most remarkable finding was that boys born without the ability to experience pain reacted in the same manner to each spanking as did the normal boys. They cried and sulked and endeavored in rather conspicuous ways to regain the love and emotional support of the parent who had spanked.

11   The upshot of Sternbach's work is that if and when spanking does cause good behavior in a child, it is not the pain involved in the spanking that motivates that youngster to behave. If pain had been the motivator, we might reasonably expect that boys born without the ability to experience pain would have been joyfully and spitefully giving their parents a very difficult time. After all, they could enjoy complete freedom to violate the wishes of their parents as frequently and in as many ways as they wanted, because no matter how severely their parents spanked them, they would never need to worry about experiencing any physical pain. Indeed, these unusual children could literally laugh out loud as their enraged parents spanked and spanked.

12   Since it does not appear to be pain that motivates good behavior, what is it that does motivate desirable behavior? The answer appears to be a close, loving, emotionally meaningful relationship with the parents. Sternbach noticed that physical punishment didn't alter the negative behavior of the children. The factors associated with a child not responding

favorably to punishment were exactly the same whether the youngster was in the group comprised of normal children or in the group comprised of those without the ability to perceive pain. If parents' behavior revealed an attitude of nonrespect or a lack of warmth and love for their offspring, that child was not likely to respond favorably to the form of discipline employed. But when a parent clearly did accept and respect his or her child, the response to punitive discipline administered by the parent was always favorable regardless of whether the youngster was in the normal group or in the unable-to-experience-pain group.

13   This means that parents who attempt to adjust the severity of pain in a spanking to the seriousness of their offspring's transgression are quite clearly wasting their time and are doing both their child and themselves a disservice. Such parents might succeed in letting off steam, but they will not succeed at benefiting either the youngster or the quality of their interrelationship.

14   Entertainer Art Linkletter is a well-known defender of spanking as a method of discipline. But Linkletter's philosophy and advice have been widely misinterpreted by parents who feel a need for support of their programmed tendency to react to their children's misbehavior with spanking behavior. Yet Linkletter has made it very clear that spanking should be used only to express caring and concern and never to cause pain. Linkletter's operational definition of spanking entails nothing more than a few slaps with the bare hands over the child's clothed buttocks. Parents who resort to painful beatings with straps, belts, hairbrushes, birch rods and the like have grossly misinterpreted both his advice and his fundamental conception of what a spanking is.

15   Simply put, such conditions as nervousness and psychological tension slow down the speed and efficiency of the intellectual thought processes. When people are nervous and tense, they do not learn as efficiently and well as they do when they are relaxed but alert. They are not able to think clearly with their normal speed and agility when they are around the punishing agents. Many parents (and teachers in our less enlightened school districts) repeatedly defeat their intentions in this regard by spanking to facilitate learning. Instead, their actions invariably create nervousness and slow down learning.

16   In addition, conditions of chronic nervousness greatly interfere with a healthy adjustment to life. People who had been frequently spanked as children often remain nervous for many years. Their nervousness greatly undermines their sociability around other people; they are often seen by others as lacking a natural, friendly spontaneity and sense of personal freedom and control over their lives. Shy, asocial people quite typically have a history of much corporal punishment.

17   Often, parents spank their children in order to relieve their own tensions and feelings of frustrated exasperation. But force is also very often indicative of an intellectual inability to defend one's point of view in a convincing manner. Indeed, it may even be indicative of the violent person's inadequate degree of confidence in the moral veracity and rightfulness of his or her own viewpoints. People who have an unconscious fear that their own position does not represent the truth are especially likely to resort to coercion and violence.

18   One of the strongest arguments against the use of harsh physical and psychological punishment is that it leads to social distance among family members. Once the social distance between parents and children has gone beyond a certain point, parents have lost the ability to constructively influence their offspring. In order for any kind of influence to exist between two people, there must be some amount of mutually enjoyable communication between them. The punitive reactions of parents very often result in the permanent cutting off of meaningful communication on certain topics. Once communication on these topics is cut off, the capacity of the parent to influence the child on matters pertinent to such topics becomes greatly reduced.

19   Parents discipline their children with the hope of influencing them. Yet the form of discipline they select very often reduces the chances for effective influence, rather than increasing it. Throughout more than half my research interviews with suburban teenagers, I found that coping with the ego-deflating insults of parents was a major problem. I also found that elementary school children often worry that if they discuss with their parents what is really on their minds they will be whipped. As youngsters grow older, their conversations with their parents often become reduced to mere trivia. Fifty-two percent of the parents I talked to complained that their offspring seldom talk to them about anything important. Many of these parents believed that this social distance was a normal and natural byproduct of their children's emergence into adolescence. Virtually none of the parents suspected that it might be due to their own approach to discipline.

20   People must first interact before they can influence one another. In addition, the more frequently two different people (or two different groups) interact with each other on an informal, mutually enjoyable basis, the more alike those two different people (or groups) become; and the more similar they become to each other in hopes, desires, attitudes, values, behavior, aspirations, dreams. More important, the more the two people (or groups) interact on this mutually enjoyable basis, the more they come to truly like and even love each other.

21   These ideas are well supported by literally hundreds of well-documented scientific research studies in such diverse fields as psychology, sociology, education, political science and anthropology. To the extent that pleasant, mutually enjoyable interaction becomes cut off as a consequence of the use of physical pain, fear and ego-deflating name-calling, to that extent the potential for true love, mutual respect and constructive influence in parent-child relationships becomes lost. In addition, the youngster's hatred and distrust of parental authority tends to generalize to a hatred and distrust of all authority.

22   Frequent use of physical punishment is strongly associated with the development of a low self-image in children. This is a scientifically established fact and is valid regardless of a parent's conscientious, well-meaning intentions. It has been established by scores of outstanding social scientists, two of the best known being Stanley Coopersmith and Morris Rosenberg.

23   Hundreds of books have been written about the self-image, not only in such scientific fields as sociology and psychology, but also in religion

and metaphysics, as well. There is scarcely a self-help book in existence among the many hundreds on the market over the past 20 years that does not emphasize at great length the crucial importance of self-esteem for success and happiness in all areas of life. Without intending to exaggerate the issue, I can confidently state that there is no variable of greater importance not only for success, effectiveness and happiness in the work place, at home among family members and in the community, but also in terms of the development of positive thinking habits (which lead to such success) and the willingness to assume personal responsibility for all of one's behaviors.

24   People with low self-images ordinarily pursue a pessimistic approach to life. They are usually loathe to assume personal responsibility for their lives because they do not see themselves as enjoying the same degree of free choice and self-determination as the next person. Hence, they blame others, and they usually display a habit of chronic negative thinking that almost always attracts to them continued unpleasant and unsatisfying experiences.

25   A strongly positive self-image is a precondition for happiness. In recent years it has become fashionable in some circles to deemphasize the desirability of happiness as an important human value. Yet the principle that happiness and self-love are prerequisites for loving and caring about others is widely accepted among contemporary psychologists.

26   Very often within the same family some children receive much more punishment than their siblings. This is why some children develop strong, healthy self-images while others in the same household grow up thinking quite poorly of themselves. In an extensive 20-year study that commenced in 1956, psychiatrists Alexander Thomas and Stella Chess found that offspring (even within the same families) are not born with the same attributes of temperament. Some youngsters are "easy" children from birth, while others seem to display certain kinds of traits that are very difficult and troublesome for many parents to deal with.

27   Parents very often make the mistake of blaming their child for displaying certain inborn traits that are not valued by their particular family. This is not to imply that traits cannot or should not be modified. In order to adjust properly to society, all children must learn to modify some of their inborn predispositions. But some children are destined to have a harder time doing this than others who had the advantage of being born with "easier" temperaments. Such youngsters require more, not less, parental understanding and patience if they are to learn desired behavior patterns without suffering severe damage to their self-esteem.

28   So, if Johnny is much naughtier than Billy was at the same age, it may be because Johnny's genes led him to be born with a more difficult, perhaps hyperactive, temperament. Spanking Johnny for his hyperactivity and comparing him negatively to his well-behaved brother Billy is bound to cause Johnny to develop a low opinion of himself that will be very resistant to change.

29   One of the most popular, albeit valid, clichés is that actions speak louder than words. Yet in a recent study, it was shown that of all the situations that are likely to cause parents to spank their children, the one most likely to do so is that of observing a son beating up his brother or

sister. It is pathetically laughable in such situations to observe a parent angrily beating his or her child with a whip while screaming at him that he or she will not tolerate violence among family members. The gross inconsistency of this is immediately apparent. When a child is presented with a pair of contradictory messages by parents, it is most likely that he or she will absorb and learn from the way those parents behave, not from what they say.

30   Children who are spanked for fighting are likely to simply be more careful in the future about not being caught in the act by their parents. Physical punishment cannot teach children anything at all about constructive ways to resolve conflicts. But spanked children have learned that the way to react to force and violence is through further and more powerful forms of force and violence. In the United States, boys are typically subjected to about three times as much corporal punishment as are girls. And it is very likely that this is one key reason why males in our society are a great deal more prone to violent and even criminal behavior. This was the basis behind the American prowar mentality of the Vietnam era. It is a mentality that is dangerous and potentially lethal. Attitudes formed within the family bear upon the larger national society.

31   Research findings dealing with the consequences of different approaches to childrearing have made it clear that frequent physical punishment teaches youngsters that the best way to deal with undesirable or frustrating behavior in their peers is through violence and the inflicting of physical pain. Albert Bandura is perhaps the best known researcher in this area. He repeatedly found that children subjected to a good deal of spanking at home tend to be far more prone to fighting and other aggressive and destructive behavior at school than those who are seldom or never spanked. He further found that such youngsters tend to be more negative and resistant to learning.

32   Passivity is a trait that is related to both low self-esteem and overdependence on others for guidance, direction and discipline. It is associated with the use of harsh physical and psychological punishment and a strict, authoritarian type of family life. Psychologist Robert R. Sears has found high degrees of passivity in strictly reared nursery-school-aged children; and he has found it to be associated with low levels of happiness and effectiveness in both girls and boys. Passive personalities have been socially programmed to react and not to act. Hence, they do not enjoy an active role in the shaping of their destinies. In addition, passive boys are occasionally seen by others as being effeminate, thus compounding their difficulties as they grow older.

33   Most parents strongly hope that their children will develop a sense of responsibility and self-discipline. One of the most frequent justifications for physical punishment is that it will help them develop these traits. But usually such strictness has just the opposite effect—children become overdependent upon *external* forms of control. When young people become too dependent on external authority figures, they fail to develop such internal forms of control as self-discipline, ego strength and creativity. Studies on the correlates of success in high-prestige, white-collar occupations have shown that people without adequately developed internal controls simply do not achieve success in those fields. Blue-collar

and lower white-collar workers must follow orders and be obedient to the wishes and directions of their superiors. But those who own the businesses, make the decisions and do the hiring and firing can afford to be dependent on no one other than their own well-disciplined selves. The incumbents of almost all the highest paid, highest prestige occupations are required to supervise themselves.

34   David P. Ausubel, one of my former psychiatry professors, once spent a year lecturing in New Zealand. At the time, the New Zealand educational system was highly authoritarian. It was widely believed that young people could not be properly educated unless they were afraid of their school instructors.

35   On one occasion, Ausubel was invited to be guest lecturer at a large high school assembly. The teachers and administrators of the school all sat in the middle rows of the large auditorium. About half the students sat behind them and about half sat in front of them. Shortly after Ausubel began lecturing, he observed that the students sitting in front of the teachers were inordinately stiff and extremely well-behaved by American standards. These students did not move or fidget in even the slightest manner. Yet, in stark contrast, he noticed that the students seated behind the faculty were silently but very conspicuously making funny faces, swinging their arms right and left in silly comic gestures—making unseemly fools of themselves. Never in all of his experience working with American high school students had Ausubel observed such immature, discourteous behavior. The remarkable aspect, however, was the grossly extreme contrast between the behavior of those students who could be seen by the faculty members and their classmates who could not.

36   Internal controls are the only real controls. They are the only controls that are likely to influence young people once the punishing authority figures are no longer hanging over their shoulder. Parents who administer corporal punishment in what they label as the child's best interests are only kidding themselves. This is especially true if they depend on their child's fear of the rod for his or her continued obedience and good behavior on a day-to-day basis. Such parents are unintentionally decreasing the chances that their offspring will emerge into mature, responsible adulthood with self-direction. They are increasing the chances that their youngster will always be a follower, ever dependent on the watchful eyes of some job supervisor.

37   One of the most common forms of sexual deviancy in the United States is sadomasochism. Our cities' so-called adult book stores are filled with books and magazines catering to the interests of "discipline lovers" and others who learned to find sexual pleasure through physical pain. Such people virtually have always had a history of a great deal of corporal punishment ("discipline") in their own backgrounds, and studies being conducted on such people today continue to reveal this. They were frequently spanked by their own parents or guardians; they are quite moralistic in justifying the use of frequent and painful corporal punishment on their own children. And they find great sexual pleasure themselves in spanking and in being spanked. The buttocks are a very sexually sensitive region of the body.

38   No variable more accurately predicts how people are likely to rear

their own offspring than the way they themselves were reared, since, as a general rule, people tend to absorb the disciplinary approaches of their parents. These remain latent until such time as they themselves have children.

39 However, scientists have been noticing that destructive techniques of parental discipline often surface in youngsters' behavior long before they have a chance to become parents themselves. A few years ago, I was living next door to a four-year-old girl who frequently displayed a bizarre pattern of play. She often beat her doll with sticks and hoses and sometimes even with heavy boards, shouting the most disparaging, obscene language at the doll.

40 One day I saw the mother run out into the backyard shouting and screaming the same obscenities at her daughter that the little girl had been screaming at her doll. The mother had a rubber hose and beat the little girl mercilessly with it as an equally merciless spasm of ego-deflating labels and obscene language came spewing forth. The incident had a profound impact on me. It represented a firsthand observation of what I later learned was a commonplace tragedy. Psychologists have long known that the way a child plays with his or her dolls is often a direct reflection of the way in which that child's parents relate to and discipline that youngster.

41 Of perhaps even greater significance are the recent finding of some ASPCA scientists. Every day, scores of dogs and cats are made to suffer unfathomable torture. Some of them are skinned alive, placed in boiling water, dismembered, blinded and so on. It is now known that most of this torture is perpetrated by children. But more important, virtually all of these children have been found, upon investigation, to have been similarly beaten and tortured by their own parents! In addition, more than two-thirds of parents adjudged guilty of inflicting the "battered-child syndrome" on their children had had a previous history of cruelty to animals.

42 Again, no one had ever manifested any compassionate feelings toward these children and their needs. Since no one ever considered their feelings or needs, they in turn never learned to develop any feelings of compassion for others—animals or humans. Often these children grow into dangerous psychopaths.

43 While the arguments against the use of physical punishment are many in number and highly convincing in substance, there is little indication in the United States today that such disciplinary approaches are losing their popularity. As a case in point, the states of New Jersey and California, and the cities of New York and Chicago, remain the only major jurisictions in the entire country where corporal punishment is illegal in the schools. Every year major efforts are made by conscientious parents and educators to change this. The issue of corporal punishment in the schools has been brought before the United States Supreme Court almost every year for the past decade; the court has persistently refused to listen to arguments pertinent to this very important issue. On April 18, 1977, they ruled five to four in favor of continuing to permit the use of corporal punishment on school children.

44   Of course, banning the use of physical punishment in the schools is not going to end its use in the home. But public schools can and should be expected to set a positive example for parents to follow. Surely the policies of our public schools must be made to reflect the best of current knowledge from such fields as child development, social psychology and human relations. Yet the hundreds of valuable insights such research has yielded have been largely ignored by most parents, teachers, educational administrators and Supreme Court "justices."

45   Many parents complain that their children constantly misbehave. They point out that their youngsters continue to misbehave no matter how much or how often they are spanked. It is no accident that parents who administer a great deal of corporal punishment are the very people who are most likely to make this complaint. Such parents are never likely to succeed at influencing their children until they recognize and act upon a key point: *chronic or persistent misbehavior is a means of communicating unfulfilled and unrecognized needs.*

46   It is not necessary that all of a youngster's needs and desires be fulfilled. But it is necessary that the parents have an awareness of those needs and that they respect and recognize their offspring for having them. A punitive approach merely serves as a blinding smokescreen; it serves to distract and sidetrack the parents from the necessary and important task of becoming aware of and coming to grips with their child's needs and felt (but not communicated) deprivations. After the youngster's felt deprivations and needs have been determined and respected, mutually acceptable steps can be worked out through which the child can have some of his or her needs met. Once this has been accomplished, the behavior of almost any chronically misbehaving youngster will drastically improve. Indeed, the parents, teachers and all other adults in the child's life will be greatly amazed by the immense improvement in that little person's everyday behavior.

ANALYSIS

structure   1. State Gilmartin's thesis.

2. List two causes of spanking.

3. List four effects of spanking.

4. List some of the methods that Gilmartin uses to support his opinions.

meaning   5. Explain "the childrearing pendulum has been moving back toward the right" (paragraph 1).

6. Explain "discipline means education" (paragraph 4).

7. What is paradoxical about the views of the moralists toward spanking and the results of studies made into the backgrounds of violent criminals?

8. What does the study of the boys who did not experience pain appear to indicate?

9. What is the importance of the self image?

10. What do spanked children learn about behavior?

11. What ideas does the story of Ausubel's experience support? (paragraphs 34–36)

12. Discuss "chronic or persistent misbehavior is a means of communicating unfulfilled and unrecognized needs" (paragraph 45).

13. What is the most important realization that parents must come to if they wish to improve the behavior of their children?

opinion   14. Express your views of spanking.

WRITING SUGGESTION

Considering your own experiences with corporal punishment, write a cause/effect paper in which you support or attack Gilmartin's views.

In the next selection, note how Thurber prepares his readers for the hilarious cause/effect sequence by letting them in on the principal cause: the fact that the whole family is a bit daft. You can best enjoy the final scene if you think of your own family milling about in night clothes in the middle of the night, shouting at each other. If your family is completely sane, you might not understand it.

James Thurber

THE NIGHT THE BED FELL

1   I suppose that the high-water mark of my youth in Columbus, Ohio, was the night the bed fell on my father. It makes a better recitation (unless, as some friends of mine have said, one has heard it five or six times) than it does a piece of writing, for it is almost necessary to throw furniture around, shake doors, and bark like a dog, to lend the proper atmosphere and verisimilitude to what is admittedly a somewhat incredible tale. Still, it did take place.

2   It happened, then, that my father had decided to sleep in the attic one night, to be away where he could think. My mother opposed the notion strongly because, she said, the old wooden bed up there was unsafe; it was wobbly and the heavy headboard would crash down on father's head in case the bed fell, and kill him. There was no dissuading him, however, and at a quarter past ten he closed the attic door behind him and went up the narrow twisting stairs. We later heard ominous creakings as he crawled into bed. Grandfather, who usually slept in the attic bed when he was with us, had disappeared some days before. (On these occasions he was usually gone six or eight days and returned growling and out of temper, with the news that the federal Union was run by a passel of blockheads and that the Army of the Potomac didn't have any more chance than a fiddler's bitch.)

Copyright © 1933, 1961 by James Thurber. From *My Life and Hard Times*, published by Harper & Row. Originally printed in *The New Yorker*.

³   We had visiting us at this time a nervous first cousin of mine named Briggs Beall, who believed that he was likely to cease breathing when he was asleep. It was his feeling that if he were not awakened every hour during the night, he might die of suffocation. He had been accustomed to setting an alarm clock to ring at intervals until morning, but I persuaded him to abandon this. He slept in my room and I told him that I was such a light sleeper that if anybody quit breathing in the same room with me, I would wake instantly. He tested me the first night—which I had suspected he would—by holding his breath after my regular breathing had convinced him I was asleep. I was not asleep, however, and called to him. This seemed to allay his fears a little, but he took the precaution of putting a glass of spirits of camphor on a little table at the head of his bed. In case I didn't arouse him until he was almost gone, he said, he would sniff the camphor, a powerful reviver. Briggs was not the only member of his family who had his crotchets. Old Aunt Melissa Beall (who could whistle like a man, with two fingers in her mouth) suffered under the premonition that she was destined to die on South High Street, because she had been born on South High Street and married on South High Street. Then there was Aunt Sarah Shoaf, who never went to bed at night without the fear that a burglar was going to get in and blow chloroform under her door through a tube. To avert this calamity—for she was in greater dread of anesthetics than of losing her household goods—she always piled her money, silverware, and other valuables in a neat stack just outside her bedroom, with a note reading: "This is all I have. Please take it and do not use your chloroform, as this is all I have." Aunt Gracie Shoaf also had a burglar phobia, but she met it with more fortitude. She was confident that burglars had been getting into her house every night for forty years. The fact that she never missed anything was to her no proof to the contrary. She always claimed that she scared them off before they could take anything, by throwing shoes down the hallway. When she went to bed she piled, where she could get at them handily, all the shoes there were about her house. Five minutes after she had turned off the light, she would sit up in bed and say "Hark!" Her husband, who had learned to ignore the whole situation as long ago as 1903, would either be sound asleep or pretend to be sound asleep. In either case he would not respond to her tugging and pulling, so that presently she would arise, tiptoe to the door, open it slightly and heave a shoe down the hall in one direction, and its mate down the hall in the other direction. Some nights she threw them all, some nights only a couple of pair.

⁴   But I am straying from the remarkable incidents that took place during the night that the bed fell on father. By midnight we were all in bed. The layout of the rooms and the disposition of their occupants is important to an understanding of what later occurred. In the front room upstairs (just under father's attic bedroom) were my mother and my brother Herman, who sometimes sang in his sleep, usually "Marching Through Georgia" or "Onward, Christian Soldiers." Briggs Beall and myself were in a room adjoining this one. My brother Roy was in a room across the hall from ours. Our bull terrier, Rex, slept in the hall.

⁵   My bed was an army cot, one of those affairs which are made wide enough to sleep on comfortably only by putting up, flat with the middle

section, the two sides which ordinarily hang down like the sideboards of a drop-leaf table. When these sides are up, it is perilous to roll too far toward the edge, for then the cot is likely to tip completely over, bringing the whole bed down on top of one, with a tremendous banging crash. This, in fact, is precisely what happened, about two o'clock in the morning. (It was my mother who, in recalling the scene later, first referred to it as "the night the bed fell on your father.")

6   Always a deep sleeper, slow to arouse (I had lied to Briggs), I was at first unconscious of what had happened when the iron cot rolled me onto the floor and toppled over on me. It left me still warmly bundled up and unhurt, for the bed rested above me like a canopy. Hence I did not wake up, only reached the edge of consciousness and went back. The racket, however, instantly awakened my mother, in the next room, who came to the immediate conclusion that her worst dread was realized: the big wooden bed upstairs had fallen on father. She therefore screamed, "Let's go to your poor father!" It was this shout, rather than the noise of my cot falling, that awakened Herman, in the same room with her. He thought that mother had become, for no apparent reason, hysterical. "You're all right, Mamma!" he shouted, trying to calm her. They exchanged shout for shout for perhaps ten seconds: "Let's go to your poor father!" and "You're all right!" That woke up Briggs. By this time I was conscious of what was going on, in a vague way, but did not yet realize that I was under my bed instead of on it. Briggs, awakening in the midst of loud shouts of fear and apprehension, came to the quick conclusion that he was suffocating and that we were all trying to "bring him out." With a low moan, he grasped the glass of camphor at the head of his bed and instead of sniffing it poured it over himself. The room reeked of camphor. "Ugf, ahfg," choked Briggs, like a drowning man, for he had almost succeeded in stopping his breath under the deluge of pungent spirits. He leaped out of bed and groped toward the open window, but he came up against one that was closed. With his hand, he beat out the glass, and I could hear it crash and tinkle on the alleyway below. It was at this juncture that I, in trying to get up, had the uncanny sensation of feeling my bed above me! Foggy with sleep, I now suspected, in my turn, that the whole uproar was being made in a frantic endeavor to extricate me from what must be an unheard-of and perilous situation. "Get me out of this!" I bawled. "Get me out!" I think I had the nightmarish belief that I was entombed in a mine. "Gugh," gasped Briggs, floundering in his camphor.

7   By this time my mother, still shouting, pursued by Herman, still shouting, was trying to open the door to the attic, in order to go up and get my father's body out of the wreckage. The door was stuck, however, and wouldn't yield. Her frantic pulls on it only added to the general banging and confusion. Roy and the dog were now up, the one shouting questions, the other barking.

8   Father, farthest away and soundest sleeper of all, had by this time been awakened by the battering on the attic door. He decided that the house was on fire. "I'm coming, I'm coming!" he wailed in a slow, sleepy voice—it took him many minutes to regain full consciousness. My mother, still believing he was caught under the bed, detected in his "I'm

coming!" the mournful, resigned note of one who is preparing to meet his Maker. "He's dying!" she shouted.

9   "I'm all right!" Briggs yelled to reassure her. "I'm all right!" He still believed that it was his own closeness to death that was worrying mother. I found at last the light switch in my room, unlocked the door, and Briggs and I joined the others at the attic door. The dog, who never did like Briggs, jumped for him—assuming that he was the culprit in whatever was going on—and Roy had to throw Rex and hold him. We could hear father crawling out of bed upstairs. Roy pulled the attic door open, with a mighty jerk, and father came down the stairs, sleepy and irritable but safe and sound. My mother began to weep when she saw him. Rex began to howl. "What the name of God is going on here?" asked father.

10   The situation was finally put together like a gigantic jig-saw puzzle. Father caught a cold from prowling around in his bare feet but there were no other bad results. "I'm glad," said mother, who always looked on the bright side of things, "that your grandfather wasn't here."

Review of Chapter 9

Ever curious, *homo sapiens* is constantly seeking causes for the effects he experiences every day. Hence the cause/effect paper is one of our most common forms of writing. But human beings see the same things in different ways for varying reasons, and complicated situations often involve a great many variables. So writers who uncover causes must write with care, and readers must read with suspicion.

The organization of the cause/effect paper varies greatly, depending on its purpose and on what aspects of the problem the writer wants to emphasize. Mitford uses examples from history to show the weaknesses of criminal classification systems. Fuller provides a highly personal and unusual description of the effects of alcohol and the struggle to escape alcoholism. Mailer sees the death of Paret through the eyes of a hot-blooded, emotional novelist; Cousins sees it through the eyes of a sophisticated, socially conscious editor. Mailer provides a chilling ringside view, then mulls it around in his mind; Cousins opens with an incident from the past, then adds scathing editorial comment.

As a child you probably heard the maxim quoted in Ben Franklin's *Poor Richard's Almanac:*

A little neglect may breed mischief:
for want of a nail the shoe was lost; for
want of a shoe the horse was lost; and
for want of a horse the rider was lost.

At that time the maxim probably seemed quite clever, perfect, and complete. It makes a good point about the tragic effect of lack of attention to detail. Today, however, a good student might wonder why the blacksmith neglected to add the nail. Was he cheating the rider? Did the horse have a sore foot? Why didn't the rider check the shoe? Didn't he eventually notice that the horse was limping? Some sources extend the maxim to say,

"For want of the rider the battle was lost." By now you, of course, realize that the correct response is, "If the outcome of the battle depended on only one rider, it probably would have been lost anyway.

EVALUATION

In addition to considering all other aspects of good writing, carefully weigh how well the writers show the relationship between causes and effects. Are the effects the logical results of the causes? Are other possibilities considered? Are the causes real or imaginary? Do the writers support their opinions adequately? Keeping these factors in mind, choose the two best selections in this chapter.

CHAPTER 10

This chapter is a smorgasbord of ideas for you to use in writing papers. It is supplementary and complementary to the other chapters. It should give you ideas for themes, help you support ideas already partially developed, spur you to do further research into a given subject, provide some deep insights into matters of life or death—or just give you a few good laughs.

Pictures, poems, proverbs, and quotations are provided as inspirational and supporting materials for narrative, descriptive, or expository writing. Many of the selections tie in with subjects presented in earlier chapters.

MAKE IT YOURS

Most writers get ideas from other writers. Whether a particular piece of writing is *yours* or not is determined by the following criteria:

1. The thesis statement must be your idea, unless you are assigned a standard subject ("Hand Guns Should Be Outlawed," etc.).
2. The ideas in the body of the work may be quoted from other sources, but they are selected, organized, and introduced by you to support your thesis. It is usually best to quote sparingly and use more than one source.
3. The sources of both direct quotations and paraphrases must be cited (direct quotations in quotation marks). The emphasis and tone of the original must be retained when words are taken out of context so that the meaning is not changed.

4. You supply all necessary transitions, make comments, and provide your own opinions.

5. You write an apt conclusion.

The questions raised and subjects suggested in the following pages are intended to stimulate your thinking, not to limit it. Hopefully, you will think of better thematic ideas than those presented and/or adapt those ideas to your own experience. Your response to a question should not be merely an answer but a well-organized theme with an introduction, body, and conclusion. Unless you are an experienced writer, it is wise to state your thesis in the introduction and to keep checking your work to be sure you are sticking to your thesis. Outlines help. Remember *organization, development, coherence,* and *unity.*

unit 1   *Patent Medicines and Home Remedies*

❖❖

Will motherwort and poplar bark cure hysterics? Should you tie an onion to a burn?

1. Write an example paper about old time remedies. It could be humorous.

2. Classify the remedies.

3. Compare patent medicines of yesterday with non-prescription medicines of today—remedies like cough syrups, sleeping pills, vitamins, Alka Seltzer, Geritol, Tums. Try to get some authoritative medical evaluation of the old and the new.

4. Using a combination of old remedies and ads, write a funny process theme telling how to cure a serious illness.

*Remedies Based on Folklore and Superstition**

RAGING MADNESS

Apply to the head cloths dipped in cold water. Or set the patient with his head under a great waterfall as long as his strength will bear, or pour cold water on his head out of a tea-kettle. Or let him eat nothing but apples for a month. Or nothing but bread and milk.

CONVULSIONS

To stop convulsions in a baby that is teething, let the mother bite off the head of a mouse.

* Adapted from *The Great Patent Medicine Era* by Adelaide Hectlinger. Copyright © 1970 by Grosset & Dunlap, Inc. Used by permission of publisher.

A RUPTURE IN CHILDREN

Boil a spoonful of egg-shells dried in an oven and powdered, in three quarters of a pint of milk. Feed the child constantly with bread boiled in this milk.

CROUP

To cure croup, give the child a teaspoon of urine three times a day. Put some hair of a croupy child into a hole bored in the wall. Plug up the hole and the croup will be cured.

RHEUMATISM

Sleep with a dog to cure rheumatism. The dog will absorb the disease and become crippled. . . . The rheumatic parts of your body are cured by wrapping an eelskin around them. . . . Wear elder leaves in your shoes to ward off rheumatism. . . . A piece of red flannel worn about the part will cure rheumatism. . . . A bee sting will cure rheumatism. . . . Wear the eyetooth of a pig. . . . Carry three potatoes in your pants pocket. . . . Carry in your pocket the triangular bone from a ham. . . . Put a copper cent into your shoe. . . . Take a chicken and cut it in two and leave all the entrails in. Put your foot right in the chicken and it will take all the rheumatism out of your body.

COUGH OR PHTHISIC

Take the dried leaves of rosemary, shred small, and smoke them in a tobacco pipe. It will help those that have a cough or phthisic, or consumption by warming and drying the thin distillations which cause these diseases.

THE KING'S EVIL OR KERNEL OF THE EARS

Take the root of bastard rhubarb, dry it, and boil it in wine. Bathe the part affected and drink a glass of it three times a day before eating. It is also good for the stone or gravel to drink the steepings of the root in Holland gin.

TO STOP VOMITING

Take green wheat or green grass, pound it and pour on boiling water and sweeten with loaf sugar. Press out the juice and let the patient drink a table-spoonful every ten minutes. Or take gum camphor pounded fine, mix it with boiling water, sweetened. The same quantity will answer for a dose as the other.

KICKAPOO

INDIAN ✳ SAGWA.

Is a compound of the virtues of Roots, Herbs,
Barks, Gums and Leaves. Its elements are

BLOOD-MAKING, BLOOD-CLEANSING
AND LIFE-SUSTAINING.

It is the Purest, Safest, Most Effectual Medicine known to the public. **By**
. its searching and cleansing qualities it drives out the foul corruptions .
. . which contaminate the blood and cause derangement and decay. . .
. . . . It stimulates and enlivens the vital functions, promotes en- . . .
. . . . . ergy and strength, restores and preserves health and in- . . . .
. . . . . fuses new life and vigor throughout the whole system. . . . . .
. . . . . No sufferer from any disease which arises from impurity . . . .
. . . of the blood need despair who will give Indian Sagwa a . . .
. . fair trial.   The sciences of Medicine and Chemistry have never . .
. produced so valuable a remedy, nor one so potent to cure all diseases .
. . . . . . arising from an impure blood. **SAGWA** will cure . . . . .

CONSTIPATION, LIVER COMPLAINT,
DYSPEPSIA, INDIGESTION, LOSS OF
APPETITE, SCROFULA, RHEUMA-
TISM, CHILLS AND FEVER,

or any Disease arising from an Impure Blood or Derangement of the
STOMACH, LIVER OR KIDNEYS.

Price, $1.00 per bottle ; 6 bottles for $5.00.

FOR SALE BY ALL DRUGGISTS.

"CURED BY LIGHTNING."

The Sun, of New-York, dated August 26, 1885, contained the following press dispatch.

CURED BY LIGHTNING.

CINCINNATI, O., AUG. 25.—Edward Burge, a railroad man, has for a number of years been suffering with a paralyzed arm. When the storm came on Saturday evening he was out in his yard, and was about to pull up a bucket of water when lightning struck his arm. He attempted to move it, and to his great delight he discovered that the stroke of lightning had made his arm alive again.

NOW, WHY IS IT

That, after five thousand years of study and practice, physicians are still unable to cure such common ailments as Dyspepsia, Indigestion, Liver and Kidney troubles?

Common sense convinces one that something must be wrong. Other branches of science, surgery, dentistry, etc., have achieved wonderful results, while medicine still remains to a great extent an *experiment*. Thinking people are exclaiming: Why all these injurious drugs? Why all these large bills and yet no cure? Surely the doctor ought to relieve me after his five thousand years of profound study. Can it be he is still groping in the dark? Let us take an illustration: Here is an ordinary headache, known to the doctor since Adam's time, and yet what physician in Europe or America can cure it?

Now, if a physician, after all the knowledge his profession has acquired in five thousand years, cannot cure a simple headache, how can he undertake to cure the more serious disorders which affect the human family?

Recently the Press was filled with reports of the meetings of the New-York County Medical Societies.

They debated thus:—In the case of a dying man, can one school consult with the other school to save the man's life? The decision was "no." Let the man die first, before either would yield. One venerable doctor with a very rich practice arose and denounced *Allopathy as murder*. An opponent equally famed, standing amongst the highest in his profession, got up and gravely assured the assembly that *Homœopathy* was the *greatest humbug of the age*.

Well, after this "showing up" of medicine, as reported in the papers, what are we poor ignorant sufferers to think?

In September, 1878, all London was astonished by a new departure in medicine,—a beautiful application of Electro-Magnetic force, which positively cured headaches, neuralgia, etc., in two to five minutes (we refer to Dr. Scott's Pure Bristle Electric Hair Brush). The people wondered, the doctors were dumbfounded, while the practical inventor was hailed as a Public Benefactor.

We could fill pages with illustrations of the gross errors of medicine, and thinking people are desiring and awaiting a new departure in therapeutics.

One is now at hand, and it threatens before long to revolutionize the old experimental schools. It has been conclusively demonstrated in the hospitals of London, as well as in large private practice, that most remarkable cures attend the application of Electro-Magnetism to diseased parts of the body. Persons thought to be dead have been restored, and diseases heretofore baffling the best medical skill have yielded to a remedy which is believed to be the "Vital Spark" itself.

It acts immediately upon the blood, nerves, and tissues, producing more benefit in a few hours than the doctor has given in weeks or months.

It has been well said, "electricity is the steam in the human engine which keeps it going and regulates its movements. It is the 'Vital Spark,' life itself, pervading all nature with power to kill or to cure."

Dr. Scott's Electric Belt.   Dr. Scott's Electric Corset.

SENT, POST-PAID, ON TRIAL.

Pall Mall Electric Ass'n, London and New-York.

(Every mail brings similar letters.)

NEWARK, N. Y. June 1.
Dr. Scott's Electric Corsets have entirely cured me of muscular rheumatism. It has also cured a severe case of headache and female troubles of eighteen years' standing.
MRS. L. C. SPENCER.

HOLLIS CENTRE, ME. Aug. 29.
I suffered severely from back trouble for years, and found no relief till I wore Dr. Scott's Electric Corsets. They cured me, and I would not be without them.
MRS. H. D. BENSON.

PEORIA, ILL.
I suffered from kidney, river, and nervous troubles for twelve years. Dr. Scott's Electric Belt entirely cured me, after all other remedies had failed. His Electric Hair Brush has cured my neuralgia. C. W. HORNISH.

NILES, MICH. Jan. 5, 1885.
Dr. Scott's Electric Corsets have cured me of acute dyspepsia, from which I had suffered for eight years. His Electric Hair Brush cures my headache every time. MRS. WM. H. PEAK.

BALTIMORE, MD.
Intense nervous debility has been my trouble for years. Physicians and their medicines did not help me. I finally derived great relief from Dr. Scott's Electric Belt. L. H. MILLER.

Probably never, since the invention of Corsets, has so large a demand been created as now exists for Dr. Scott's Electric Corsets and Belts. They are worn daily in over eight thousand families in the city of New-York alone.

If you have *any* pain, ache, or ill-feeling from any cause, if you seem "pretty well," yet lack energy and do not "feel up to the mark," if you suffer from disease, we beg you to at once try these remarkable curatives. They cannot and do not injure like medicine. Always doing good, never harm. *There is no shock or sensation felt in wearing them.* There is no waiting a long time for results; Electro-magnetism acts quickly,—generally the first week, more frequently the first day, and often even during the first hour they are worn their wonderful curative powers are felt.

The celebrated DR. W. A. HAMMOND, of New-York, formerly Surgeon-General of the U. S. Army, lately lectured upon this subject, and advised all medical men to make trial of these agencies, describing at the same time most remarkable cures he had made, even in cases which would seem hopeless.

The Corsets do not differ in appearance from those usually worn, as we substitute our flat steel magnetods in place of the ordinary corset-steels. They are all equally charged, differing only in quality and design. They are elegant in shape and finish, made after the best French pattern, and warranted satisfactory in every respect. Those who have tried them say they will wear no others. Most of the above applies equally well to the Electric Belt for gents or ladies.

The prices are as follows: **$1.00, $1.50, $2.00,** and **$3.00** for the Corsets, and **$3.00** each for the Belts. We make these in dove and white only. They are sent out in a handsome box, accompanied by a silver-plated compass, by which the Electro-magnetic influence can be tested. If you cannot get them in your town, we will send either kind to any address, post-paid, on receipt of price, with 20 cents added for packing or registration, and we guarantee safe delivery into your hands. Remit in post-office money-order, draft, check, or in currency by registered letter. In ordering, kindly state exact size of Corset usually worn; or, where the size is not known, take a measurement of the waist over the linen. This can be done with a piece of common string, which send with your order. Remit to

GEO. A. SCOTT, 842 Broadway. N. Y.

THE ITCH

Make a syrup of the juice of sorrel and fumitory. This is a sovereign remedy for that troublesome disorder. Use it inwardly, and the juice of sorrel and vinegar, as a wash, outwardly.

STOMACH BLEEDING

Take one pound of yellow dock root, dry it thoroughly, and pound it fine. Boil this in a quart of milk, and strain it off. Use one gill three times a day, also one pill a day, made of turpentine, from the end of a white pine log, and honey, equal parts. This will heal the vessels that leak.

HYSTERICS

Take the leaves of motherwort and thoroughwort, and poplar bark, from the root of a tree. Pound these fine and sift them through a fine sieve. Mix with molasses and make it into pills, and take four of them when the disorder is coming on. This will settle the head, and make every thing as calm as a clock!

WEAKNESS AND GENERAL DEBILITY

Take of lovage root half a pound, four ounces of burdock roots, and half a pound of comfrey roots to four quarts of water, and let it boil moderately for the space of two hours, strain it off and then continue to boil it down to one quart, add half a pint of the best Holland gin, and one pound of honey, or loaf sugar will do if honey cannot be procured; put it into a bottle and cork it tight for eight and forty hours, when it will be fit for use. Dose, a table-spoonful three times a day before eating. This syrup has been known to perform a great many cures after every other remedy had failed and the most celebrated physicians' skill entirely baffled.

CANKER SORES

Take plaintain, honeysuckle, sage, and rosemary, equal parts, and boil them in sour wine; add thereto a little honey and alum. Wash the mouth with this as often as necessary. A few times will be sufficient. It is very harmless, but not more so than it is healing.

CONSUMPTIVE COUGH OR BREAST PAIN

Take a table-spoonful of tar, three spoonfuls of honey, the yolks of three eggs, beat them well together, then add half a pint of wine, and beat them again. Then cork it up tight for use. Take a teaspoonful three times a day, before eating. Be sure to drink nothing but barley tea for your constant tea.

BURNS

Take an onion and cut it in halves, warm it a very little, (but not roast it, for that decreases its strength, and consequently its virtues) bind it on the affected part. It will stop the soreness and inflammation, by drawing out the humors, which always accompany a burn, if not prevented.

WORMS IN CHILDREN

There are many things good for children in this case. The leaves of sage, powdered fine, and mixed with a little honey, a tea-spoonful for a dose; or flour of sulphur, mixed with honey, is good for worms.

DEAFNESS, SINGING IN THE EARS, ETC.

Take the juice of sow-thistle, and heat it with a little oil of bitter almonds, in the shell of a pomegranate, and drop some of it into the ears. It is a good remedy for deafness, singings, and other diseases of the head and ears.

INFLAMMATION OF THE HEART, ETC.

Make a decoction of red roses with wine, apply it to the region of the heart, with a sponge; or let the leaves remain in, and bring them on, over where your heart beats, shifting them often. This is very good for St. Anthony's fire, and many other diseases of the stomach, also for pains in the head, and hot and inflamed eyes. Be sure to remember that red roses strengthen the heart, liver, stomach, and retentive faculties.

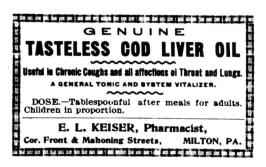

GENUINE
TASTELESS COD LIVER OIL

Useful in Chronic Coughs and all affections of Throat and Lungs.

A GENERAL TONIC AND SYSTEM VITALIZER.

DOSE.—Tablespoonful after meals for adults. Children in proportion.

E. L. KEISER, Pharmacist,

Cor. Front & Mahoning Streets,   MILTON, PA.

unit 2 *Lighthouse on the Lake*

❖❖❖

Write a detailed description of this wintery view. Does it bring to mind a similar scene or, perhaps, a story? Does it make you think of loneliness or peace? Tell of daily life in a lighthouse or another isolated place.

Photo courtesy the Cleveland Press

unit 3   *Love and Marriage*

❖❖

1. Define *love.*
2. Tell how you have fallen in love and/or out of it. Use quotes from this unit where appropriate.
3. Write of the causes of love—and the effects.
4. Compare and contrast the various views of love.
5. Tell one of the love stories in your life.
6. Use some of these quotes in a critique of Elegy IV from Ovid's *Art of Love* in Section 4A.

Quotes on Love*

Many a man has fallen in love with a girl in a light so dim he would not have chosen a suit by it.
> MAURICE CHEVALIER, news summaries, July 17, 1955.

An archeologist is the best husband any woman can have: the older she gets, the more interested he is in her.
> AGATHA CHRISTIE, news reports of March 9, 1954.

In love we find a joy which is ultimate because it is the ultimate truth.
> RABINDRANATH TAGORE, *Creative Unity,* 1922

I've sometimes thought of marrying—and then I've thought again.
> NOEL COWARD, *Theatre Arts,* Nov. 1956.

Love is an energy which exists of itself. It is its own value.
> THORNTON WILDER, on theme of *The Bridge of San Luis Rey; Time,* Feb. 3, 1958.

Bitterness imprisons life; love releases it. Bitterness paralyzes life; love empowers it. Bitterness sours life; love sweetens it. Bitterness sickens life; love heals it. Bitterness blinds life; love anoints its eyes.
> HARRY EMERSON FOSDICK, *Riverside Sermons,* Harper & Row, 1958.

Love is our highest word, and the synonym of God.
> RALPH WALDO EMERSON, "Love," *Essays,* 1841.

> * All quotations from the 1950s on are from *Contemporary Quotations,* compiled by James B. Simpson, published 1964 by Thomas Y. Crowell Co., and used by permission of Father Simpson. Other quotations are from *The World Treasury of Religious Quotations.*

Love is an act of endless forgiveness, a tender look which becomes a habit.
PETER USTINOV, *Christian Science Monitor,* Dec. 9, 1958.

He who practices the law without loving does not practice the law, because the first commandment is love. And he who loves while scorning the law does not love, because the law is the first will of Him Who loves us, and Whom we love.
JACQUES MARITAIN, *Art and Poetry,* 1943.

. . . Man can live his truth, his deepest truth, but cannot speak it. It is for this reason that love becomes the ultimate human answer to the ultimate human question. Love, in reason's terms, answers nothing. We say that *Amor vincit omnia,* but, in truth, love conquers nothing—certainly not death—certainly not chance. What love does is to arm. It arms the worth of life in spite of life . . .
ARCHIBALD MACLEISH, on his Broadway play, *J. B., Time,* Dec. 22, 1958.

Love is the noblest frailty of the mind.
JOHN DRYDEN (1631–1700), *The Indian Emperor.*

Love is a malady without a cure.
JOHN DRYDEN (1631–1700), *Palamon and Arcite.*

You can see them alongside the shuffleboard courts in Florida or on the porches of the old folks' homes up north: an old man with snow-white hair, a little hard of hearing, reading the newspaper through a magnifying glass; an old woman in a shapeless dress, her knuckles gnarled by arthritis, wearing sandals to ease her aching arches. They are holding hands, and in a little while they will totter off to take a nap, and then she will cook supper, not a very good supper, and they will watch television, each knowing exactly what the other is thinking, until it is time for bed. They may even have a good, soul-stirring argument, just to prove that they still really care. And through the night they will snore unabashedly, each resting content because the other is there. They are in love, they have always been in love, although sometimes they would have denied it. And because they have been in love they have survived everything that life could throw at them, even their own failures.
ERNEST HAVEMANN, in concluding article in his series, "Love and Marriage," *Life,* Sept. 29, 1961.

The Senior Prom is the point at which we learn how well we are doing thus far. A date means we are popular with at least one other person and, therefore, we are potentially lovable. Reassured, we press on.
JULIAN HUXLEY.

Every creature, being a more or less remote derivation of infinite love, is therefore the fruit of love and does not move except through love.
POPE PIUS XII, *Address,* October 23, 1940.

So long as the emotional feelings between the couple are right, so long as there is mutual trust and love, their bodies will invariably make the appropriate responses.

DR. DAVID R. MACE, *Time,* March 10, 1958.

Man has survived everything, and we have only survived it on our optimism, and optimism means faith in ourselves, faith in the everydayness of our lives, faith in our universal qualities, and above all, faith in love.

EDWARD STEICHEN, comment about photographic exhibit "The Family of Man," NBC-TV, 1955.

A lady of 47 who has been married 27 years and has six children knows what love really is and once described it for me like this: "Love is what you've been through with somebody."

JAMES THURBER, *Life,* March 14, 1960.

I would like to have engraved inside every wedding band, *Be kind to one another.* This is the Golden Rule of marriage, and the secret of making love last through the years.

RANDOLPH RAY, *My Little Church Around the Corner,* Simon and Schuster, 1957.

To be in love is merely to be in a state of perpetual anesthesia.

H. L. MENCKEN, recalled in reports of his death, Jan. 29, 1956.

Great lovers will always be unhappy because, for them, love is of supreme importance.

CESARE PAVESE, Italian author, *The Burning Brand,* Walker & Co., 1961.

Love is a dweller in strange places and has no proper address. It is no more remarkable to find it lighting the dim marble halls of a palace than blazing on the humble hearth, and the house that knows it not is dark and cold indeed. It is the penchant of poets to crown love with roses, discover it beside a limpid stream or in verdant meadows, but a lover knows this has no bearing on the matter, and given love, the desert springs with flowers.

MARY PARRISH, "All the Love in the World," *McCall's,* June, 1961.

How do you know love is gone? If you said that you would be there at seven and you get there by nine, and he or she has not called the police yet—it's gone.

MARLENE DIETRICH, *Marlene Dietrich's ABC's,* Doubleday, 1961.

The truth [is] that there is only one terminal dignity—love. And the story of a love is not important—what is important is that one is capable of love. It is perhaps the only glimpse we are permitted of eternity.

HELEN HAYES, *Guideposts,* Jan. 1960.

. . . Love is a hole in the heart.

BEN HECHT, in his play, *Winkelberg,* produced in New York in Jan., 1958.

How much do we know about love? The first thing we know about love is that, for most of us, it is the most absorbing and interesting subject in existence. There is an enormous range of meanings in this one little word "love." There are mother love and self-love, father love and children's love for their parents; there are brotherly love and love of one's home and one's country; love of money and love of power; making love and loving food; there are music lovers, sports lovers, bird lovers, sun lovers. Preachers insist that we should love God; Jesus adjures us to love our enemies. Love clearly includes all these usages: but the love in which one can be is the pre-eminent love for most of us.

JULIAN HUXLEY, "All About Love," *Look,* July 12, 1955.

unit 4   *To Kiss a Frog*

❖❖❖

It's good to act silly sometimes—to do something unusual or crazy. Did you ever enter a frog in a jumping contest, compete in a soap box derby, or try to pick up a greased watermelon? Write about it.

Wide World Photos

unit 5　*Sexism*

❖❖

1. Use the following quotes to argue that women are truly inferior to men.

2. Use the quotes to argue that, since most religious works were written, interpreted, and transcribed by men, such writings are, indeed, sexist.

3. Use the quotes to support or attack the idea of having women clergy—priests, ministers, rabbis, etc.

4. Use some of the quotes in discussing "Tales with a Point of View" in Section 4C.

5. Find examples of sexism in other writing.

A Sampling of Sexist Quotes

The glory of a man is knowledge, but the glory of a woman is to renounce knowledge.　—Chinese proverb

Do not trust a good woman, and keep away from a bad one.
　—Portuguese proverb

Women are sisters nowhere.　—West African proverb

Whenever a woman dies there is one quarrel less on earth.
　—German proverb

Never trust a woman, even though she has given you ten sons.
　—Chinese proverb

In childhood a woman must be subject to her father; in youth, to her husband; when her husband is dead, to her sons. A woman must never be free of subjugation.　—*The Hindu Code of Manu, V*

I thank thee, O Lord, that thou hast not created me a woman.
　—Daily Orthodox Jewish Prayer (for a male)

There is a good principle which created order, light, and man, and an evil principle which created chaos, darkness, and woman.
　—Pythagoras

We may thus conclude that it is a general law that there should be naturally ruling elements and elements naturally ruled . . . the rule of the freeman over the slave is one kind of rule; that of the male over the female

another . . . the slave is entirely without the faculty of deliberation; the female indeed possesses it, but in a form which remains inconclusive . . .
—ARISTOTLE, *Politics*

If thy wife does not obey thee at a signal and a glance, separate from her.
—*Sirach* 25:26

When a woman thinks . . . she thinks evil.
—SENECA

Creator of the heavens and the earth, He has given you wives from among yourselves to multiply you, and cattle male and female. Nothing can be compared with Him.
—*Holy Koran of Islam*

And the rib, which the Lord God had taken from man, made he a woman and brought her unto the man. And Adam said, This is now bone of my bone, and flesh of my flesh; she shall be called Woman, because she was taken out of Man.
—*Genesis* 2:22–23

How can he be clean that is born of a woman?
—*Job,* 4:4

Suffer women once to arrive at an equality with you, and they will from that moment become your superiors.
—CATO THE ELDER, 195 B.C.

Let the women learn in silence with all subjection . . . I suffer not a woman to usurp authority over men, but to be in silence.
—ST. PAUL

Wives, submit yourselves unto your husbands . . . for the husband is the head of the wife, even as Christ is the head of the church.
—*Ephesians* 5:23–24

The five worst infirmities that afflict the female are indocility, discontent, slander, jealousy, and silliness . . . Such is the stupidity of woman's character, that it is incumbent upon her, in every particular, to distrust herself and to obey her husband.
—*Confucian Marriage Manual*

God created Adam lord of all living creatures, but Eve spoiled it all.
—MARTIN LUTHER

All witchcraft comes from carnal lust, which is in women insatiable.
—KRAMER AND SPRENGER, Inquisitors, *Malleus Maleficarum, c.* 1486

A man in general is better pleased when he has a good dinner than when his wife talks Greek.
—SAMUEL JOHNSON

The whole education of women ought to be relative to men. To please them, to be useful to them, to make themselves loved and honored by them, to educate them when young, to care for them when grown, to counsel them, to console them, and to make life sweet and agreeable to them— these are the duties of women at all times and what should be taught them from their infancy.
—JEAN JACQUES ROUSSEAU

Women have no moral sense; they rely for their behavior upon the men they love.
—LA BRUYERE

Most women have no characters at all.
—ALEXANDER POPE

I never knew a tolerable woman to be fond of her own sex.
—JONATHAN SWIFT

Man for the field and woman for the hearth:
Man for the sword and for the needle she:
Man with the head and woman with the heart:
Man to command and woman to obey;
All else confusion.
—ALFRED, LORD TENNYSON

unit 6   *Go, Team, Go!*

❖•❖

1. Describe the action up to and including the scene in the picture, from the point of view of the runner. Include his thoughts as he runs. Write in the first person if you wish.

2. Describe the feelings of a rookie defensive tackle as he goes for the runner.

3. Describe the runner's girlfriend, watching in the crowd.

4. Consider how three different types of girlfriends might view the same scene.

5. Tell of a critical point in a game in which you played.

6. Someone is critically injured in this play. Write a cause/effect paper about it.

Photo by Tony Tomsic, courtesy the Cleveland Press

unit 7   *Are Lists for the Listless?*

❖❖❖

Who would bother to write a book of lists, and who would bother to read it? *The Book of Lists* by David Wallechinsky and Irving and Amy Wallace was on several best seller lists, so apparently many people have bothered to read it.

1. Compare the problems of Abigail Van Buren's readers with those of Ann Landers.

2. Consider why people write to strangers (newspaper columnists) about their most personal problems. Get opinions from psychologists to support your thesis.

3. Write about bathtubs and the things that happen in them. Perhaps you can write a funny theme in which you argue against taking any baths at all.

4. Discuss some of the famous "boners" and find some more.

5. Get *The Book of Lists* and try to figure out why so many people have read it.

6. Write about other lists such as dictionaries, sports records, important dates, etc.

WONDERFUL BONERS

1. DAN O'LEARY'S HOME RUN

O'Leary, of the Port Huron baseball team, came to bat against Peoria with the score tied. O'Leary hit what may have been the first home run of his career. After rounding the bases, he was declared out. He had run around the bases the wrong way.

2. THE $2 MILLION COMMA

An unidentified congressional clerk was instructed to write: "All foreign fruit-plants are free from duty." Instead, he wrote: "All foreign fruit, plants are free from duty." It cost the U.S. government $2 million before a new session of Congress could rectify the error.

3. O'NEILL'S INCREDIBLE DIRECTIONS

When Nobel prizewinner Eugene O'Neill wrote his play *Where the Cross Is Made,* he gave these stage directions for one scene: "His right arm had been amputated at the shoulder and the sleeve on that side hangs flabbily. Then he goes over to the table, and sits down, resting his elbows, his chin in his hands, staring somberly before him."

4. THE MATERIALISTIC MINT

Many years ago, the U.S. Mint printed on a run of its gold coins: "In Gold We Trust."

From *The Book of Lists* (renumbered). Copyright © 1977 by David Wallechinsky, Irving Wallace, and Amy Wallace. By permission of William Morrow & Company.

5. TOPSY-TURVY ART

The U.S. National Academy of Design held an art competition and awarded second place to a work by Edward Dickinson—which the judges then learned had been hanging upside down.

6. DEFOE'S MEMORY LAPSE

In his immortal novel *Robinson Crusoe,* author Daniel Defoe had his shipwrecked castaway try to salvage some goods: "I resolved, if possible, to get to the ship; so I pulled off my clothes, for the weather was hot to extremity, and took to the water." After the naked Crusoe climbed aboard the ship: "I found that all the ship's provisions were dry; and being well disposed to eat, I went to the bread room and filled my pockets with biscuits."

7. PINTO VERSUS PINTO

During a wrestling match in Providence, R.I., Count George Zaryoff squared off against Stanley Pinto. During the proceedings, Pinto became entangled in the ringside ropes, and in trying to extricate himself his shoulders touched flat against the mat for 3 secs. He had succeeded in pinning himself and lost the match.

8. THE MEMORABLE STOLEN BASE

In a baseball game, Babe Herman, the Brooklyn Dodgers' star outfielder and slugger, stole second base—with the bases loaded.

9. THE SMOKE-FILLED ROOMS

After completing construction of the Howard Hotel in Baltimore, the contractors installed boilers and started fires—before discovering they had forgotten to build a chimney.

10. MAD JUSTICE

In 1863, Paul Hubert, of Bordeaux, France, was convicted of murder and sentenced to life in jail. After Hubert had served 21 years in solitary confinement, his case was reopened—and only then was it found he had been convicted of murdering himself.

FAMOUS EVENTS THAT HAPPENED IN THE BATHTUB

1. POISONING OF PELIAS

According to Greek mythology, Medea murdered Jason's uncle (Pelias, king of Thessaly) by giving him a bath in a vat of deadly poison which she falsely claimed would restore his lost youth.

2. MURDER OF AGAMEMNON

Shortly after his return from the Trojan War, the Greek hero Agamemnon was murdered by his wife, Clytemnestra, who struck him twice with an ax while he was relaxing in the tub.

3. MORPHY'S DEATH

Paul Morphy of New Orleans defeated famous chess players when he was still a child. As an adult, he could play eight games simultaneously while blindfolded. Some people consider him the greatest chess player who ever lived, but from the age of 22 until his death on July 10, 1884, at 47, he played no more chess. Believing that people were trying to poison him or burn his clothes, Morphy became a virtual recluse. On one oppressively hot day he returned from a walk and took a cold bath. In the tub he died from what doctors described as "congestion of the brain or apoplexy, which was evidently brought on by the effects of the cold water on his overheated body."

4. MARAT'S ASSASSINATION

Jean-Paul Marat played an active part in the French Revolution. As editor of the journal *L'Ami du peuple*, he became known as an advocate of extreme violence. The moderate Girondists were driven out of Paris and took refuge in Normandy. There, some of them met and influenced a young woman named Charlotte Corday. Convinced that Marat must die, she went to Paris and bought a butcher knife. When she arrived at Marat's house on July 13, 1793, he was taking a bath. (He spent many hours in the tub because of a painful skin condition.) Overhearing Corday, he asked to see her. They discussed politics for a few minutes; then Corday drew her knife and stabbed Marat to death in the bathtub.

5. SMITH'S MURDERS

George Joseph Smith of England earned his living by his almost hypnotic power over women. In 1910, he met Bessie Mundy, married her (without mentioning that he already had a wife), and disappeared with her cash and clothes. Two years later they met by chance and began living together again. After Smith persuaded Bessie to write a will in his favor, he took her to a doctor on the pretense that she suffered from fits. (Both she and the doctor took his word for it.) A few days later she was found dead in the bathtub, a cake of soap clutched in her hand. Everyone assumed she had drowned during an epileptic seizure. Smith married two more women—Alice Burnham and Margaret Lofty—took out insurance policies on their lives, and described mysterious ailments to their doctors. They, too, were found dead in their bathtubs. When Alice Burnham's father read of Margaret Lofty's death, he was struck by its similarity to his daughter's untimely end. The police were notified, and Smith was tried for murder and sentenced to be executed. His legal wife, Edith, testified at the trial that she could remember only one occasion when Smith himself took a bath.

6. CARROLL'S ORGY

America was shocked by reports of an orgy on February 22, 1926, at the Earl Carroll Theatre, New York, N.Y., after a performance of his *Vanities*. To climax a midnight party onstage, a bathtub was filled with champagne and a nude model climbed in, while the men lined up and filled their glasses from the tub. This was during the Prohibition era, so a federal grand jury immediately began an inquiry into whether or not the tub really did contain liquor and, if so, who had supplied it. Earl Carroll, the producer who staged the party, was convicted of perjury for telling the grand jury that no wine had been in the bathtub. He was sentenced to a year and a day in prison, plus a $2,000 fine. After he suffered a nervous breakdown on the way to the penitentiary, his fellow prisoners were ordered never to mention bathtubs in his presence.

7. KING HAAKON'S FALL

On June 29, 1955, the reign of King Haakon VII, who had ruled Norway from the time of its independence in 1905, effectively came to an end when the beloved monarch fell in the royal bathtub at his palace in Oslo. The elderly king lingered on for over two years before succumbing on September 21, 1957, to complications resulting from his fall.

8. GLENN'S CAREER

The momentum of what contemporary experts considered to be an unstoppable political career was interrupted in 1964 when astronaut hero John Glenn fell in the bathtub and had to withdraw from his race for senator from Ohio. He was finally elected to the Senate in 1974.

RATING THE CLEANLINESS OF 6 EUROPEAN PEOPLES

Here is the consumption of soap, in ounces of soap per person per year:

1. British Isles   40
2. Switzerland   37
3. Germany   34
4. Sweden   33
5. France   22.6
6. Netherlands   22.2

SOURCE: Swiss Union of Soap and Detergent Manufacturers, 1974.

ABIGAIL VAN BUREN'S READERS' 7 MOST UNUSUAL PROBLEMS

1. "I'm a bus driver and want some information on how to become a shepherd."
2. "I want to have a child but don't even have a boyfriend. Can you line me up with somebody?"
3. "I hear there is life after death. If that is true, can you put me in touch with my Uncle LeRoy Albert from Victoria, Tex.?"
4. "Will you please send me all the information you have on the rhythm method? I'm learning how to dance."
5. "I'm a 50-year-old widow and my doctor says I need a husband or the equivalent. Would it be all right if I borrowed my sister's husband? It's all right with them."
6. "My husband burns the hair out of his nose with a lighted match. And he thinks I'm crazy because I voted for Goldwater."
7. "I can't trust my husband. He cheats so much I'm not even sure my last baby is HIS."

From *The Book of Lists* (renumbered). By permission of Ann Landers and Field Newspaper Syndicate.

ANN LANDERS' READERS' 7 MOST UNUSUAL PROBLEMS

1. The man who hid his wife's dentures so she couldn't go out and vote for a Democrat.
2. The man who wanted to be buried in his 1939 Dodge.
3. The woman who wrote to inquire about who owned the walnuts from the tree which grew on her property but very close to the neighbor's property. Most of the nuts were falling on the neighbor's property and she felt that since it was her tree which produced the nuts, she was entitled to them. (Answer: The neighbor could use the nuts that fell on her property, but couldn't sell them.)
4. The woman whose husband was going to have a transsexual operation. She wanted to know what the children should call their father after the operation. "Daddy" didn't seem appropriate for a "woman." (Answer: They can call him "Bob" or "Bill" or whatever he changes his name to—probably "Mary" or "Sue".)
5. The totally bald woman who used to remove her wig at poker games and place it on her chips for luck.
6. The man who kept a pig in his apartment and insisted the pig was a wonderful "watchdog." The neighbors complained.
7. The woman who did her housework in the nude and enjoyed it thoroughly until one day she went to the basement to do her laundry and was surprised by the meter reader.

ABIGAIL VAN BUREN'S READERS' 10 MOST COMMON PROBLEMS

1. "My wife doesn't understand me."
2. "My husband never gives me any money."
3. "My parents don't trust me."
4. "My grandchildren never come to visit me."
5. "We never hear from our married kids unless they want something."
6. "My boyfriend keeps wanting me to 'prove my love.' "
7. "My girlfriend wants to get married and I'm not ready."
8. "My neighbor keeps dropping in uninvited."
9. "How does a nice woman meet a nice man?"
10. "How does a nice man meet a nice woman?"

ANN LANDERS' READERS' 10 MOST COMMON PROBLEMS

1. *Sexual problems between husband and wife:* "I'm not getting enough" or "I'm getting too much" or "He's impotent" or "She's frigid."

From *The Book of Lists.* By permission of Ann Landers and Field Newspaper Syndicate.

2. *Cheating spouses:* Men used to be the cheaters nine times out of ten. Now it's almost 50-50.
3. *Problems with in-laws:* "They are too demanding of our time." "They interfere." "They spoil our children."
4. *Teenagers complaining about parents who don't understand them:* "They're living in the olden days" or "They never talk to us about anything that matters."
5. *Teenage love:* "How can I be sure it's the real thing?" or "He likes someone else" or "He never takes me anyplace, he just wants to park and make out" or "Where can I get the pill?"
6. *Loneliness:* "How can a respectable girl" (or guy) "meet people?"
7. *Physical appearance problems:* These include weight, birthmarks, crooked teeth, baldness, acne, and being flat-chested, too short, or too tall.
8. *Pregnant girls:* "Should I have an abortion?" "Should I marry him?" "Should I keep my baby?" "How do I tell my parents?"
9. *Problems at work:* "My boss is on the make, I don't want to lose my job—but I can't stand him." Or "Someone in this store has terrible body odor. What can I do?"
10. *Drug, tobacco, and alcohol addiction:* "My parents smoke. I hate it. How can I get them to stop?" "How do I get my husband" (or wife, or friend) "off the booze?" Or "My parents are drunk all the time. I'm ashamed to have any friends in." Or "My best friend is on LSD or heroin." Or "Is marijuana harmful?"

unit 8   *Loneliness, Regimentation, Fear*

❖•❖

Overwhelmed by the Bureaucracy? Are we just numbers in a computer? Stuck in a rut? Struck by the idea that life is fragile, fleeting, elusive?

Use one or more of the poems and pictures in this unit to develop a theme. Refer back to any materials in earlier chapters that apply. Support your thesis with one or more methods of development.

Are the gloomy predictions of a regimented 1984 unavoidable? Will robots like those pictured replace us, or will we, ourselves, become mindless machines? (See "Life Cycle of Common Man" and "The Unknown Citizen" in this section; "The Emerging Plastic Image of Man," Section 4C, and "George Orwell's *1984*—How Close Are We?" in Section 6C.) Will robots provide us with a life of luxury or create unemployment and other problems? Will they vie for your girlfriend or boyfriend? Compare life today with a robot-run world of tomorrow. Write a cause/effect paper about a world run by robots. Describe such a world in detail.

Wide World Photos

W. H. Auden

THE UNKNOWN CITIZEN

(To JS/07/M/378
This Marble Monument
Is Erected by the State)

He was found by the Bureau of Statistics to be
One against whom there was no official complaint,
And all the reports on his conduct agree
That, in the modern sense of an old-fashioned word, he was a saint,
For in everything he did he served the Greater Community.   5
Except for the War till the day he retired
He worked in a factory and never got fired,
But satisfied his employers, Fudge Motors Inc.
Yet he wasn't a scab or odd in his views,
For his Union reports that he paid his dues,   10
(Our report on his Union shows it was sound)
And our Social Psychology workers found

Copyright 1940 and renewed 1968 by W. H. Auden. Reprinted from *Collected Poems,* by W. H. Auden, edited by Edward Mendelson. By permission of Random House, Inc. and Faber & Faber Ltd.

That he was popular with his mates and liked a drink.
The Press are convinced that he bought a paper every day
And that his reactions to advertisements were normal in every way. [15]
Policies taken out in his name prove that he was fully insured,
And his Health-card shows he was once in hospital but left it cured.
Both Producers Research and High-Grade Living declare
He was fully sensible to the advantages of the Installment Plan
And had everything necessary to the Modern Man, [20]
A phonograph, a radio, a car and a frigidaire.
Our researchers into Public Opinion are content
That he held the proper opinions for the time of year;
When there was peace, he was for peace; when there was war, he went. [25]
He was married and added five children to the population,
Which our Eugenist says was the right number for a parent of his
    generation,
And our teachers report that he never interfered with their education.
Was he free? Was he happy? The question is absurd:
Had anything been wrong, we should certainly have heard.

Howard Nemerov

LIFE CYCLE OF COMMON MAN

Roughly figured, this man of moderate habits,
This average consumer of the middle class,
Consumed in the course of his average life span
Just under half a million cigarettes,
Four thousand fifths of gin and about [5]
A quarter as much vermouth; he drank
Maybe a hundred thousand cups of coffee,
And counting his parents' share it cost
Something like half a million dollars
To put him through life. How many beasts [10]
Died to provide him with meat, belt and shoes
Cannot be certainly said.
              But anyhow,
It is in this way that a man travels through time,
Leaving behind him a lengthening trail [15]
Of empty bottles and bones, of broken shoes,
Frayed collars and worn out or outgrown
Diapers and dinnerjackets, silk ties and slickers.

Given the energy and security thus achieved,
He did . . . ? What? The usual things, of course, [20]
The eating, dreaming, drinking and begetting,

From *The Collected Poems of Howard Nemerov,* University of Chicago Press, 1977.
Used by permission of Howard Nemerov.

And he worked for the money which was to pay
For the eating, et cetera, which were necessary
If he were to go on working for the money, et cetera,
But chiefly he talked. As the bottles and bones   25
Accumulated behind him, the words proceeded
Steadily from the front of his face as he
Advanced into the silence and made it verbal.
Who can tally the tale of his words? A lifetime
Would barely suffice for their repetition;   30
If you merely printed all his commas the result
Would be a very large volume, and the number of times
He said "thank you" or "very little sugar, please,"
Would stagger the imagination. There were also
Witticisms, platitudes, and statements beginning   35
"It seems to me" or "As I always say."

Consider the courage in all that, and behold the man
Walking into deep silence, with the ectoplastic
Cartoon's balloon of speech proceeding
Steadily out of the front of his face, the words   40
Borne along on the breath which is his spirit
Telling the numberless tale of his untold Word[1]
Which makes the world his apple, and forces him to eat.

[1] *Logos,* the principle of creation and order.

Amy Lowell

PATTERNS

I walk down the garden-paths,
And all the daffodils
Are blowing, and the bright blue squills.
I walk down the patterned garden-paths
In my stiff, brocaded gown.   5
With my powdered hair and jeweled fan,
I too am a rare
Pattern. As I wander down
The garden-paths.

My dress is richly figured,   10
And the train
Makes a pink and silver stain
On the gravel, and the thrift
Of the borders.
Just a plate of current fashion,   15

"Patterns" by Amy Lowell from *The Complete Poetical Works of Amy Lowell.* Copyright 1955 by Houghton Mifflin Company. Used by permission of the publisher.

Tripping by in high-heeled, ribboned shoes.
Not a softness anywhere about me,
Only whalebone and brocade.
And I sink on a seat in the shade
Of a lime tree. For my passion   20
Wars against the stiff brocade.
The daffodils and squills
Flutter in the breeze
As they please.
And I weep;   25
For the lime-tree is in blossom
And one small flower has dropped upon my bosom.

And the plashing of waterdrops
In the marble fountain
Comes down the garden-paths.   30
The dripping never stops.
Underneath my stiffened gown
Is the softness of a woman bathing in a marble basin,
A basin in the midst of hedges grown
So thick, she cannot see her lover hiding,   35
But she guesses he is near,
And the sliding of the water
Seems the stroking of a dear
Hand upon her.
What is Summer in a fine brocaded gown!   40
I should like to see it lying in a heap upon the ground.
All the pink and silver crumpled up on the ground.

I would be the pink and silver as I ran along the paths,
And he would stumble after,
Bewildered by my laughter.   45
I should see the sun flashing from his sword-hilt and the buckles on
        his shoes.
I would choose
To lead him in a maze along the patterned paths,
A bright and laughing maze for my heavy-booted lover.
Till he caught me in the shade,   50
And the buttons of his waistcoat bruised my body as he clasped me,
Aching, melting, unafraid.
With the shadows of the leaves and the sundrops
And the plopping of the waterdrops,
All about us in the open afternoon—   55
I am very like to swoon
With the weight of this brocade,
For the sun sifts through the shade.

Underneath the fallen blossom
In my bosom,   60
Is a letter I have hid.

It was brought to me this morning by a rider from the Duke.
"Madam, we regret to inform you that Lord Hartwell
Died in action Thursday se'nnight.
As I read it in the white, morning sunlight,
The letters squirmed like snakes.
"Any answer, Madam?" said my footman.
"No," I told him.
"See that the messenger takes some refreshment.
No, no answer."
And I walked into the garden,
Up and down the patterned paths,
In my stiff, correct brocade.
The blue and yellow flowers stood up proudly in the sun,
Each one.
I stood upright too,
Held rigid to the pattern
By the stiffness of my gown.
Up and down I walked,
Up and down.

In a month he would have been my husband.
In a month, here, underneath this lime,
We would have broke the pattern;
He for me, and I for him,
He as Colonel, I as Lady,
On this shady scat.
He had a whim
That sunlight carried blessing.
And I answered, "It shall be as you have said."
Now he is dead.

In Summer and in Winter I shall walk
Up and down
The patterned garden-paths
In my stiff, brocaded gown.
The squills and daffodils
Will give place to pillared roses, and to asters, and to snow.
I shall go
Up and down,
In my gown.
Gorgeously arrayed,
Boned and stayed.
And the softness of my body will be guarded from embrace
By each button, hook, and lace.
For the man who should loose me is dead,
Fighting with the Duke in Flanders,
In a pattern called a war.
Christ! What are patterns for?

Paul Simon

PATTERNS

The night set softly
With the hush of falling leaves
Casting shivering shadows
On the houses through the trees
And light from a street lamp   5
Paints a pattern on my wall
Like the pieces of a puzzle
Or a child's uneven scrawl.

Up a narrow flight of stairs
In a narrow little room   10
As I lie upon my bed
In the early evening gloom.
Impaled on my wall
My eyes can dimly see
The pattern of my life   15
And the puzzle that is me.

From the moment of my birth
To the instant of my death
There are patterns I must follow
Just as I must breathe each breath.   20
Like a rat in a maze
The path before me lies
And the pattern never alters
Until the rat dies.

And the pattern still remains   25
On the wall where darkness fell
And it's fitting that it should
For in darkness I must dwell.
Like the color of my skin
Or the day that I grow old   30
My life is made of patterns
That can scarcely be controlled.

Copyright © 1965 Paul Simon. Used by permission.

Do you feel alone in a crowd (see "The Universal Waiting Room," Section 3B), or do you believe that we are all tied together by mutual needs, feelings, and problems? Are friends drifting away? Can we, as a society, learn brotherly and sisterly love? Can we find ways to live together and laugh together? Define *loneliness* or *alienation.* Write a cause/effect paper dealing with a specific period when you felt lonely or alienated.

The Subway by George Tooker, 1950. Egg tempera on composition board. 18 x 36 inches. Collection of the Whitney Museum of American Art. Juliana Force Purchase.

The Shriek by Edvard Munch, signed 1896. Lithograph, 13 × 10 inches.
The Museum of Modern Art, New York. Matthew T. Mellon Fund.

The day seems pleasant enough. The boats are at anchor in calm waters. Why should this woman shriek? Do you ever want to scream for no apparent reason?

Percy Bysshe Shelley

OZYMANDIAS

I met a traveler from an antique land
Who said: Two vast and trunkless legs of stone
Stand in the desert. . . . Near them, on the sand,
Half sunk, a shattered visage lies, whose frown,
And wrinkled lip, and sneer of cold command,   5
Tell that its sculptor well those passions read
Which yet survive, stamped on these lifeless things,
The hand that mocked them, and the heart that fed:
And on the pedestal these words appear:
"My name is Ozymandias, King of Kings: 10
Look on my works, ye Mighty, and despair!"
Nothing beside remains. Round the decay
Of that colossal wreck, boundless and bare
The lone and level sands stretch far away.

Arthur Guiterman

ON THE VANITY OF EARTHLY GREATNESS

The tusks that clashed in mighty brawls
Of mastodons, are billiard balls.

The sword of Charlemagne the Just
Is ferric oxide known as rust.

The grizzly bear whose potent hug   5
Was feared by all, is now a rug.

Great Caesar's bust is on the shelf,
And I don't feel so well myself!

"On the Vanity of Earthly Greatness" by Arthur Guiterman from *Gaily the Troubadour.* Copyright © 1936, reprinted by permission of Louise H. Sclove.

unit 9   *Cry Terror!*

❖❖

The following chart of terrorist types is from *Crusaders, Criminals, Crazies* by the psychiatrist Frederick J. Hacker. Generally speaking, terrorism from below is perpetrated by a group or individual not in power; terror from above is promoted by those in power, usually to suppress the opposition.

1. Use the information in the chart for example, classification, cause/effect, and comparison/contrast papers.

2. In addition you may want to research some specific acts of terrorism or study the history of terrorism.

3. You may want to give examples of specific hijacking or bombing incidents or write a case history of one terrorist.

TERRORISM FROM BELOW

Crazy	*Criminal*	*Crusading*
MOTIVATION		
Self-centered and sacrificial	Selfish and self-protective	Unselfish and sacrificial
Thought processes: highly personal, often nonrational or irrational	Thought processes: task-oriented, rational, conventional in terms of prevailing values	Thought processes: task-oriented, functionally rational[1] but unconventional in terms of prevailing values
Sometimes delusional	Realistic	Realistic, often in service of unrealistic ends
Abstract goals	Concrete goals	Concrete and abstract goals
Anticipated gain: psychological and idiosyncratic	Anticipated gain: personal and material	Anticipated gain: collective, symbolic, publicity, or material
Often "incomprehensible"	Commonly "understandable"	"Understandable" to sympathizers, "senseless" to antagonists
Cry for help, self-dramatization (psychodrama), therapeutic attempt, attempt at self-cure	Materially, not psychologically, oriented	Attention-getting, ostentatious, dramatic, spectacular, publicity-conscious
Amateurish M.O.[2]	Professional, mostly repetitive M.O.	Theatrical M.O. follows trends and fashions

Reprinted from *Crusaders, Criminals, Crazies: Terror and Terrorism in Our Time* by Frederick J. Hacker, M.D., with the permission of W. W. Norton & Company, Inc. Copyright © 1976 by Frederick J. Hacker.

[1] According to Karl Mannheim, a distinction is to be made between functional rationality, referring to the appropriate relationship between ends and means, and substantive rationality, referring to the "appropriateness" of ends.

[2] M.O.: modus operandi, method of procedure.

Crazy	Criminal	Crusading
High risk taking	High risk avoidance	Indifferent to high risk
Predominantly inward-directed aggression, intrapunitive, suicidal	Predominantly outward-directed aggression, extrapunitive, homicidal	Intrapunitive and extrapunitive, suicidal and homicidal

CAST

Crazy	Criminal	Crusading
Loners or small groups, not organized	Loners or organized in a business-like (e.g., syndicates, corporations) or familylike (e.g., clan, brotherhood) manner, often subject to terror from above (Mafia)	Small or large groups, organized in armylike manner (e.g., leagues, fronts, units), with hierarchical command structure, often submissive to terror from above
Unstable, immature, often distractible and inept individuals with weak ego and overt behavior disturbances	Detached, often dehumanized individuals, often unstable and inept but also often with seemingly intact ego and without overt behavior disturbances	Fanatical individuals, often with seemingly intact ego, without overt behavior disturbances
Conspicuous through bizarre conduct or attire	Mostly inconspicuous	Inconspicuous
Often overt sexual disturbance	No overt sexual disturbance	No overt sexual disturbance, little or no overt sexual interest
Unpredictable, vacillating, hesitating	Predictable, mostly determined, ruthless	Predictably unpredictable, determined, ruthless
Indifferent to immediate success	Exclusively interested in concrete immediate success	Predominantly interested in immediate and long-range publicity and success
Frequently imitative	Frequently imitative	Frequently innovative and violence-escalating
Eager for alliances with audience, often on any terms.	Disinterested in alliances but interested in specific deals	Interested in deals and alliances on their own terms
Cannot be deterred by ordinary means, can be persuaded but not bought	Can be deterred by ordinary means, can be bought but not persuaded	Cannot be deterred by ordinary means, incorruptible

VICTIMS

Crazy	Criminal	Crusading
Selection: random or according to delusional system (with attraction to the powerful and prominent)	Selection: purely instrumental (the rich and prominent for trade and blackmail value)	Selection: for symbolic and/or publicity value, often from emotional, highly charged enemy target group as instruments for barter but may become targets for brainwashing and eventual allies
Highly endangered for short periods of time	Danger varying according to response; the more professional the criminal, the less endangered the victim	After initial phase, danger almost entirely dependent upon responses

	Crazy	*Criminal*	*Crusading*
OBJECTS (AUDIENCE)			
	Selection: random or vaguely defined target group, visualized as possible allies and helpers	Selection: usually small groups, such as the victim's family	Selection: largest group possible (the nation, the world)
	Recipients of moral appeals	Recipients of business propositions	Recipients of specific blackmail threats and vague moral appeals
REACTION OF OBJECTS			
	High ambivalence	Indignation not tempered by ambivalence	High ambivalence
	Merciless removal ("Kill him; he's crazy anyway") or pity (poor-devil phenomenon)	Buying offers and/or severe punishment	Extreme measures (e.g., repressive counteraction, death penalty) advocated by antagonists; understanding advocated by sympathizers
	Emphasis on protection rather than punishment	Emphasis on punishment and deterrence	Emphasis on punishment for protection and deterrence by antagonists; emphasis on little or no individual punishment by sympathizers
	Quick retaliation or advocacy of flexible negotiations	Advocacy of immediate negotiations, often with the use of guile and trickery	Various coping styles; show of strength (e.g., no negotiation, no concession), but negotiations obligatory if victims are sufficiently valuable

TERROR FROM ABOVE

	Crazy	*Criminal*	*Crusading*
MOTIVATION			
	Same as terrorism	Same as terrorism	Same as terrorism
CAST			
	Erratic, bizarre conduct with emphasis on self-aggrandizement	Professional conduct of administrators and executors in tight business organizations demanding discipline and submission, strict division of labor	Professional conduct of generals and soldiers in military organizations demanding discipline and submission with specific rules for propaganda and image making
	Untrained, often unskilled	Often well trained and highly skilled	Often well trained and highly skilled
	Often manipulated	Often manipulators	Often manipulated manipulators

	Crazy	*Criminal*	*Crusading*
VICTIMS	Same as terrorism	Same as terrorism	Same as terrorism
OBJECTS (AUDIENCE)	Selection: random, vague, and inconsistent, no discernible pattern	Selection: captive limited target groups	Selection: captive total population, everyone a potential victim
REACTION OF OBJECTS	Wait-and-see attitude	Quick, limited response, often through manoeuvers, tricks, and without moral scruples	Ambivalent reaction according to political conviction and/or gravity of threat
	Attempted exploitation of terrorist's self-destructive tendencies (give enough rope to hang)	Attempted deals and short-range accommodations, limited submission, or escape attempts, frequently, long-range accommodation and submission	Short-range escape attempts or "inner" escape by demonstrative apathy; different coping devices depending on degree and duration of "total institution"; frequently long-range accommodation, submission, and conversion (joining)
	Ridicule and faked submission	Indignation and disgust	Indignation and disgust, sometimes changing to resignation or enthusiasm

unit 10 *How Should We Teach Our Young?*

❖❖

The following articles are from a symposium in the *Saturday Review of Education,* March 1973. Written in response to the question, "How will we raise our children in the year 2000?" many of the statements reflect the turmoil of the '60s—the Vietnam War, the Peace Movement, the reaction of students against regimentation, and the desire for a more creative, more imaginative educational system.

1. What do *you* think education should be like in the year 2000? Support your views with quotes from these and other sources.

2. Compare and contrast some of the different views.

3. Classify the views presented.

4. What are some of the principal causes and effects of problems in our current educational system? Use comments from this unit to support your views. Get other comments.

5. Define *education.*

HOW WILL WE RAISE OUR CHILDREN IN THE YEAR 2000?

Gloria Steinem

1   The year 2000. It has a hopeful, science-fiction ring, so perhaps we can predict that by then there will be an understanding of how caste functions in our child-rearing operations, that there will be a concerted effort to eliminate all the giant and subtle ways in which we determine human futures according to the isolated physical differences of race or sex.

2   That statement may sound simple or unnatural to many of us reading it now. Simple—to those of us who accept the fact that individual differences far outstrip the group differences based on race or sex. Unnatural—to those of us who assume that physical differences pervade and shape all human capabilities. But it seems to me that the problem of caste is the most profound and revolutionary of the crises we must face. Only by attacking the patriarchal and racist base of social systems of the past—tribal or industrial, capitalist or socialist—can we begin to undo the tension and violence and human waste that this small globe can no longer afford, and that the powerless, caste-mark majority of this world will no longer tolerate.

3   By the year 2000 we will, I hope, raise our children to believe in human potential, not God. Hopefully, the raising of children will become both an art and a science: a chosen and a loving way of life in both cases. Whether children are born into extended families or nuclear ones, into communal groups or to single parents, they will be wanted—a major difference from a past in which, whatever the sugar coating, we have been made to feel odd or unnatural if we did not choose to be biological parents. Children will be raised by and with men as much as women; with old people, as well as with biological or chosen parents; and with other children. For those children of single parents or nuclear families, the community must provide centers where their peers and a variety of adults complete the human spectrum. For those children born into communal groups or extended families, the community must provide space to be alone in and individual, one-to-one teaching. The point is to enlarge personal choice, to produce for each child the fullest possible range of human experience without negating or limiting the choices already made by the adults closest to her or to him.

4   It used to be said that this country was a child-centered one. Nothing could be further from the truth. Children have been our lowest priority, both in economic and emotional spending. They also have been looked upon as a caste, although a temporary one. And that caste has been exploited as labor by relatives as well as by business people. It has been used as a captive audience or a way of seeking social status. It has finally been reduced to the status of object—a possession of that caste known as adults.

© Saturday Review, 1973. All rights reserved.

By the year 2000 there should be no one way of raising children; there should be many ways—all of them recognizing that children have legal and social rights that may be quite separate and different from the rights or desires of the adults closest to them. At last we should be nurturing more individual talents than we suppress.

Nikki Giovanni

1   In a science fiction comic book a long time ago I read a story called "The Death Machine." A man stumbled into Doctor X's office and noticed a machine by an open window. He fiddled with the dials and put in his name and the year and day. The dials lit up, and the machine sent out a card that said, "You will be struck by lightning and killed at 6:00 tomorrow morning." The man was fascinated. He pressed a button labeled "Death Averted" and jumped five years in time. He saw that he would be rich and successful—but that he was going to be in an airplane accident. Then he pressed "Death Averted" and went ten years ahead. This time he had a lovely wife and happy children—but there was going to be a business disaster and he would commit suicide. Again he pressed "Death Averted" and went ahead fifteen years. The man was so busy seeing what a wonderful, successful, happy life he would have that he didn't see that dawn was coming. He paid no attention to the open window and the rising wind. And then, suddenly, the man was struck dead by lightning. At 6:00 a.m.

2   There is a message for all of us in this story. We have the potential to create a comfortable world with justice and integrity as building blocks; yet we are unwilling to try. We have read of the fall of great empires, both Black and non-Black: still, we think we will somehow escape their fate. But all we are doing is pressing our own "Death Averted" button.

3   I will not be raising children in the year 2000. If America learns something about grace and mercy, perhaps I will be blessed to enjoy my grandchildren. This can happen only if, just as we have touched the inner realms of space, we seek the inner space of mankind. We do not need a power change, though that would be better than the situation we have: we need a change in the way we conceive of power. Most of us today are afraid—in our homes and on the streets—but instead of boosting the economy through our frantic purchasing of locks and bolts, we should learn that we cannot shut ourselves in or others out. We must try to get along.

4   We are no longer the young, innocent nation making honest mistakes on the road to greatness. We are an insidious group of power mongers who, through simple attrition, have won our way into prominence. Senility breeds corruption.

5   I can only hope that in 2000 some young couple still has enough faith in life to choose to affirm it.

Billy Graham

1   About 3,000 years ago the king of ancient Israel wrote: "Lo, children are a heritage of the Lord: and the fruit of the womb is his reward. As arrows are in the hand of a mighty man; so are children of thy youth. Happy is the man who has his quiver full of them. . . ." (Psalms 127:3-5). If the core of truth in this quotation has remained unchanged for three millennia, there is no reason to believe that it will change in the next twenty-seven years. Children have always been the delight and joy of most parents, and they are still the symbol of the eternal marriage between love and duty.

2   The possibilities presented in some modern writings have given the false impression to many that the institution of the family is dead. The grotesque concepts of "purchased embryos," "bioparents," and "homosexual daddies" would lead some to believe that the ancient and time-honored life of the family is doomed to extinction. The bizarre and sensational make the headlines, but, thankfully, all the "way-out" experiments of our technological age are not always adopted by the masses.

3   In my opinion history has, for the most part, moved in a straight line. It is true that marriage is undergoing stress and strain today, but it will survive. The turbulence of a technological world will perhaps make for even stronger family ties. The family has historically been a refuge, a haven, from the stresses and strains of life—and, I believe, it will be strengthened and reinforced by the rigors, novelties, and transience of modern pressures.

4   Today's so-called generation gap is to some degree a figment of our imaginations, and I believe it will be somewhat closed by the year 2000. The extreme permissiveness so evident in the Seventies will be replaced by a more normal and proper discipline. We are suffering through a reaction to the Victorian Age; adults live under certain restrictions, and life is easier when these are learned in early life.

5   The word *love,* which has been bandied about a great deal of late and which means many things to many people, will become more important to the family of the future. And, of course, the family of the future must have faith. The pressures demanding an inner faith will not be lessened in the year 2000. In all probability they will be greatly increased.

6   Thus, the time-honored virtues, which have augured well for the family since the beginning of time, will not be replaced by startling innovations. They will endure with parents and children until the end of time.

Urie Bronfenbrenner

1   The future of the nation's children depends on the future of the nation's families, and the American family is in a period of significant change.

2   • In 1971 43 percent of the nation's mothers worked outside the home; in 1948 the figure was only 18 percent. One in every three mothers with children under six is working today.

3   • As more mothers have gone to work, the number of other adults in the family who could care for the child has decreased. Fifty years ago about half of all households included at least one other adult besides the parents; today that figure is below 5 per cent.

4   • In 1970 almost a quarter of all children were living in single-parent families, nearly double the rate for a decade ago. Almost half the mothers who are single parents of children under six are now in the labor force, and a third of these are working full time.

5   • Among families that are intact and well-off economically, research results indicate that parents are spending less time in activity with their children. Although the rats are gone, the rat race still prevails. The adults, as well as the children, have become victims of the mounting pressures.

6   In today's world children are deprived not only of parents but of adults in general. The resulting vacuum is filled by the television screen and the age-segregated peer group.

7   What is needed is a change in our patterns of living that will bring adults and children back into each other's lives. To effect such a change will require profound modifications in our social and economic institutions. Among the most needed reforms are increased opportunity and status for part-time jobs; flexible work schedules so that one parent can be at home when children return from school; enhancement of the status and power of women in all walks of life—both on the job and at home; the breaking down of the wall between school and community so that children become acquainted with the world of work and parents and other adults besides teachers can take an active part in activities at school; the inclusion, as an integral part of the high school curriculum, of supervised experience in the care of younger children; and, above all, the provision of adequate health and child-care services, housing, and income maintenance to the millions of American families whose resources are insufficient to insure normal development for a growing child.

8   Whether we are willing to take such measures will determine the balance of inadequacy and competence, alienation and commitment in the next generation of Americans. If we fail, it will not be for lack of resources or of viable alternatives but for lack of will.

Abbie Hoffman

1   By the year 2000 technology will have taken over so much of the stuff we now call work that the Protestant ethic—demanding postponement of pleasure and kowtowing to sin, guilt, and repression in order to keep the wheels turning—will be obsolete along with the internal combustion engine, two-dimensional television, and daily birth-control pills.

2   In times past people started developing careers at the ripe age of

seven, married at twelve or thirteen, had kids, and died of the chill at twenty. People went from infancy to adulthood. In fact, the whole notion of childhood is a relatively recent idea. By 2000 the cybernetic revolution will be driving toward the discovery of the fountain of youth. Childhood will be increasingly prolonged. There will not be such pressure to abandon dreams, adventure, frivolity, idealism, and romance and "get down to business." Thus, more kids will be having kids. Information about contraception and a variety of scientific advances in that area will provide humans with unlimited choices. A global consciousness will develop to keep the numbers down. Neither the species nor your Aunt Sadie is going to pressure you into making babies. Child having and child rearing will be more a part of the play sphere of life than the work sphere.

3   Since this will be a much healthier way to go about things, upbringing will be extremely permissive. Kids will be born out of love. It'll just be another way of making a friend. Laying your trip or your hands on the kid (adult chauvinism) will be frowned on by society.

4   Naturally, sex roles will be as blurred as age roles. There will simply be no need for sharp sex differences. The number of different styles of family situations available would boggle the mind of a present-day computer.

5   Advances in video-tape equipment and cable TV, especially the capacity to broadcast from the home to central "schools," combined with less-demanding work roles, will allow parents and children the opportunity to experience each other's education in the home.

6   Now, since sexual taboos are going to be reduced to a smidgen of psychic energy and since child rearing is going to be done for fun and since pregnancy might even be totally separated from the sexual act, we'll be ready for the culmination of the sexual revolution, namely "polymorphous incest." When the Oedipal conflict bites the dust, anything can happen. It'll seem quite natural for our kids to be making it with their kids. Isn't that what waterbeds are really all about?

Elizabeth Janeway

1   Some of the people who will be raising children in the year 2000 are already here with us. My grandson is four, and my granddaughter is two. It's a little early to say what their future plans will be, but if their childhood influences them, they will remember growing up in a supportive network of relationships with adults who are not their parents. By some quirk they possess an actual, if dispersed, extended family on both sides; just as important is the "Mothers' Mafia" of the neighborhood, which will take over an extra child when a parent is ill or away. The extended family may vanish, but the informal mothering (and fathering) by neighboring parents will, I suspect, grow stronger.

2   "The family," said Talcott Parsons, "is a sub-system of society." The family is not, and never can be, a unit complete in itself. But it is harder today than it ever has been for children to move from family base

to an adult place in society, because the connecting links are so few. One reason is that the family has lost the vital economic role it used to have when it was the focus of much necessary work. For the first time in history no one, male or female, can make an adequate living at home. The factory system put an end to the economic function of the family group, and children now grow up without a clue as to the ordinary process of earning their keep.

3   A solution I would like to recommend is the establishment of enriching and exciting child-care facilities at industrial plants, commercial centers, educational establishments—everywhere that parents go to work. These would be *model* care facilities, cosponsored by unions and imaginative educators, with programs offered by libraries, museums, musical conservatories, and theater and dance groups, the inheritors of ethnic and cultural traditions. Directed by a professional core, these places should engage, use, and entertain a coming-and-going population of children of all ages, adults of both sexes and all the generations that could be called on, interacting, teaching each other, connecting. The separation of work life from actual living is taking a terrible toll on the workers of our nation. God knows, I don't propose the child care I'm talking about as a way to orient children to the drab, desperate, mechanized kind of work that is distressing us today. But I suspect that *reuniting* living and working is going to be necessary for all of us, and I think that children-where-you-work can be influential in humanizing work, just as work-where-you-grow-up can be informative and exciting for children.

4   Overall, my great hope for the year 2000 is the reintegration of the parts of our world that started to come apart when the machines moved in. We can't do without the machines, but we've been scared of them too long. Damn it, are we mice or are we men? Does it take a woman to ask that question? Then thank God the women's movement has arrived to stand up and shout for liberation for the human race—beginning with our children.

Catharine Barrett

1   At this critical moment no one can say with certainty whether we are at the brink of a colossal disaster or whether this is indeed mankind's shining hour. But it is certain that dramatic changes in the way we will raise our children in the year 2000 are indicated, particularly in terms of schooling, and that these changes will require new ways of thinking. Let me propose three.

2   First, we will help all of our people understand that school is a concept and not a place. We will not confuse "schooling" with "education." The school will be the community; the community, the school. Students, parents, and teachers will make certain that John Dewey's sound advice about schooling the whole child is not confused with nonsense about the school's providing the child's whole education.

3   We will need to recognize that the so-called "basic skills," which

currently represent nearly the total effort in elementary schools, will be taught in one quarter of the present school day. The remaining time will be devoted to what is truly fundamental and basic—time for academic inquiry, time for students to develop their own interests, time for a dialogue between students and teachers. When this happens—and it's near—the teacher can rise to his true calling. More than a dispenser of information, the teacher will be a conveyor of values, a philosopher. Students will learn to write love letters and lab notes. We will help each child build his own rocket to his own moon.

4   Finally, if our children are to be human beings who think clearly, feel deeply, and act wisely, we will answer definitely the question "Who should make what decisions?" Teachers no longer will be victims of change; we will be agents of change.

Bruno Bettelheim

1   It's always risky to try to peer into the future. But when one does, the more reliable estimates usually come from predicting on the basis of the past rather than extrapolating from the present.

2   In past centuries mankind divided itself into two distinct groups when it came to child rearing. The vast majority formed what can be called a traditional group—they raised their children in very much the same way they themselves had been raised. (This pattern still holds for much of the world.) In contrast to these was the tiny group of innovators who tried something different. The latter group's numbers began to increase somewhat in the last century and especially in the last few decades, but it still remains quite a small minority.

3   Using psychoanalytic terms, the overwhelming majority of parents identify positively with their own parents, whose ways of behaving they internalized as children. Hence, in all essentials they act toward their children as they were acted upon by their own parents. For instance, modern mores have it that teen-agers ought to be given more freedom to come and go as they please. And greater affluence has made it possible to spend more money on children. Here are two apparent great changes. But the parents' internalized values have not changed. So although modern parents let their teenagers act much more independently, they have severe private misgivings about it and in subtle ways they make the children feel guilty.

4   Distinct from parents who have internalized, and who reflect, their own parents' values, however indirectly, is that much smaller number of persons who negatively identify with their own parents. Deciding that they themselves were brought up all wrong, such parents become determined to raise their children better than they were raised. As youngsters, they were not permitted to do things their own way. So, as parents, they insist vigorously that their own child make his own decisions. But there's an irony here: the liberated parents' insistence that their child make up

his own mind is really just another way of saying that he must do as his parents think best.

5   After all this, what are my predictions? It seems clear that while there will be changes in the externals, things will remain pretty much the same as far as the most basic issues are concerned. The vast majority of parents will continue to bring up their children in more or less traditional ways. This conclusion is supported by the turning inward that characterizes many of our citizens today, the tendency to turn away from broader issues and toward the narrower circle of the family as a means to fulfillment. On the other side, the children who are brought up today in so-called freedom may, through negative identification with their parents, raise their own children quite strictly. To balance out matters, some of the youngsters raised quite strictly today will, again through negative identification, bring up their own youngsters in so-called freedom.

6   Ample lip service has been paid to psychoanalytic views on child rearing—views that could radically change attitudes toward bringing up children. But little real attention has been given them and even less implementation. The widespread popularity presently enjoyed by theories of behavior modification suggests that today, as in the past, most people are committed to the idea that some know best how others should act. "Acceptable" behavior is either forced onto individuals or indirectly induced in them through bribes—the token economy of behavior modification. All of this, unfortunately, makes it quite unlikely that an essential reform of child-rearing methods is close at hand. Much as reform might be desired, it's not knocking at the door in 1973, and I doubt it will be in the year 2000 either.

George B. Leonard

1   We need no prophecy to inform us that many of the organizing principles of our present way of life have become outmoded and even self-destructive. The year 2000, if it is to come in peace, will see a gentler, more sensitive world. The technologically advanced nations will have stabilized the production and consumption of energy and will be seeking equitable means to distribute the stuff of a less-extravagant economy. The human urge to create and explore will turn from physical to spiritual frontiers, to areas we now term, for lack of a vocabulary, as mystical. Standardized, *dis-eased* human components will not be needed for this enterprise. Child rearing will be considerably altered.

2   Even today young children help provide a model for our transformation. Their multiple consciousness, their tendency to see life force in all things, their superb imagination and spectacular learning ability—these capacities will be valued, not crushed. The present socialization process serves primarily to force the child's perception into single vision, into our bizarre, historically aberrant Western consciousness. The process is so traumatic that it creates in almost every one of us the condition known as childhood amnesia. In transformed society we will be en-

couraged to remember, not forget, our own existence, to multiply and expand, not limit, our consciousness.

3   Drug abuse, a symptom of a society in its death throes, will no longer be a problem. Where heightened perceptions are sanctioned and reinforced by an effective social group, a drug generally can only get in the way of such perception.

4   Schooling will be different. No longer will we worry about teaching our children to read books, while totally ignoring their inability to read their own bodies. (Perhaps the only required courses of the future will be dance and body-energy awareness.) No longer will we blind ourselves with petty and generally fruitless manipulations of "achievement scores," while totally ignoring the skills of survival in a new world. We shall by no means ignore the cognitive material that today, ineffectively taught, makes up the bulk of schooling. But we shall start teaching our children to put themselves together rather than splitting mind from body, intellect from emotions.

5   The family of the future will be larger, less narrowly defined. No one will be childless; no one will lack for affection. The outworn roles of "man" and "woman" will be discarded. As high-pressure sex becomes less important, all of life will become more erotic. Indeed, as roles and classes and even separate nations fade in importance, we may see the emergence of a family as wide as all humankind, a family that can weep together, laugh together, and share the common ecstasy of a world in transformation.

Bobby Seale

1   I will not be raising children in the year 2000, but I am involved in how children are being raised now, and I can speculate about how they will raise *their* children in the year 2000.

2   The children in the Black Panther party's Intercommunal Youth Institute learn that the world—the universe—is their classroom. And we begin this learning process early—between the ages of two and a half and three.

3   We want our youth to understand and know the world as it exists. The best way to do this is to bring them into contact with the world in practical ways, working in their own community 60 per cent of the time and in their classrooms only 40 per cent of the time.

4   What each child learns is how to investigate the real world. We see our children as smaller people, not as curious little objects for our own pleasure and self-satisfaction. Truthfully speaking, the conditions of Black people are not like those of the people who exist in the mainstream of this society. We want to show our children *how* to think about the world around them, not *what* to think.

5   Our students participate in determining the policies that govern them. They criticize each other (and their instructors) in order to correct mistakes and mistaken ideas. If they violate the rules that they themselves

helped to make, then they are criticized before the collective. All of this is done with the understanding that we criticize with love, never with hatred. Never are children called stupid, dull, or dumb. No one child is forced to make a better grade than another. There are no grades. There is no negative competition. There is only the competition that will produce enthusiasm and prove, through action, that our capabilities are endless.

6   Our children are now capable of thinking out problems that we were sheltered from at their age, and I am sure that they will be able to teach their children even more in the year 2000. Their exchange of information with us now is evidence of this ability. Already they are teaching us many things. Hopefully, the youth of today will help to lead us toward liberation and freedom.

Margaret Mead

1   Changes in methods of child rearing are important not only because they contribute to changes in the character of the future citizens of the planet but because making changes in the way children are raised affects the character of those who raise them—parents, teachers, physicians, legislators. How children will be raised in the year 2000 can only be a more or less informed guess by someone who has specialized in the relationship of child rearing to other aspects of culture. But how we should raise our children is necessarily a program for a better future and a citizenry that can better deal with the great issues of the next century.

2   I hope that they will be raised in neighborhoods where they have warm relationships with many older people—grandparents or surrogate grandparents, teen-agers, currently unmarried adults, who have time to teach children special skills. I hope that such contacts will mean that children will no longer be confined to the isolated nuclear family in suburbs and housing developments, where all of the families are of the same class and ethnic group and have children of approximately the same age.

3   I hope that we will have redesigned our cities and suburbs so that there is a real outdoors for all little children's play, so that they can experience the unpredictability and endless fascination of growing things and be rescued from their current boredom with only-too-predictable toys and school tasks.

4   I hope that men and women will have come to design their married lives as parents who share, in many different styles, both the domestic tasks of homemaking and the tasks that contribute to the public life of the country, with all division of labor based on temperament and skill rather than on sex membership. Providing such an upbringing for children is the easiest and most efficient way to bring up children who will be persons first—individuals able to use their full potentialities—and members of one sex or the other second.

5   I hope that children can be raised with the recognition that since war can no longer protect any country, it is no longer appropriate to raise boys who will someday be asked to kill and die and girls who will concur

in these activities. If boys are not raised to be soldiers, it will be easier to relax those political frontiers that are now powerless to protect us against the new enemies: nuclear death, overpopulation strangulation, ecological death of sea and air. We can relax the lines around the small family and around the state and raise children in continually widening circles of affection for family, community, country, and planet—children who will care enough for each circle to be willing to make any sacrifice for its well-being and who will not find life stale and meaningless, as they so often do now, but will find it exacting, exhilarating, and significant.

Isaac Asimov

1   Let us assume that we still have a working technological society in the year 2000 (something that is by no means to be taken as certain). The price for that will be a nation (even a world, perhaps) that will have solved the population problem and that will recognize the necessity of achieving not merely a stable population but one that will decline to some optimum value.

2   Given such a policy, there will be far fewer children than there are today, and, therefore, each will be more individually valued. It should be clear, under those circumstances, that children are wards of society in general and not merely the property of their biological progenitors. Children, few in number and therefore not to be wasted, must be used wisely, as would be true of any resource that was at once crucially important and in short supply.

3   Nothing should then take precedence over effective and useful education; no talent should be more highly regarded than that of the great teacher; no money can be better spent than that which brings the teacher and the child together.

4   What is the mechanism by which children will be taught in the year 2000? Closed-circuit television? Teaching machines? Pills designed to increase learning ability? To a certain extent this is irrelevant. How we teach is unimportant if what we teach is all wrong.

5   But then what will we teach? Something that can be easily described? For instance, we could envision a totally computerized society and suggest that computer programming be taught from kindergarten on. Yet there is no point in listing subjects, for no such list is useful.

6   Suppose, for instance, that society *is* totally computerized, so that more and more work can be done without the direct intervention of the human hand or brain. Surely, it will not take the entire population to design and maintain the computers and to construct programs for them.

7   Indeed, we can easily imagine a twenty-first-century technological world that will be, in essence, a world of idleness. People will do what pleases them, and it will be the business of education to see to it that children learn their options, that each child has a chance to probe his own abilities and desires and find out what really will interest him most.

8   Ideally, we will have education for diversity, for clearly that child is

most fascinating and valuable who discovers an unusual interest in himself, one that he can then share with a world that without him would be deprived of that interest. It may be the invention of a new branch of chemistry or of new games to be played with matchsticks—what's the difference? There will be enough children who will find the desire within themselves to play with computers and with the universe and therefore end by running the earth. They also serve who only play with matchsticks.

9   In the end, diversity rests on the human gene pool and the variety within it. The human gene pool is the ultimate resource, and the more diverse that pool is—the larger the number of individual gene-types for future combination and recombination—the better off humanity is.

10   Exposure to diversity, both cultural and genetic, is an absolute good and will, in time to come, be an integral and essential part of education. It is to be hoped that by the year 2000 we will recognize that nothing can be worse for the development of a child than to have him live in a world in which everyone is and does very much as he himself is and does.

Index

Humanities Can Irrigate Deserts, The (Delattre), 260–63

I

In Business (Thomas), 19–20
Inferences, 3
Inner Shalimar . . . Outer Shalimar, 50
Insectivore to Cultural Ape (Morris), 33–36
Instruments of Power: Naming and Defining
(Bosmajian), 230–34
I'll Have One of Each (Engel and Houlgate),
108

J

JANEWAY, Elizabeth, 331–32
Joseph Stalin (Kennan), 58
Joy of Sports, The (Novak), 236–38
Juan Chicoy (Steinbeck), 60–61
Just a Tad Different, 81

K

KAZIN, Alfred, 54
KELTY, Matthew, 186–88
KENNAN, George F., 58
Kennedy (Sorenson), 90–92
Kiowa Grandmother, A (Momaday), 58–59
Kitchen, The (Kazin), 54–55
Knoxville: Summer 1915 (Agee), 67–68
KRONENBERGER, Louis, 125–27

L

LANDERS, Ann, 312
"Learning" to Give Up (Rosenfeld), 252–55
LEONARD, George B., 334–35
Life Cycle of Common Man (Nemerov),
315–16
"Life" on Death Row, 248–49
LIPSYTE, Robert, 239–44
Logical fallacies, 3–5
  after this—because of this, 4
  arguing in a circle, 4
  attacking the person instead of the
    idea, 4
  avoiding the point, 4
  begging the question, 4
  card stacking, 5
  either/or syndrome, 4
  false analogies, 4
  faulty inferences, 3
  overgeneralizations, 3
Love Is a Fallacy (Shulman), 134–41
Love quotes, 300–303
LOWELL, Amy, 316–18

M

MACCOBY, Michael, 128–33
Machiavelli and Guicciardini (Barzini),
146–47
MAILER, Norman, 58, 265–69
MALISHCHAK, Richard, 247
Matrimonial ads, 46–48
MAUGHAM, Somerset W., 59
McCARTHY, Mary, 53
McCULLOGH, Colleen, 71–73
MEAD, Margaret, 336–37
Meaning of Cliché, The (Evans and Evans),
219–20
Meggie Cleary's Birthday (McCullogh),
71–73
MENNINGER, Karl, 249
MGB—The Well Coordinated Athlete, 51
MILLER, Merle, 22–23
MITFORD, Jessica, 188–92, 256–60
MOMADAY, N. Scott, 52, 58
Monastic Way of Death, The (Kelty), 186–88
Moore, Dinty (Alexander), 57
MOOREHEAD, Alan, 82–83
MORRIS, Desmond, 33–36
MUIR, Edward, 115
MUNCH, Edvard, 321
My Search for Sobriety (Fuller), 270–77

N

NADER, Laura, 251–52
NATAL, James, 165–69
NEMEROV, Howard, 315
Newtonian Relativity Principle, The (Barnett),
86–88
Night the Bed Fell, The (Thurber), 287–90
NOLEN, William, 193–96
NOVAK, Michael, 236–38

O

OMMANNEY, F. D., 111–12
On the Vanity of Earthly Greatness (Guiter-
man), 322
Organization, of theme, 2
Origin of Death, The, 9
Outline, 25
Overgeneralization, 3
OVID, 83–84
Ozymandius (Shelley), 322

P

PACKARD, Vance, 100–103
Paper Wedding Gown, The (Toffler), 88–90
Paperback Best Sellers, 107
PARKS, Gordon, 84–85
Patterns (Lowell), 316–18